Ayu
Watanabe

L♥DK

エルディーケー

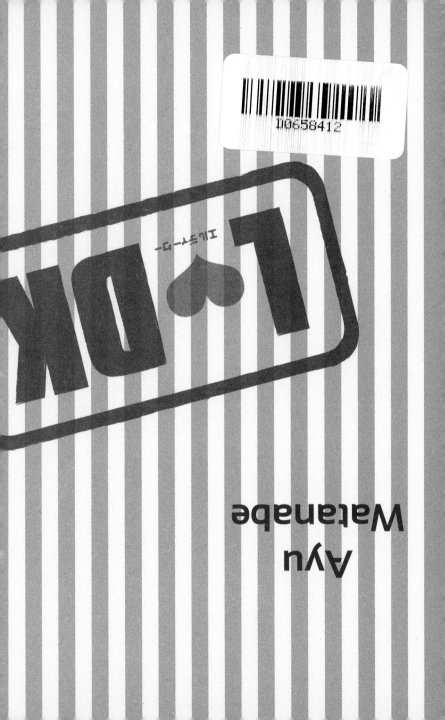

L♥DK

Ayu Watanabe

7

Contents

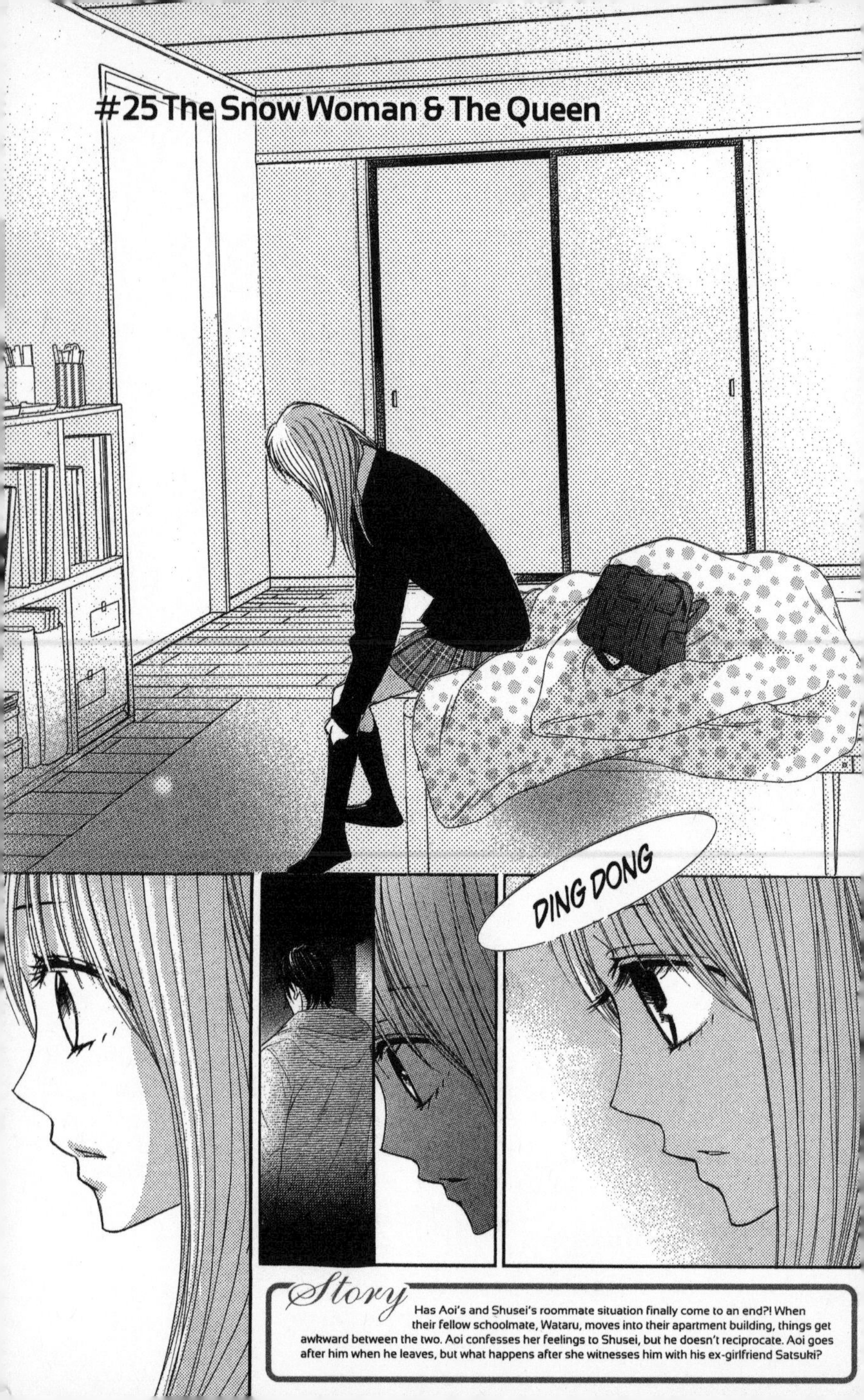
#25 The Snow Woman & The Queen
DING DONG
Story
Has Aoi's and Shusei's roommate situation finally come to an end?! When their fellow schoolmate, Wataru, moves into their apartment building, things get awkward between the two. Aoi confesses her feelings to Shusei, but he doesn't reciprocate. Aoi goes after him when he leaves, but what happens after she witnesses him with his ex-girlfriend Satsuki?

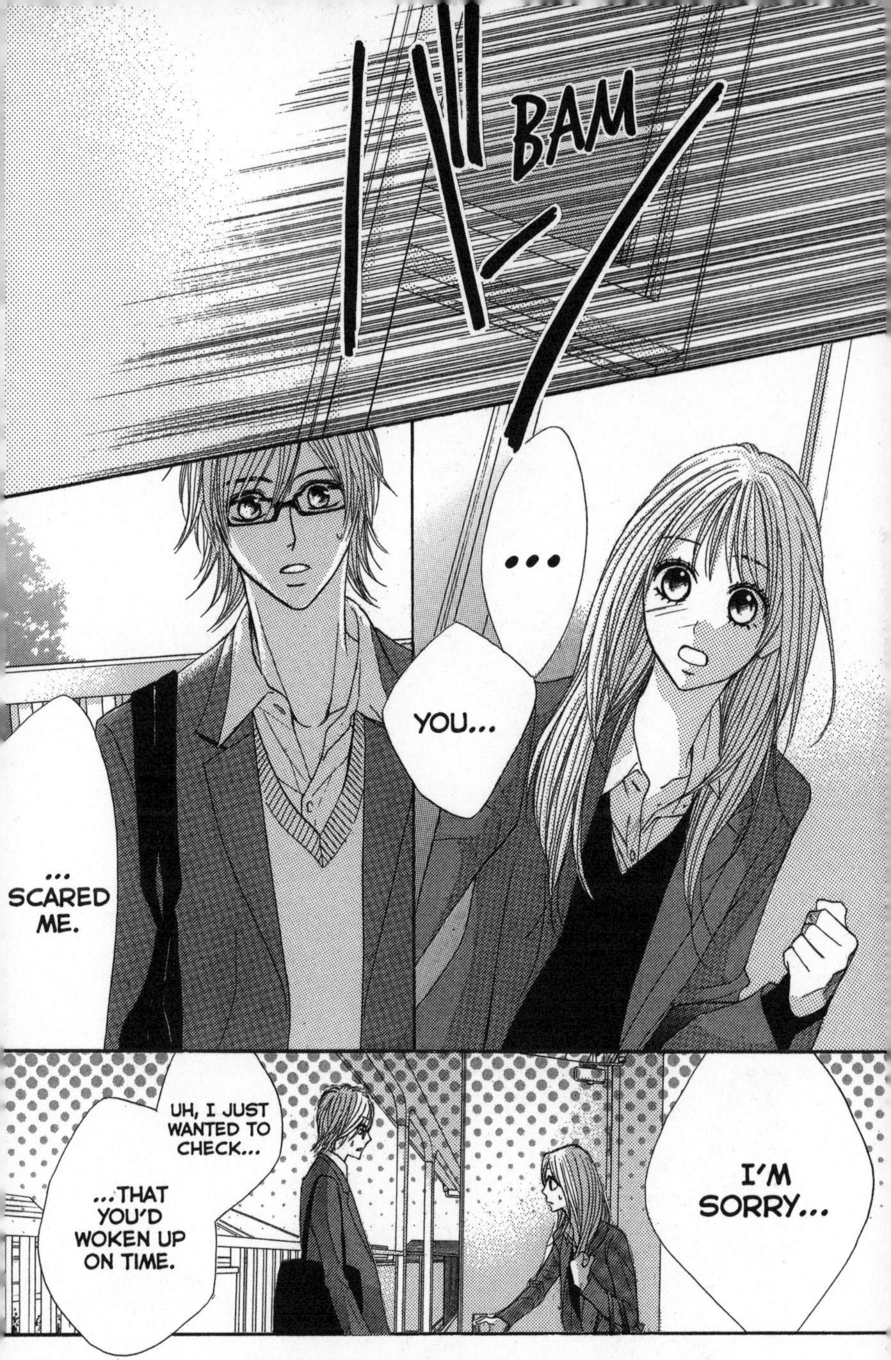
BAM
...
YOU...
...SCARED ME.
I'M SORRY...
UH, I JUST WANTED TO CHECK...
...THAT YOU'D WOKEN UP ON TIME.

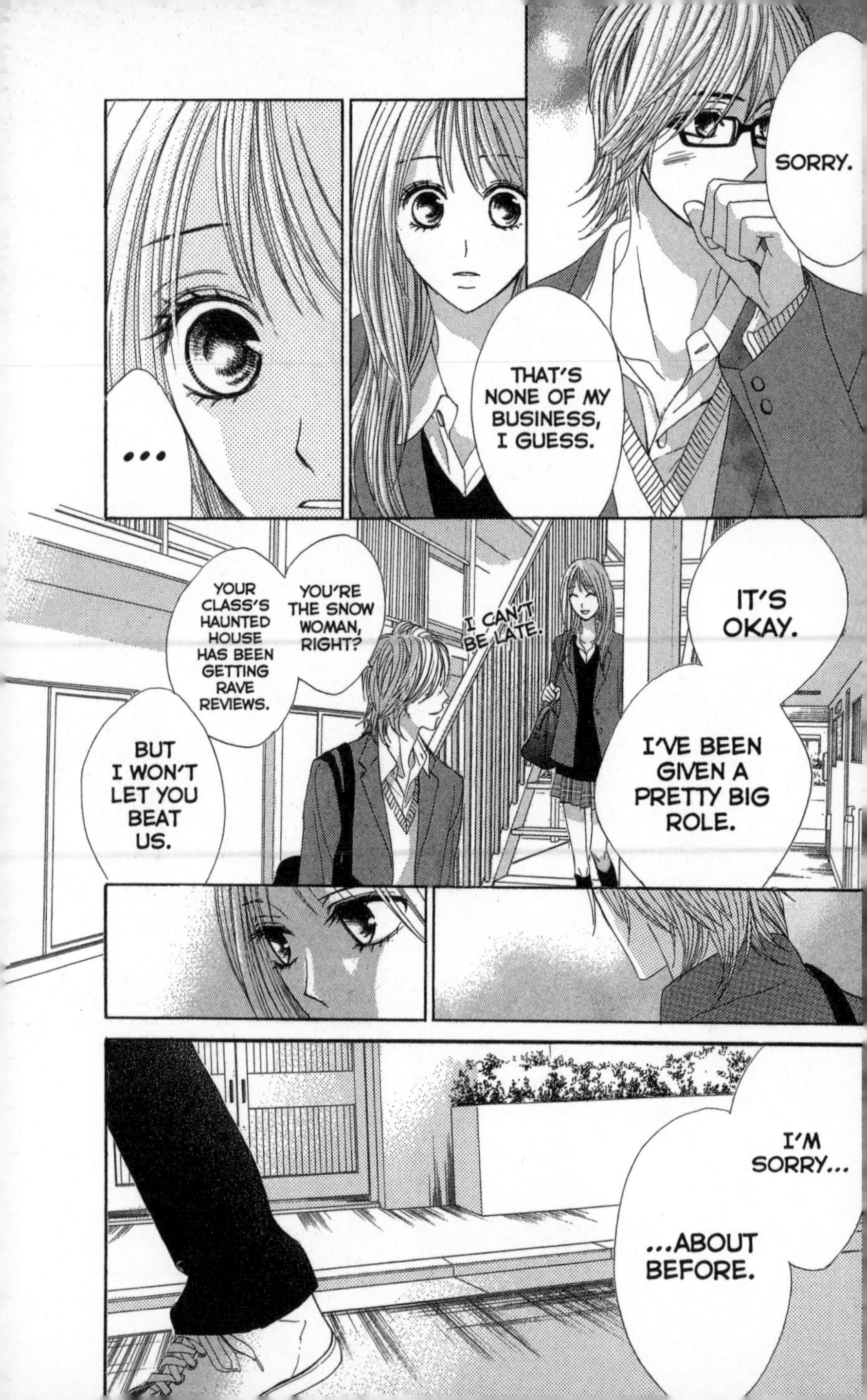
SORRY.
THAT'S NONE OF MY BUSINESS, I GUESS.
...
IT'S OKAY.
I'VE BEEN GIVEN A PRETTY BIG ROLE.
I CAN'T BE LATE.
YOU'RE THE SNOW WOMAN, RIGHT?
YOUR CLASS'S HAUNTED HOUSE HAS BEEN GETTING RAVE REVIEWS.
BUT I WON'T LET YOU BEAT US.
I'M SORRY...
...ABOUT BEFORE.

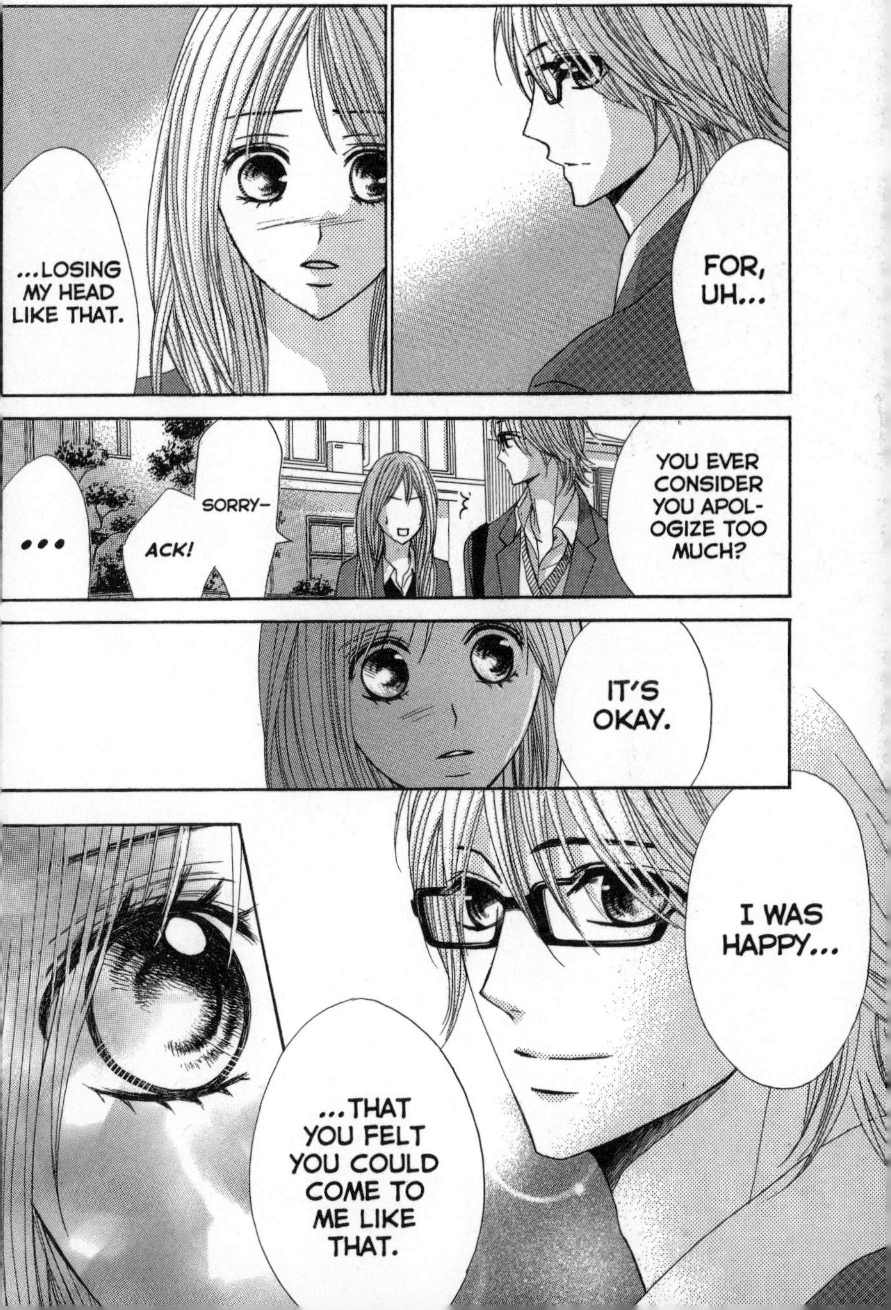
FOR, UH...
...LOSING MY HEAD LIKE THAT.
YOU EVER CONSIDER YOU APOLOGIZE TOO MUCH?
SORRY—
ACK!
...
IT'S OKAY.
I WAS HAPPY...
...THAT YOU FELT YOU COULD COME TO ME LIKE THAT.

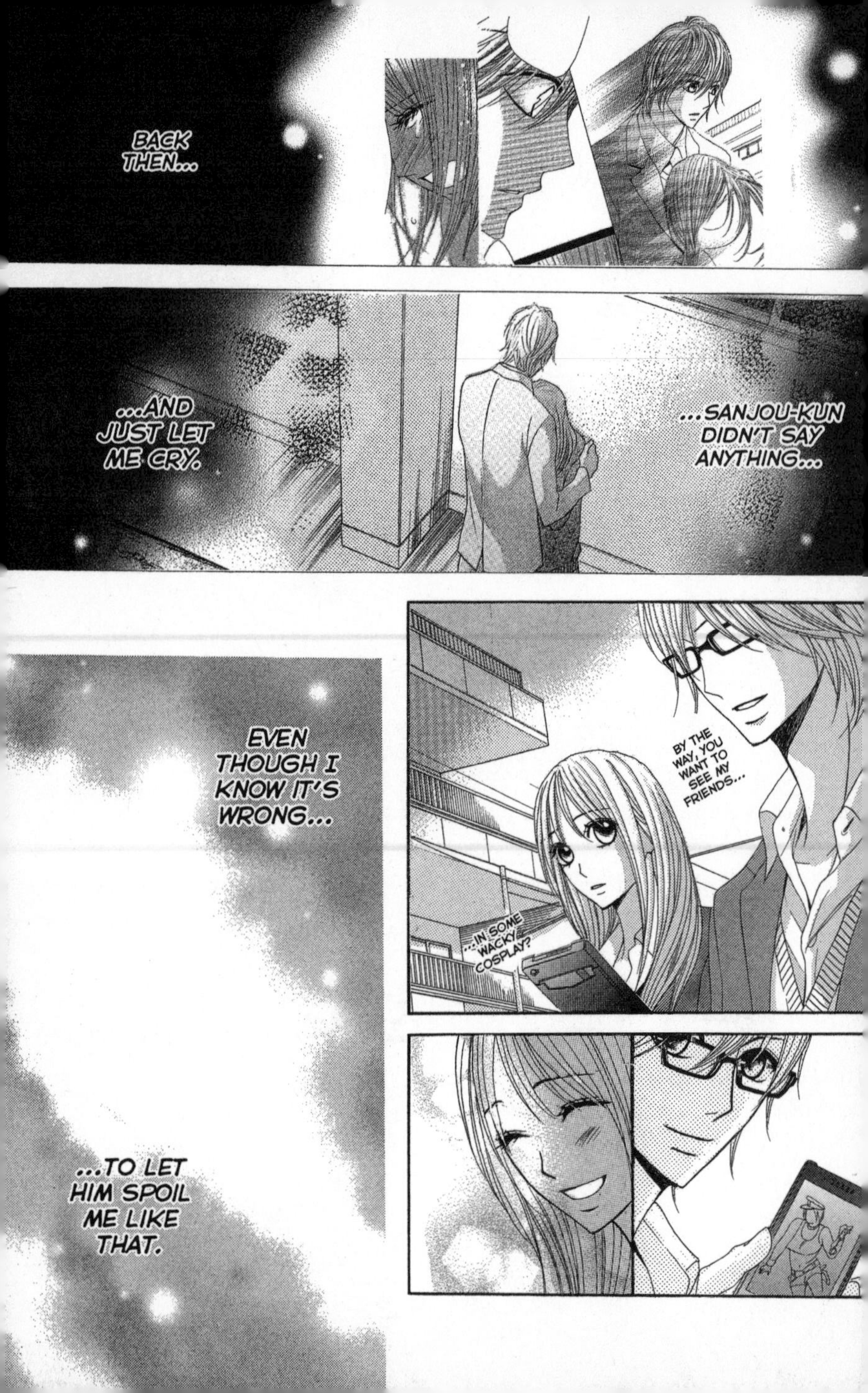
BACK THEN...
...SANJOU-KUN DIDN'T SAY ANYTHING...
...AND JUST LET ME CRY.
BY THE WAY, YOU WANT TO SEE MY FRIENDS...
...IN SOME WACKY COSPLAY?
EVEN THOUGH I KNOW IT'S WRONG...
...TO LET HIM SPOIL ME LIKE THAT.

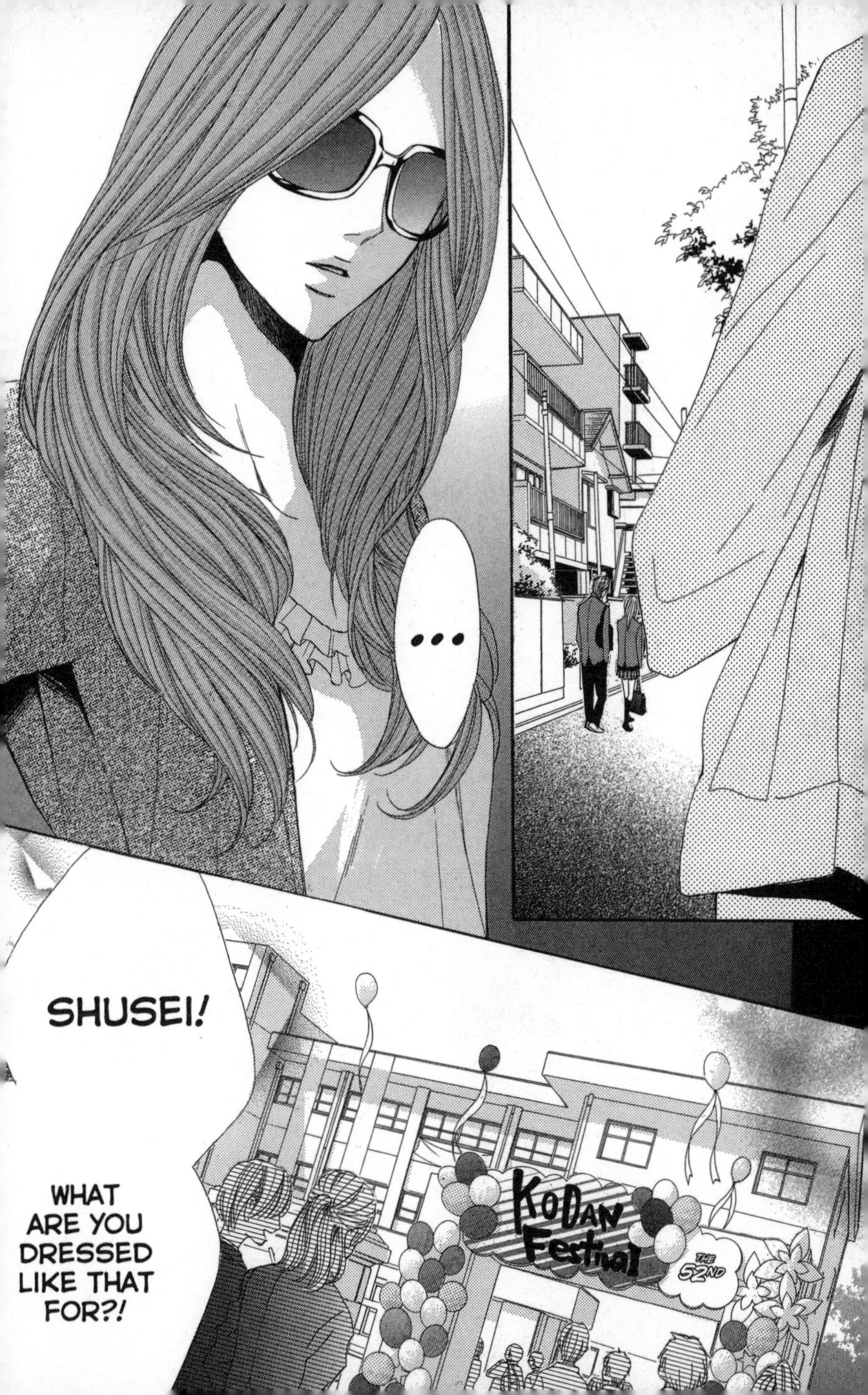
...
SHUSEI!
WHAT ARE YOU DRESSED LIKE THAT FOR?!
KODAN Festival
THE 52ND

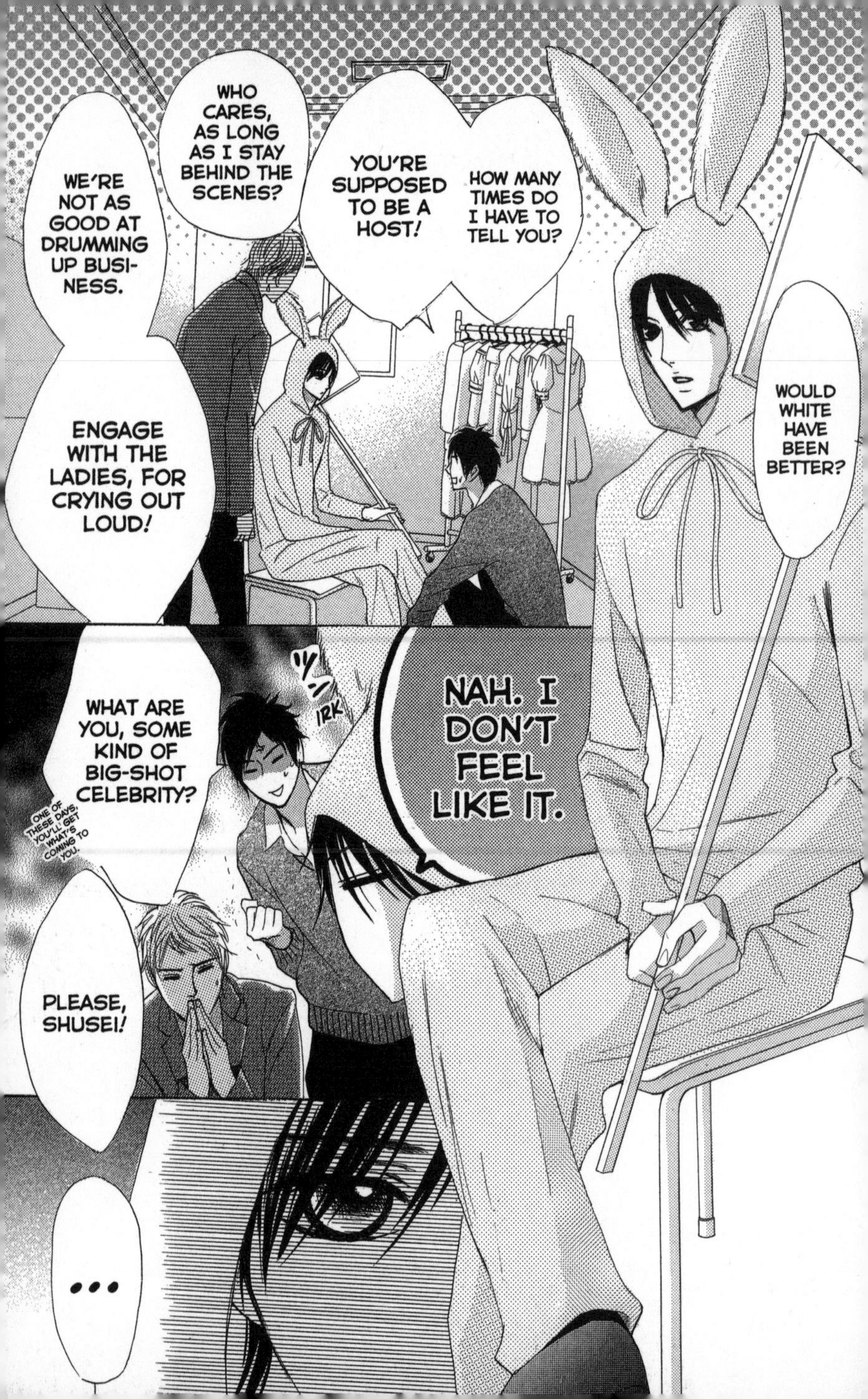
HOW MANY TIMES DO I HAVE TO TELL YOU?
YOU'RE SUPPOSED TO BE A HOST!
WHO CARES, AS LONG AS I STAY BEHIND THE SCENES?
WE'RE NOT AS GOOD AT DRUMMING UP BUSI-NESS.
ENGAGE WITH THE LADIES, FOR CRYING OUT LOUD!
WOULD WHITE HAVE BEEN BETTER?
NAH. I DON'T FEEL LIKE IT.
IRK
WHAT ARE YOU, SOME KIND OF BIG-SHOT CELEBRITY?
ONE OF THESE DAYS, YOU'LL GET WHAT'S COMING TO YOU.
PLEASE, SHUSEI!
...

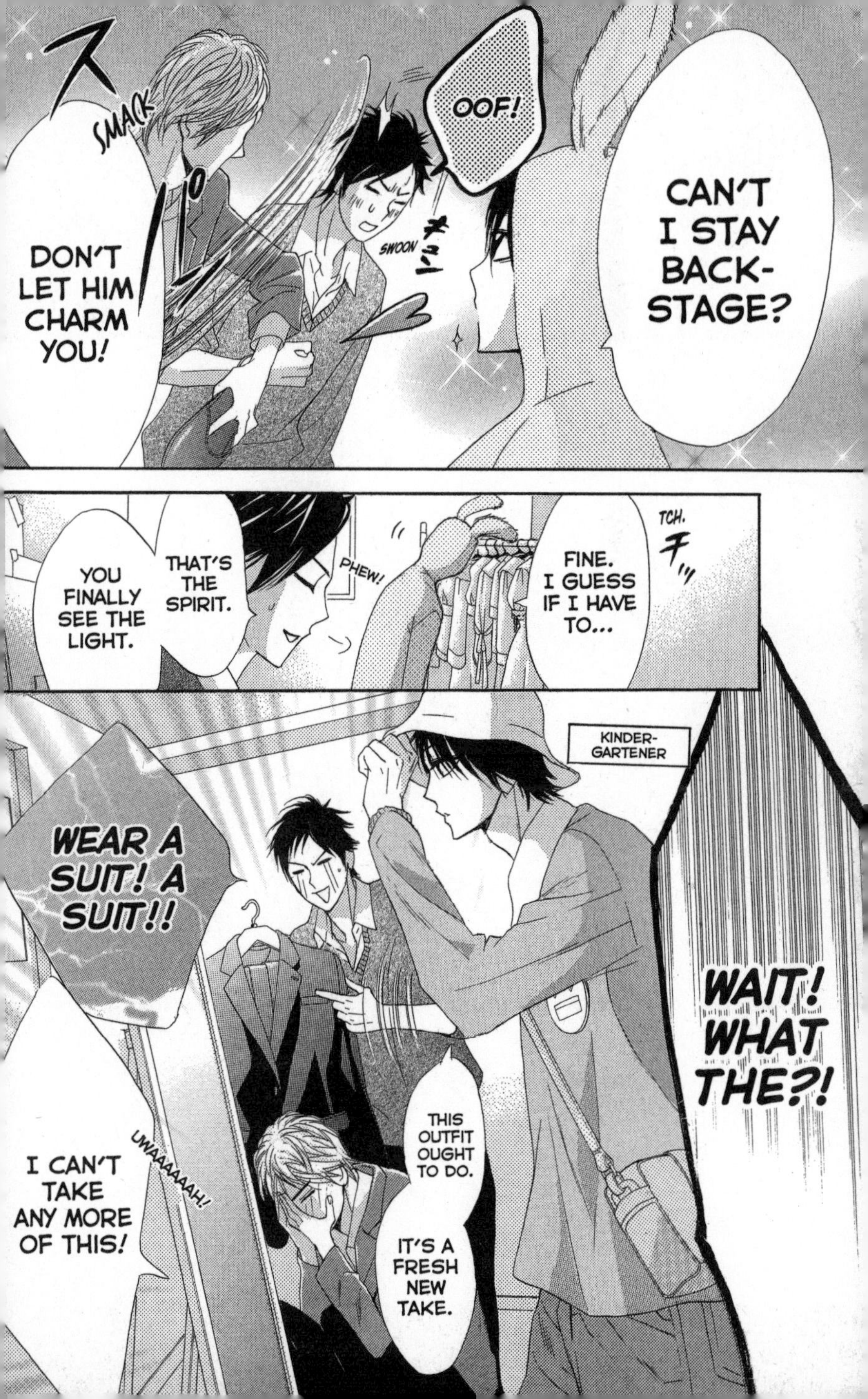
CAN'T I STAY BACK-STAGE?
OOF!
SWOON
SMACK
DON'T LET HIM CHARM YOU!
TCH.
FINE. I GUESS IF I HAVE TO...
PHEW!
THAT'S THE SPIRIT.
YOU FINALLY SEE THE LIGHT.
KINDER-GARTENER
WAIT! WHAT THE?!
WEAR A SUIT! A SUIT!!
THIS OUTFIT OUGHT TO DO.
IT'S A FRESH NEW TAKE.
UWAAAAAAAH!
I CAN'T TAKE ANY MORE OF THIS!

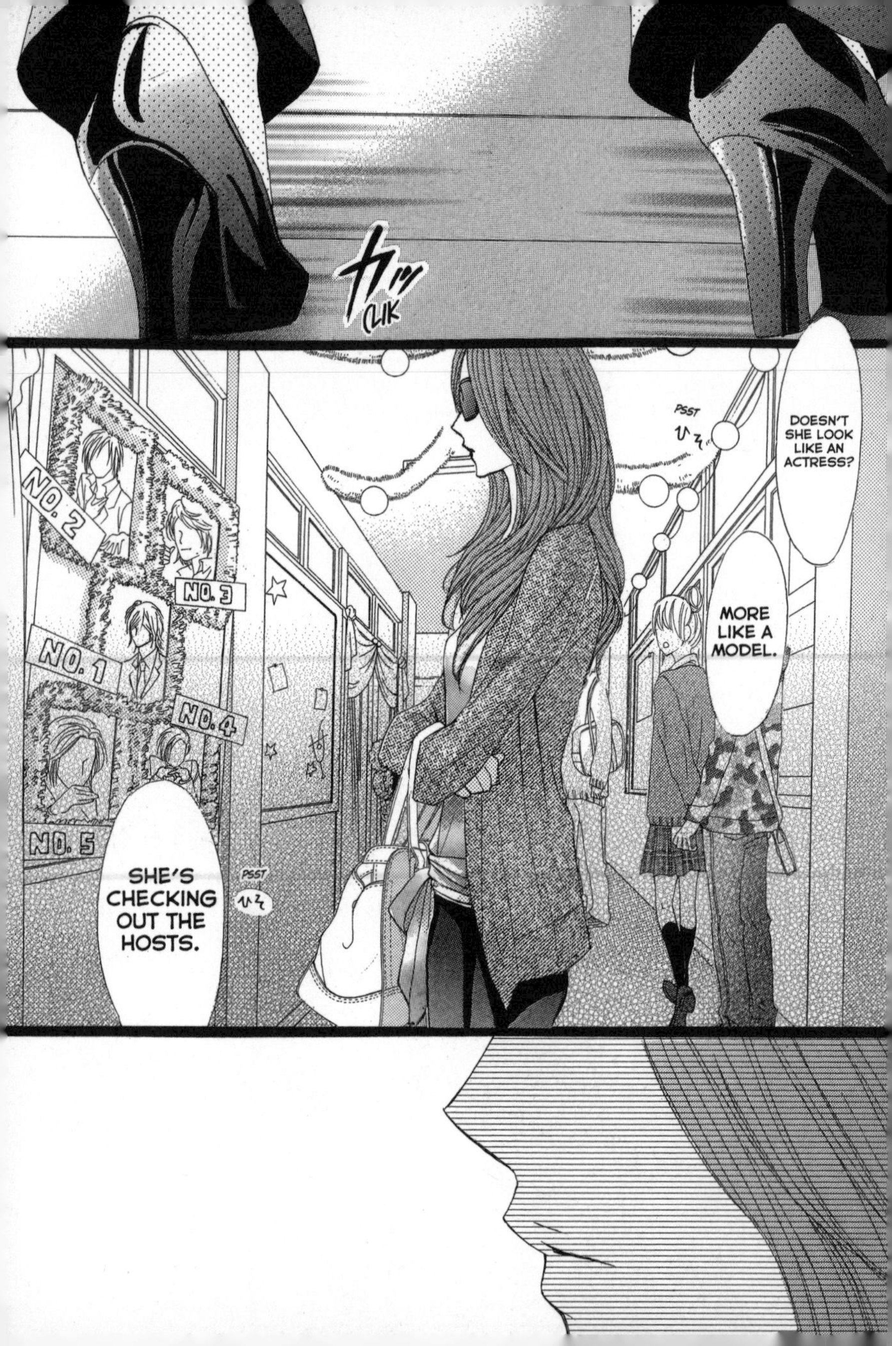
カッ
CLIK
DOESN'T SHE LOOK LIKE AN ACTRESS?
MORE LIKE A MODEL.
PSST
ひそ
NO. 2
NO. 3
NO. 1
NO. 4
NO. 5
SHE'S CHECKING OUT THE HOSTS.
PSST
ひそ

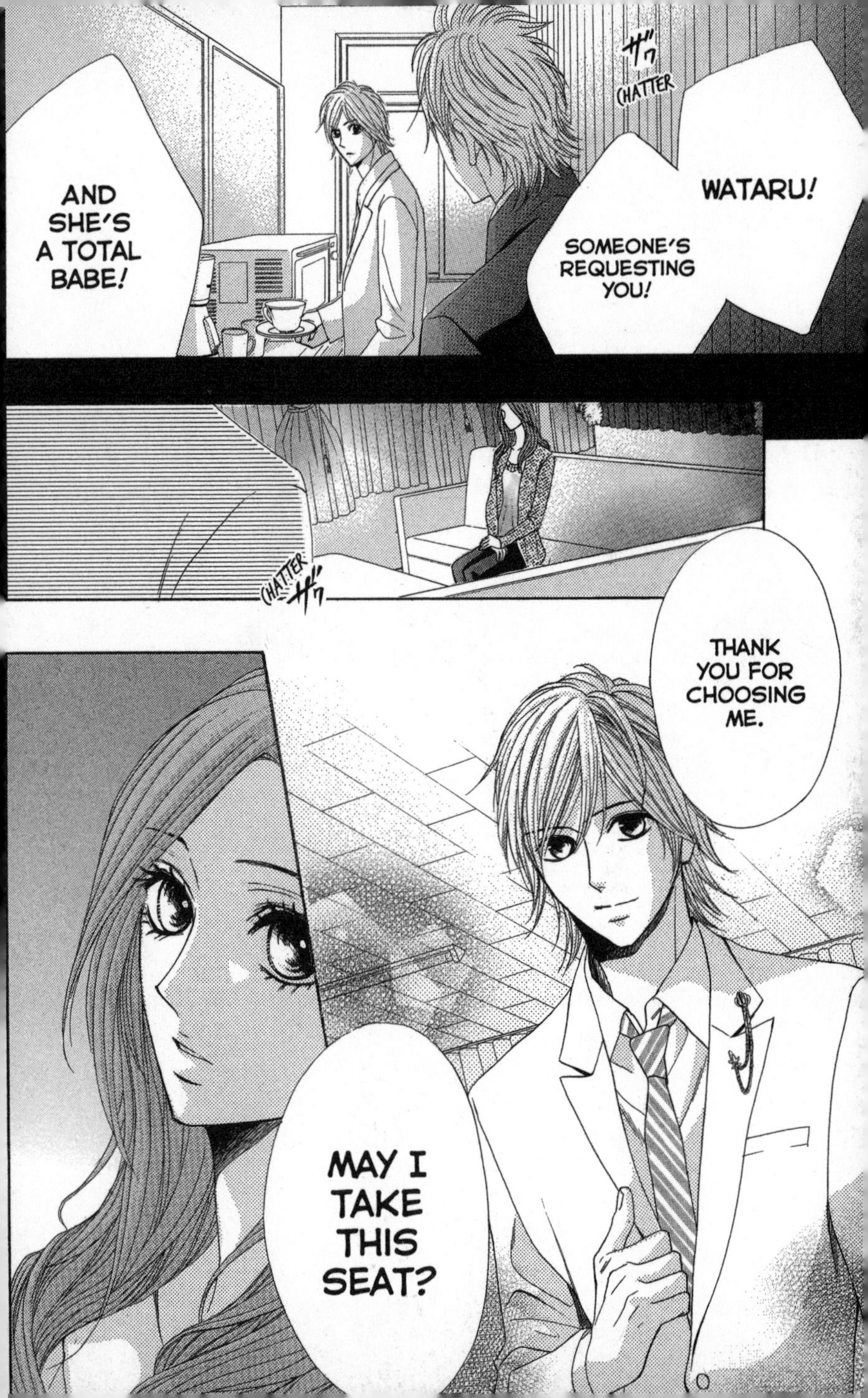
CHATTER
WATARU!
SOMEONE'S REQUESTING YOU!
AND SHE'S A TOTAL BABE!
CHATTER
THANK YOU FOR CHOOSING ME.
MAY I TAKE THIS SEAT?

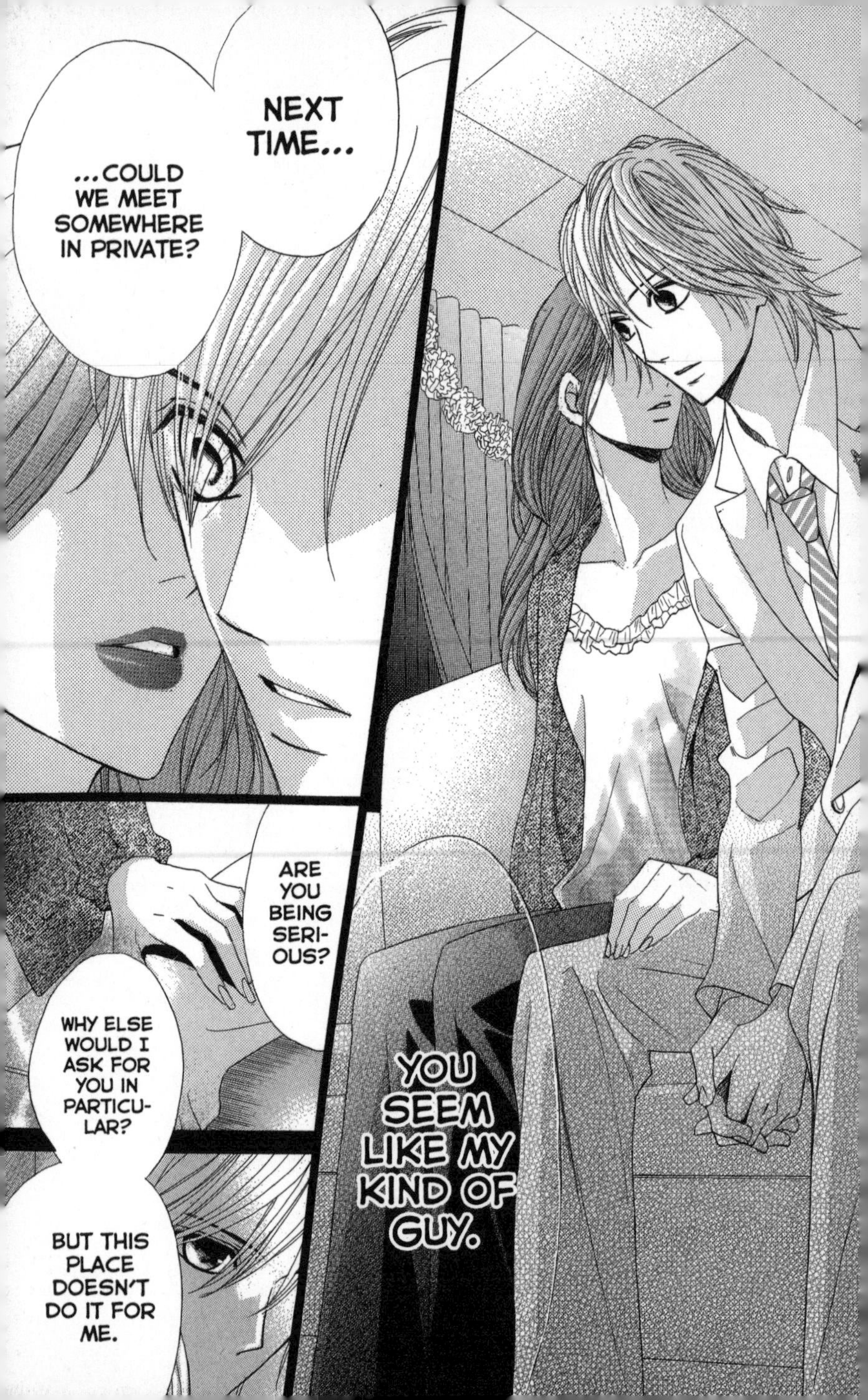
YOU SEEM LIKE MY KIND OF GUY.
NEXT TIME...
...COULD WE MEET SOMEWHERE IN PRIVATE?
ARE YOU BEING SERI-OUS?
WHY ELSE WOULD I ASK FOR YOU IN PARTICU-LAR?
BUT THIS PLACE DOESN'T DO IT FOR ME.

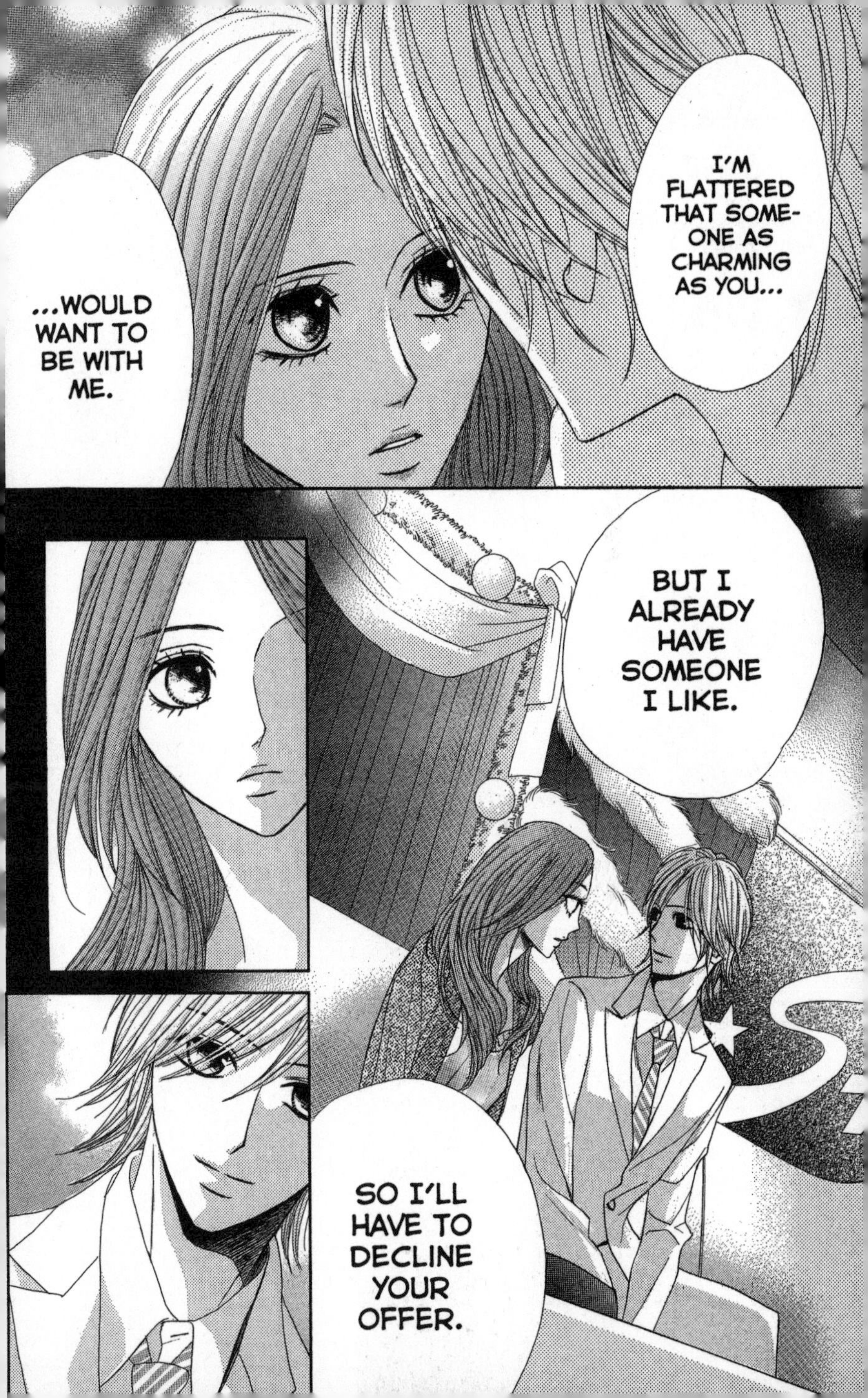
I'M FLATTERED THAT SOME-ONE AS CHARMING AS YOU...
...WOULD WANT TO BE WITH ME.
BUT I ALREADY HAVE SOMEONE I LIKE.
SO I'LL HAVE TO DECLINE YOUR OFFER.

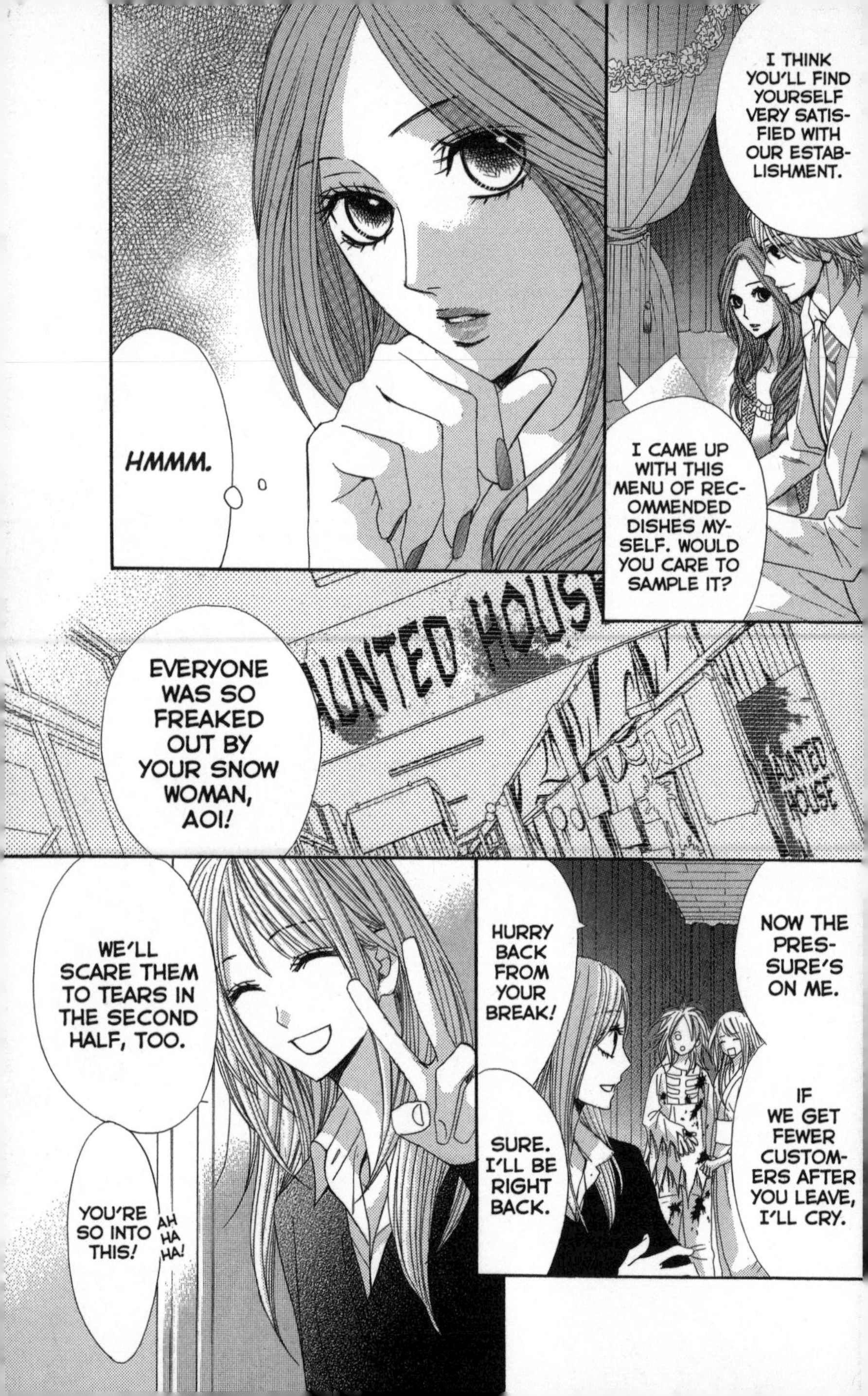
I THINK YOU'LL FIND YOURSELF VERY SATIS-FIED WITH OUR ESTAB-LISHMENT.
I CAME UP WITH THIS MENU OF REC-OMMENDED DISHES MY-SELF. WOULD YOU CARE TO SAMPLE IT?
HMMM.
EVERYONE WAS SO FREAKED OUT BY YOUR SNOW WOMAN, AOI!
NOW THE PRES-SURE'S ON ME.
HURRY BACK FROM YOUR BREAK!
IF WE GET FEWER CUSTOM-ERS AFTER YOU LEAVE, I'LL CRY.
SURE. I'LL BE RIGHT BACK.
WE'LL SCARE THEM TO TEARS IN THE SECOND HALF, TOO.
YOU'RE SO INTO THIS!
AH HA HA!

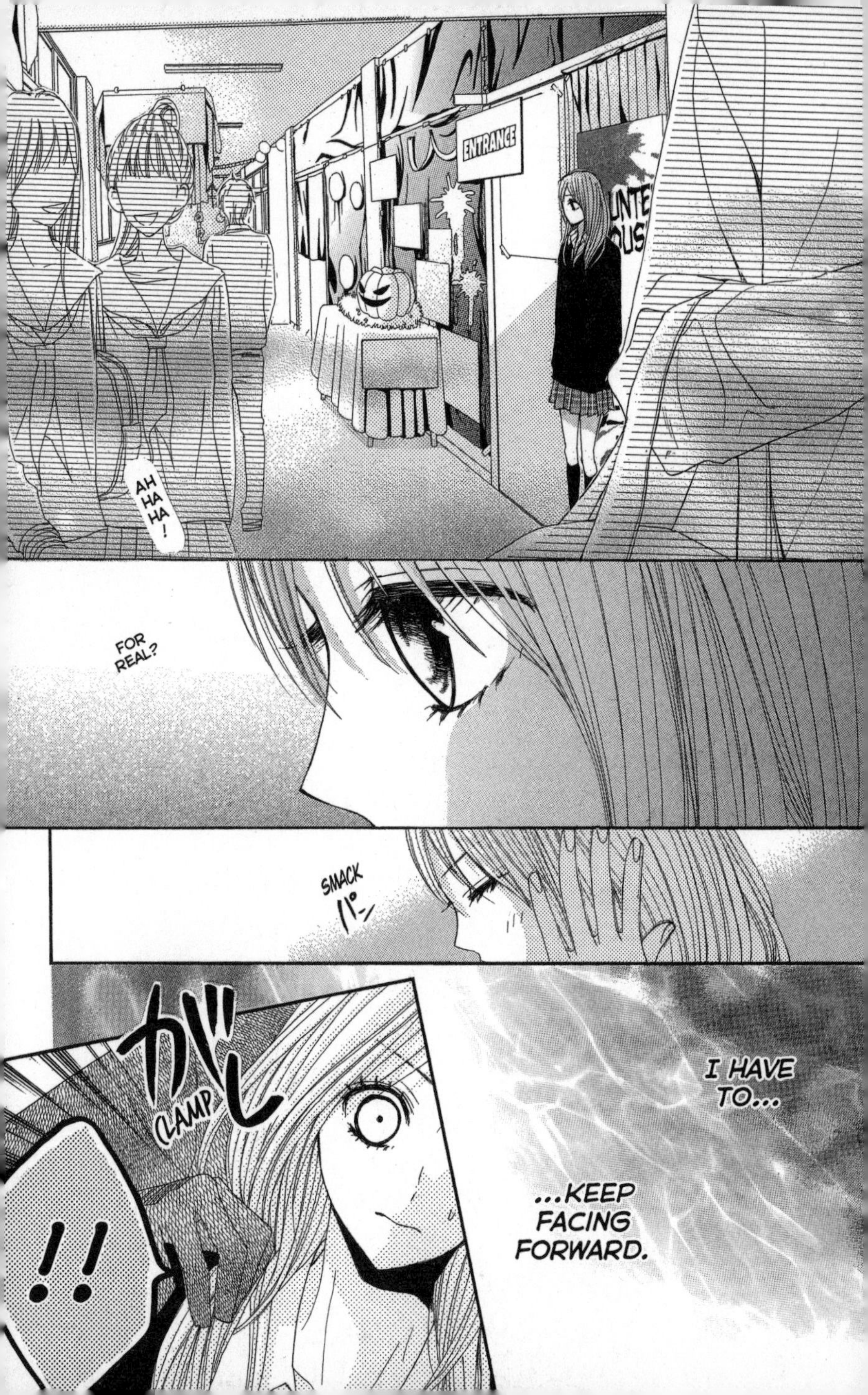
ENTRANCE
AH HA HA!
FOR REAL?
SMACK
パン
I HAVE TO...
...KEEP FACING FORWARD.
がし
CLAMP
!!

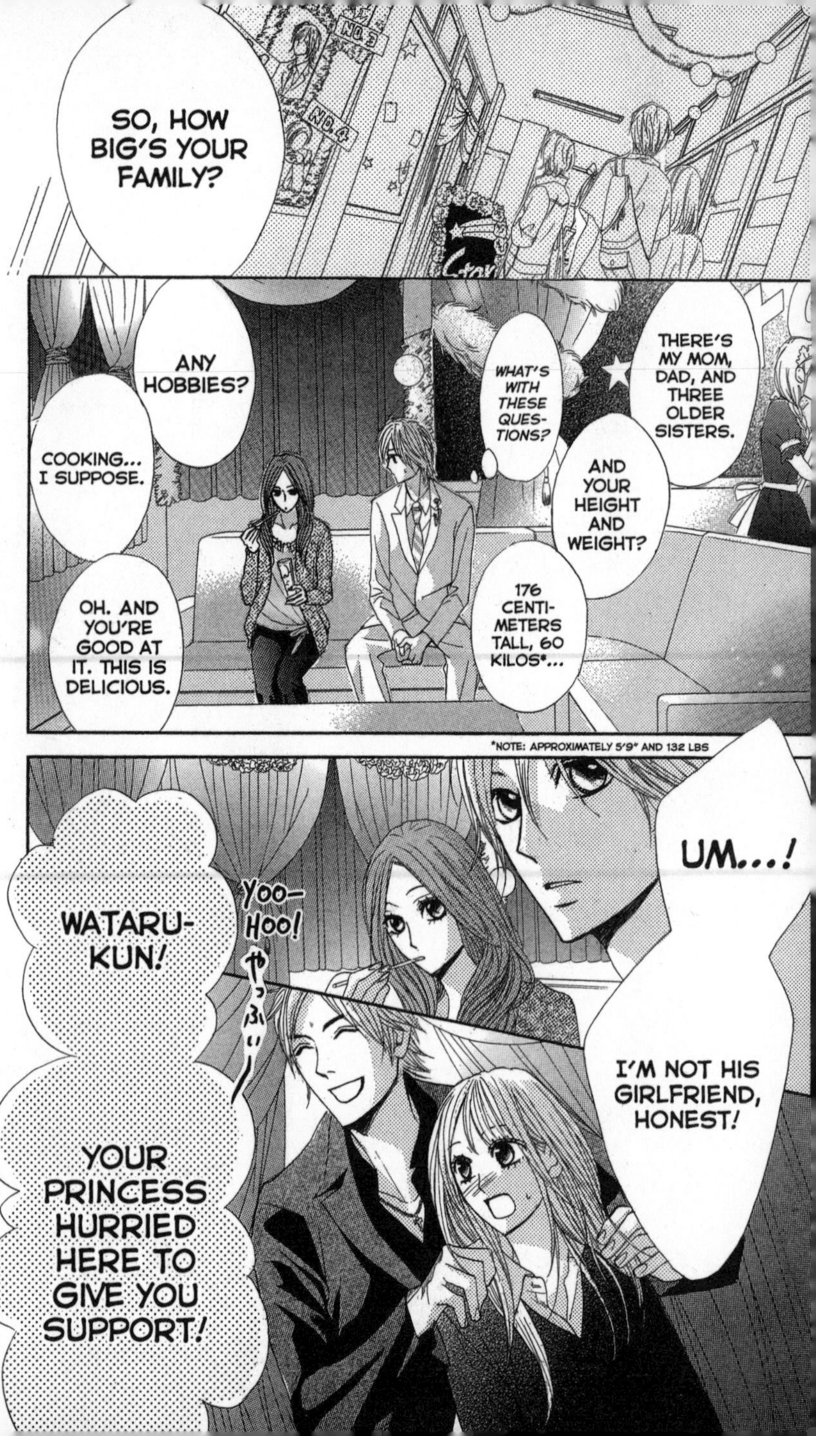
SO, HOW BIG'S YOUR FAMILY?
THERE'S MY MOM, DAD, AND THREE OLDER SISTERS.
WHAT'S WITH THESE QUES-TIONS?
AND YOUR HEIGHT AND WEIGHT?
176 CENTI-METERS TALL, 60 KILOS*...
ANY HOBBIES?
COOKING... I SUPPOSE.
OH. AND YOU'RE GOOD AT IT. THIS IS DELICIOUS.
UM...!
I'M NOT HIS GIRLFRIEND, HONEST!
YOO-HOO!
やっふぃー
WATARU-KUN!
YOUR PRINCESS HURRIED HERE TO GIVE YOU SUPPORT!

*NOTE: APPROXIMATELY 5'9" AND 132 LBS

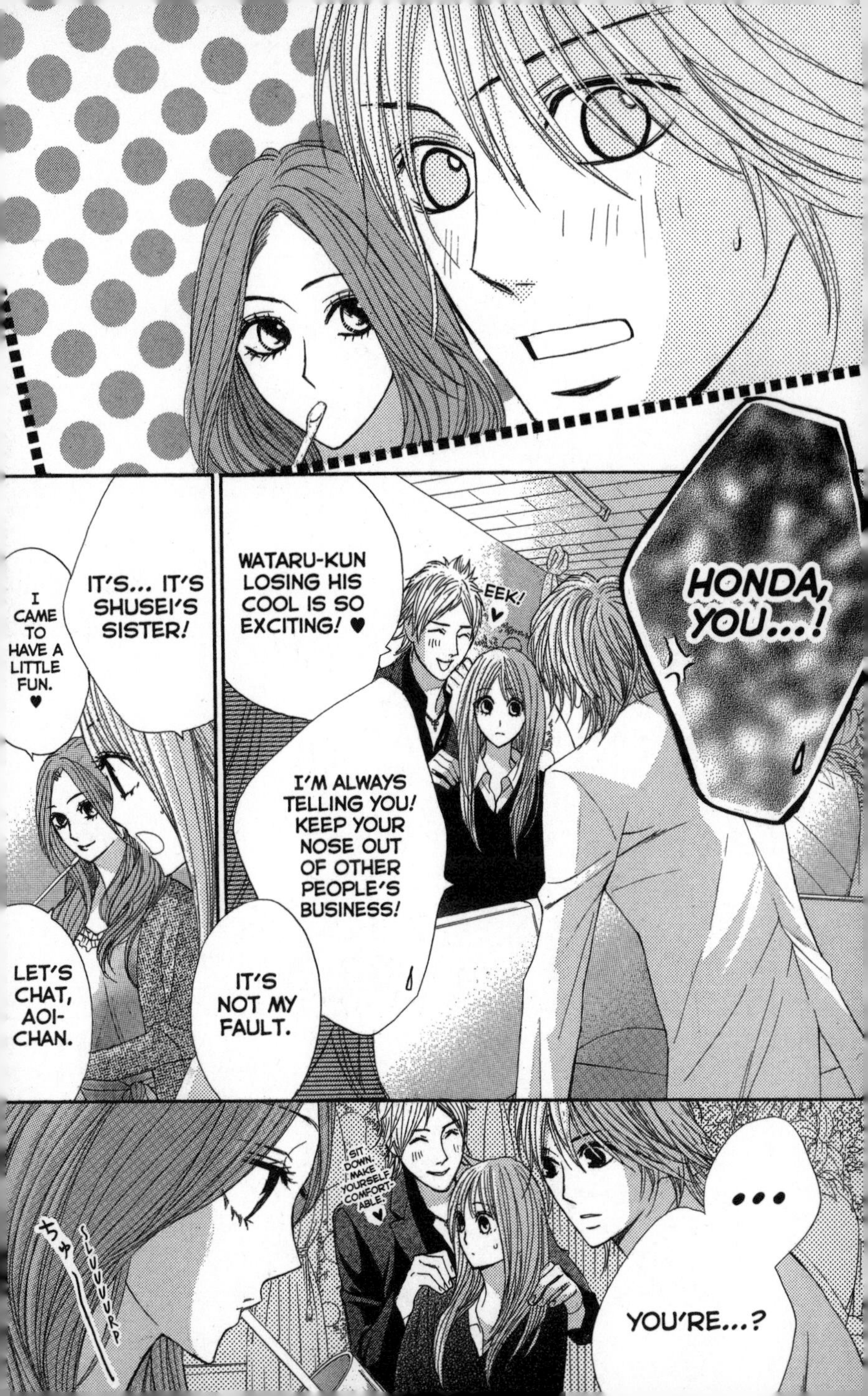
HONDA, YOU...!
WATARU-KUN LOSING HIS COOL IS SO EXCITING! ♥
EEK! ♥
I'M ALWAYS TELLING YOU! KEEP YOUR NOSE OUT OF OTHER PEOPLE'S BUSINESS!
IT'S NOT MY FAULT.
IT'S... IT'S SHUSEI'S SISTER!
I CAME TO HAVE A LITTLE FUN. ♥
LET'S CHAT, AOI-CHAN.
...
YOU'RE...?
SIT DOWN. MAKE YOURSELF COMFORT-ABLE. ♥
ちゅー
SLUUUURP

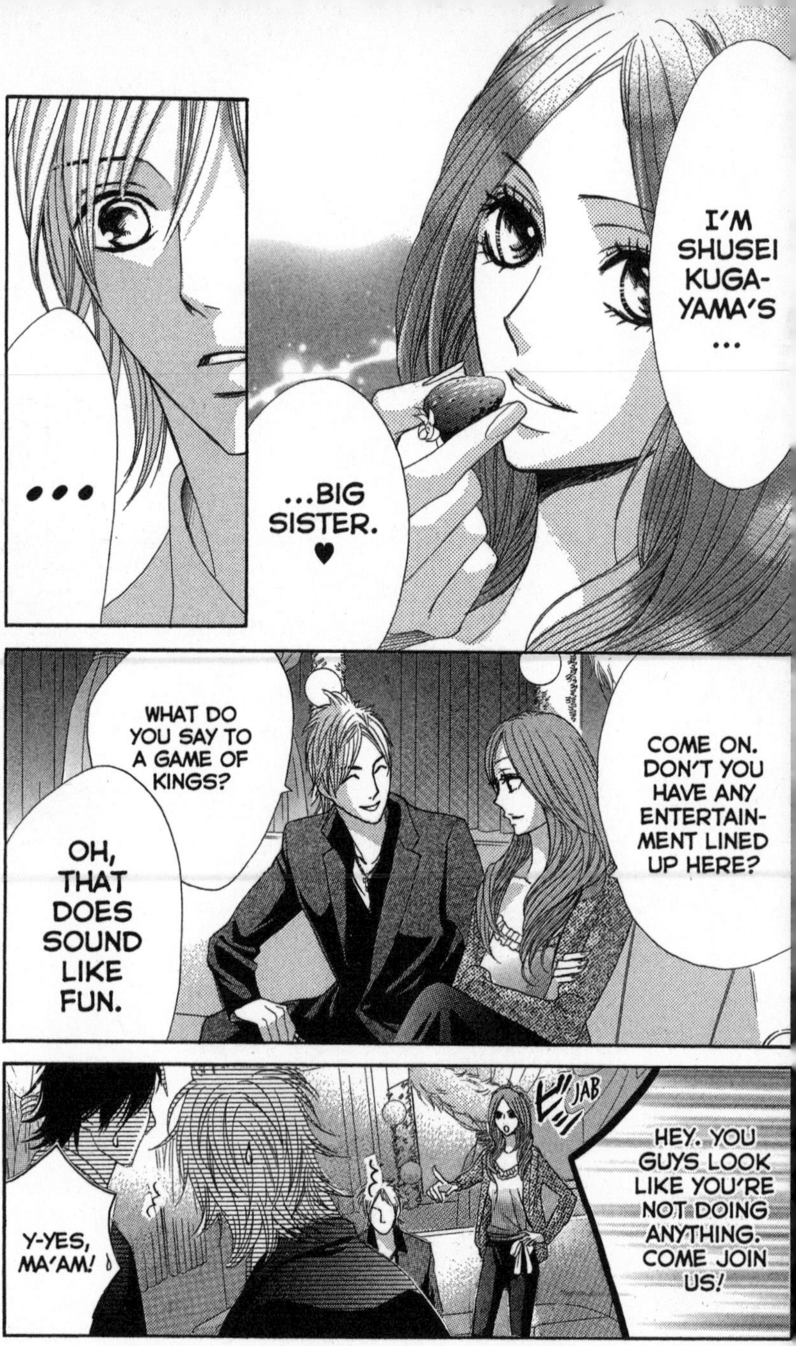
I'M SHUSEI KUGA-YAMA'S ...
...BIG SISTER. ♥
•••
COME ON. DON'T YOU HAVE ANY ENTERTAIN-MENT LINED UP HERE?
WHAT DO YOU SAY TO A GAME OF KINGS?
OH, THAT DOES SOUND LIKE FUN.
JAB
HEY. YOU GUYS LOOK LIKE YOU'RE NOT DOING ANYTHING. COME JOIN US!
Y-YES, MA'AM!

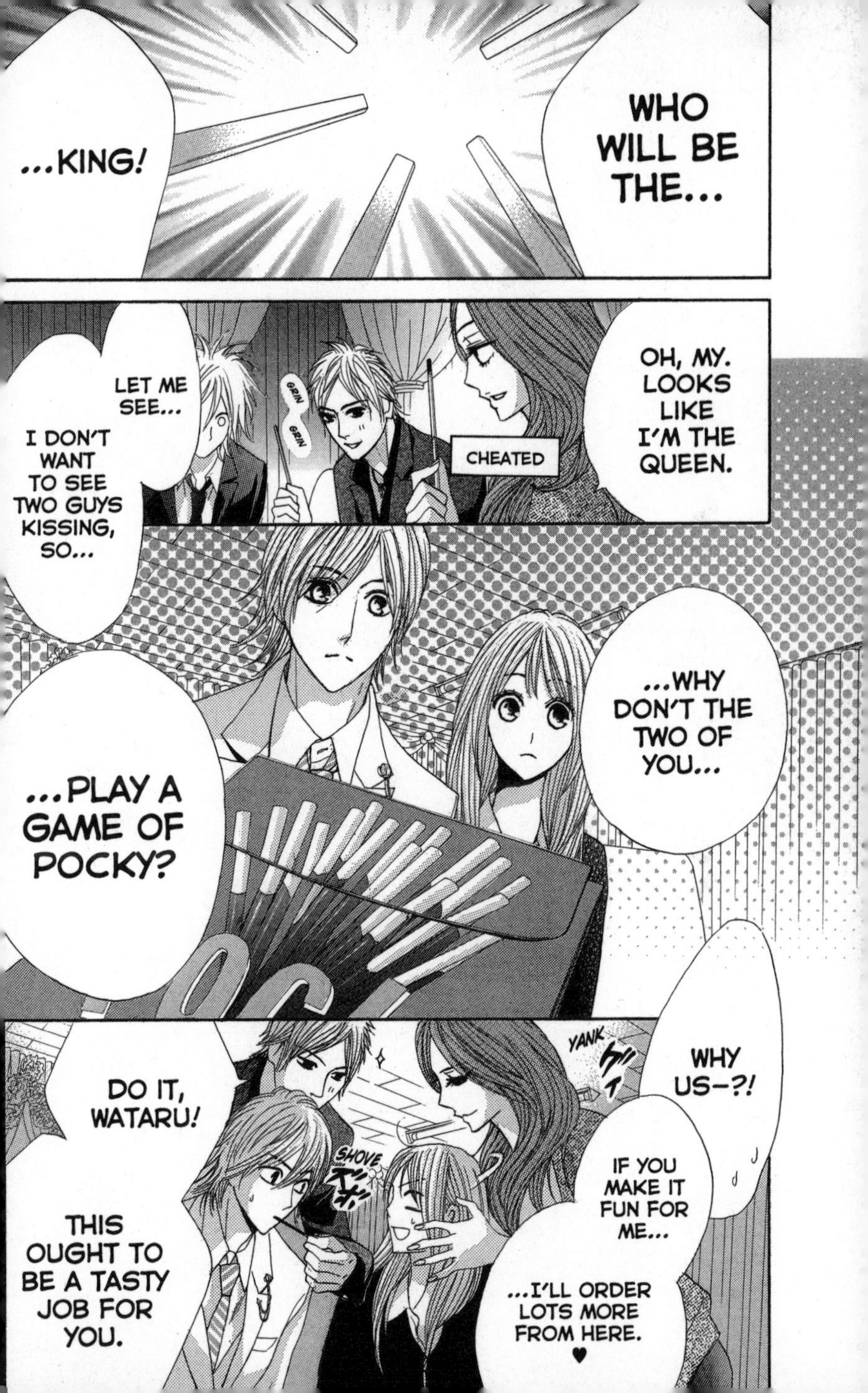
WHO WILL BE THE...
...KING!
OH, MY. LOOKS LIKE I'M THE QUEEN.
CHEATED
GRIN GRIN
LET ME SEE...
I DON'T WANT TO SEE TWO GUYS KISSING, SO...
...WHY DON'T THE TWO OF YOU...
...PLAY A GAME OF POCKY?
WHY US—?!
YANK
IF YOU MAKE IT FUN FOR ME...
...I'LL ORDER LOTS MORE FROM HERE. ♥
SHOVE
DO IT, WATARU!
THIS OUGHT TO BE A TASTY JOB FOR YOU.

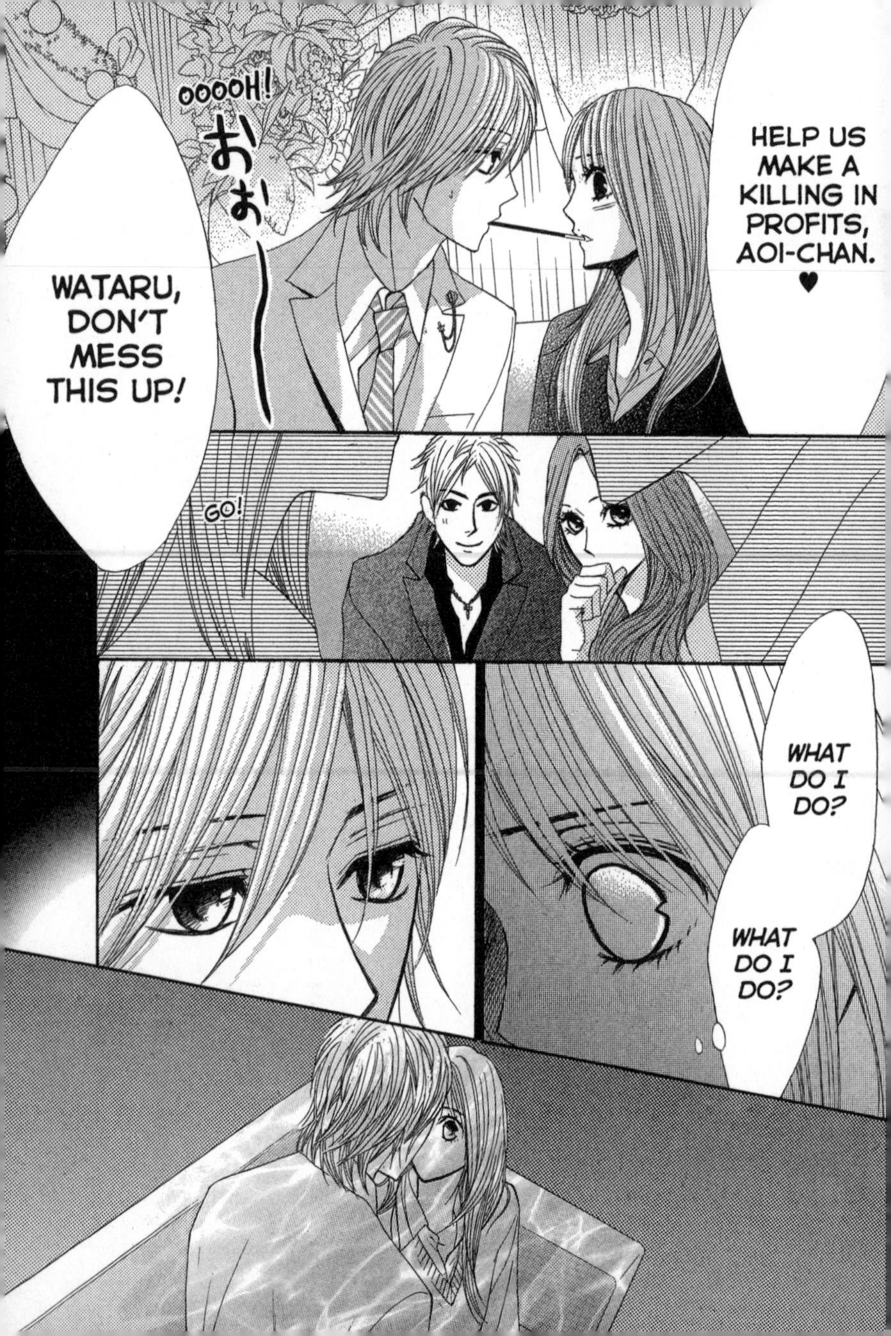
HELP US MAKE A KILLING IN PROFITS, AOI-CHAN. ♥
OOOOH!
おぉー
WATARU, DON'T MESS THIS UP!
GO!
WHAT DO I DO?
WHAT DO I DO?

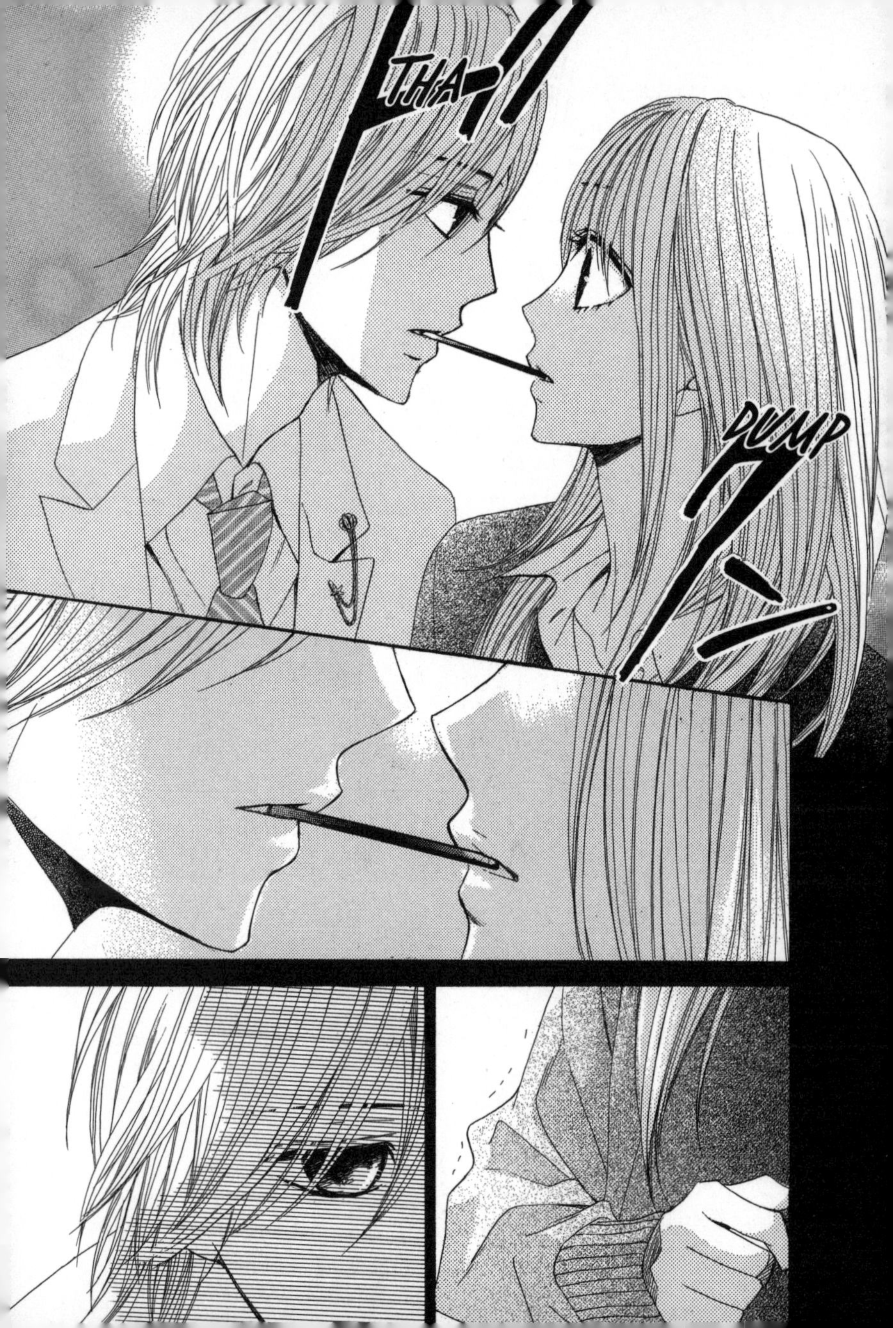
THA-
DUMP

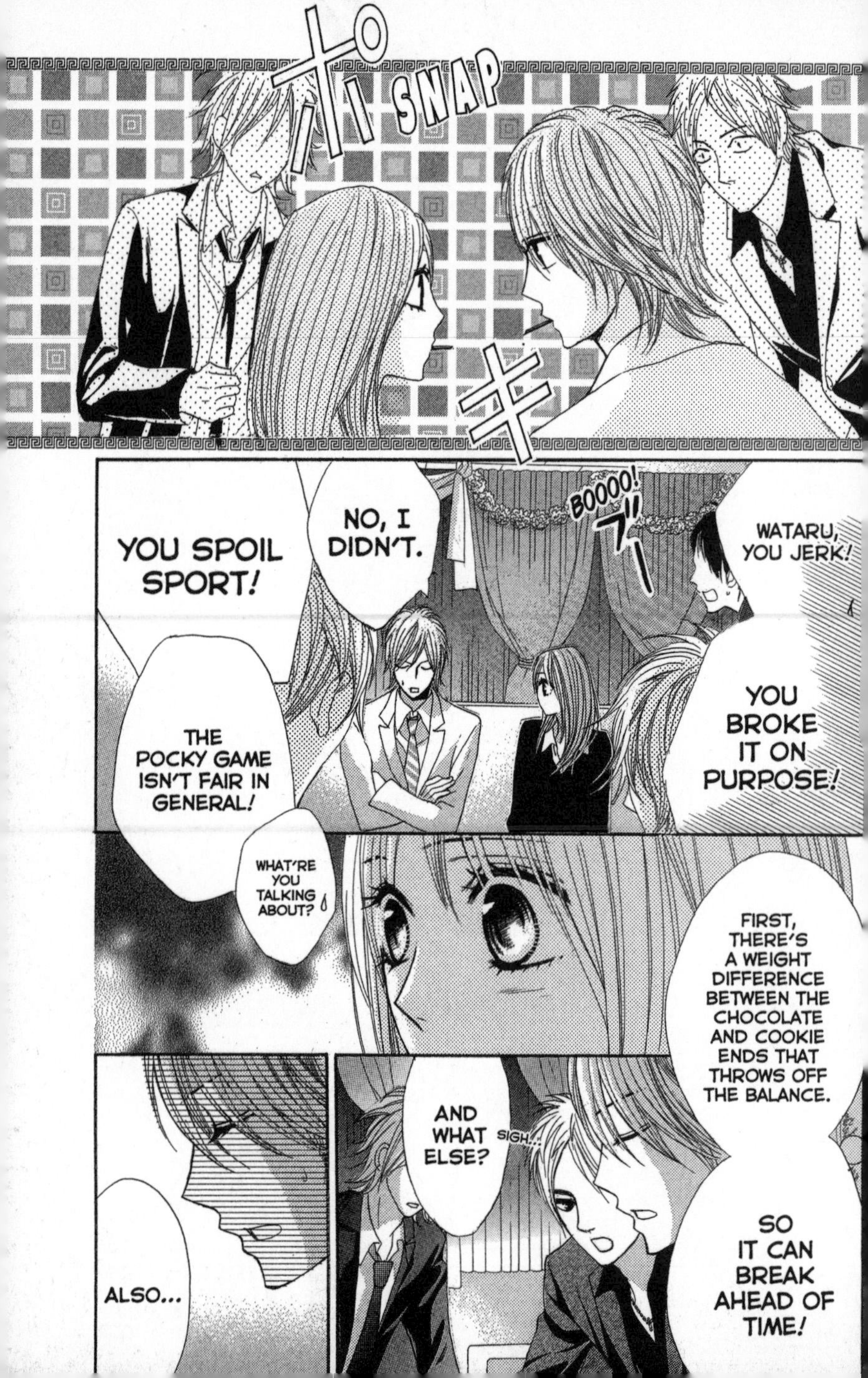
SNAP
WATARU, YOU JERK!
YOU BROKE IT ON PURPOSE!
BOOOO!
NO, I DIDN'T.
YOU SPOIL SPORT!
THE POCKY GAME ISN'T FAIR IN GENERAL!
FIRST, THERE'S A WEIGHT DIFFERENCE BETWEEN THE CHOCOLATE AND COOKIE ENDS THAT THROWS OFF THE BALANCE.
WHAT'RE YOU TALKING ABOUT?
SO IT CAN BREAK AHEAD OF TIME!
SIGH...
AND WHAT ELSE?
ALSO...

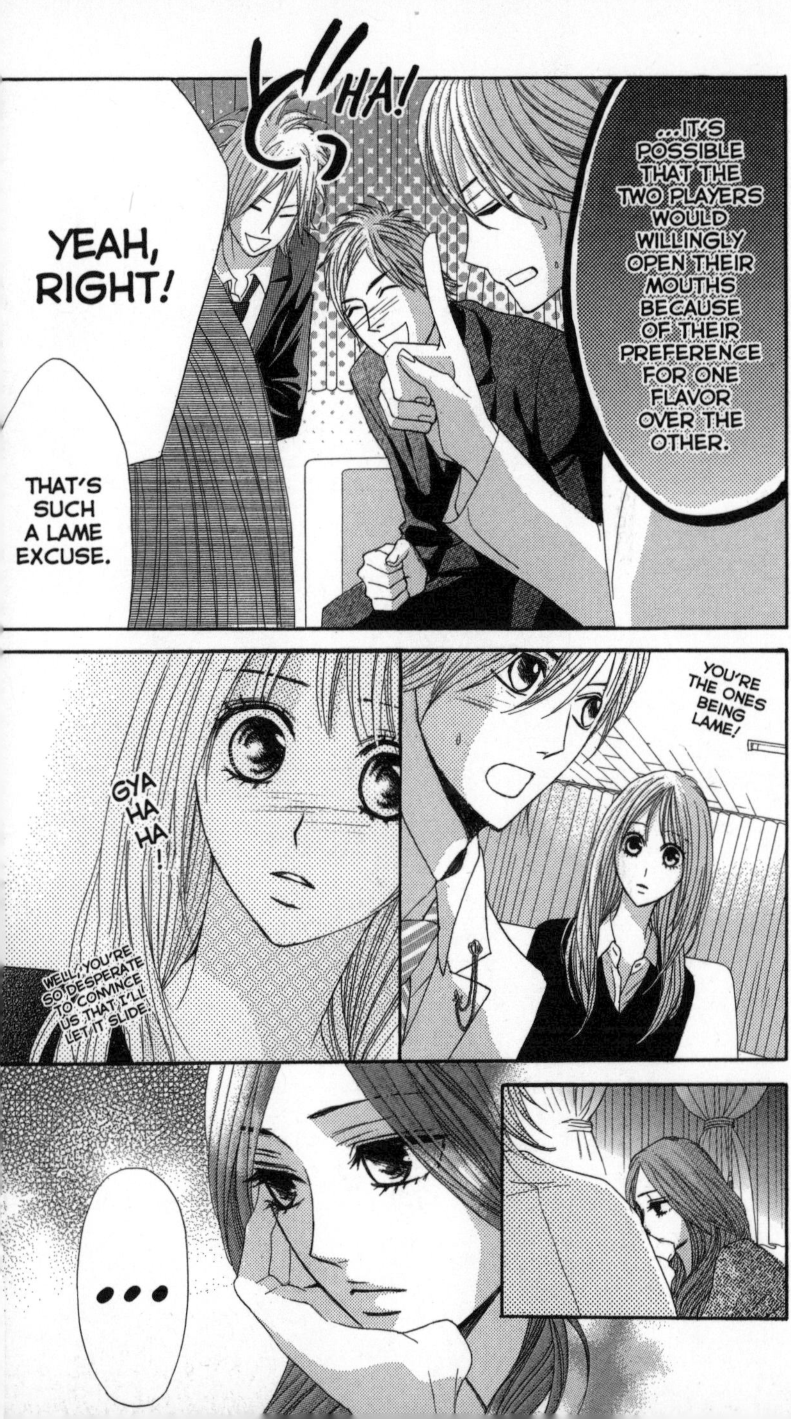
...IT'S POSSIBLE THAT THE TWO PLAYERS WOULD WILLINGLY OPEN THEIR MOUTHS BECAUSE OF THEIR PREFERENCE FOR ONE FLAVOR OVER THE OTHER.
HA!
YEAH, RIGHT!
THAT'S SUCH A LAME EXCUSE.
YOU'RE THE ONES BEING LAME!
GYA HA HA!
WELL, YOU'RE SO DESPERATE TO CONVINCE US THAT I'LL LET IT SLIDE.
...

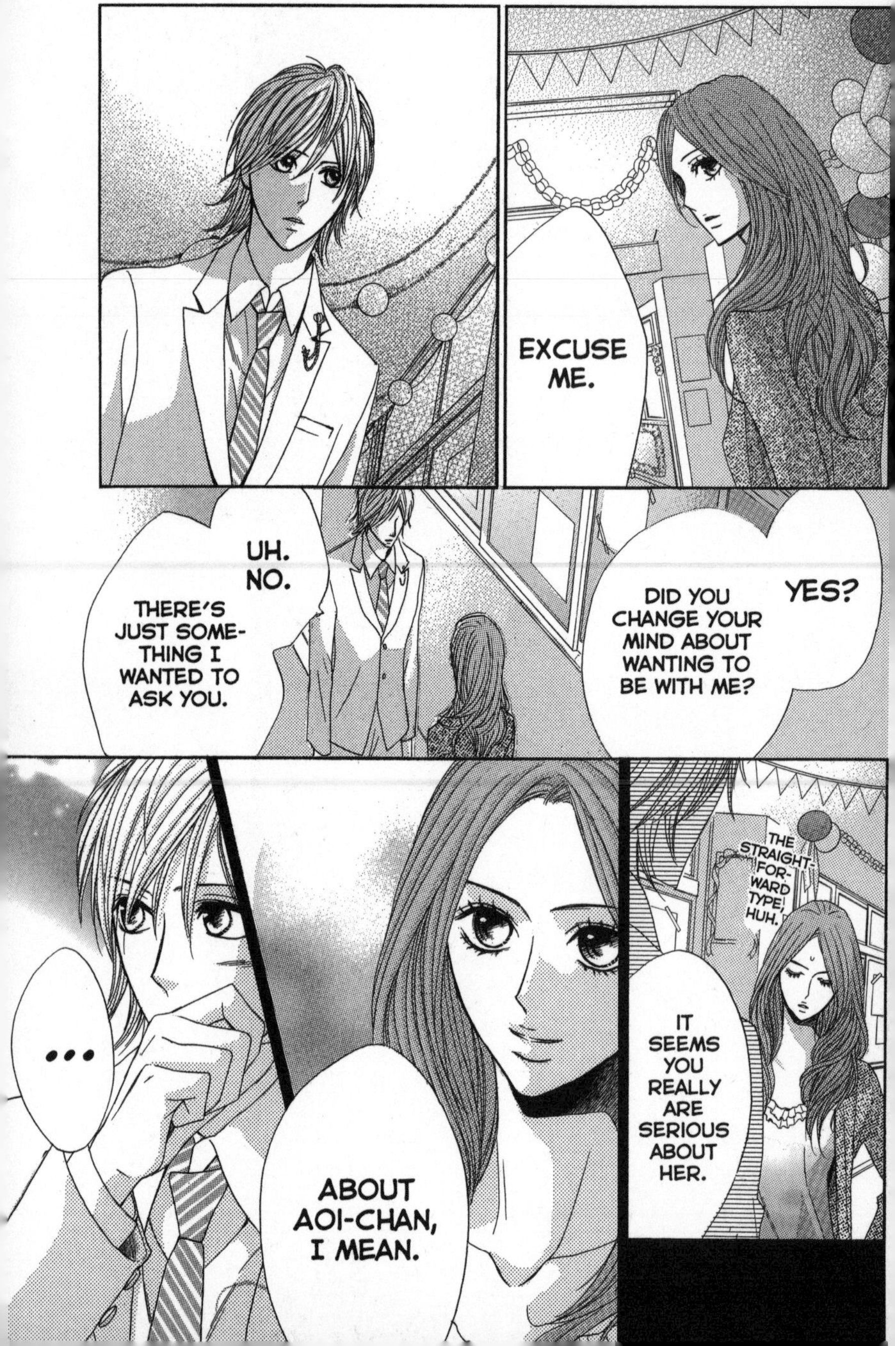
EXCUSE ME.
YES?
DID YOU CHANGE YOUR MIND ABOUT WANTING TO BE WITH ME?
UH. NO.
THERE'S JUST SOME-THING I WANTED TO ASK YOU.
THE STRAIGHT-FOR-WARD TYPE, HUH.
IT SEEMS YOU REALLY ARE SERIOUS ABOUT HER.
ABOUT AOI-CHAN, I MEAN.
...

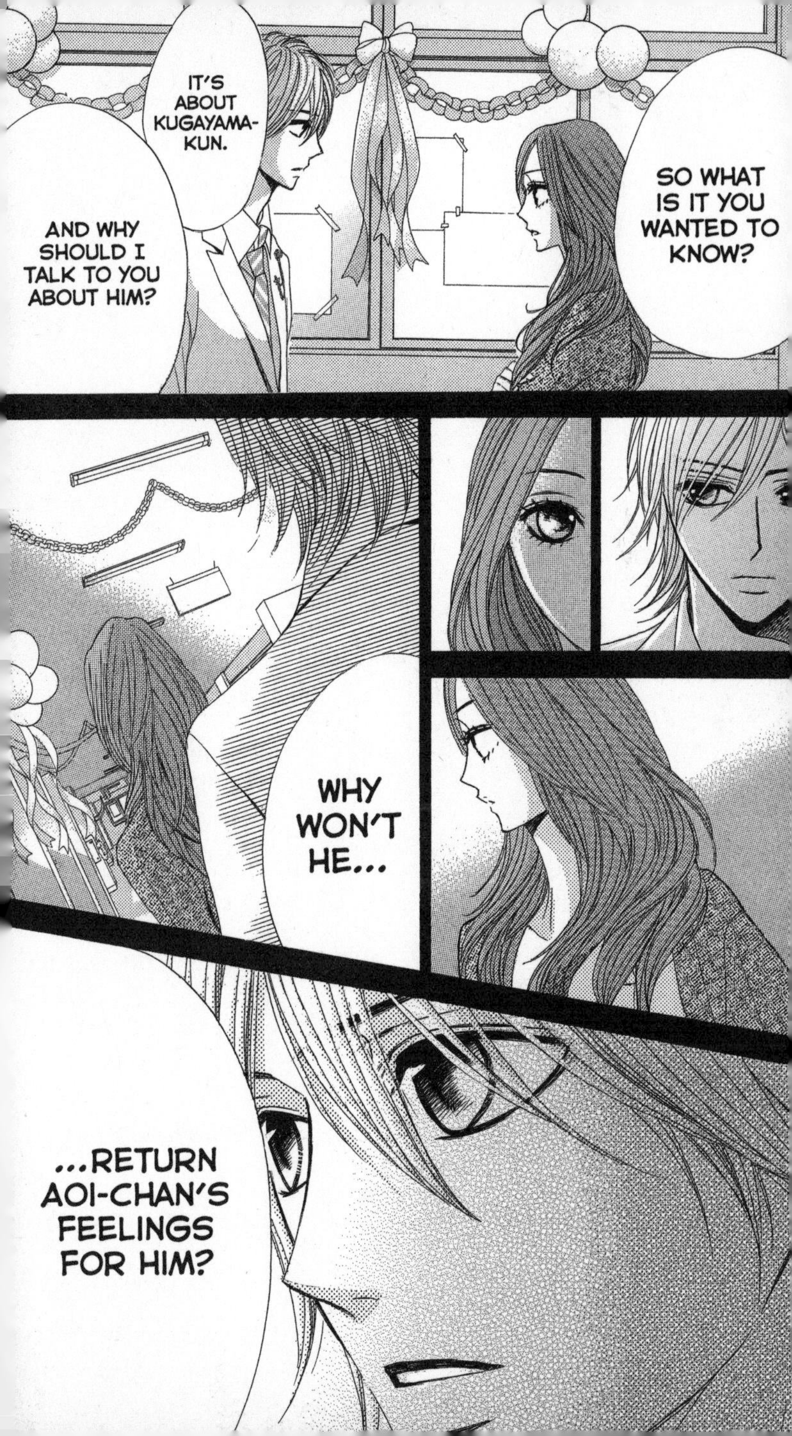
SO WHAT IS IT YOU WANTED TO KNOW?
IT'S ABOUT KUGAYAMA-KUN.
AND WHY SHOULD I TALK TO YOU ABOUT HIM?
WHY WON'T HE...
...RETURN AOI-CHAN'S FEELINGS FOR HIM?

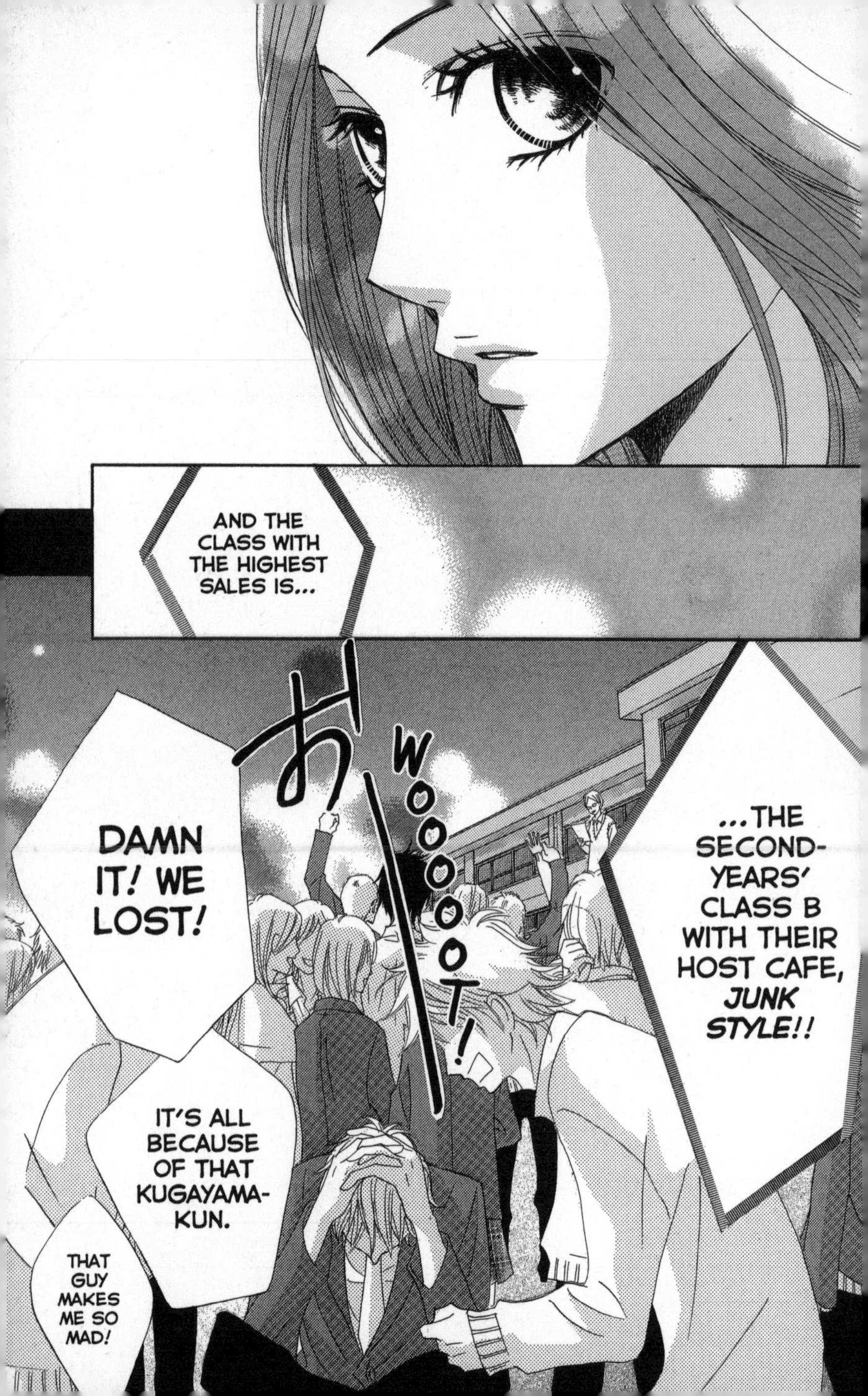
AND THE CLASS WITH THE HIGHEST SALES IS...
...THE SECOND-YEARS' CLASS B WITH THEIR HOST CAFE, JUNK STYLE!!
お
WOOOOOOT!
DAMN IT! WE LOST!
IT'S ALL BECAUSE OF THAT KUGAYAMA-KUN.
THAT GUY MAKES ME SO MAD!

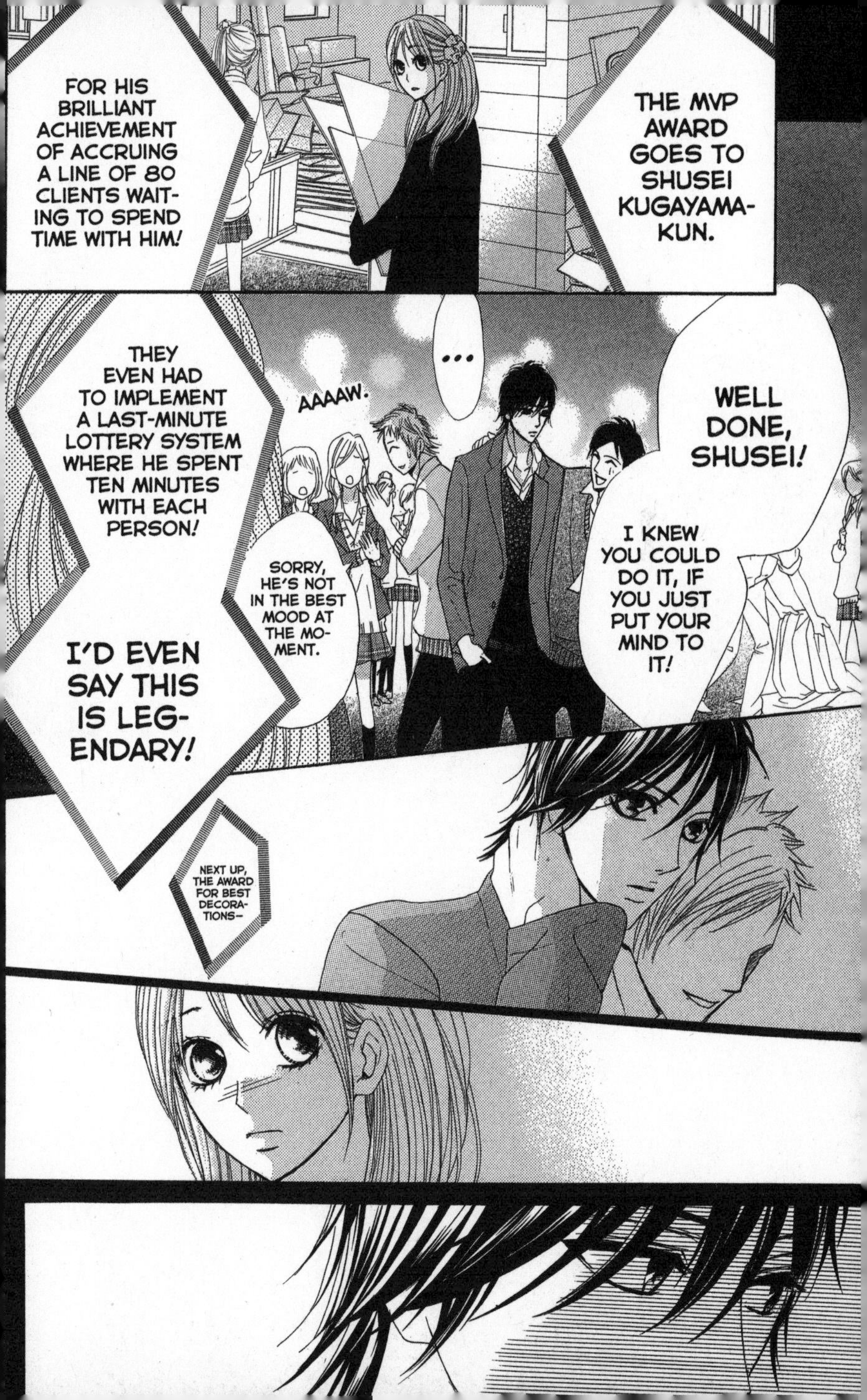
THE MVP AWARD GOES TO SHUSEI KUGAYAMA-KUN.
FOR HIS BRILLIANT ACHIEVEMENT OF ACCRUING A LINE OF 80 CLIENTS WAIT-ING TO SPEND TIME WITH HIM!
WELL DONE, SHUSEI!
I KNEW YOU COULD DO IT, IF YOU JUST PUT YOUR MIND TO IT!
...
AAAAW.
SORRY, HE'S NOT IN THE BEST MOOD AT THE MO-MENT.
THEY EVEN HAD TO IMPLEMENT A LAST-MINUTE LOTTERY SYSTEM WHERE HE SPENT TEN MINUTES WITH EACH PERSON!
I'D EVEN SAY THIS IS LEG-ENDARY!
NEXT UP, THE AWARD FOR BEST DECORA-TIONS—

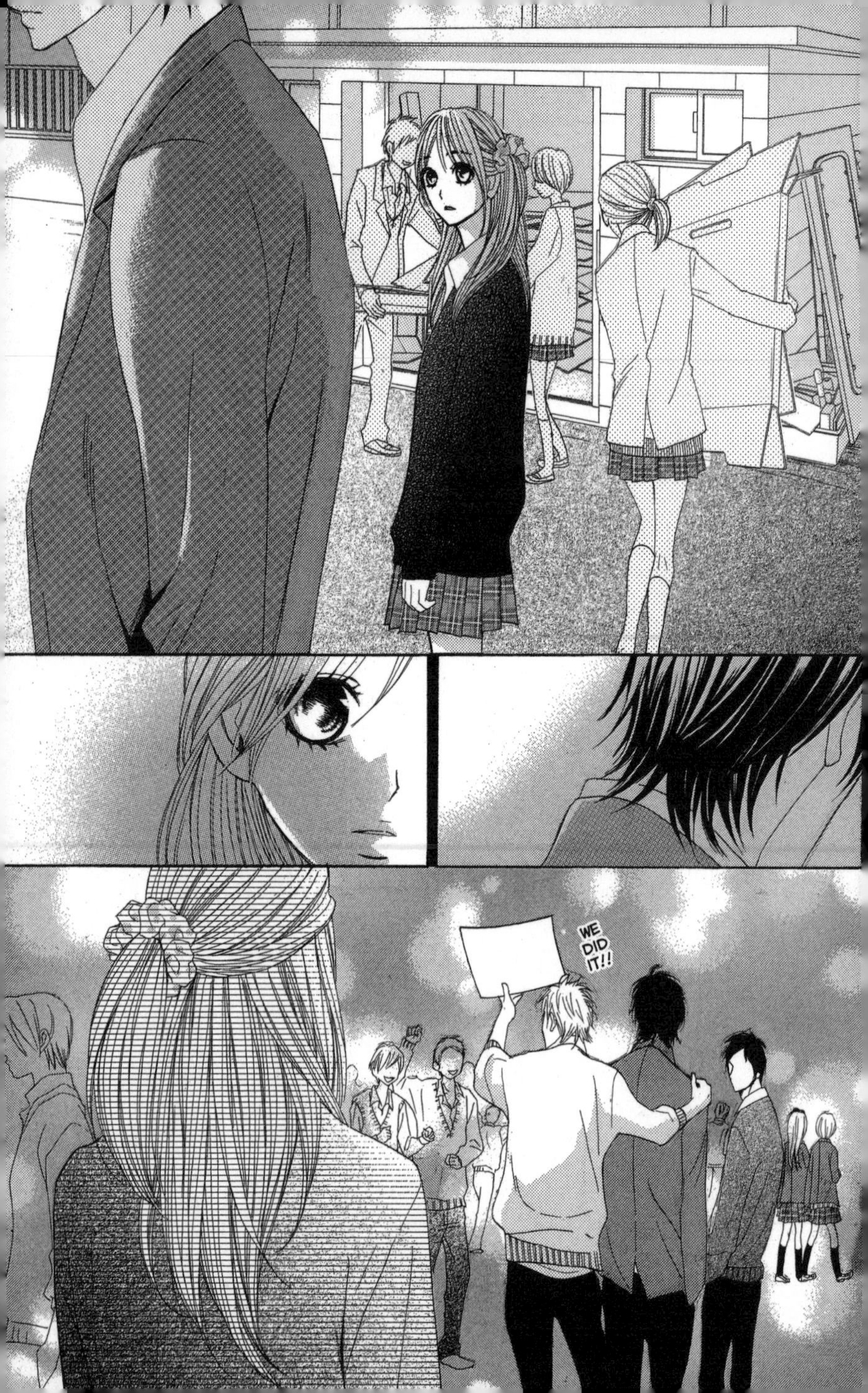
WE DID IT!!

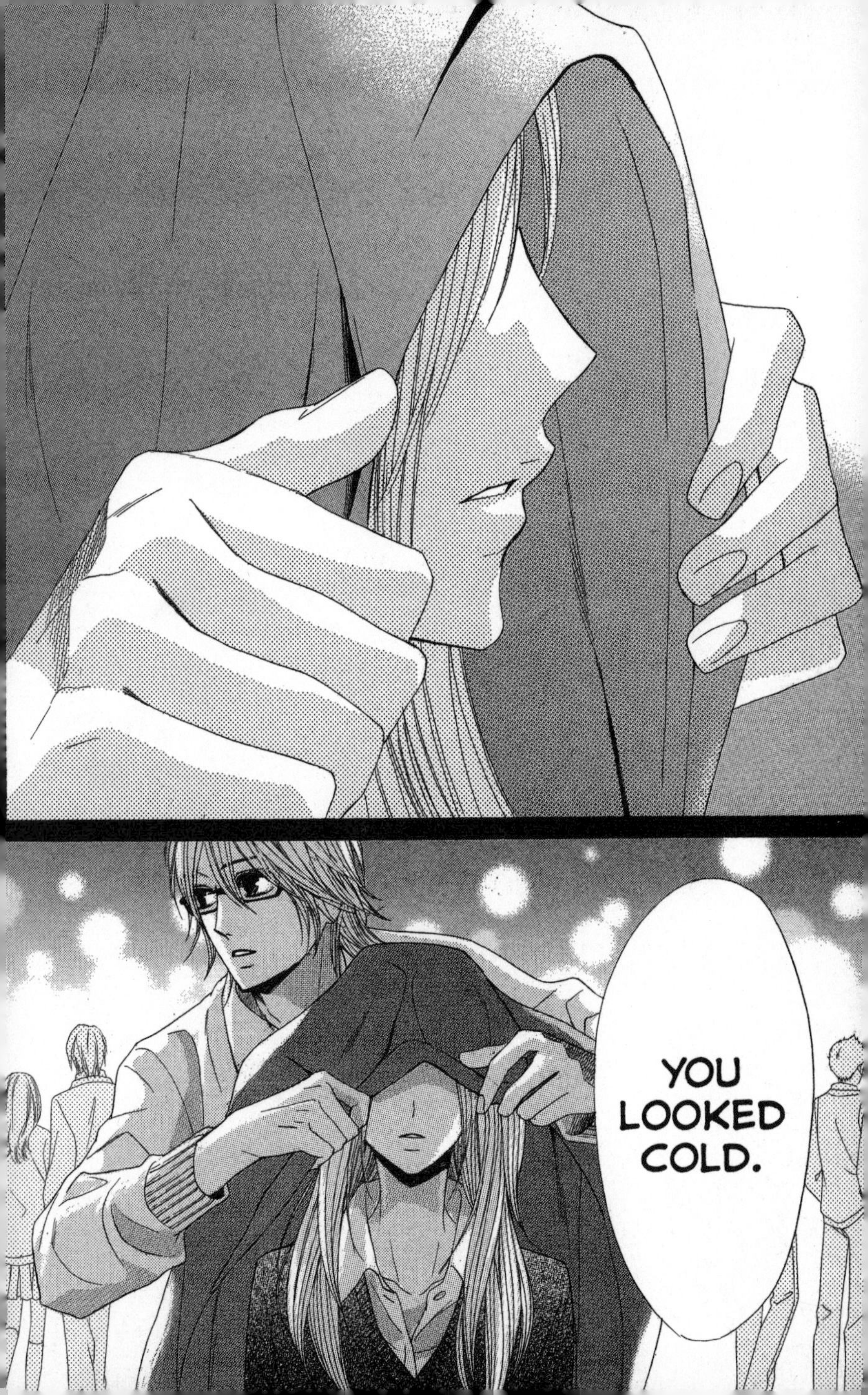
YOU LOOKED COLD.

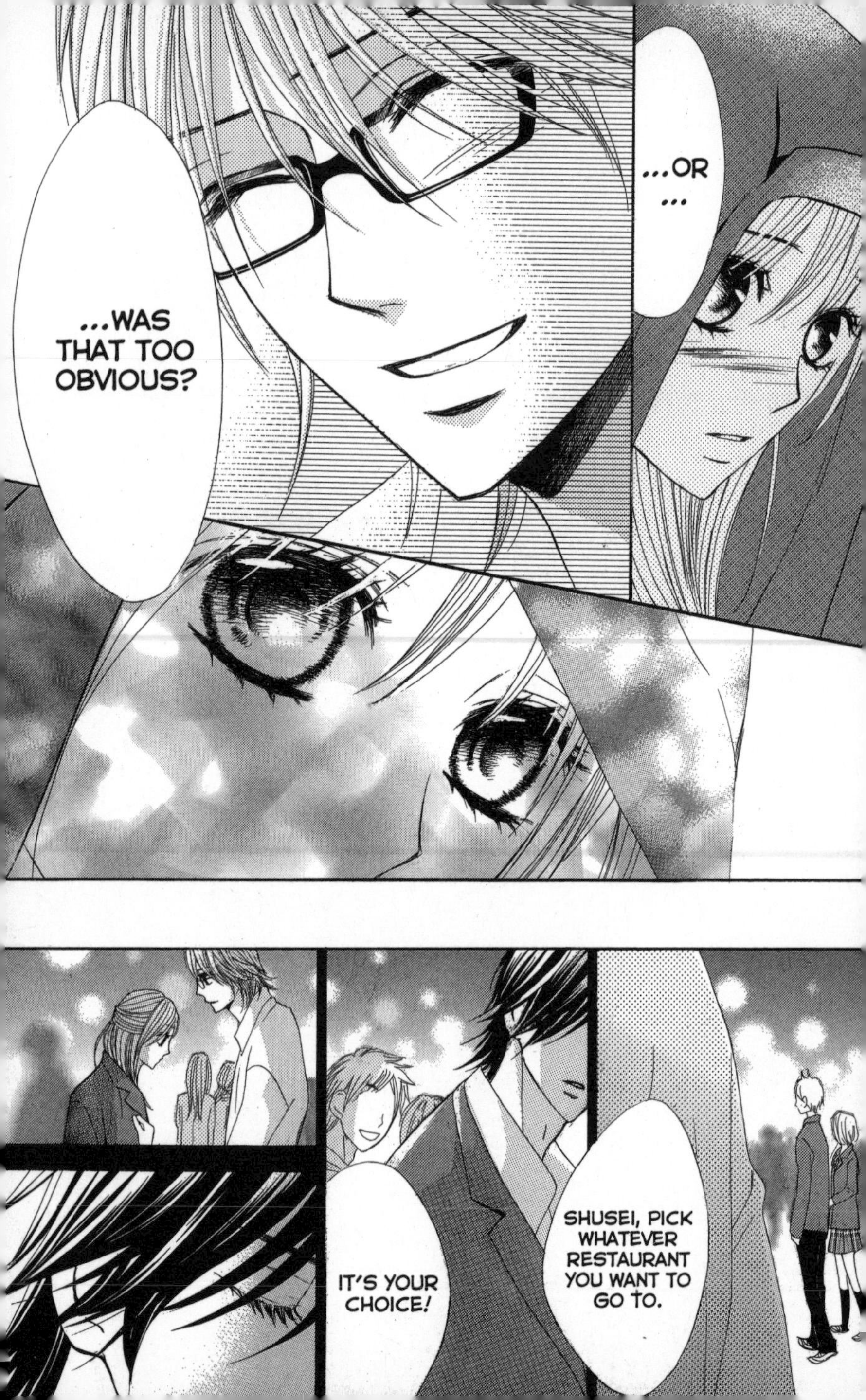
...OR ...
...WAS THAT TOO OBVIOUS?
SHUSEI, PICK WHATEVER RESTAURANT YOU WANT TO GO TO.
IT'S YOUR CHOICE!

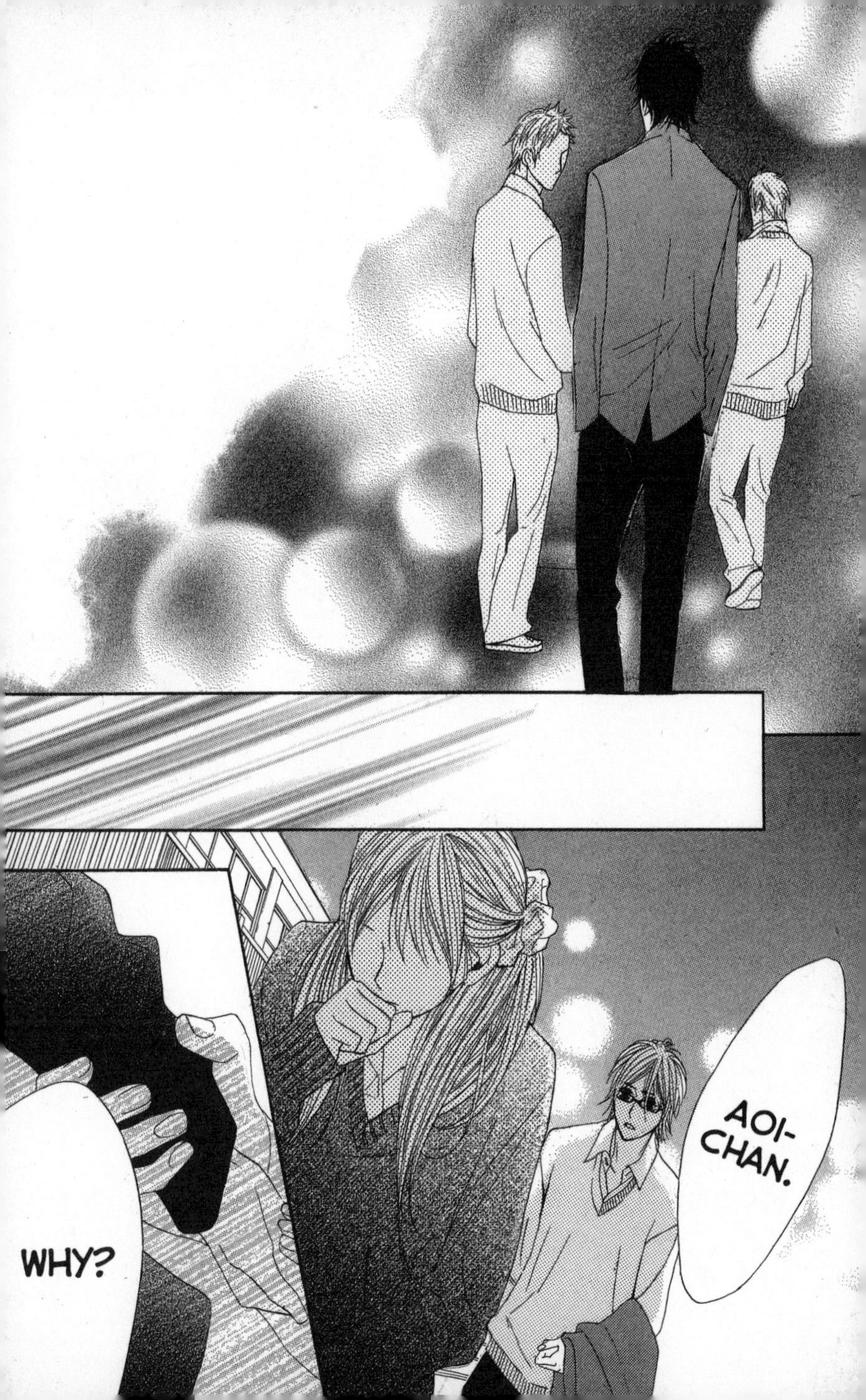

AOI-CHAN.
WHY?

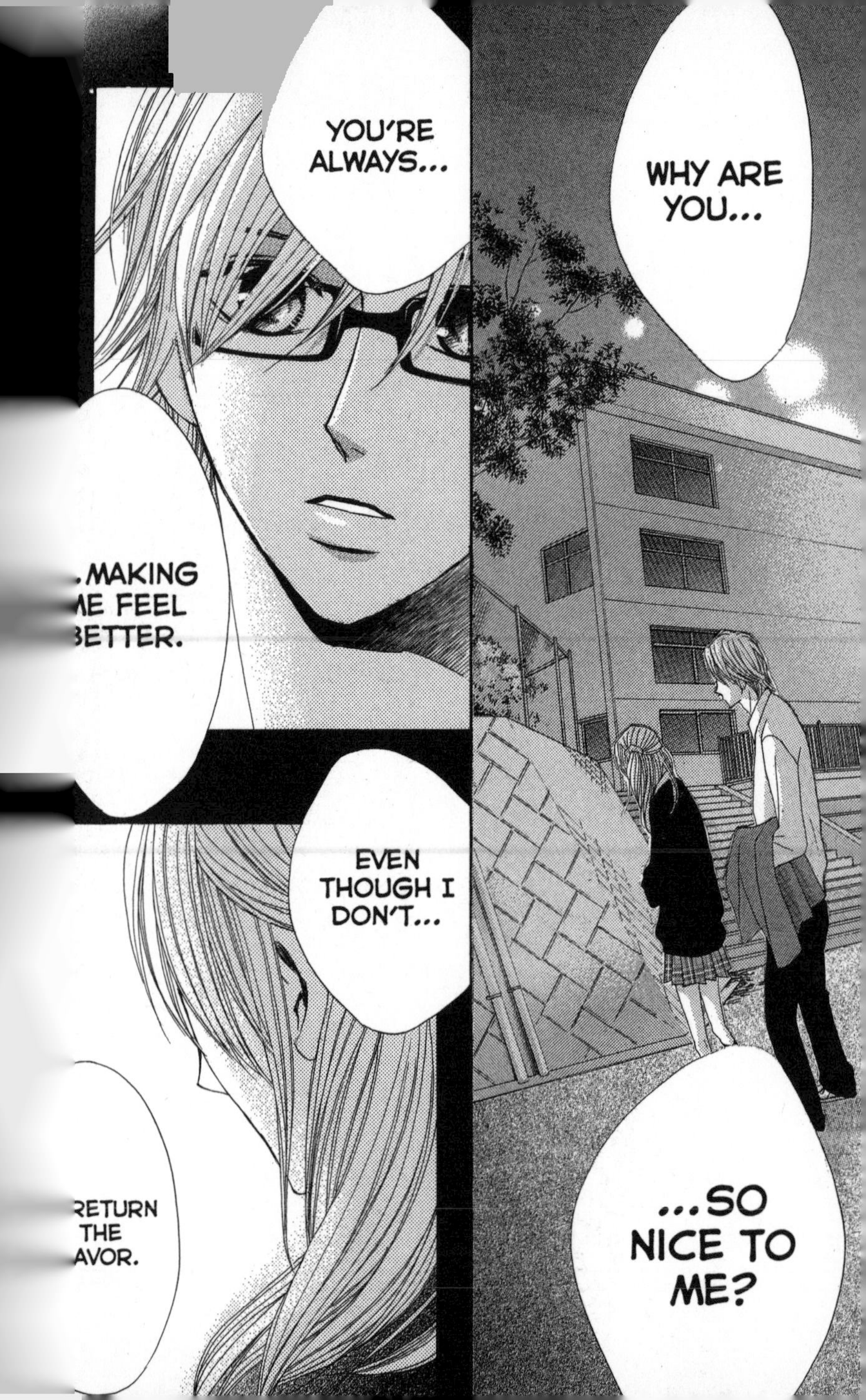
WHY ARE YOU...
...SO NICE TO ME?
YOU'RE ALWAYS...
...MAKING ME FEEL BETTER.
EVEN THOUGH I DON'T...
RETURN THE FAVOR.

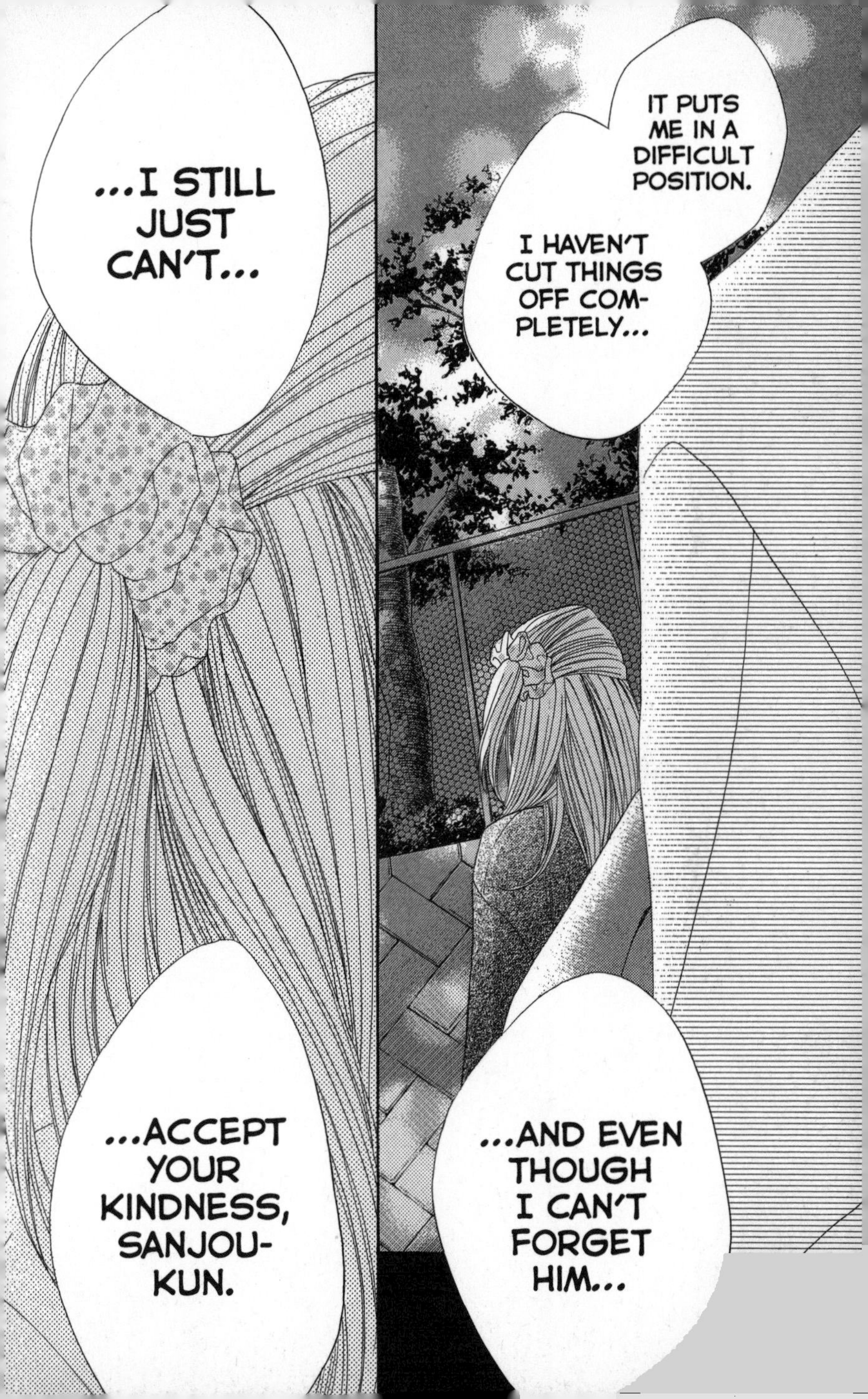
IT PUTS ME IN A DIFFICULT POSITION.
I HAVEN'T CUT THINGS OFF COM-PLETELY...
...AND EVEN THOUGH I CAN'T FORGET HIM...
...I STILL JUST CAN'T...
...ACCEPT YOUR KINDNESS, SANJOU-KUN.

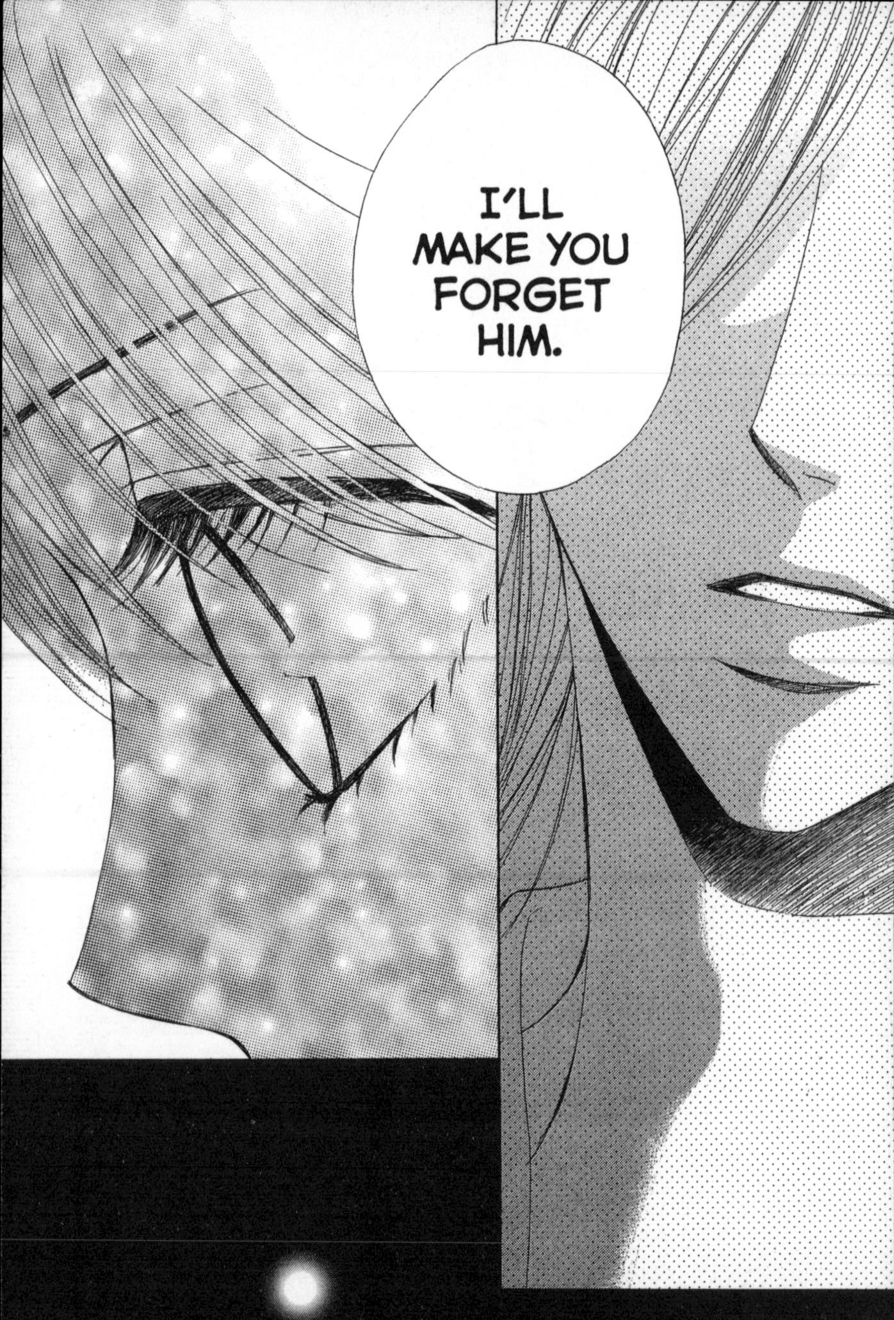
I'LL MAKE YOU FORGET HIM.

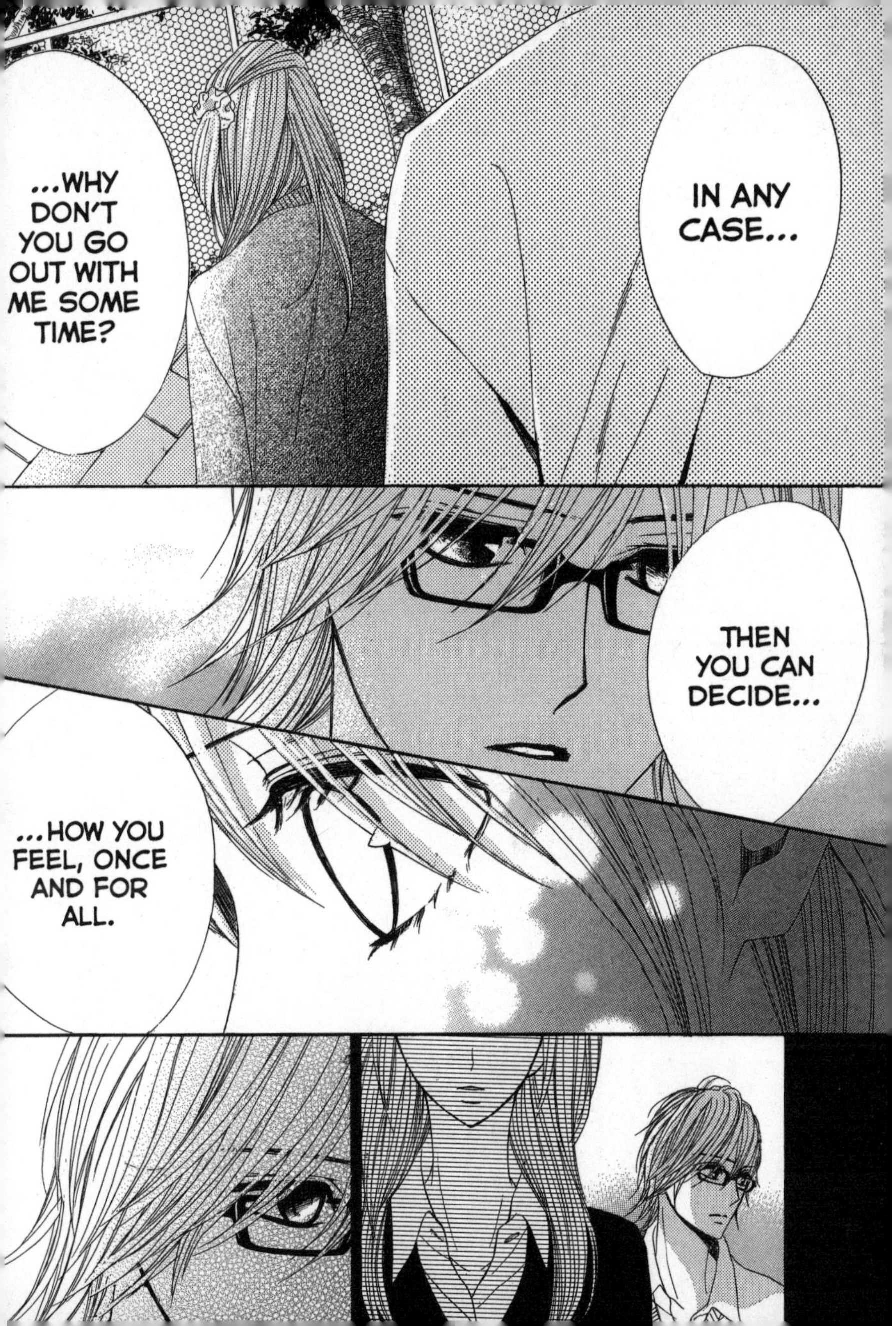
IN ANY CASE...
...WHY DON'T YOU GO OUT WITH ME SOME TIME?
THEN YOU CAN DECIDE...
...HOW YOU FEEL, ONCE AND FOR ALL.

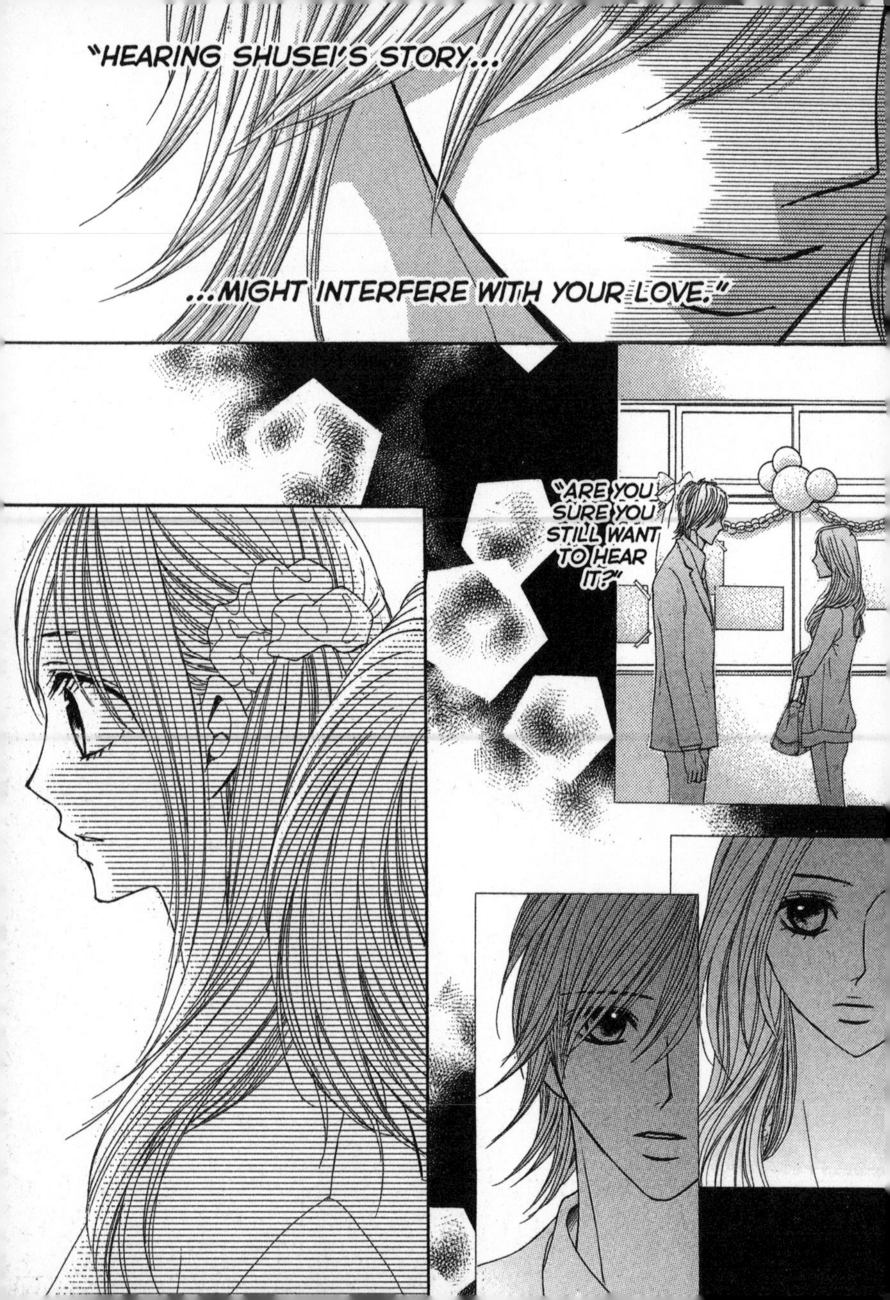
"HEARING SHUSEI'S STORY...
...MIGHT INTERFERE WITH YOUR LOVE."
"ARE YOU SURE YOU STILL WANT TO HEAR IT?"

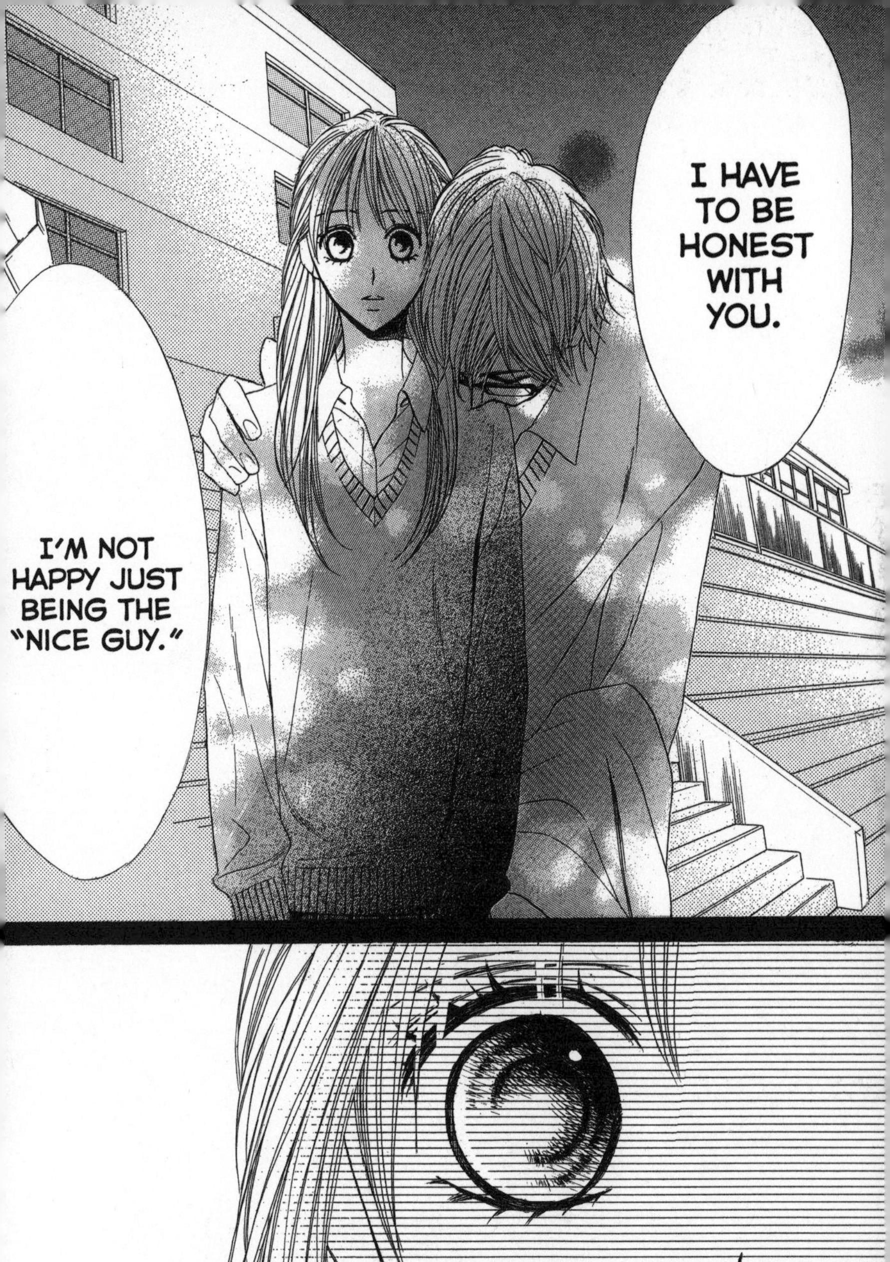
I HAVE TO BE HONEST WITH YOU.
I'M NOT HAPPY JUST BEING THE "NICE GUY."

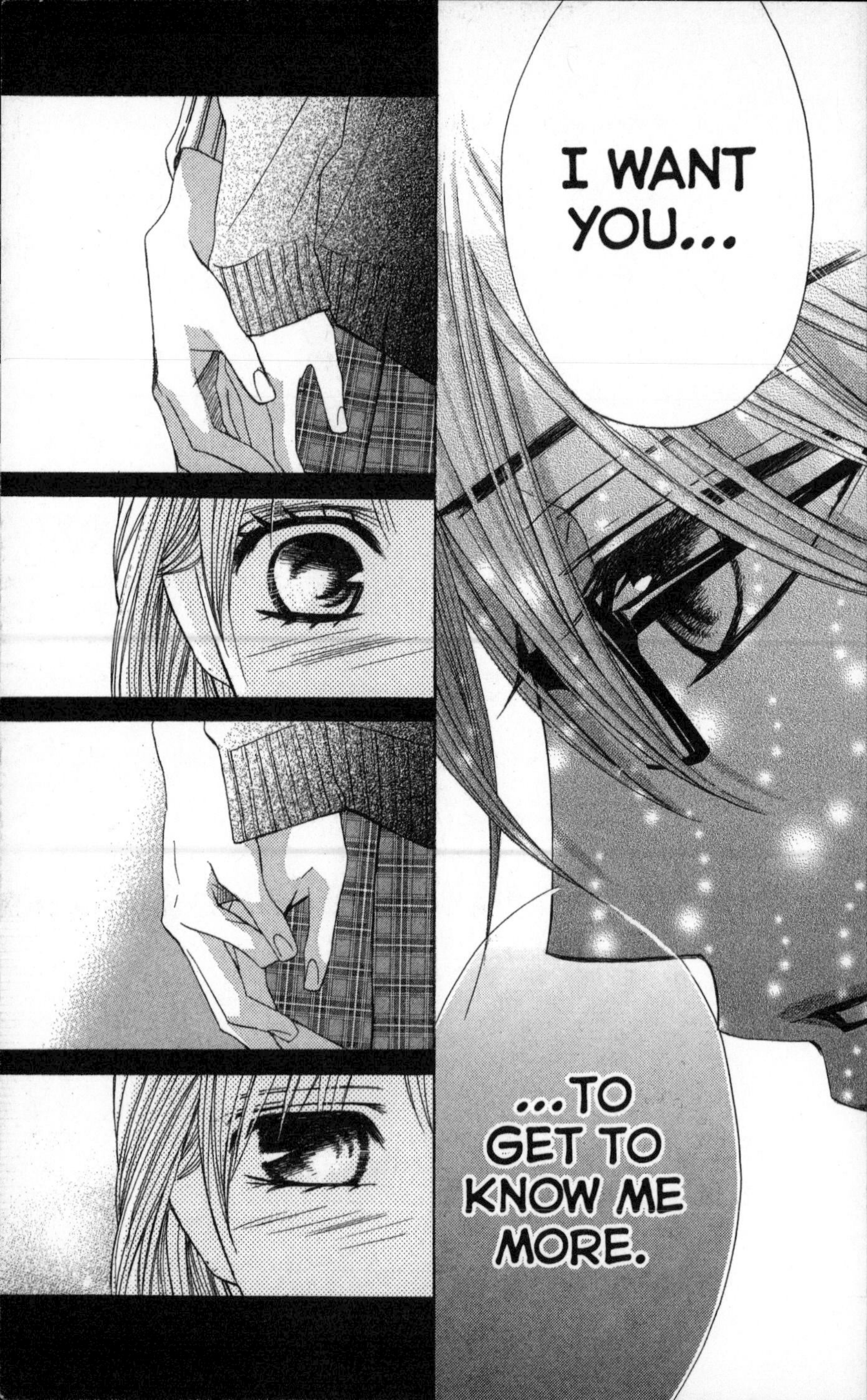
I WANT YOU...
...TO GET TO KNOW ME MORE.

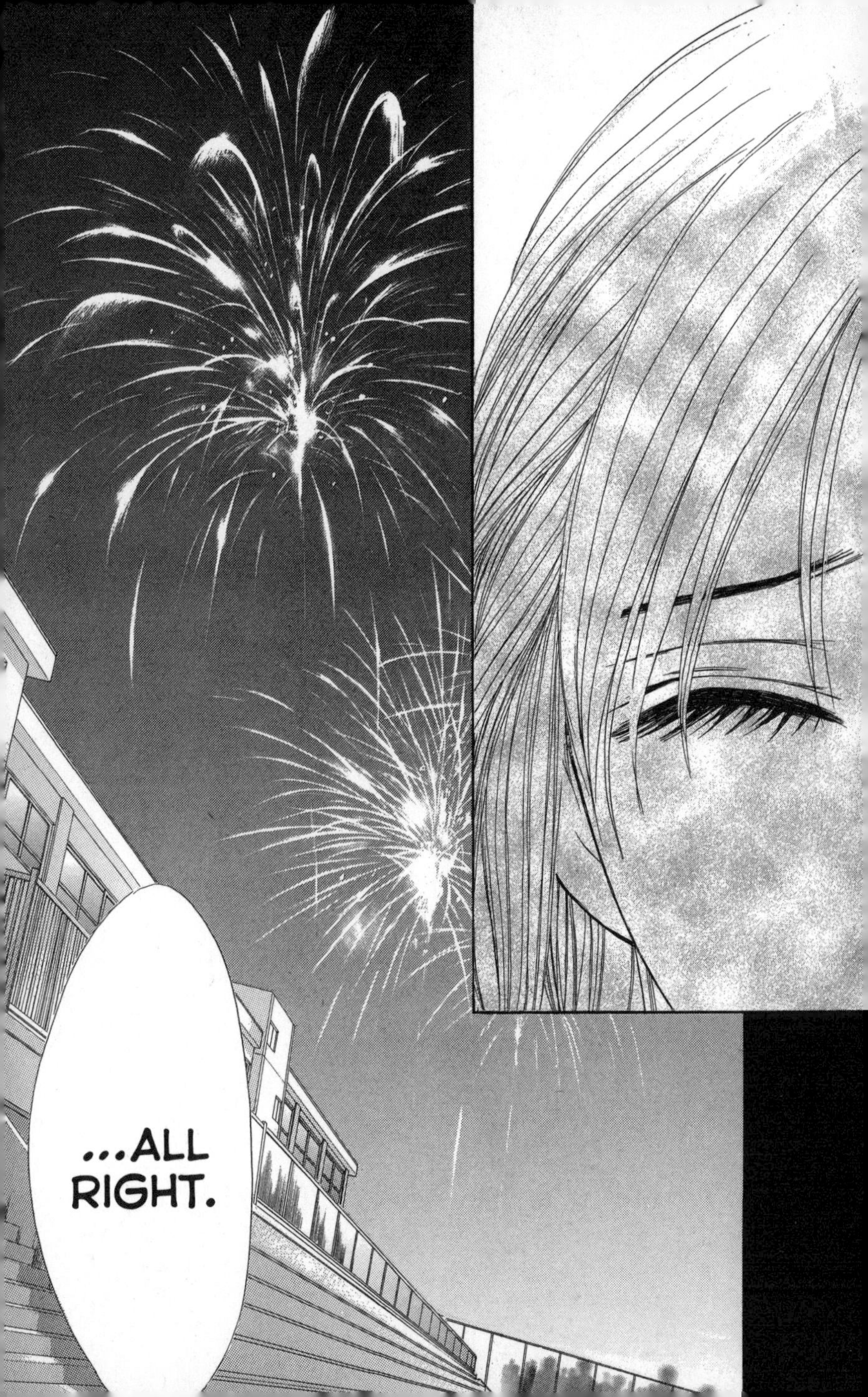
...ALL RIGHT.

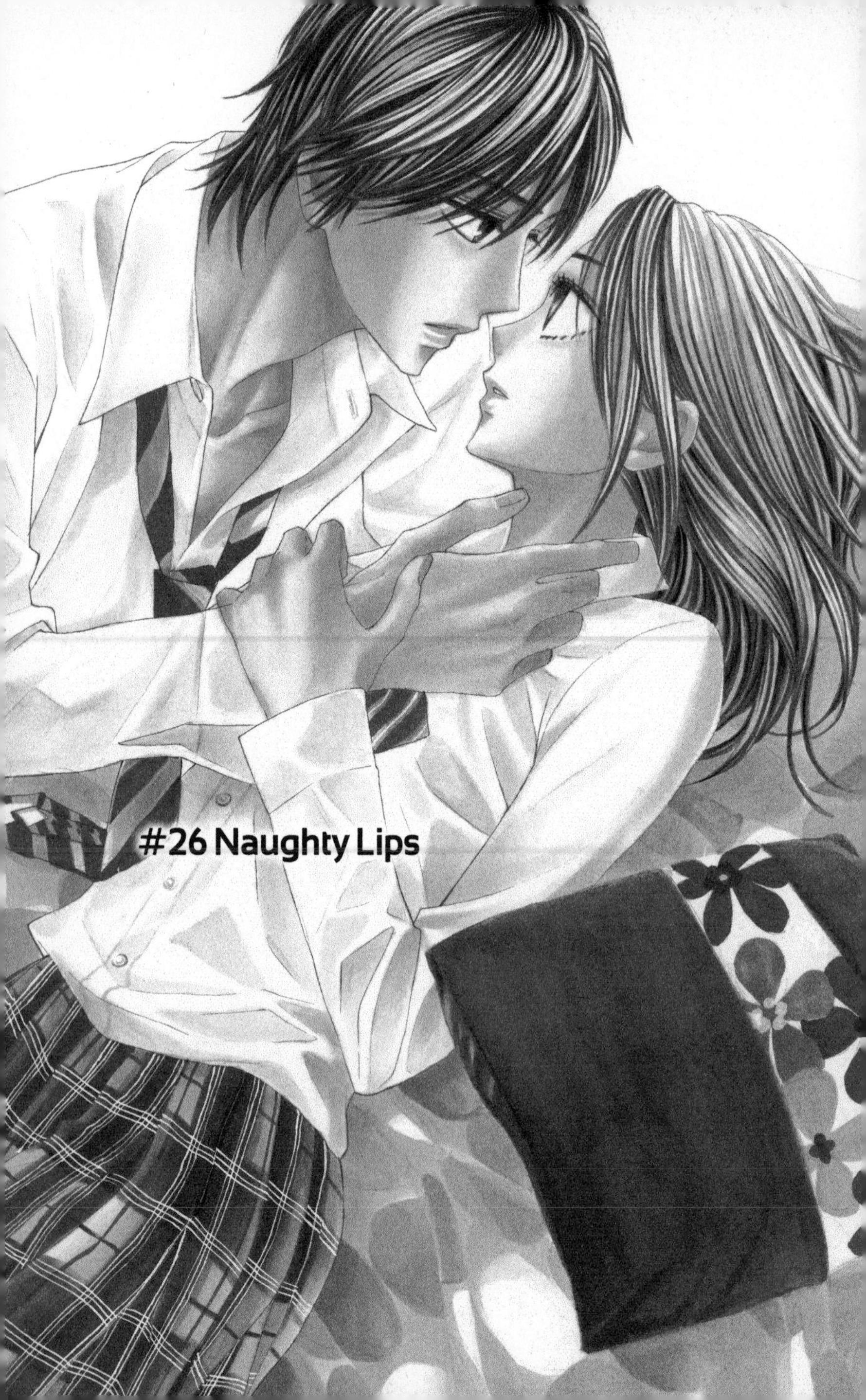
#26 Naughty Lips

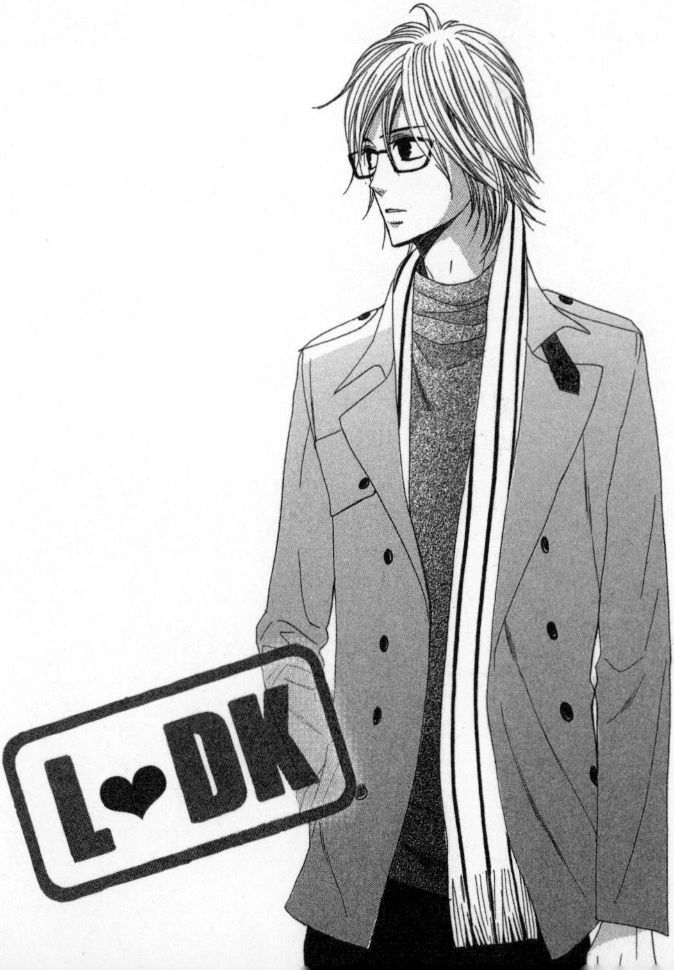
L♥DK

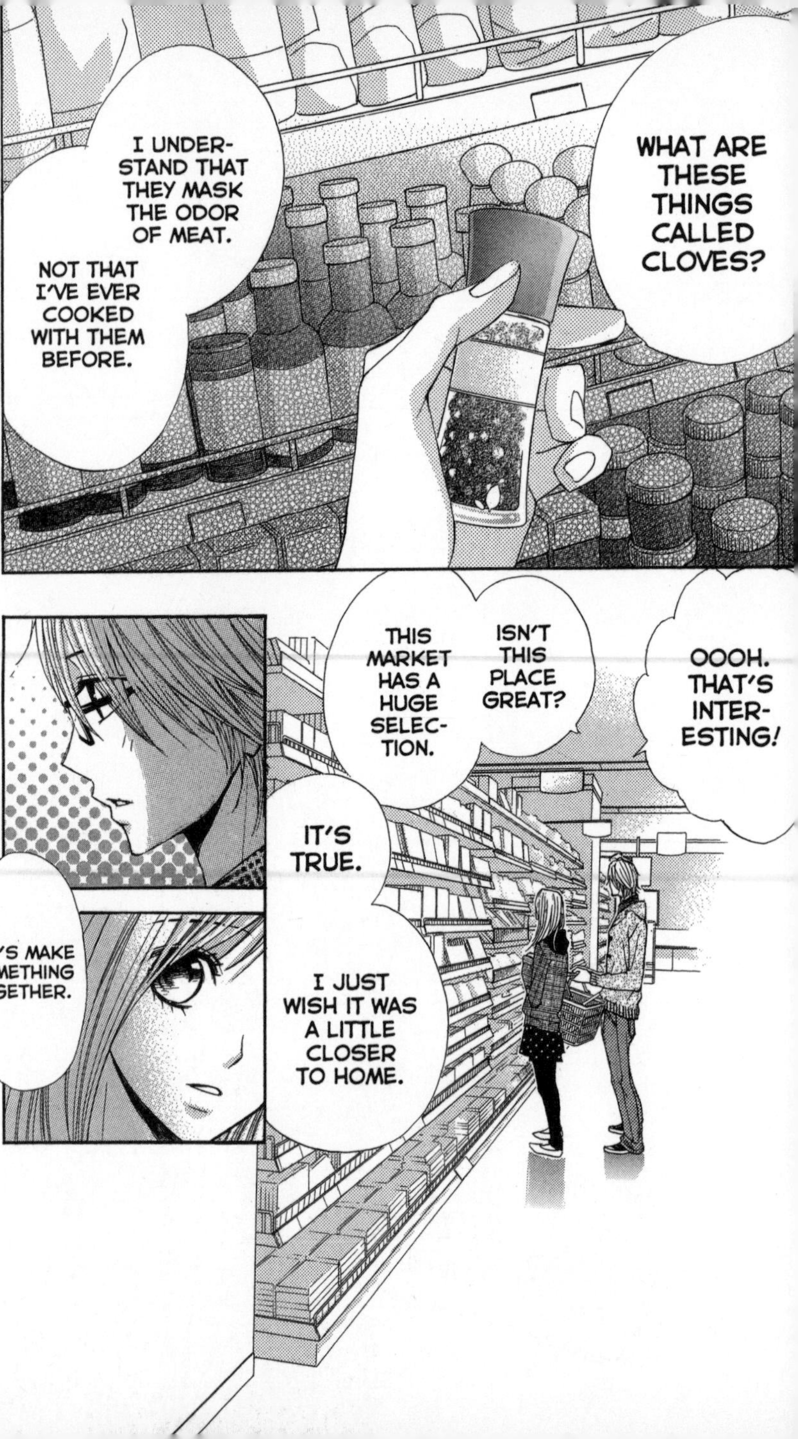
WHAT ARE THESE THINGS CALLED CLOVES?
I UNDER-STAND THAT THEY MASK THE ODOR OF MEAT.
NOT THAT I'VE EVER COOKED WITH THEM BEFORE.
OOOH. THAT'S INTER-ESTING!
ISN'T THIS PLACE GREAT?
THIS MARKET HAS A HUGE SELEC-TION.
IT'S TRUE.
I JUST WISH IT WAS A LITTLE CLOSER TO HOME.
LET'S MAKE SOMETHING TOGETHER.

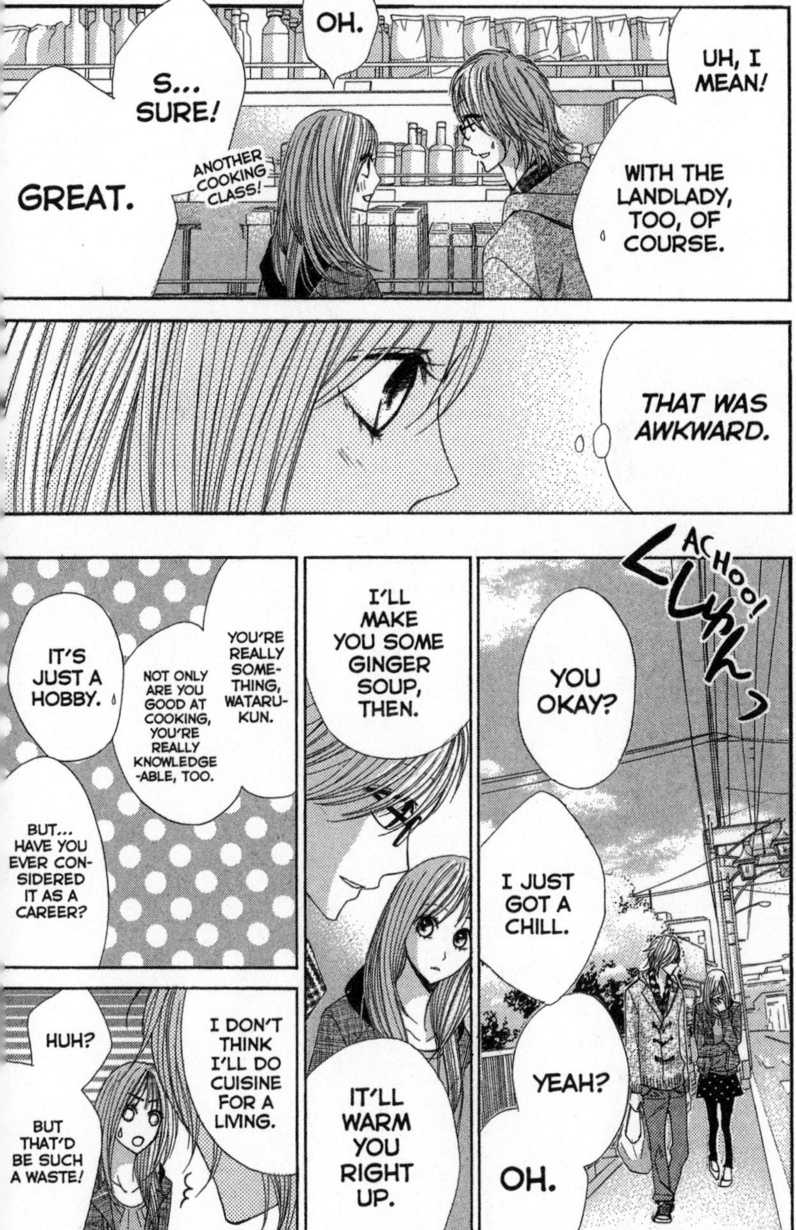
UH, I MEAN!
OH.
WITH THE LANDLADY, TOO, OF COURSE.
S... SURE!
ANOTHER COOKING CLASS!
GREAT.
THAT WAS AWKWARD.
ACHOO!
くしゅん
YOU OKAY?
I JUST GOT A CHILL.
YEAH?
OH.
I'LL MAKE YOU SOME GINGER SOUP, THEN.
IT'LL WARM YOU RIGHT UP.
YOU'RE REALLY SOMETHING, WATARU-KUN.
NOT ONLY ARE YOU GOOD AT COOKING, YOU'RE REALLY KNOWLEDGE-ABLE, TOO.
IT'S JUST A HOBBY.
BUT... HAVE YOU EVER CONSIDERED IT AS A CAREER?
I DON'T THINK I'LL DO CUISINE FOR A LIVING.
HUH?
BUT THAT'D BE SUCH A WASTE!

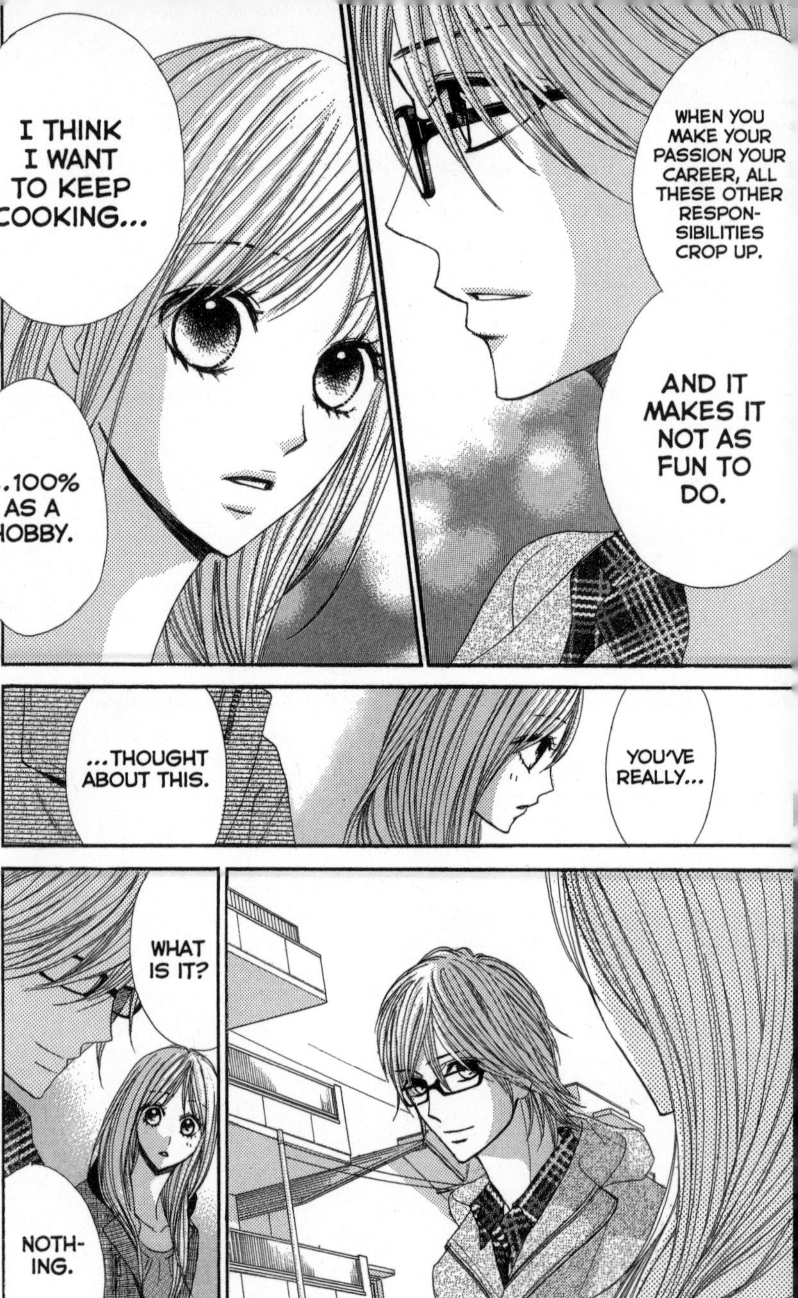
WHEN YOU MAKE YOUR PASSION YOUR CAREER, ALL THESE OTHER RESPON-SIBILITIES CROP UP.
AND IT MAKES IT NOT AS FUN TO DO.
I THINK I WANT TO KEEP COOKING...
...100% AS A HOBBY.
YOU'VE REALLY...
...THOUGHT ABOUT THIS.
WHAT IS IT?
NOTH-ING.

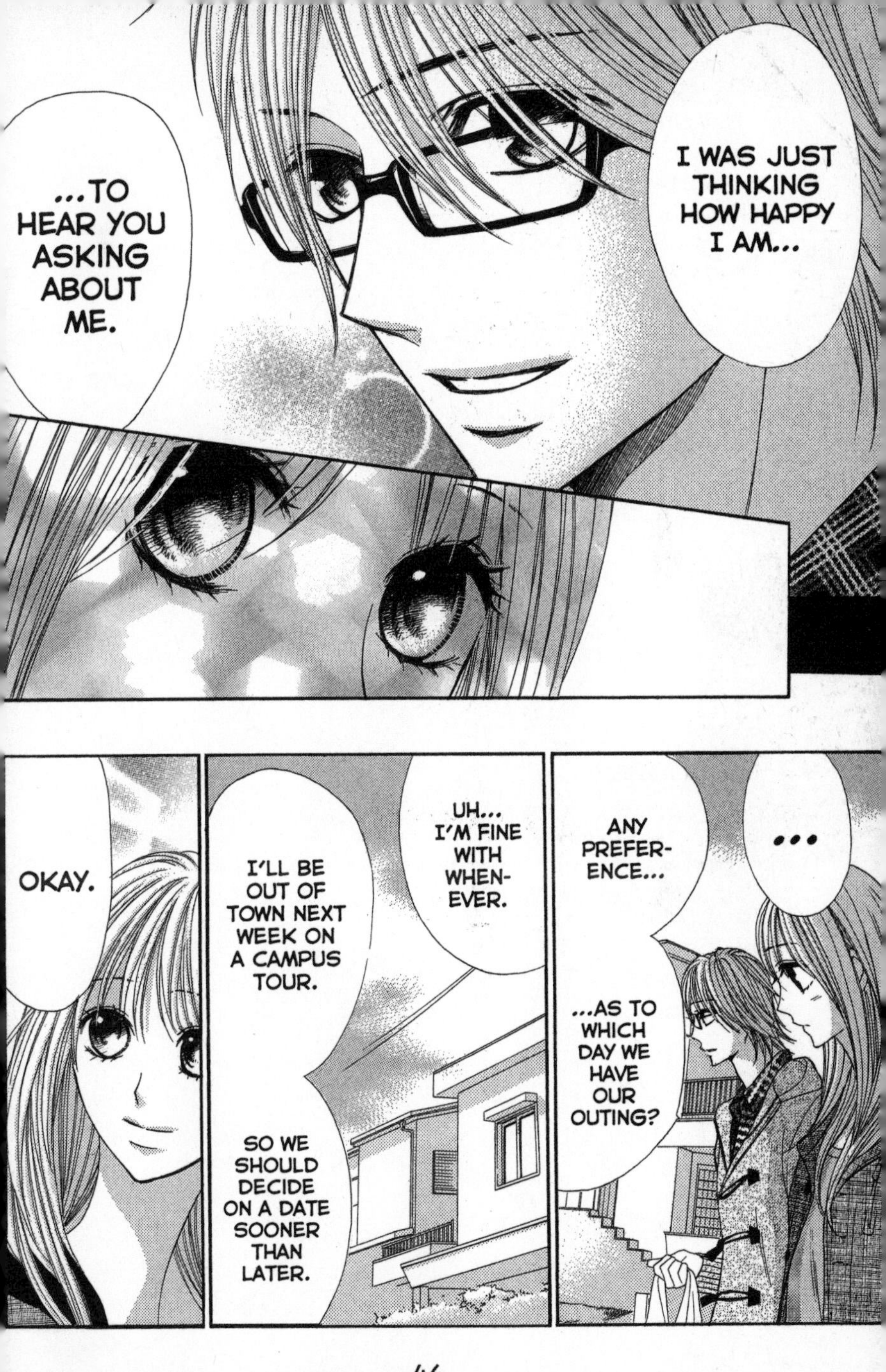
I WAS JUST THINKING HOW HAPPY I AM...
...TO HEAR YOU ASKING ABOUT ME.
...
ANY PREFERENCE...
...AS TO WHICH DAY WE HAVE OUR OUTING?
UH... I'M FINE WITH WHENEVER.
I'LL BE OUT OF TOWN NEXT WEEK ON A CAMPUS TOUR.
SO WE SHOULD DECIDE ON A DATE SOONER THAN LATER.
OKAY.

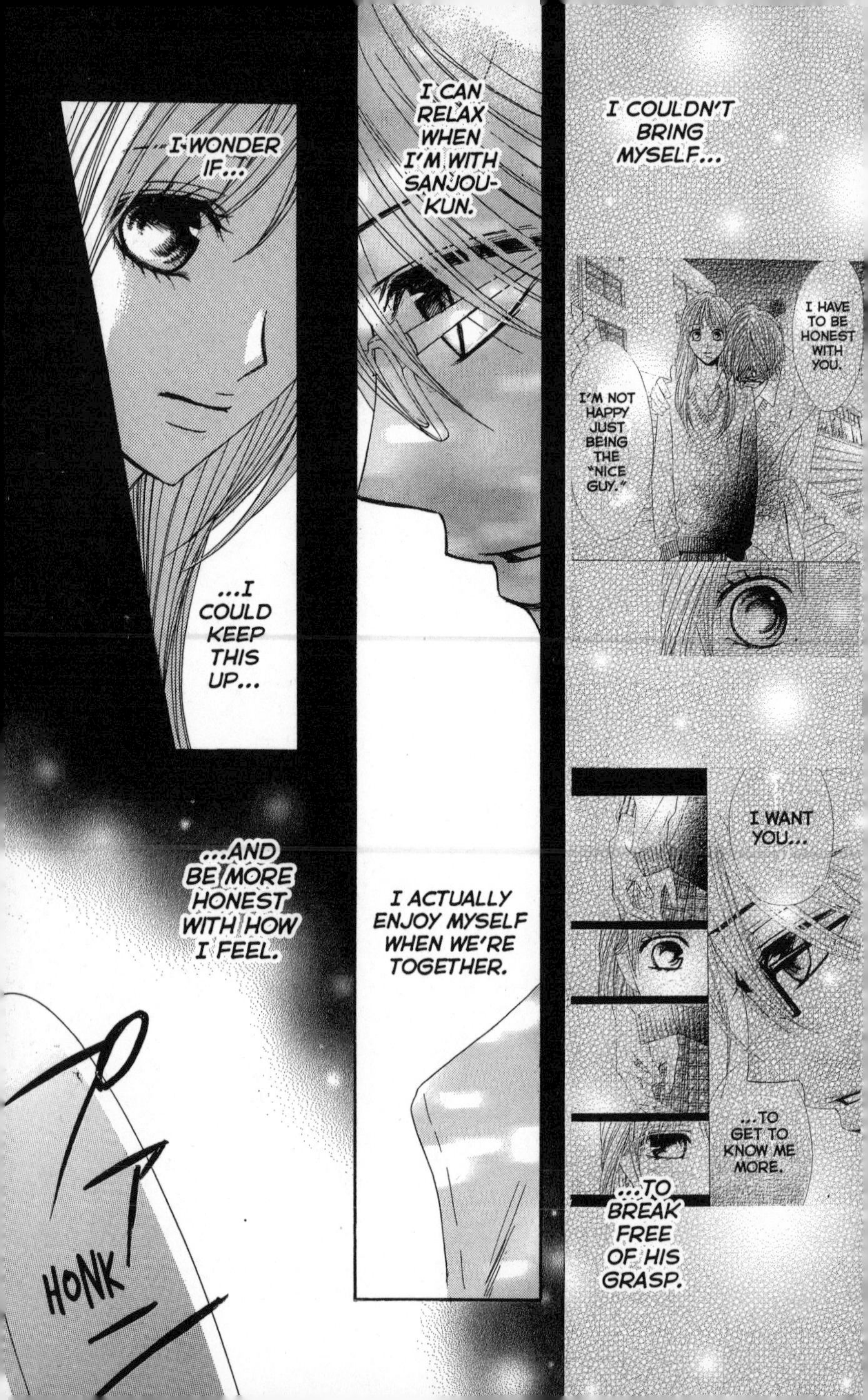
I COULDN'T BRING MYSELF...
I HAVE TO BE HONEST WITH YOU.
I'M NOT HAPPY JUST BEING THE "NICE GUY."
I WANT YOU...
...TO GET TO KNOW ME MORE.
...TO BREAK FREE OF HIS GRASP.
I CAN RELAX WHEN I'M WITH SANJOU-KUN.
I ACTUALLY ENJOY MYSELF WHEN WE'RE TOGETHER.
I WONDER IF...
...I COULD KEEP THIS UP...
...AND BE MORE HONEST WITH HOW I FEEL.
HONK

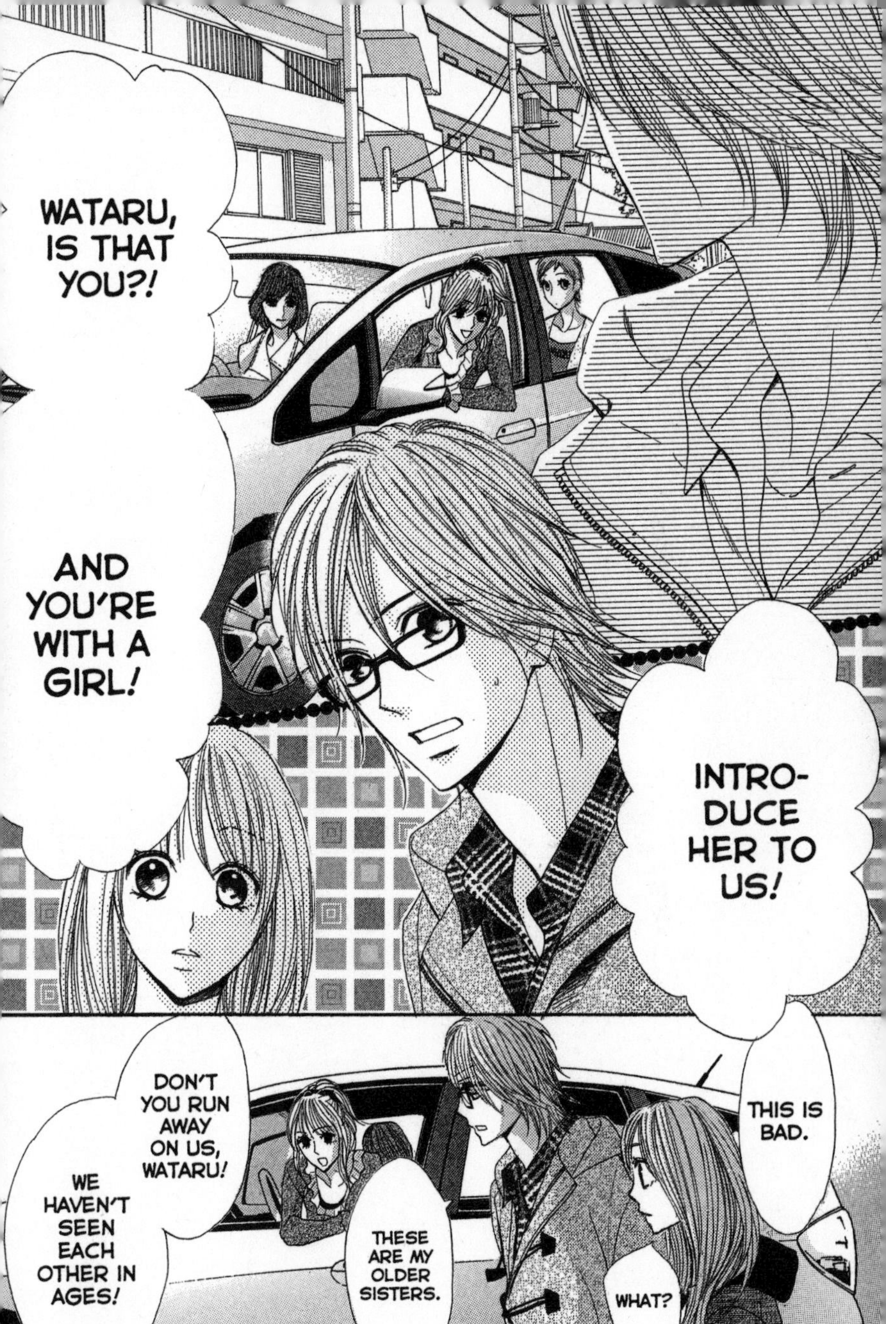
WATARU, IS THAT YOU?!
AND YOU'RE WITH A GIRL!
INTRO-DUCE HER TO US!
THIS IS BAD.
DON'T YOU RUN AWAY ON US, WATARU!
WE HAVEN'T SEEN EACH OTHER IN AGES!
THESE ARE MY OLDER SISTERS.
WHAT?

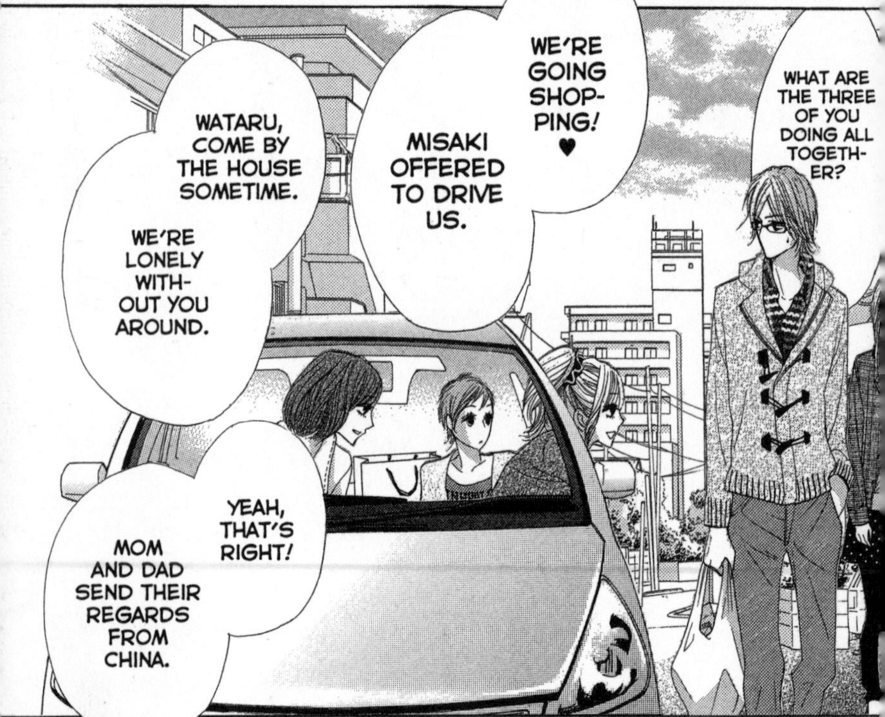
WHAT ARE THE THREE OF YOU DOING ALL TOGETH-ER?
WE'RE GOING SHOP-PING! ♥
MISAKI OFFERED TO DRIVE US.
WATARU, COME BY THE HOUSE SOMETIME.
WE'RE LONELY WITH-OUT YOU AROUND.
YEAH, THAT'S RIGHT!
MOM AND DAD SEND THEIR REGARDS FROM CHINA.

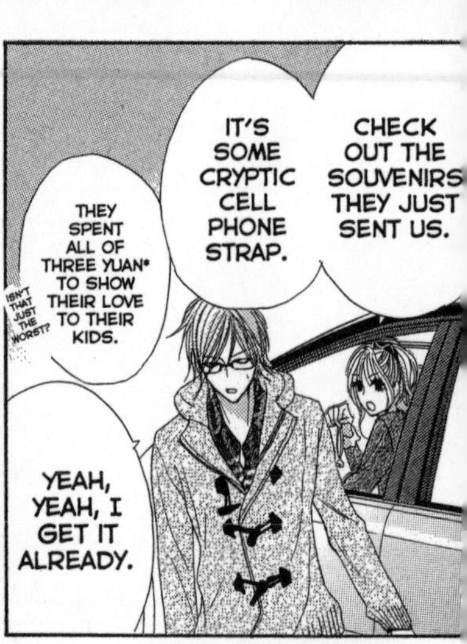
CHECK OUT THE SOUVENIRS THEY JUST SENT US.
IT'S SOME CRYPTIC CELL PHONE STRAP.
THEY SPENT ALL OF THREE YUAN* TO SHOW THEIR LOVE TO THEIR KIDS.
ISN'T THAT JUST THE WORST?
YEAH, YEAH, I GET IT ALREADY.

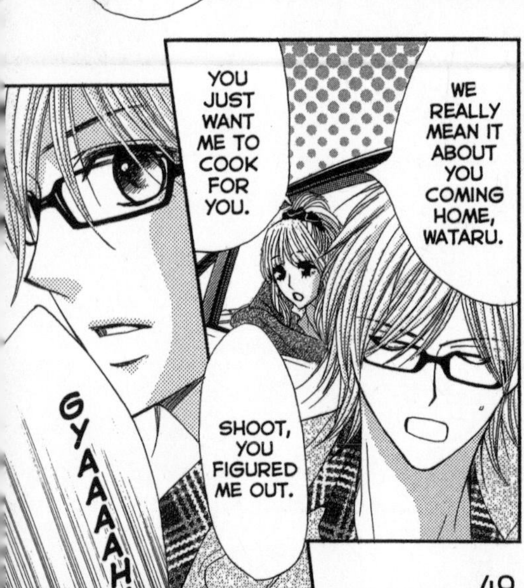
WE REALLY MEAN IT ABOUT YOU COMING HOME, WATARU.
YOU JUST WANT ME TO COOK FOR YOU.
SHOOT, YOU FIGURED ME OUT.
GYAAAAH!

*NOTE: THREE YUAN EQUALS APPROXIMATELY $0.50 USD.

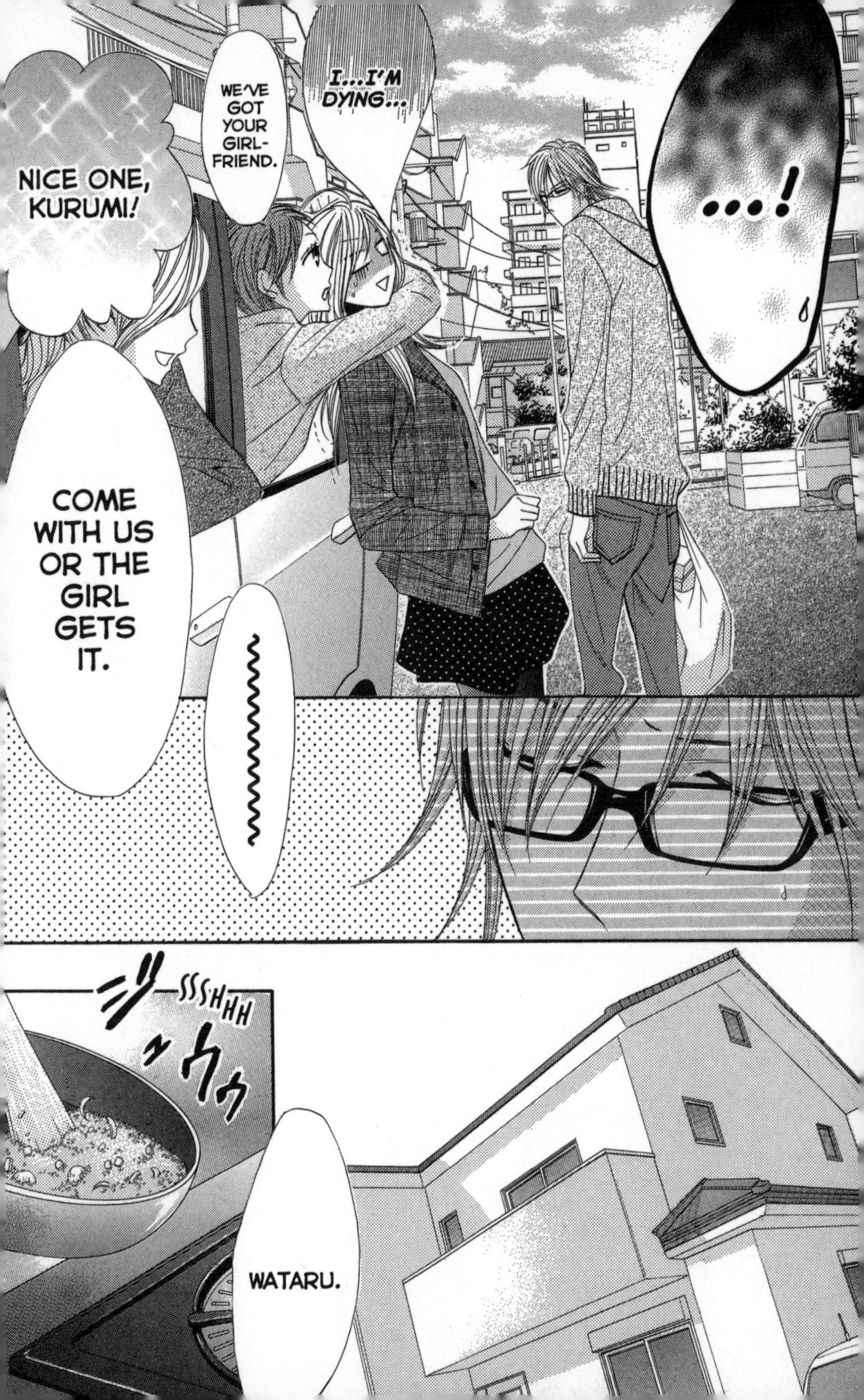
...!
I...I'M DYING...
WE'VE GOT YOUR GIRL-FRIEND.
NICE ONE, KURUMI!
COME WITH US OR THE GIRL GETS IT.
ジュウゥ
SSSHHH
WATARU.

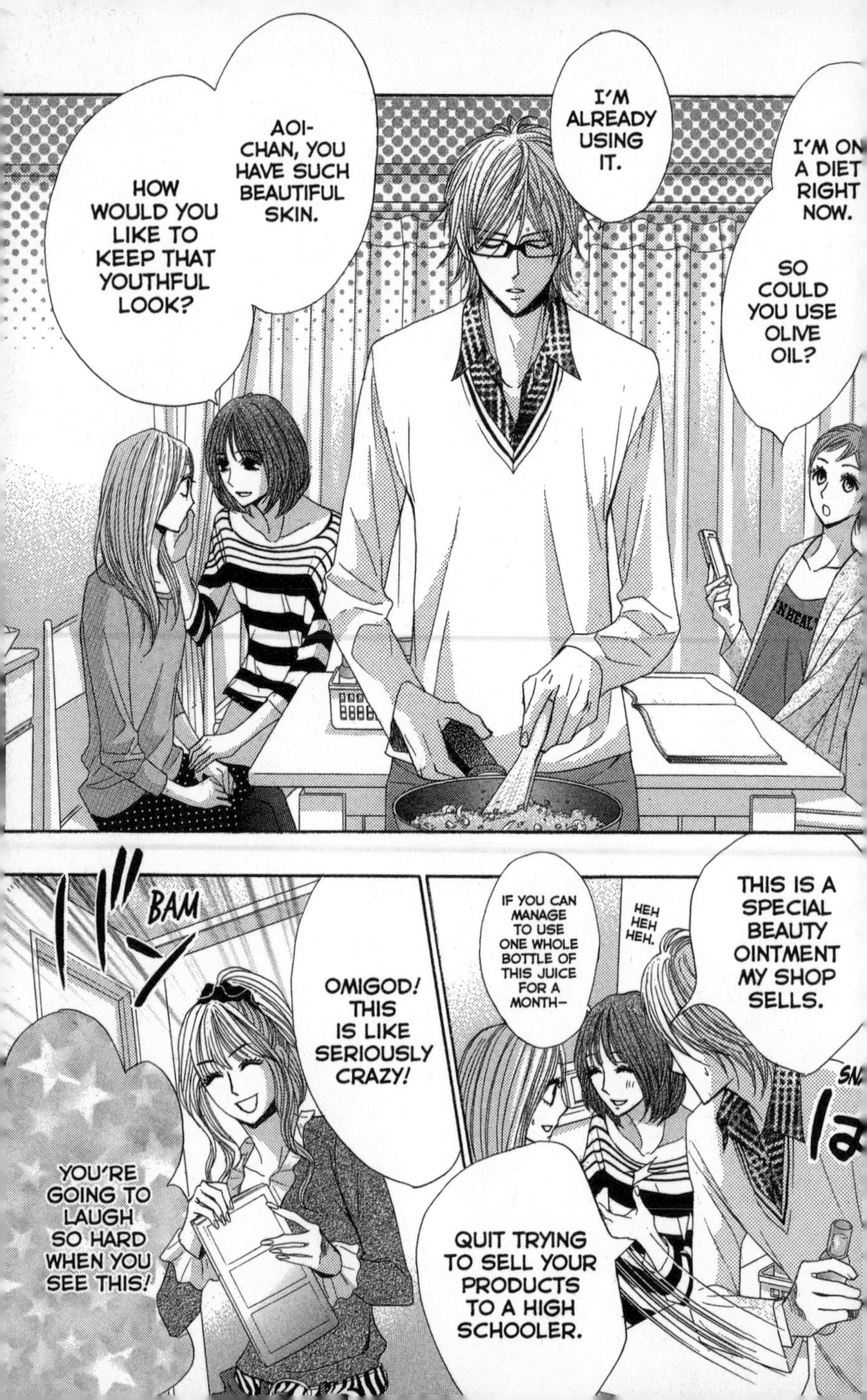
I'M ON A DIET RIGHT NOW.
SO COULD YOU USE OLIVE OIL?
I'M ALREADY USING IT.
AOI-CHAN, YOU HAVE SUCH BEAUTIFUL SKIN.
HOW WOULD YOU LIKE TO KEEP THAT YOUTHFUL LOOK?
THIS IS A SPECIAL BEAUTY OINTMENT MY SHOP SELLS.
HEH HEH HEH.
IF YOU CAN MANAGE TO USE ONE WHOLE BOTTLE OF THIS JUICE FOR A MONTH–
QUIT TRYING TO SELL YOUR PRODUCTS TO A HIGH SCHOOLER.
BAM
OMIGOD! THIS IS LIKE SERIOUSLY CRAZY!
YOU'RE GOING TO LAUGH SO HARD WHEN YOU SEE THIS!

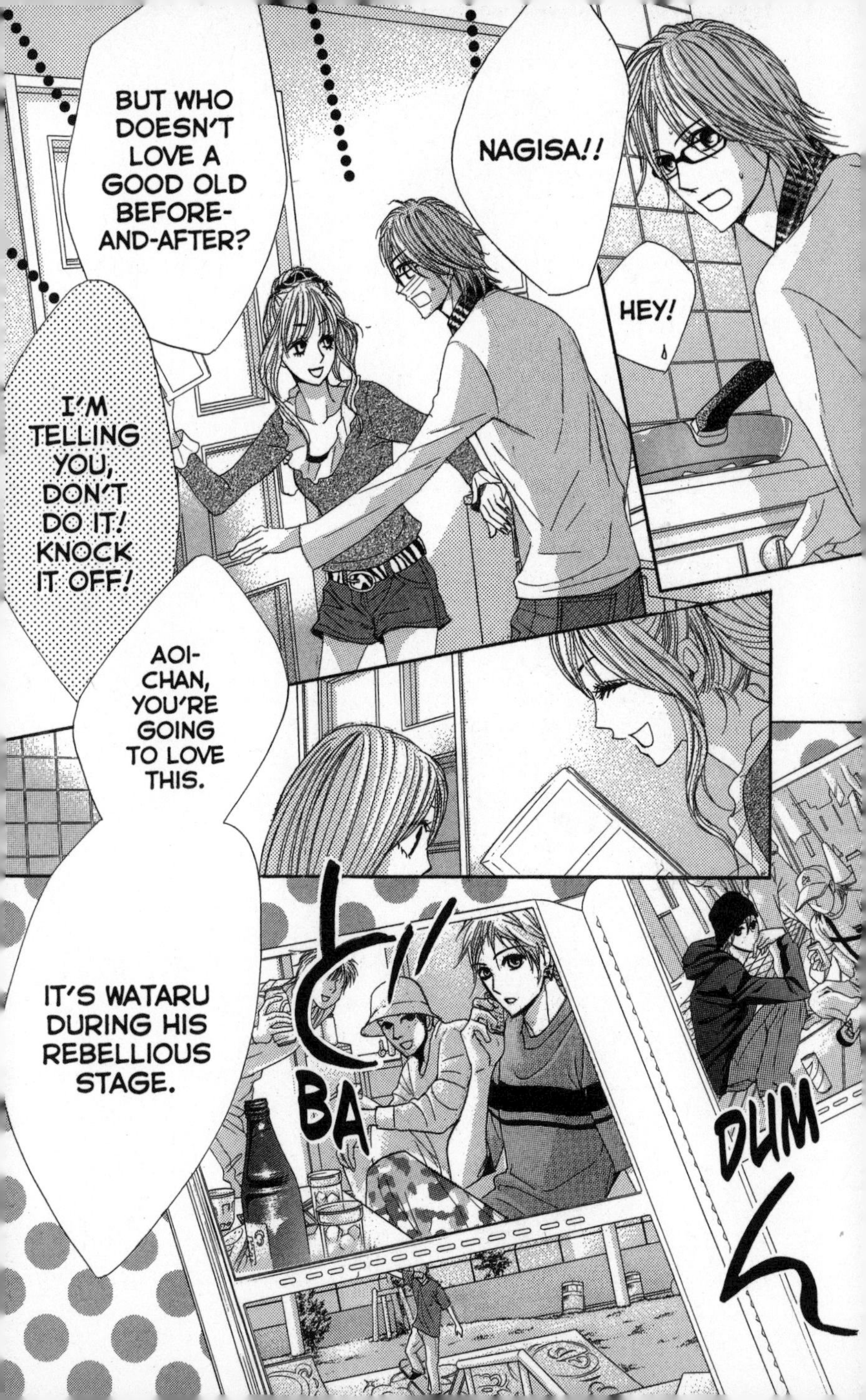
NAGISA!!
HEY!
BUT WHO DOESN'T LOVE A GOOD OLD BEFORE-AND-AFTER?
I'M TELLING YOU, DON'T DO IT! KNOCK IT OFF!
AOI-CHAN, YOU'RE GOING TO LOVE THIS.
DUM
BA
IT'S WATARU DURING HIS REBELLIOUS STAGE.

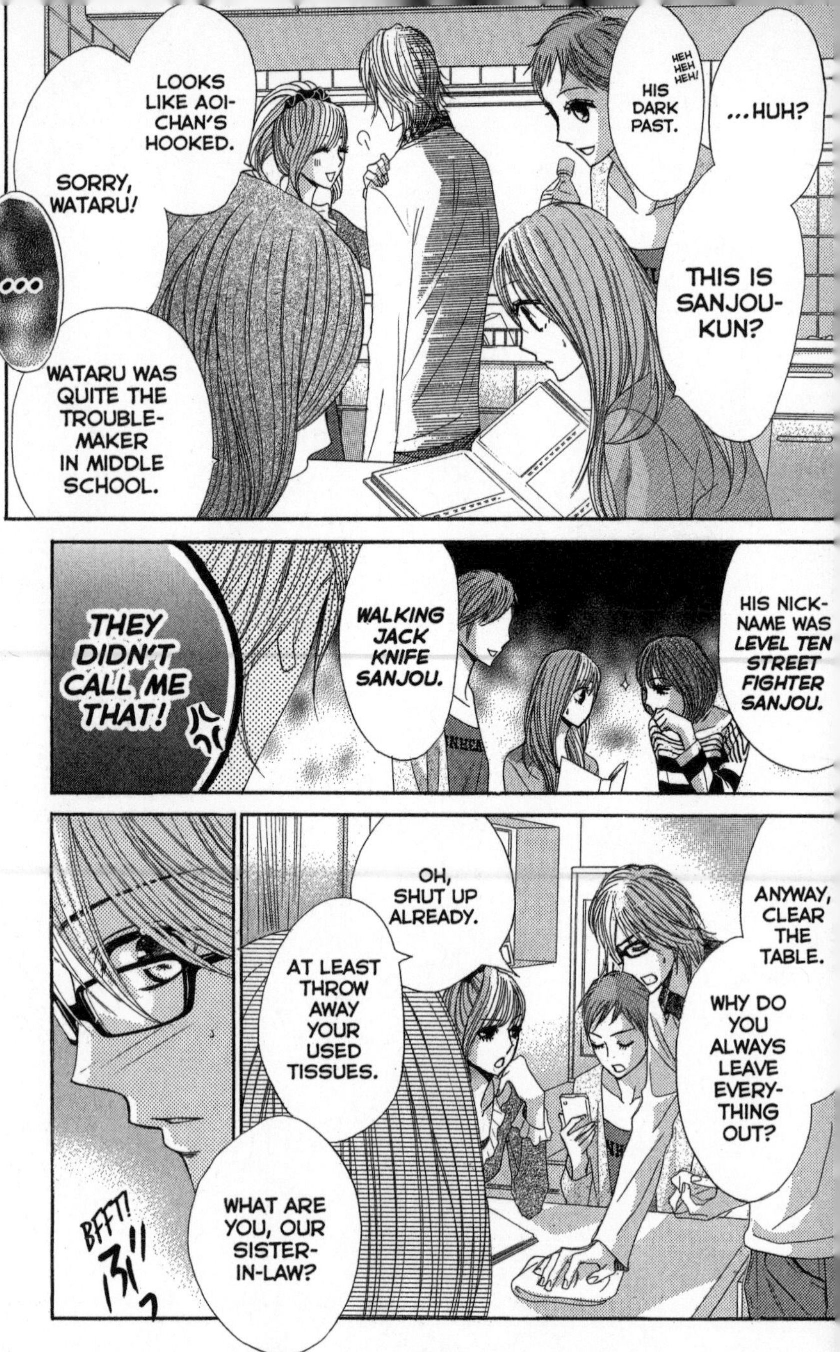
...HUH?
HEH HEH HEH!
HIS DARK PAST.
THIS IS SANJOU-KUN?
LOOKS LIKE AOI-CHAN'S HOOKED.
SORRY, WATARU!
...
WATARU WAS QUITE THE TROUBLE-MAKER IN MIDDLE SCHOOL.
HIS NICK-NAME WAS LEVEL TEN STREET FIGHTER SANJOU.
WALKING JACK KNIFE SANJOU.
THEY DIDN'T CALL ME THAT!
ANYWAY, CLEAR THE TABLE.
WHY DO YOU ALWAYS LEAVE EVERY-THING OUT?
OH, SHUT UP ALREADY.
AT LEAST THROW AWAY YOUR USED TISSUES.
WHAT ARE YOU, OUR SISTER-IN-LAW?
BFFT!

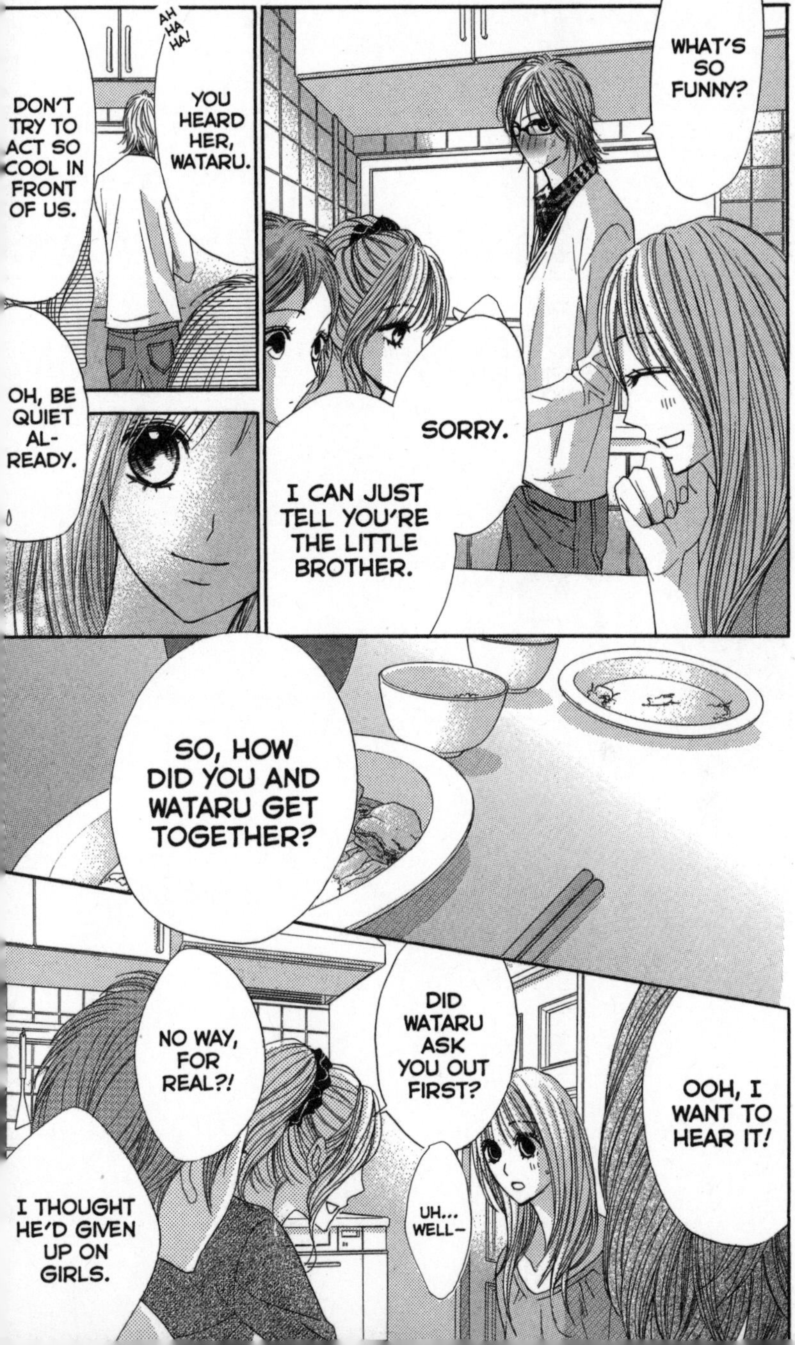
WHAT'S SO FUNNY?
SORRY.
I CAN JUST TELL YOU'RE THE LITTLE BROTHER.
AH HA HA!
YOU HEARD HER, WATARU.
DON'T TRY TO ACT SO COOL IN FRONT OF US.
OH, BE QUIET AL-READY.
SO, HOW DID YOU AND WATARU GET TOGETHER?
OOH, I WANT TO HEAR IT!
DID WATARU ASK YOU OUT FIRST?
NO WAY, FOR REAL?!
UH... WELL–
I THOUGHT HE'D GIVEN UP ON GIRLS.

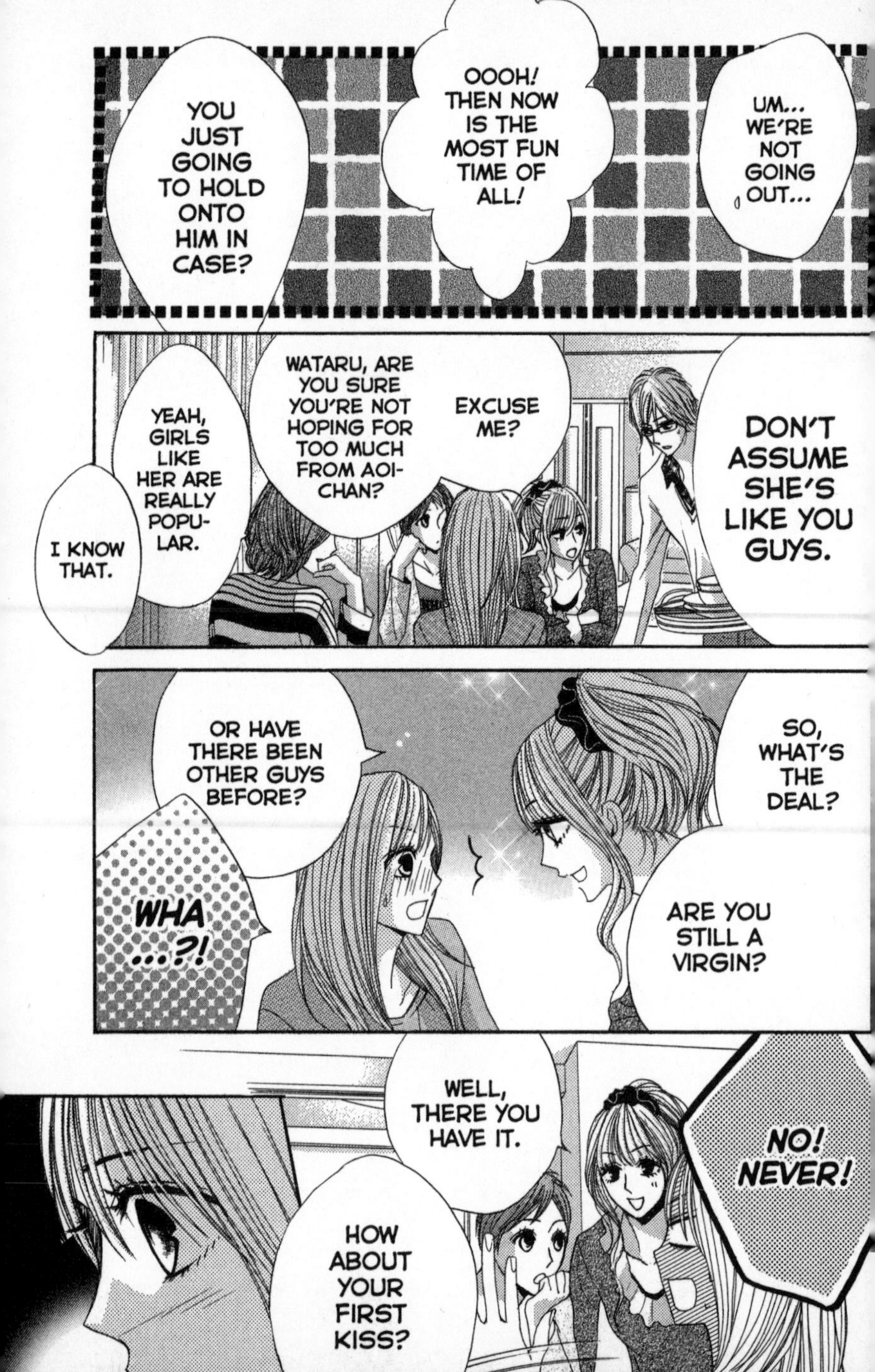
UM... WE'RE NOT GOING OUT...
OOOH! THEN NOW IS THE MOST FUN TIME OF ALL!
YOU JUST GOING TO HOLD ONTO HIM IN CASE?
DON'T ASSUME SHE'S LIKE YOU GUYS.
EXCUSE ME?
WATARU, ARE YOU SURE YOU'RE NOT HOPING FOR TOO MUCH FROM AOI-CHAN?
YEAH, GIRLS LIKE HER ARE REALLY POPU-LAR.
I KNOW THAT.
SO, WHAT'S THE DEAL?
ARE YOU STILL A VIRGIN?
OR HAVE THERE BEEN OTHER GUYS BEFORE?
WHA...?!
NO! NEVER!
WELL, THERE YOU HAVE IT.
HOW ABOUT YOUR FIRST KISS?

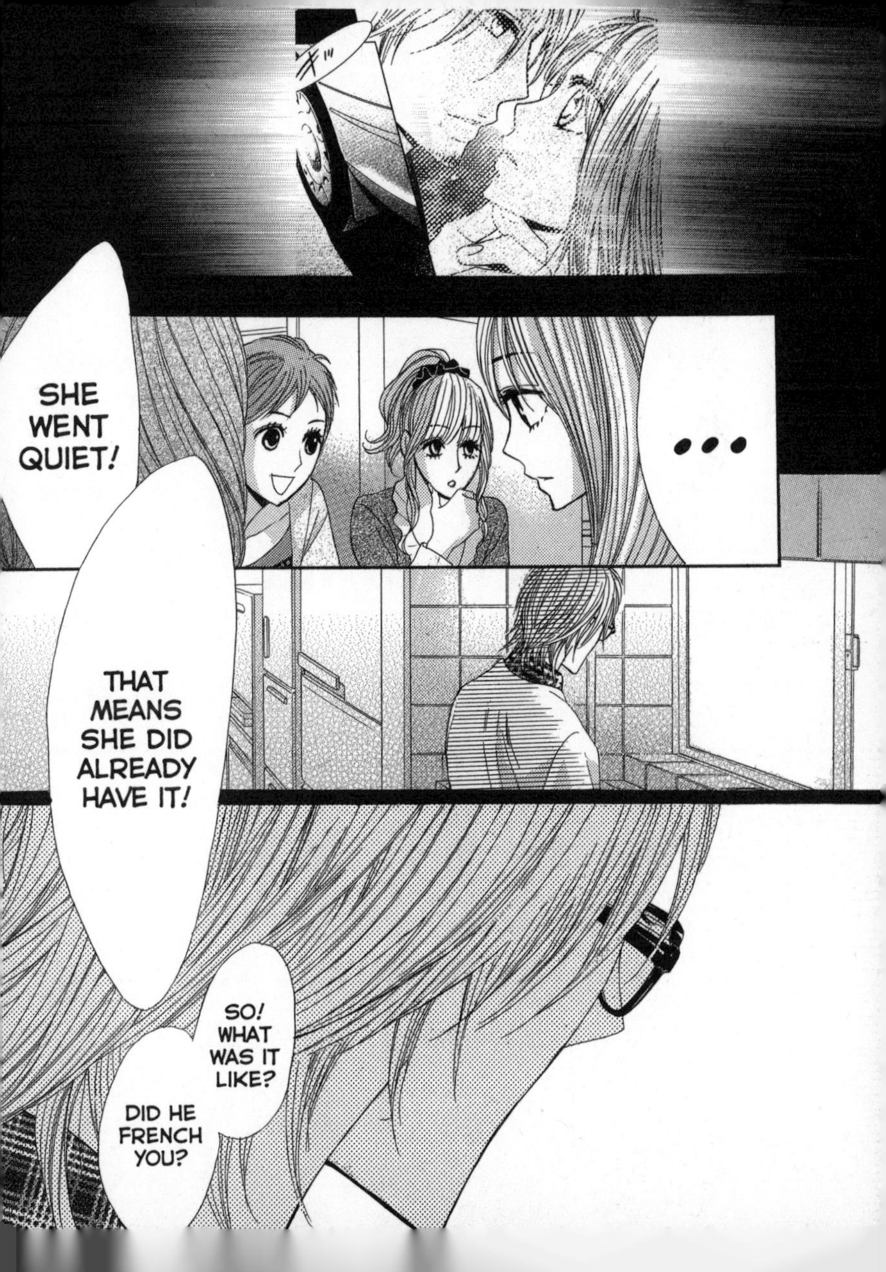
ギッ
...
SHE WENT QUIET!
THAT MEANS SHE DID ALREADY HAVE IT!
SO! WHAT WAS IT LIKE?
DID HE FRENCH YOU?

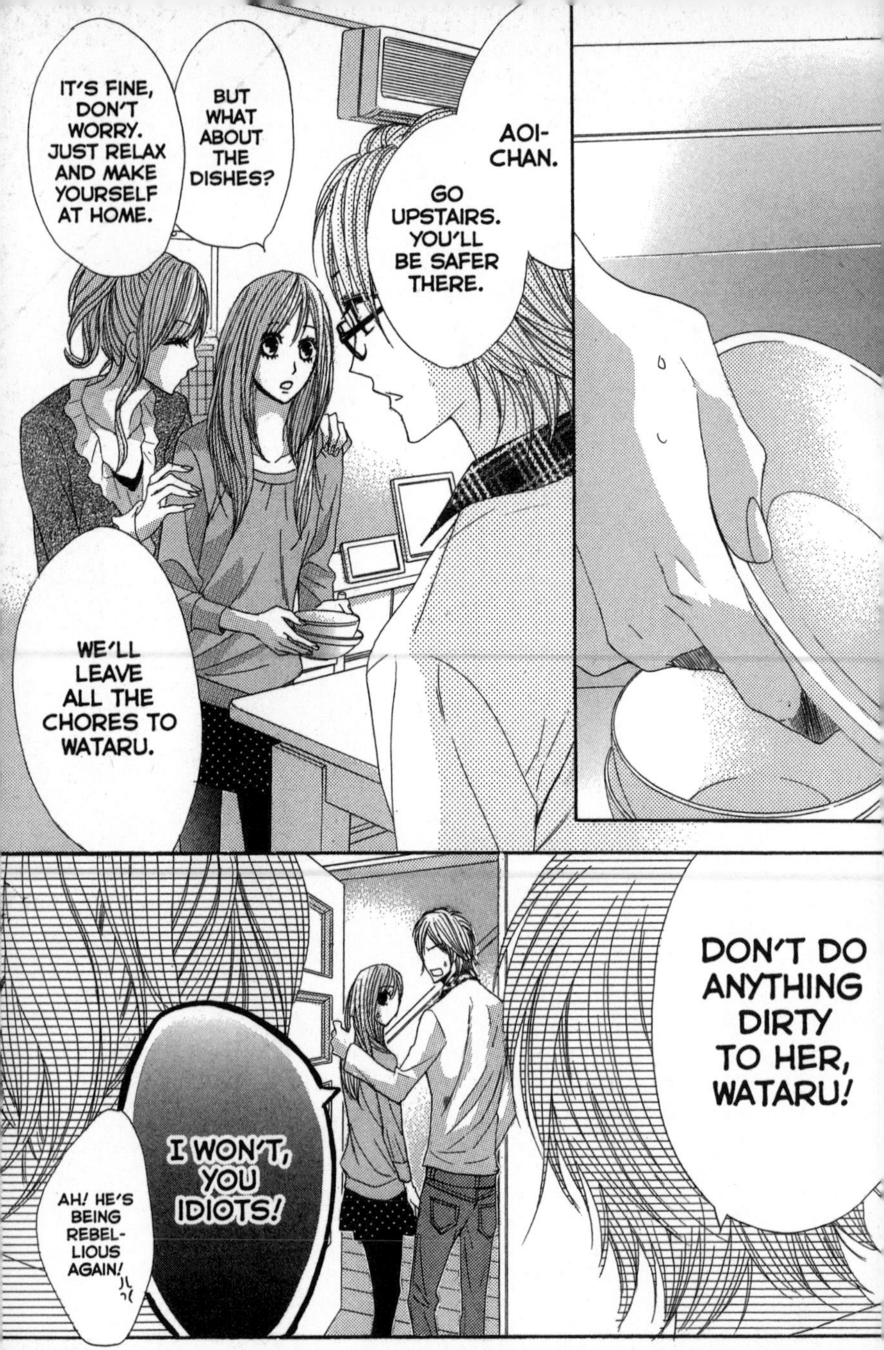
AOI-CHAN.
GO UPSTAIRS. YOU'LL BE SAFER THERE.
BUT WHAT ABOUT THE DISHES?
IT'S FINE, DON'T WORRY. JUST RELAX AND MAKE YOURSELF AT HOME.
WE'LL LEAVE ALL THE CHORES TO WATARU.
DON'T DO ANYTHING DIRTY TO HER, WATARU!
I WON'T, YOU IDIOTS!
AH! HE'S BEING REBEL-LIOUS AGAIN!

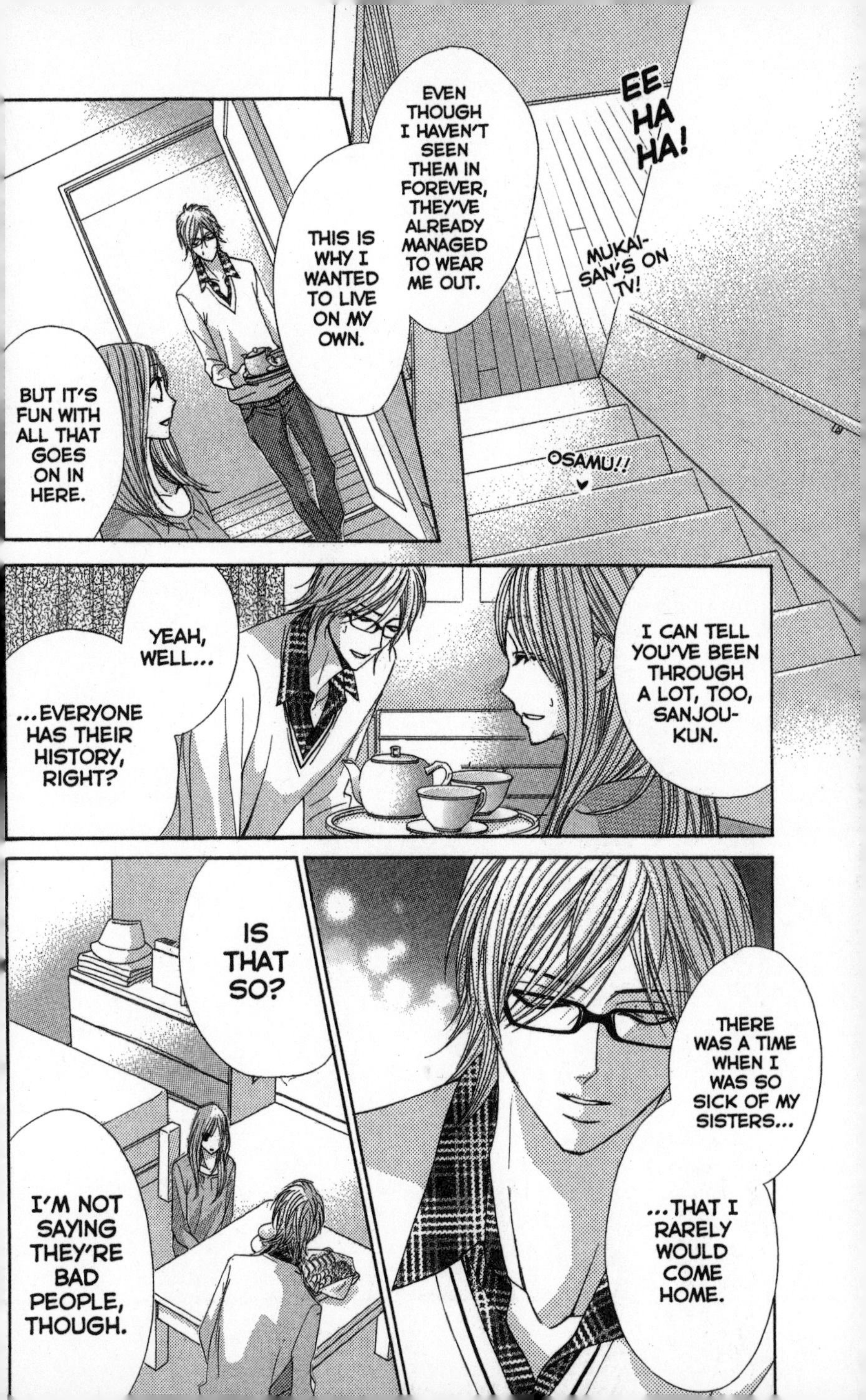
EE HA HA!
MUKAI-SAN'S ON TV!
OSAMU!! ♥
EVEN THOUGH I HAVEN'T SEEN THEM IN FOREVER, THEY'VE ALREADY MANAGED TO WEAR ME OUT.
THIS IS WHY I WANTED TO LIVE ON MY OWN.
BUT IT'S FUN WITH ALL THAT GOES ON IN HERE.
I CAN TELL YOU'VE BEEN THROUGH A LOT, TOO, SANJOU-KUN.
YEAH, WELL...
...EVERYONE HAS THEIR HISTORY, RIGHT?
THERE WAS A TIME WHEN I WAS SO SICK OF MY SISTERS...
...THAT I RARELY WOULD COME HOME.
IS THAT SO?
I'M NOT SAYING THEY'RE BAD PEOPLE, THOUGH.

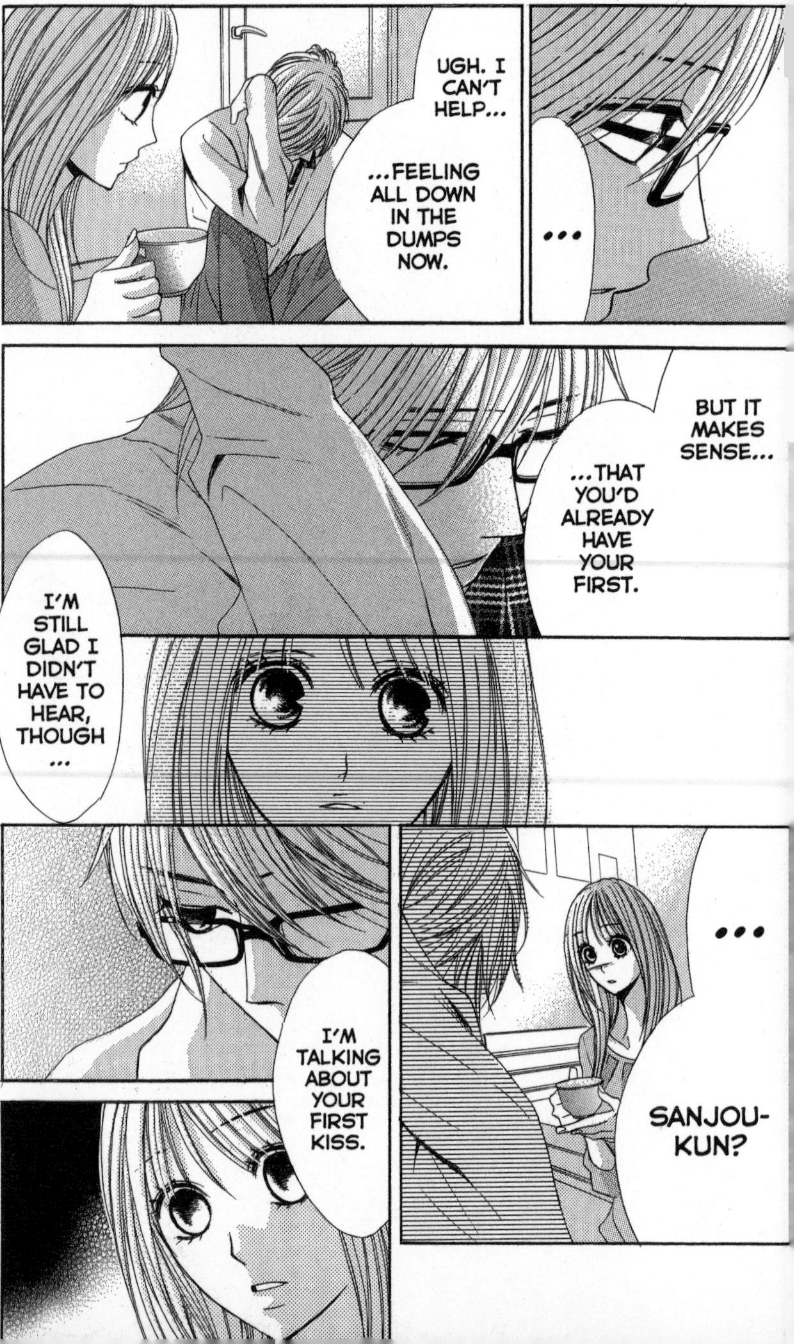
...
UGH. I CAN'T HELP...
...FEELING ALL DOWN IN THE DUMPS NOW.
BUT IT MAKES SENSE...
...THAT YOU'D ALREADY HAVE YOUR FIRST.
I'M STILL GLAD I DIDN'T HAVE TO HEAR, THOUGH...
...
SANJOU-KUN?
I'M TALKING ABOUT YOUR FIRST KISS.

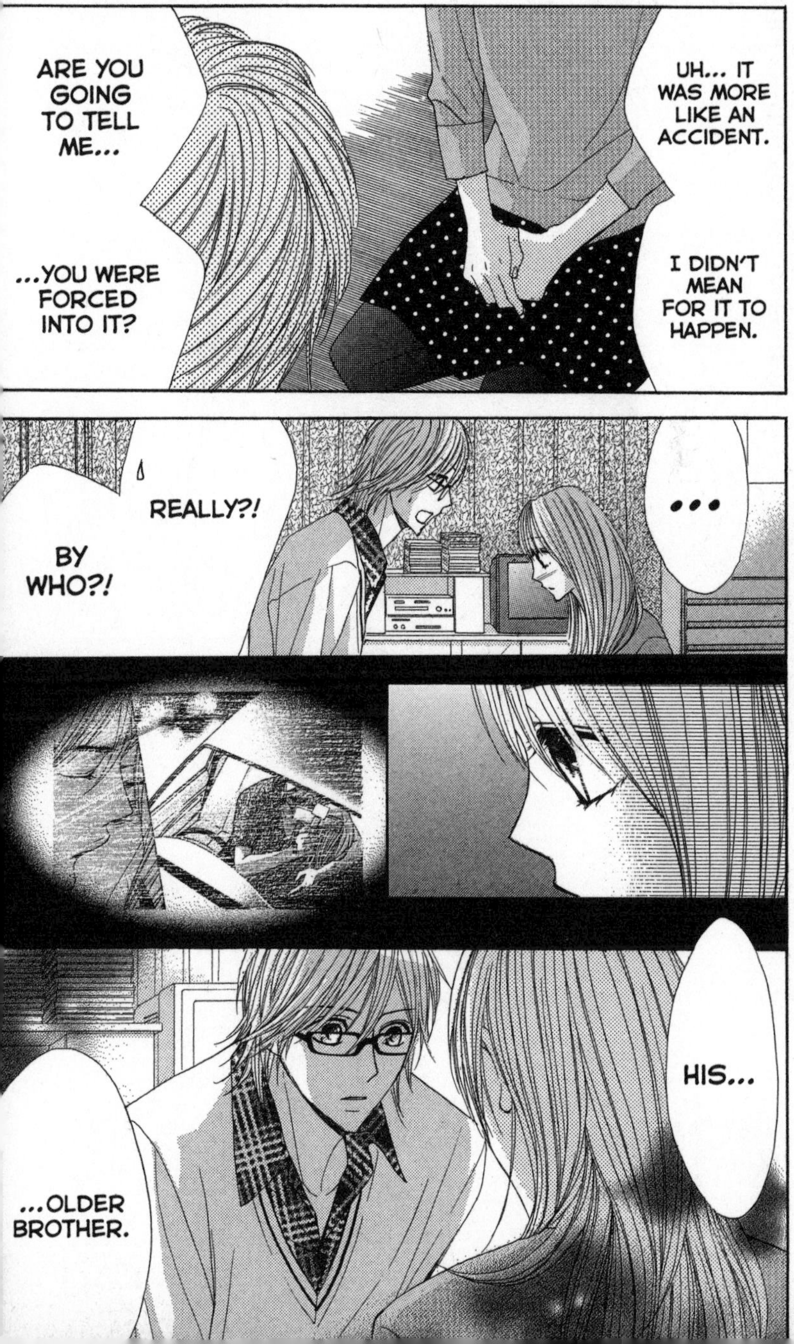
UH... IT WAS MORE LIKE AN ACCIDENT.
I DIDN'T MEAN FOR IT TO HAPPEN.
ARE YOU GOING TO TELL ME...
...YOU WERE FORCED INTO IT?
...
REALLY?!
BY WHO?!
HIS...
...OLDER BROTHER.

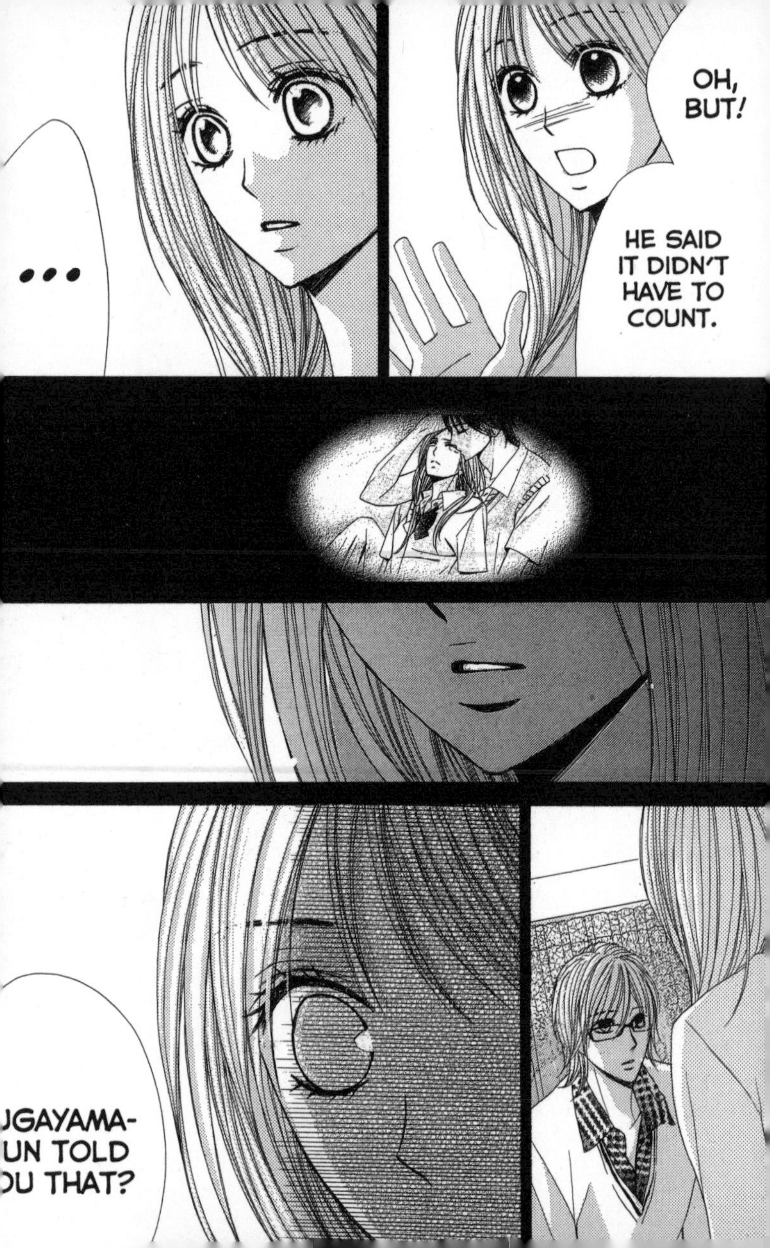
OH, BUT!
HE SAID IT DIDN'T HAVE TO COUNT.
...
UGAYAMA-UN TOLD OU THAT?

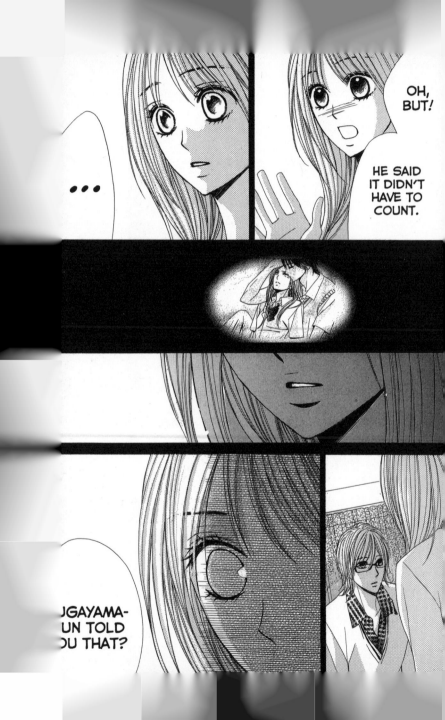

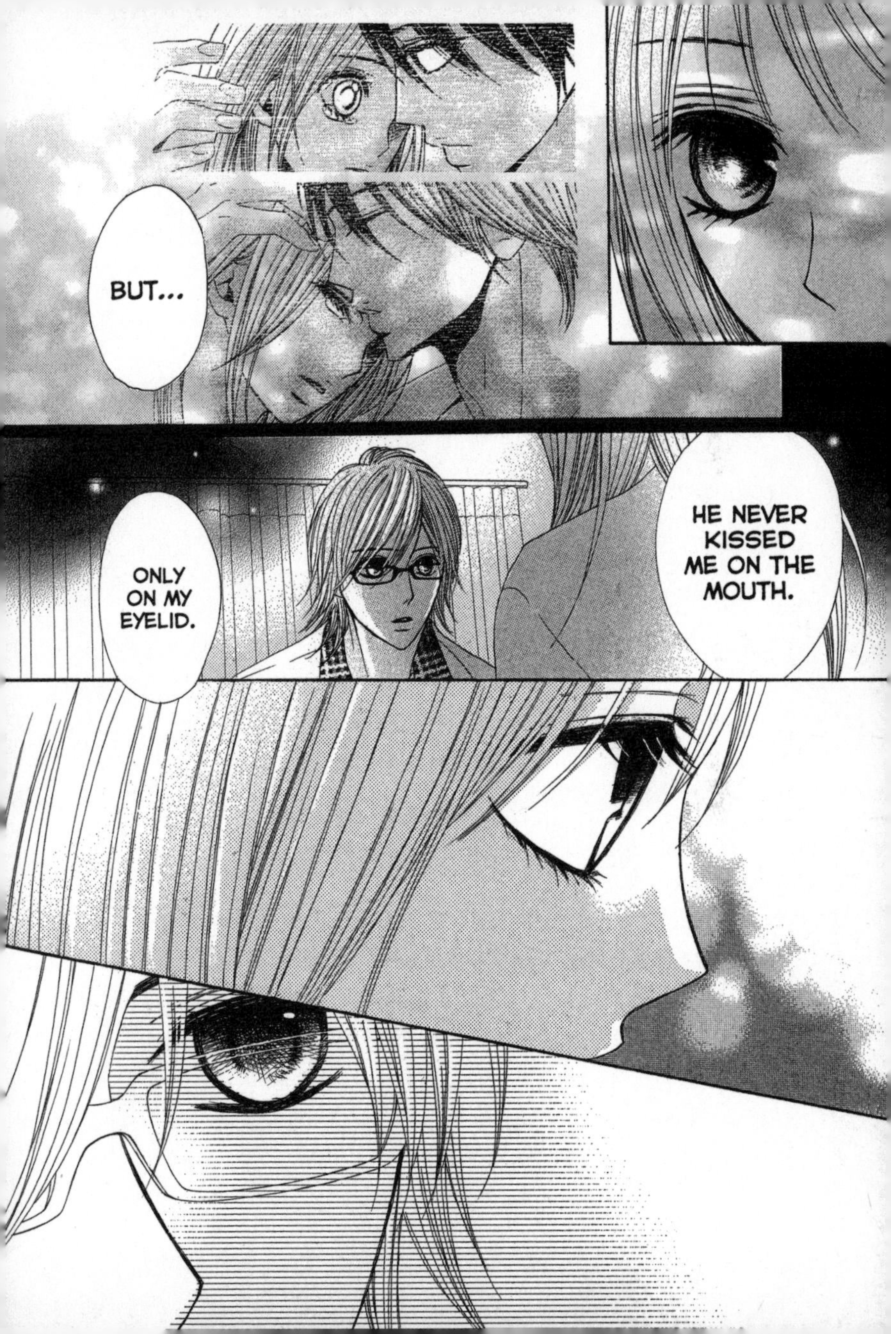
BUT...
HE NEVER KISSED ME ON THE MOUTH.
ONLY ON MY EYELID.

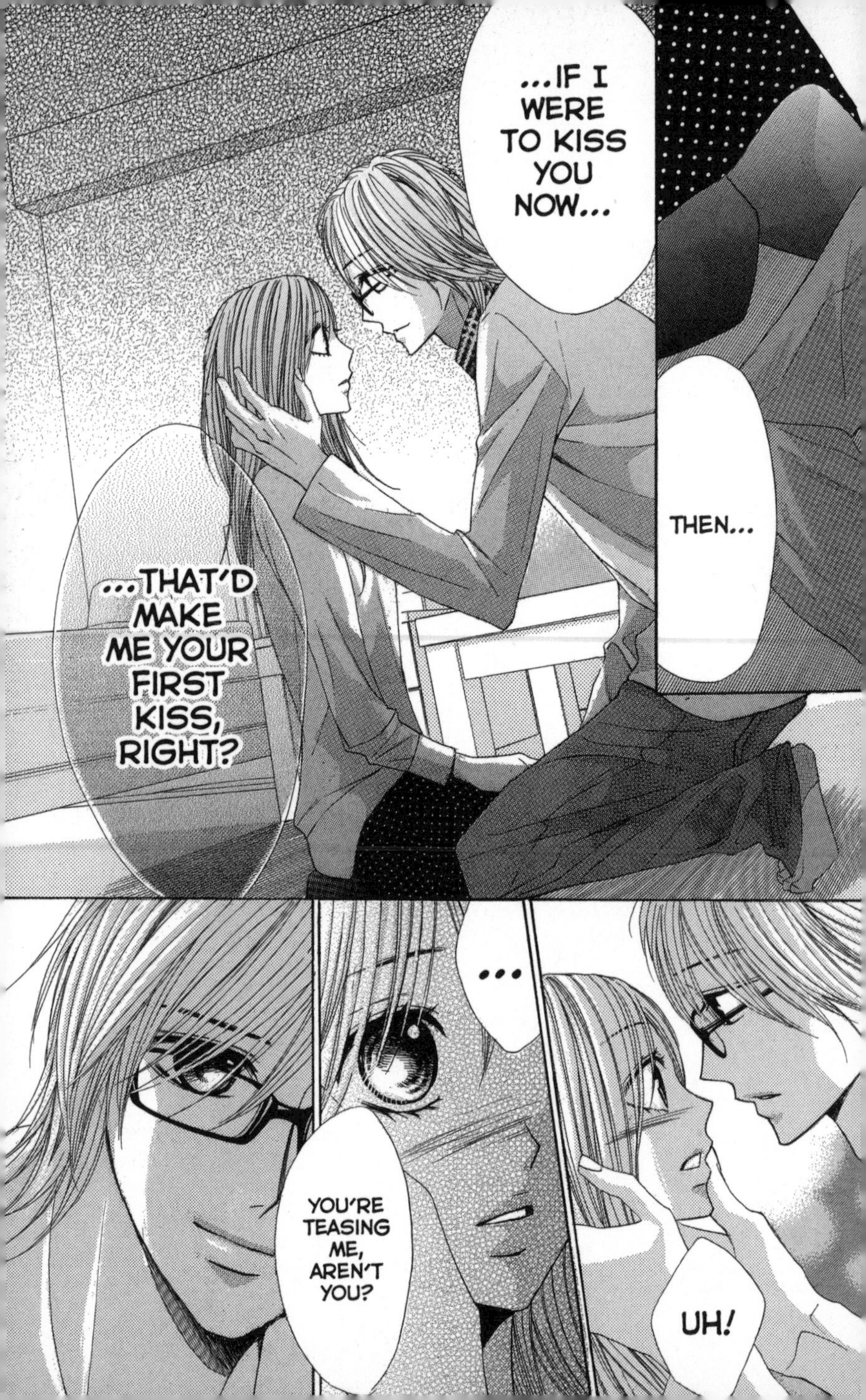
THEN...
...IF I WERE TO KISS YOU NOW...
...THAT'D MAKE ME YOUR FIRST KISS, RIGHT?
UH!
...
YOU'RE TEASING ME, AREN'T YOU?

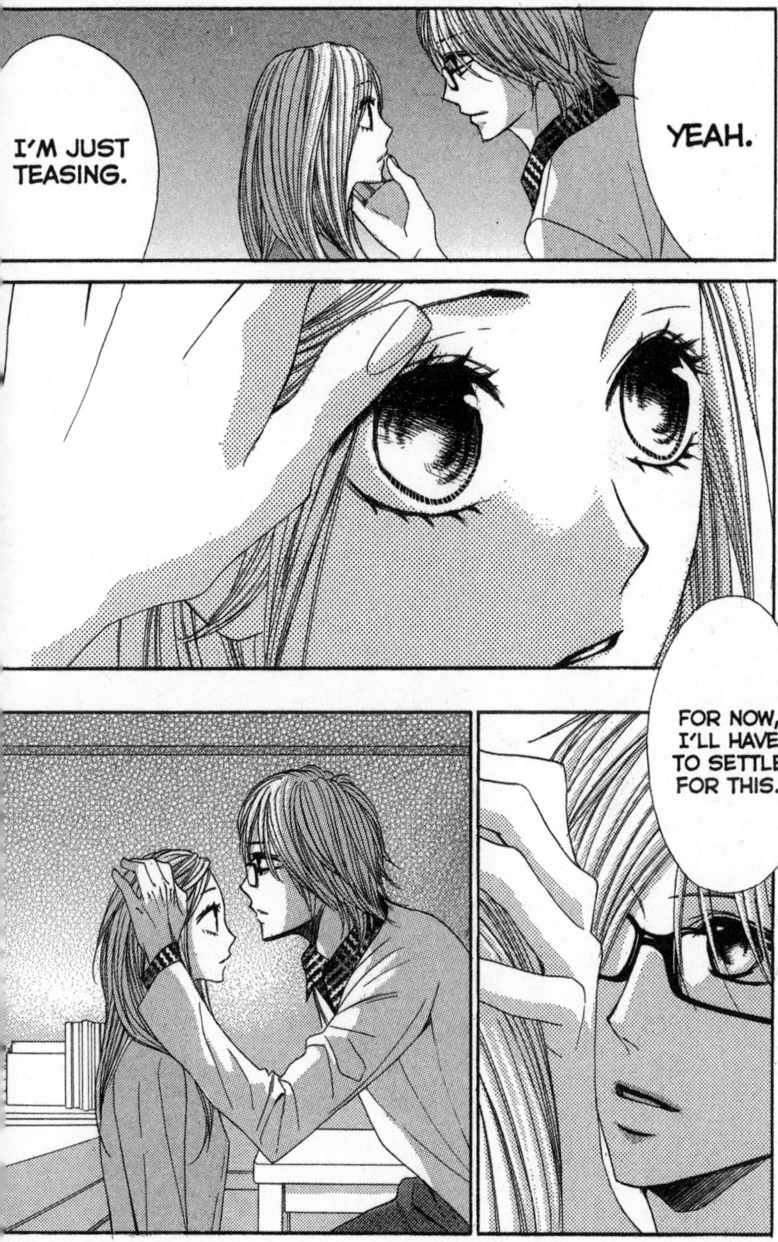
YEAH.
I'M JUST TEASING.
FOR NOW, I'LL HAVE TO SETTLE FOR THIS.

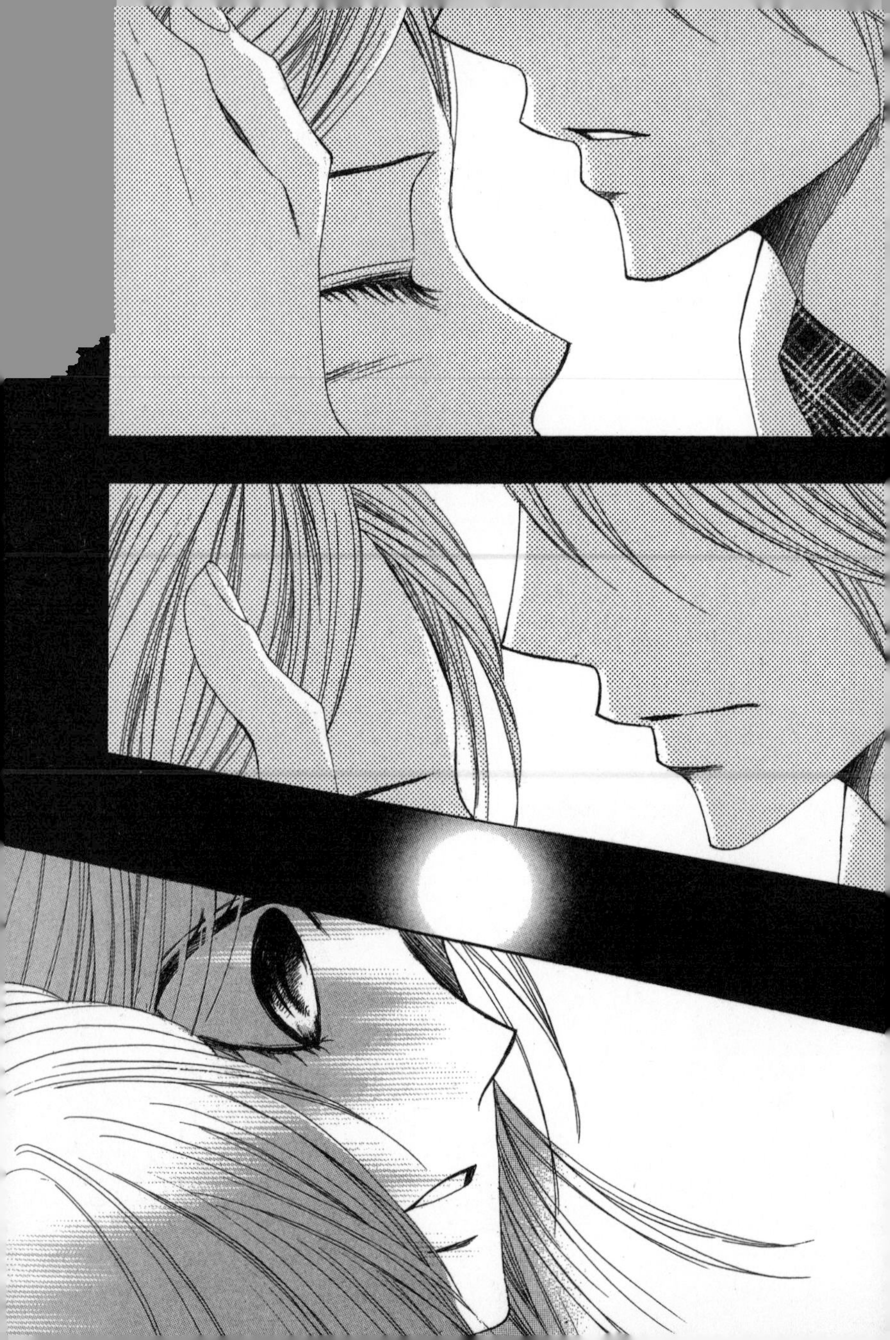

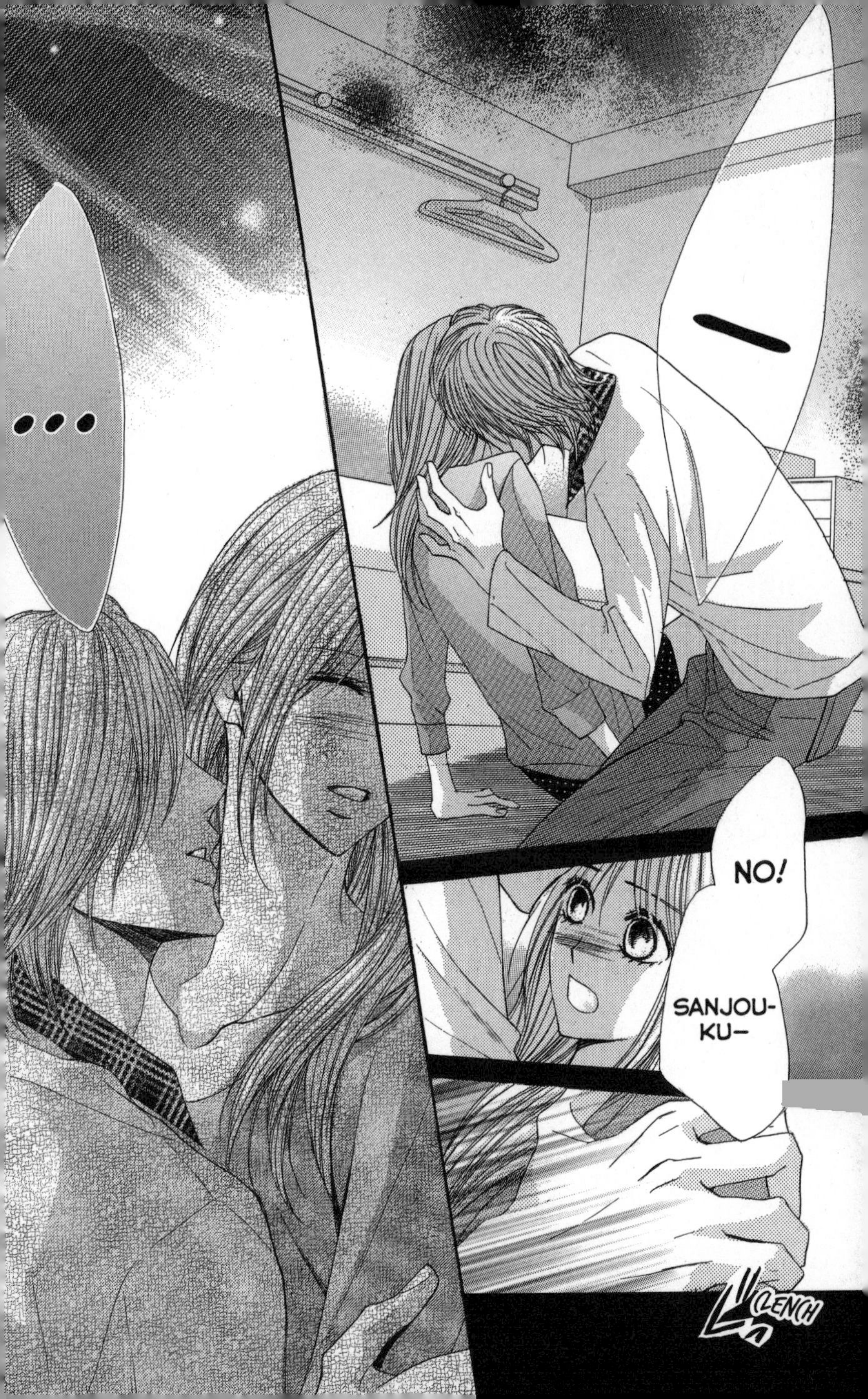

–
...
NO!
SANJOU-KU–
CLENCH

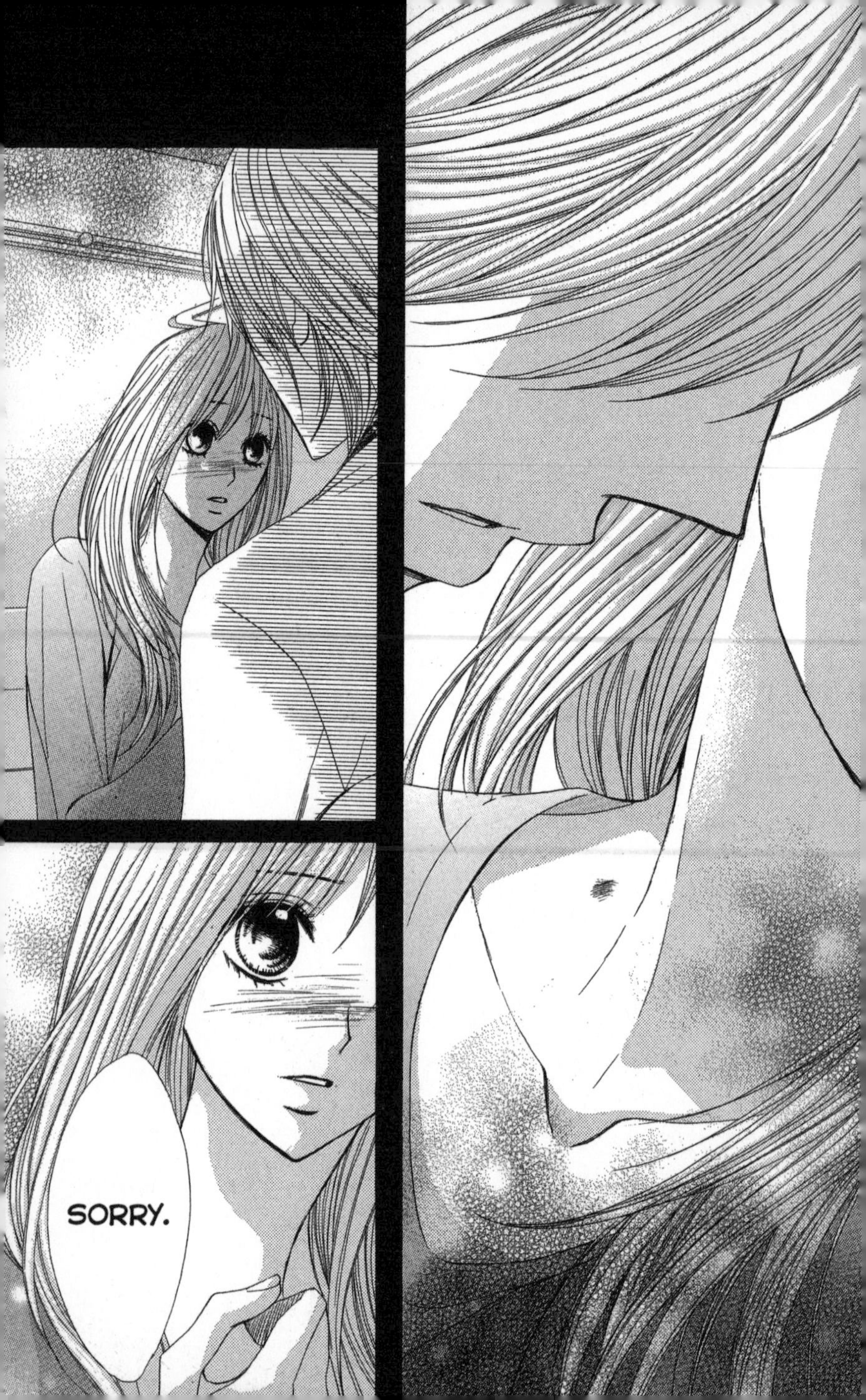
SORRY.

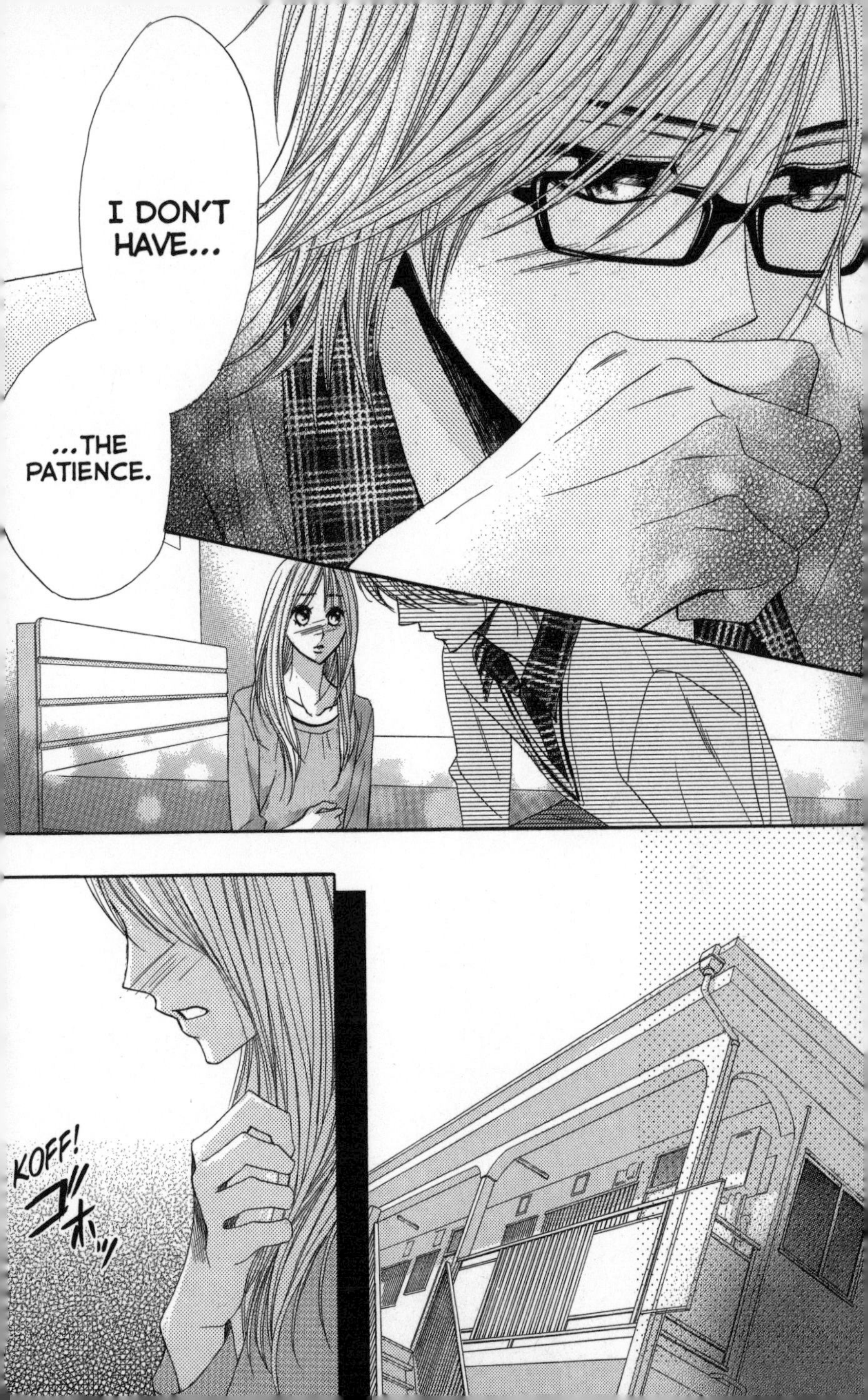
I DON'T HAVE...
...THE PATIENCE.
KOFF!
ゴホッ

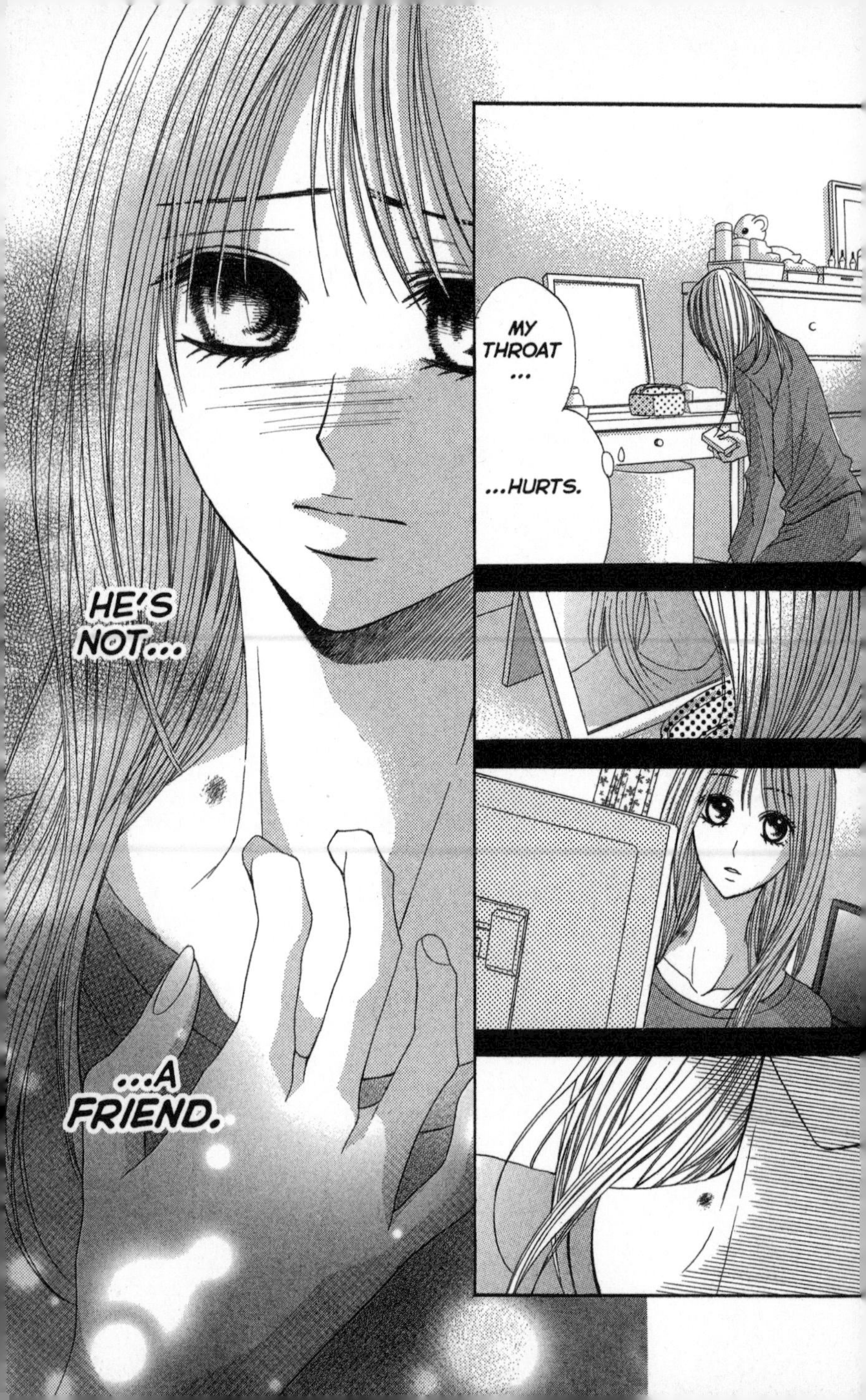
MY THROAT ...
...HURTS.
HE'S NOT...
...A FRIEND.

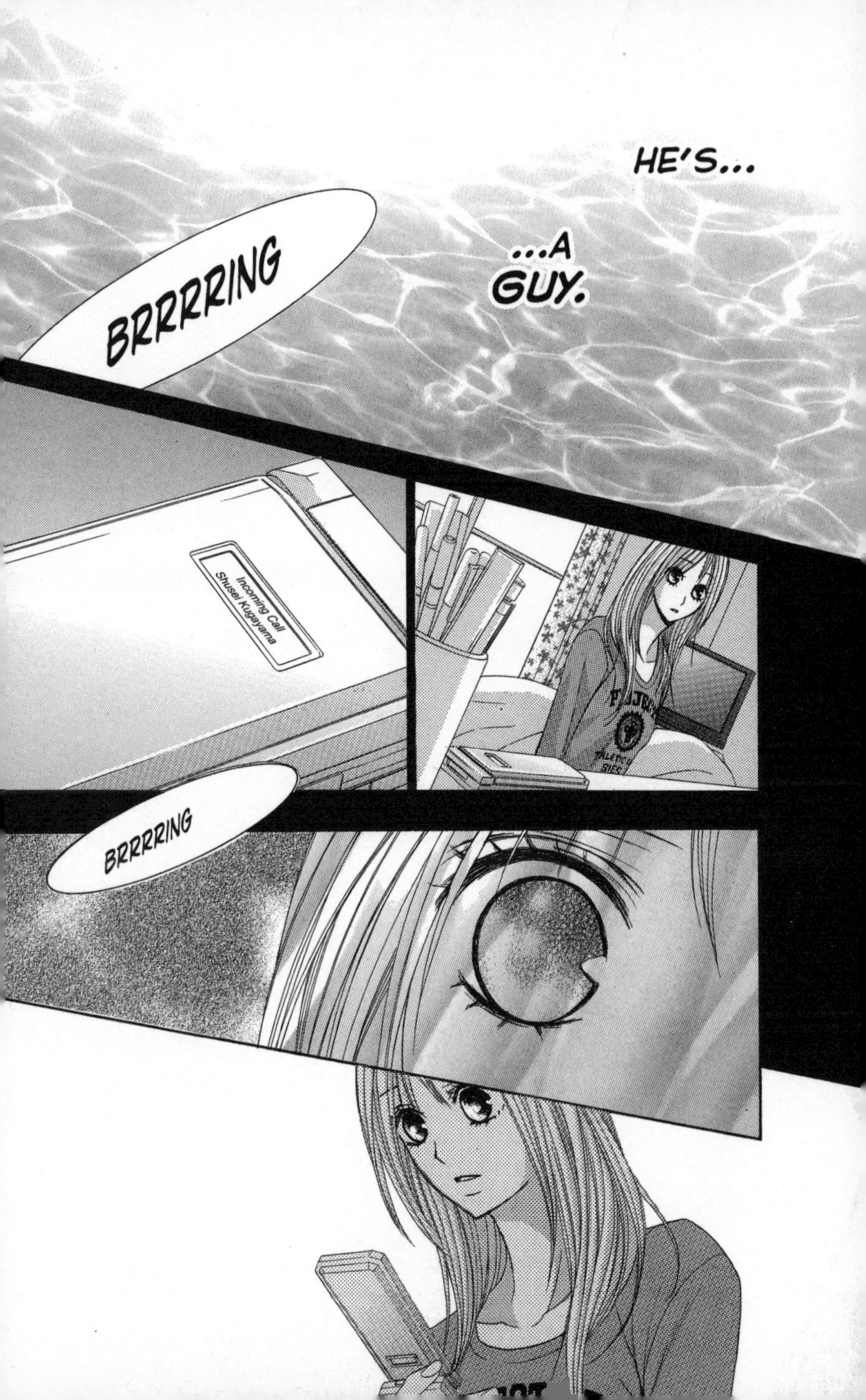
HE'S...
...A GUY.
BRRRRING
Incoming Call
Shusei Kugayama
BRRRRING

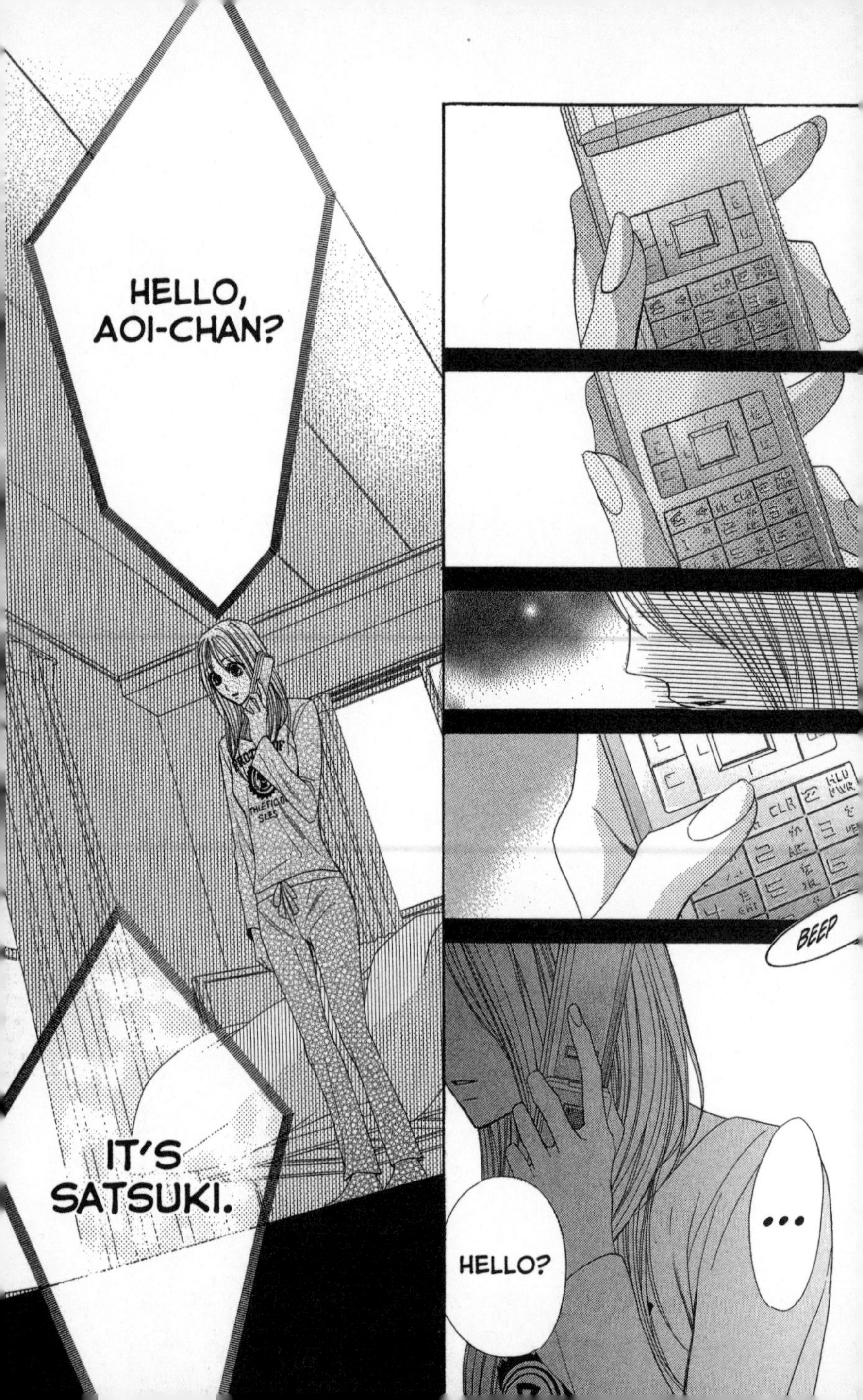
BEEP
...
HELLO?
HELLO, AOI-CHAN?
IT'S SATSUKI.

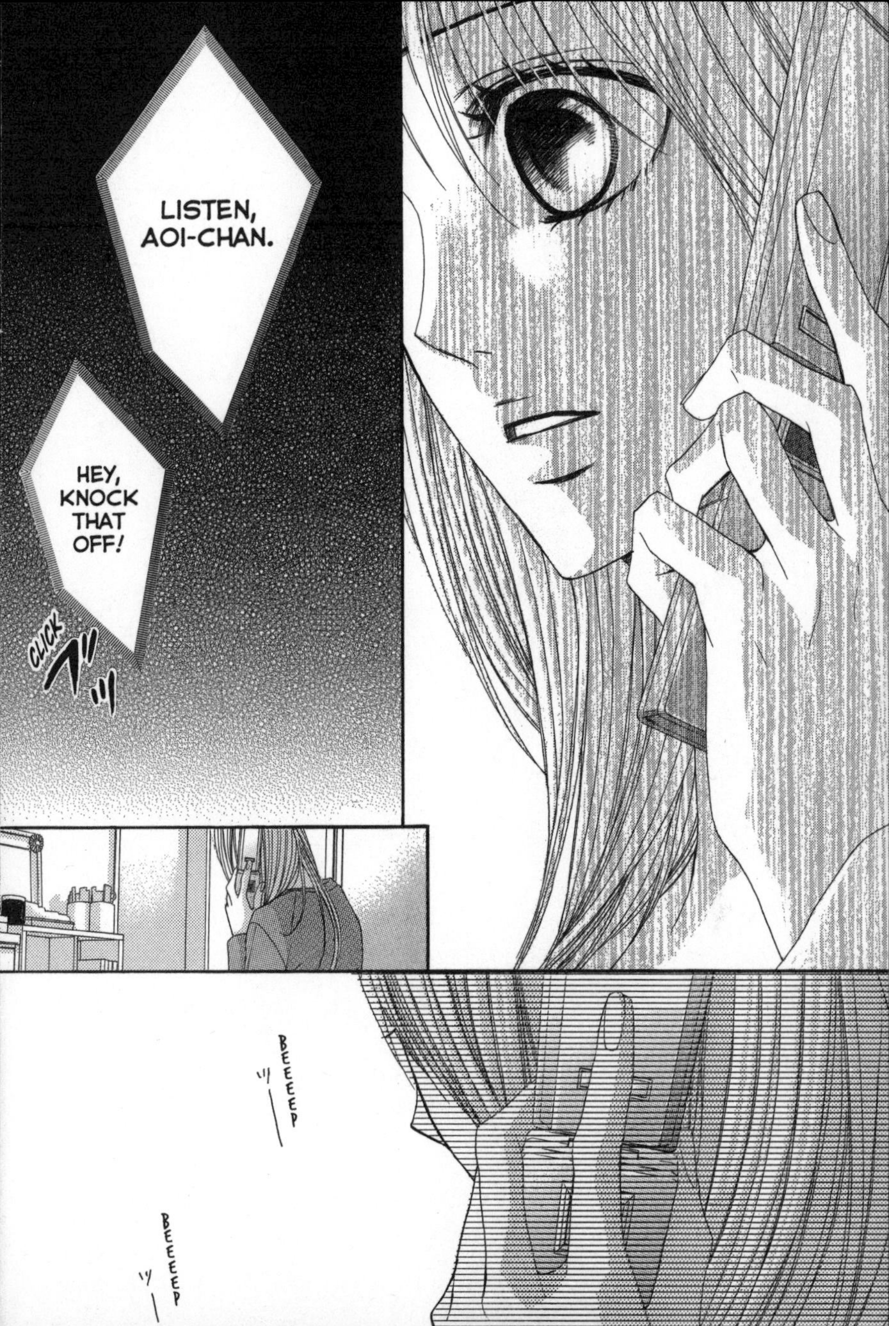
LISTEN, AOI-CHAN.
HEY, KNOCK THAT OFF!
CLICK
BEEEEEP
BEEEEEP

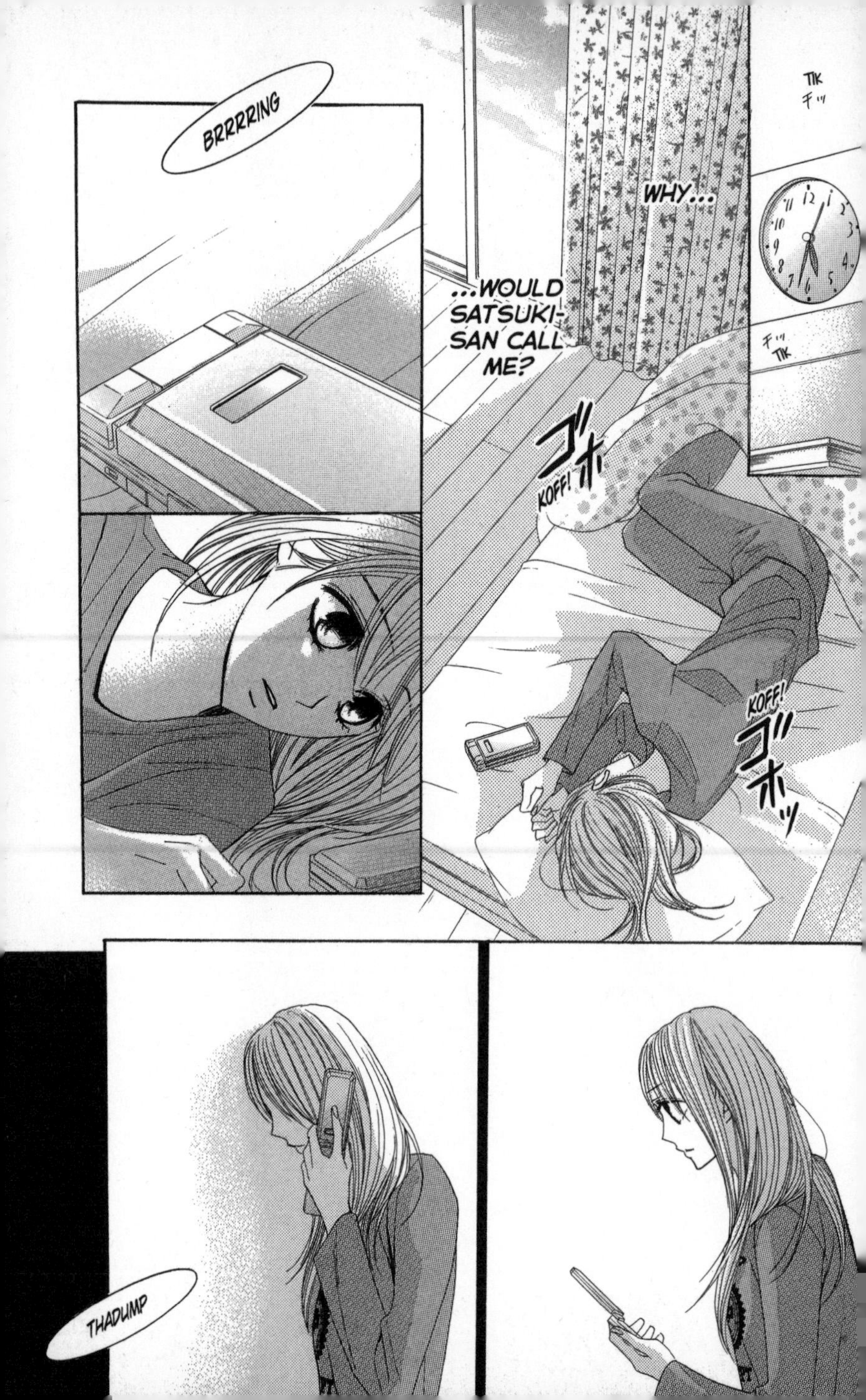
TIK
チッ
WHY...
...WOULD SATSUKI-SAN CALL ME?
チッ
TIK
ゴホ
KOFF!
KOFF!
ゴホッ
BRRRRING
THADUMP

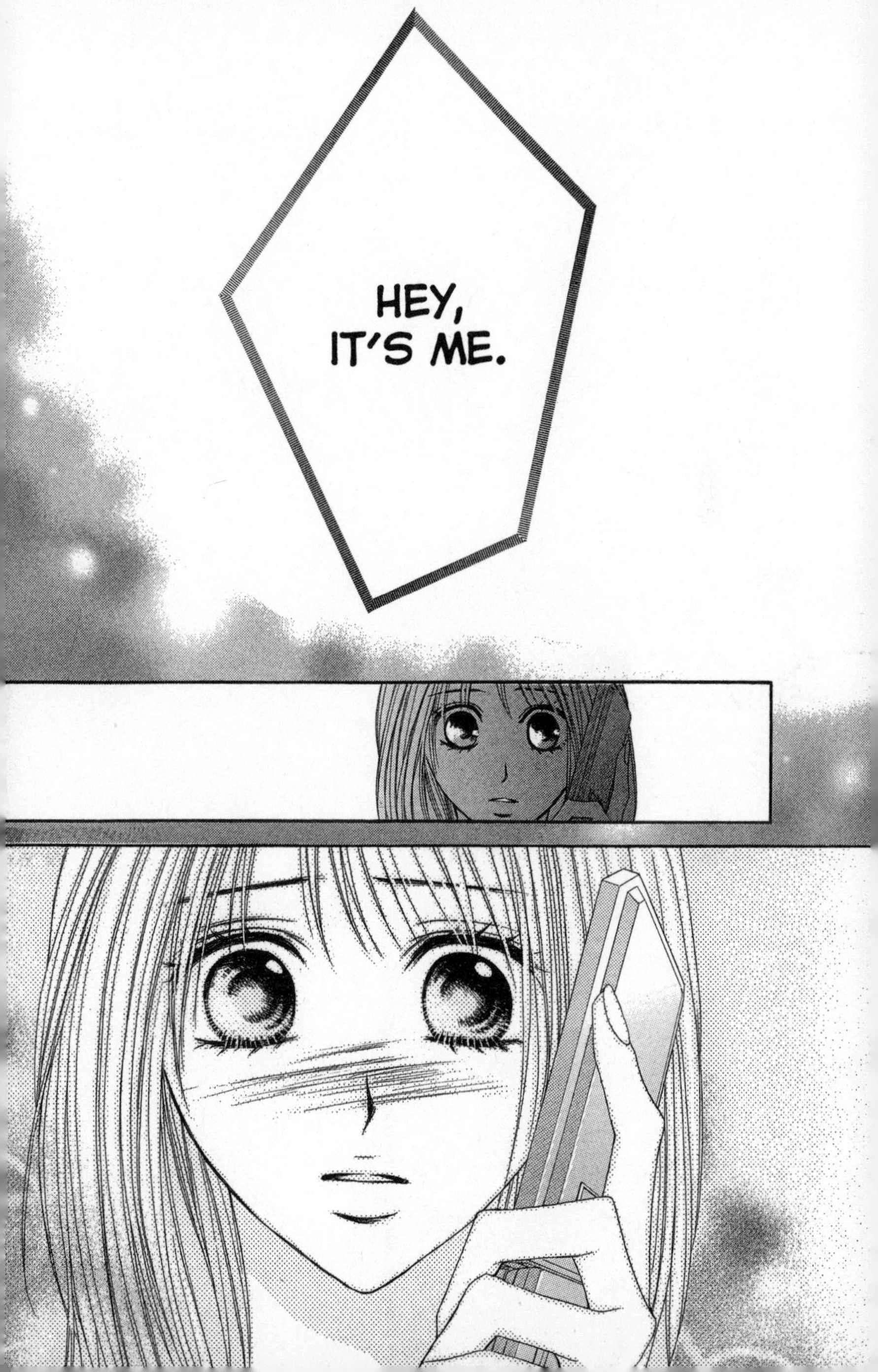
HEY, IT'S ME.

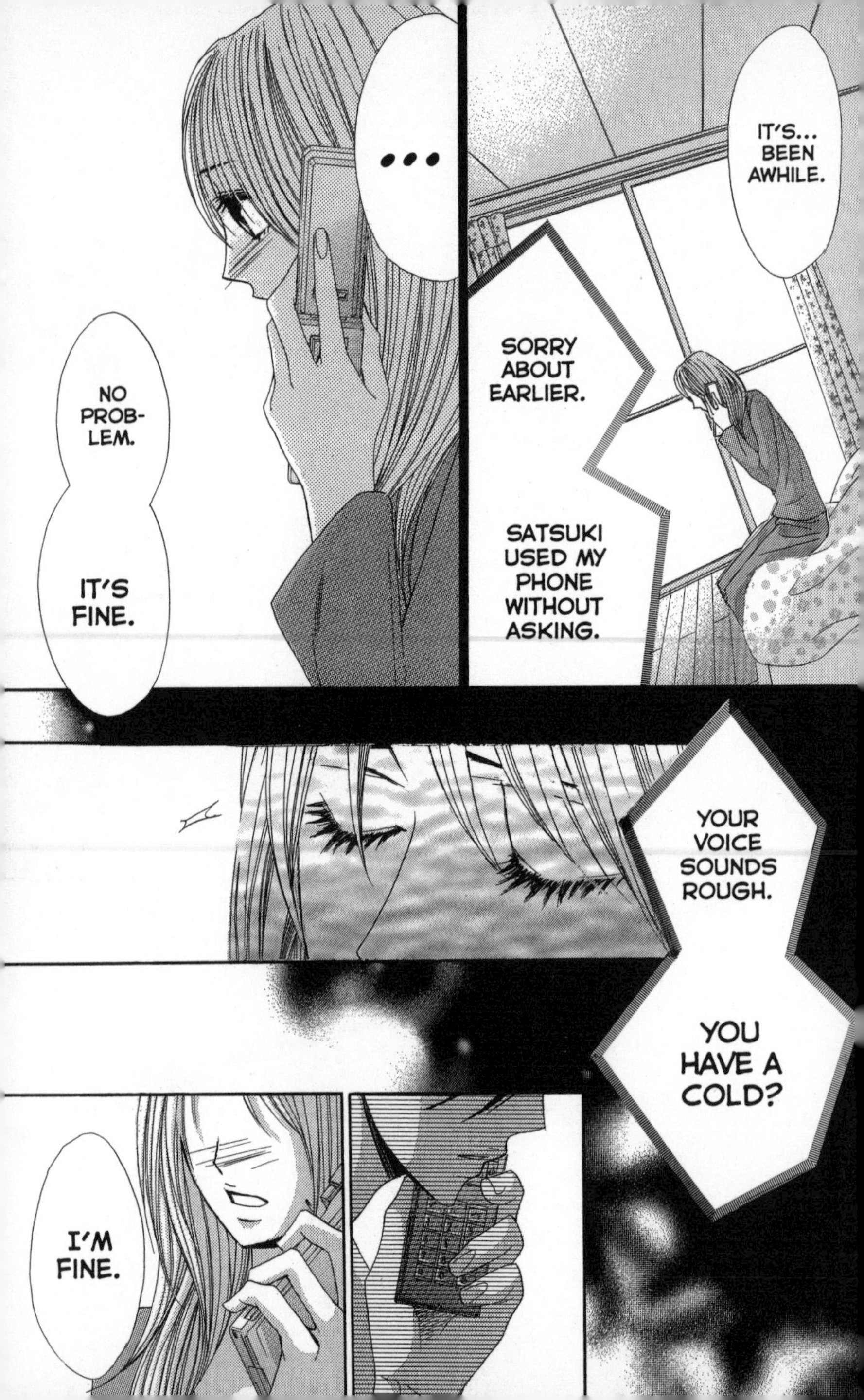
IT'S... BEEN AWHILE.
SORRY ABOUT EARLIER.
SATSUKI USED MY PHONE WITHOUT ASKING.
...
NO PROB- LEM.
IT'S FINE.
YOUR VOICE SOUNDS ROUGH.
YOU HAVE A COLD?
I'M FINE.

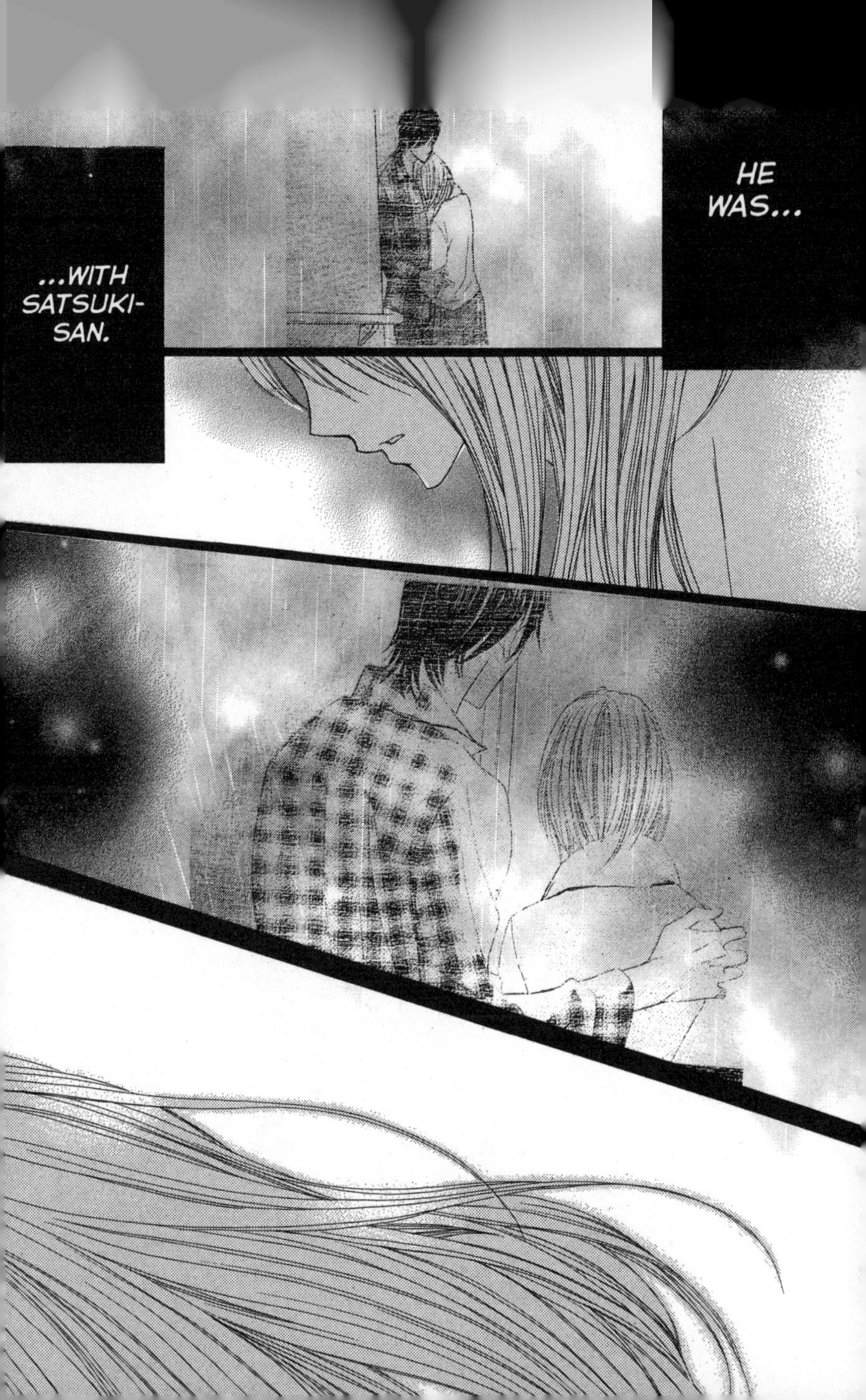

HE WAS...
...WITH SATSUKI-SAN.

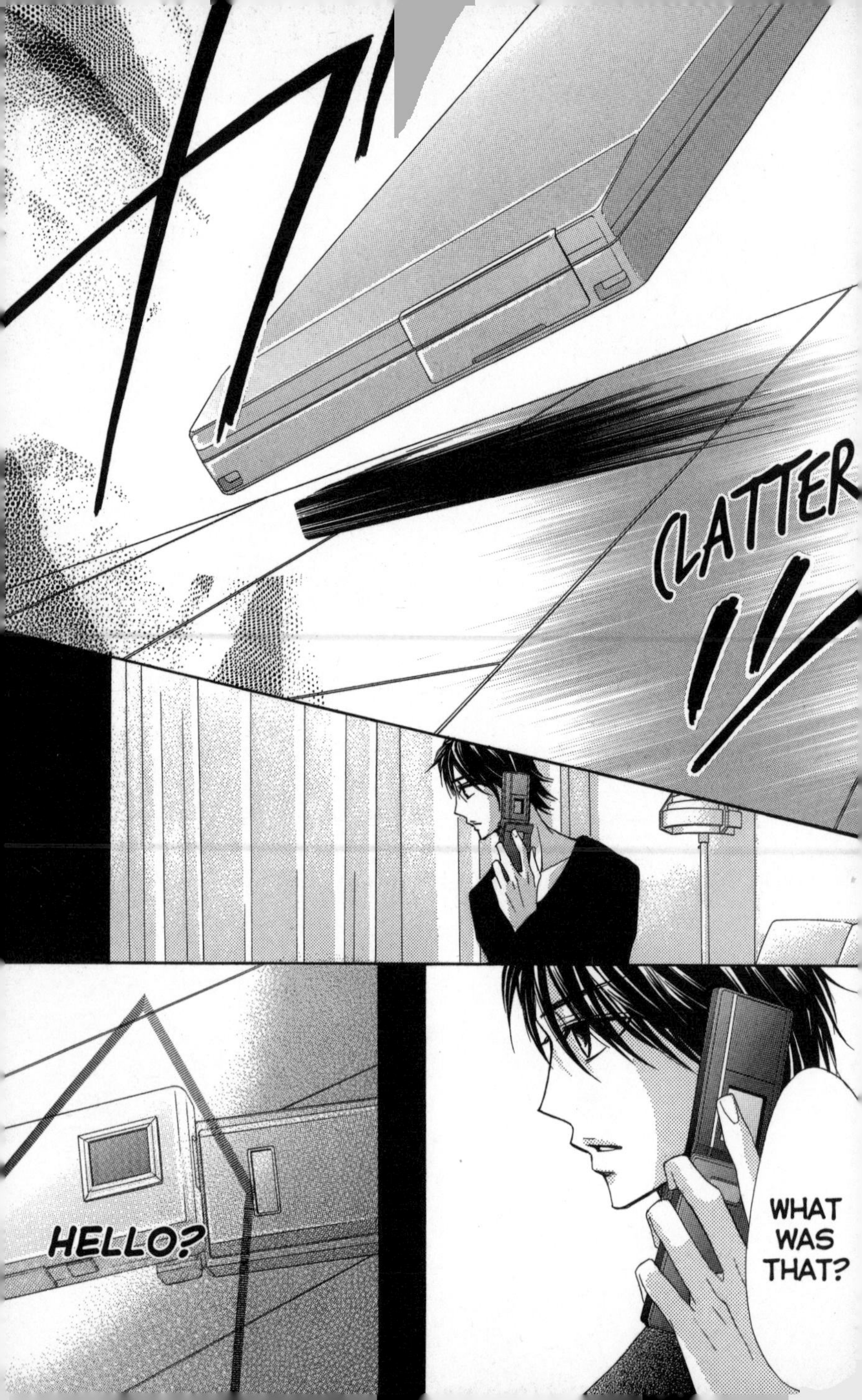
CLATTER
WHAT WAS THAT?
HELLO?

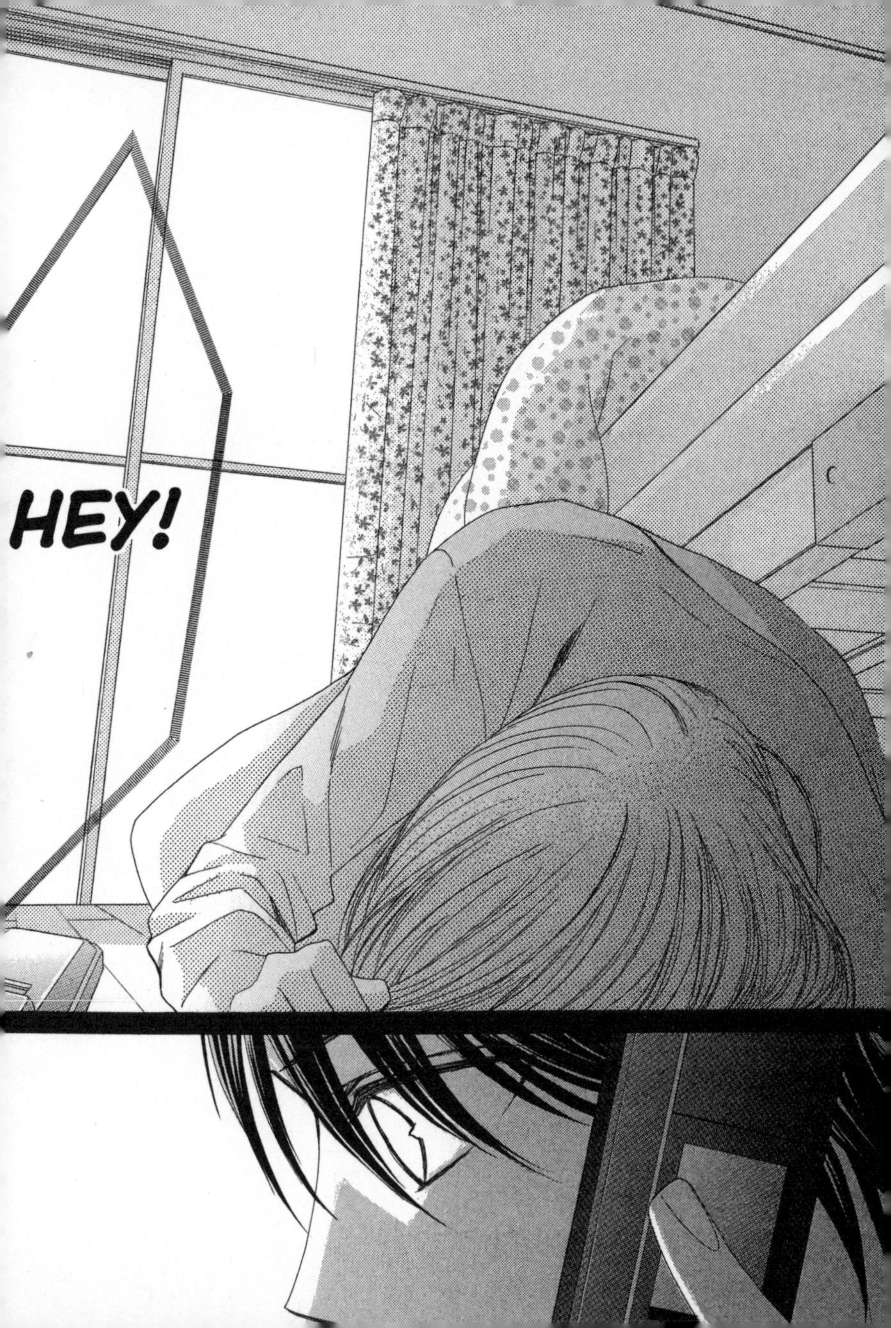
HEY!

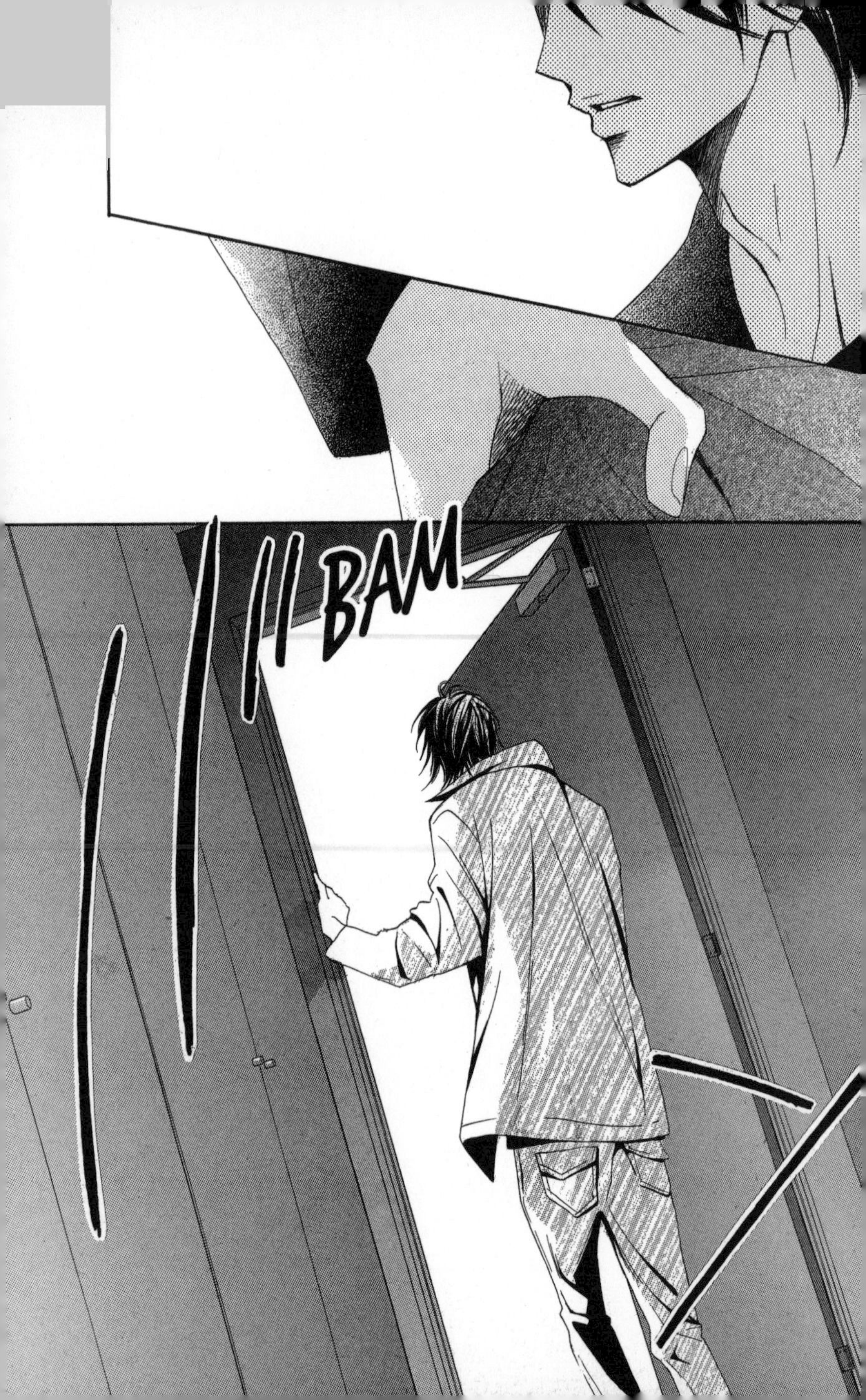
BAM

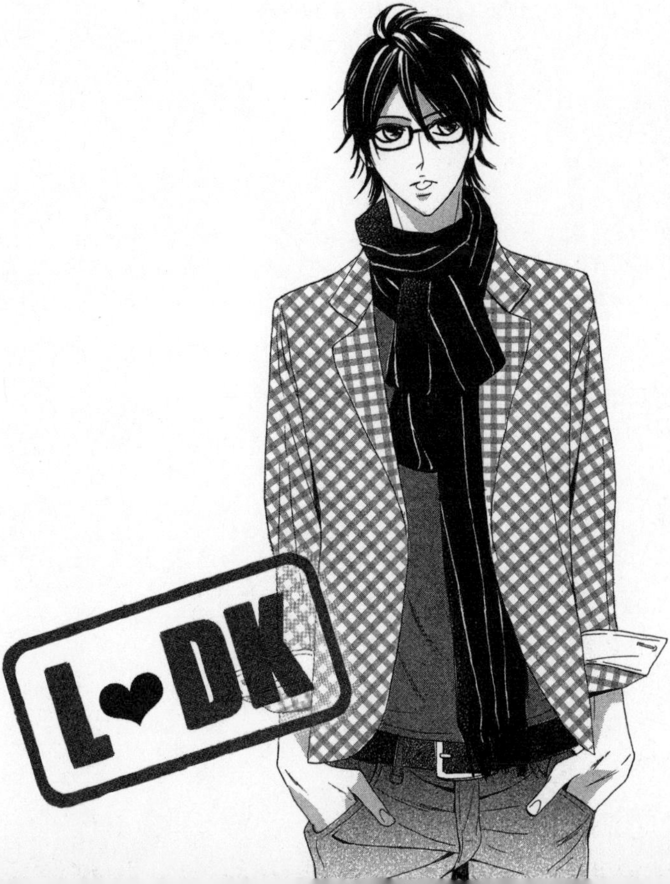
L♥DK

#27 The Three Who Pass Each Other

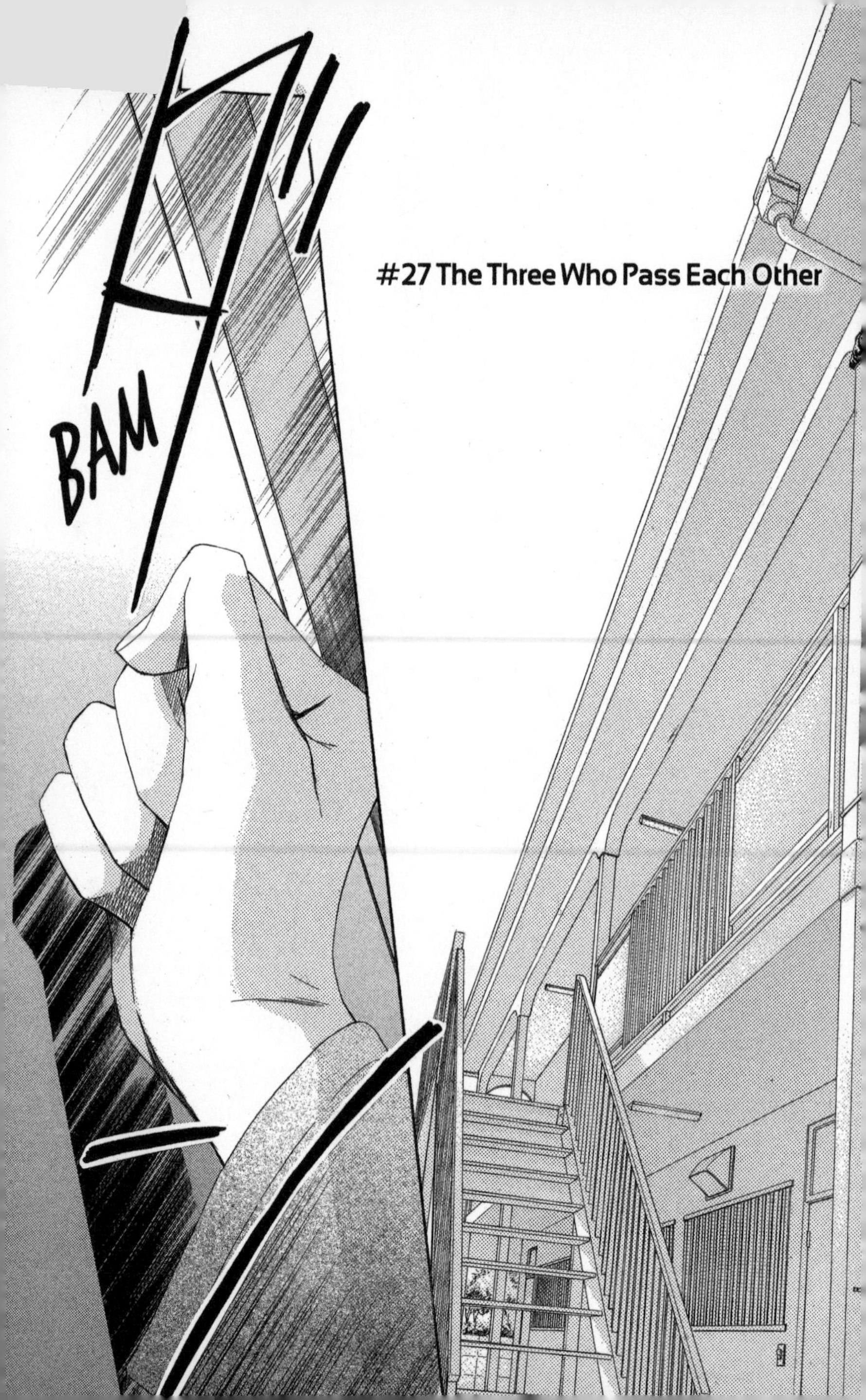
BAM

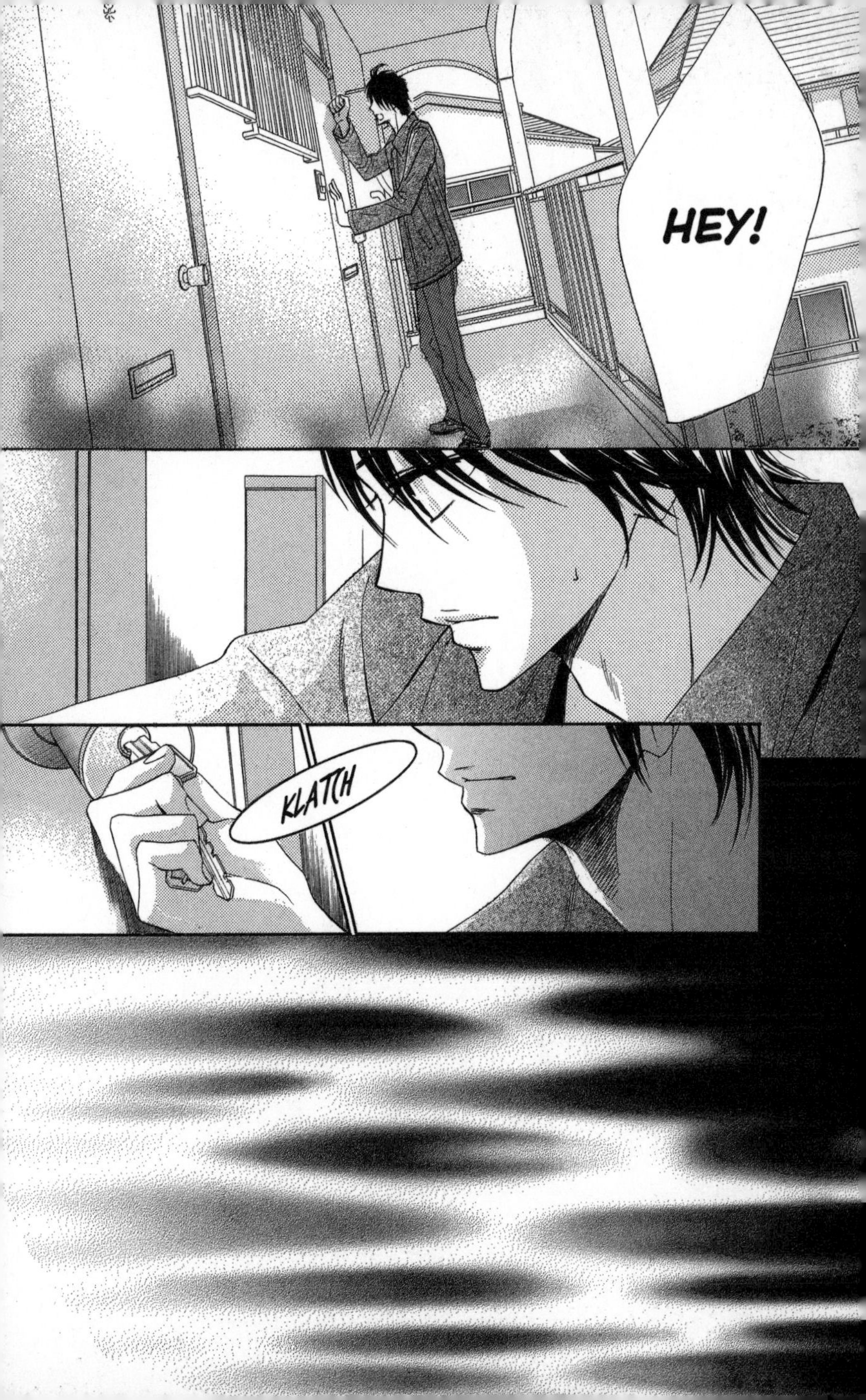
HEY!
KLATCH

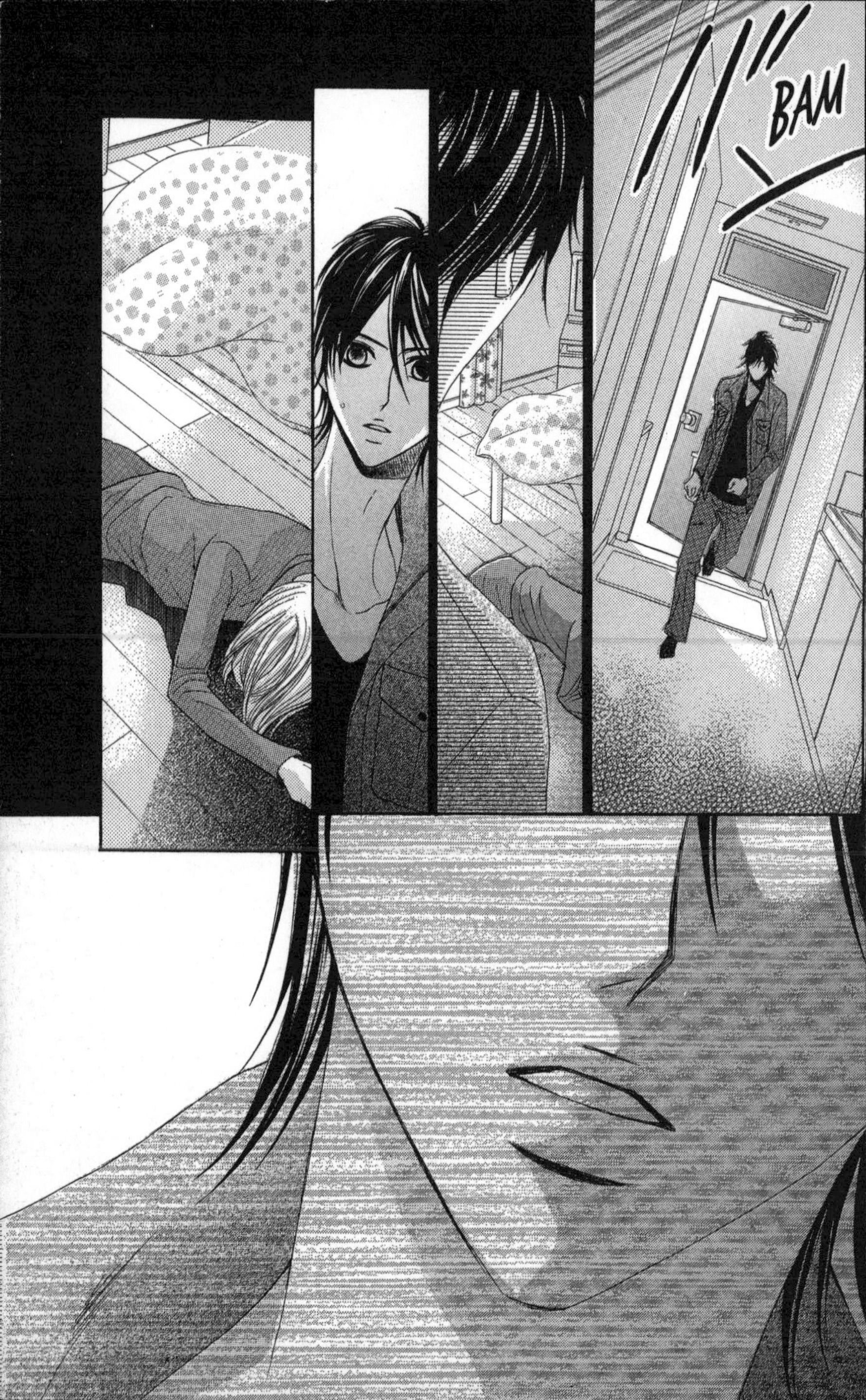
BAM

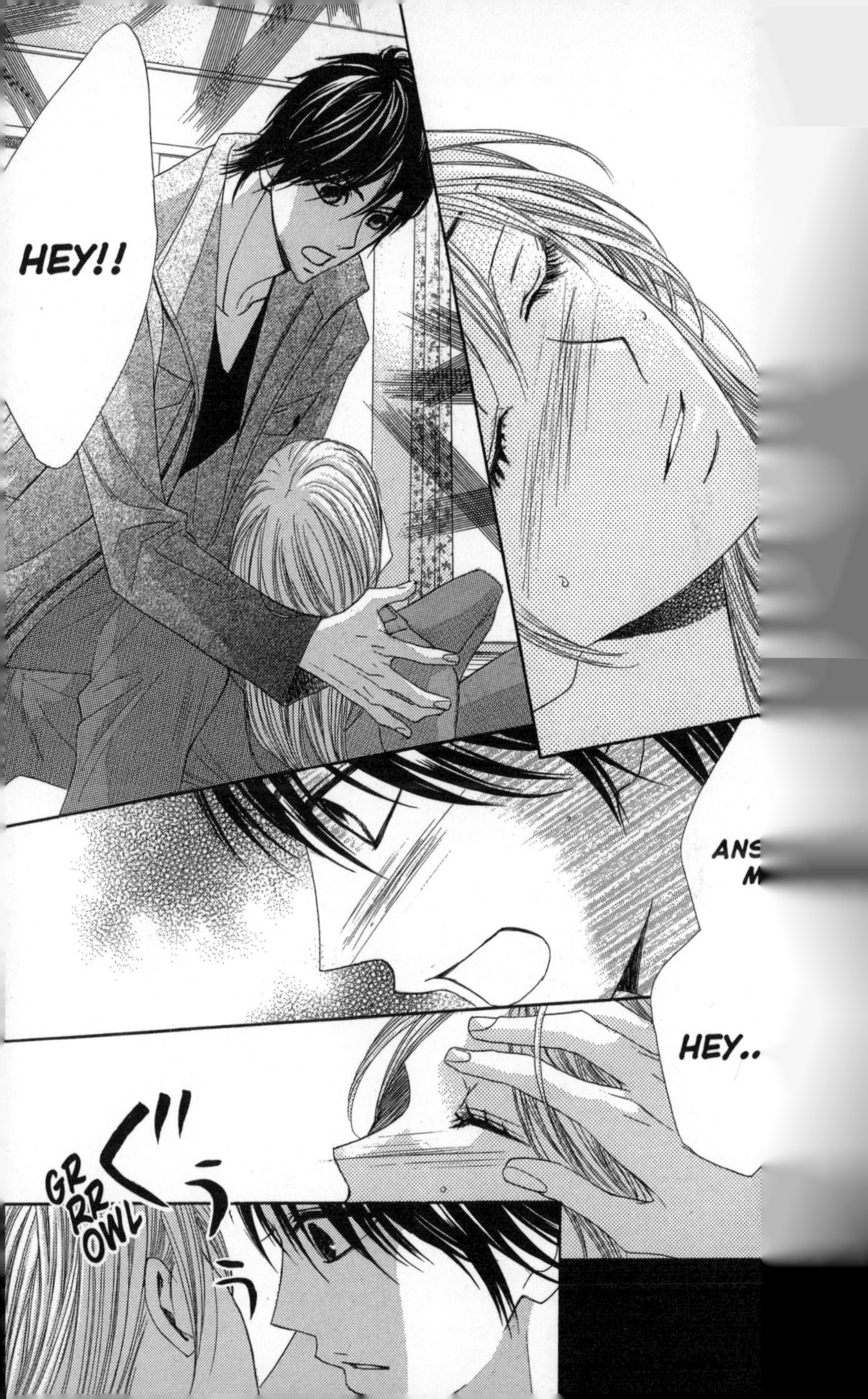
HEY!!
ANS
M
HEY..
GR RR OWL
ぐぅ

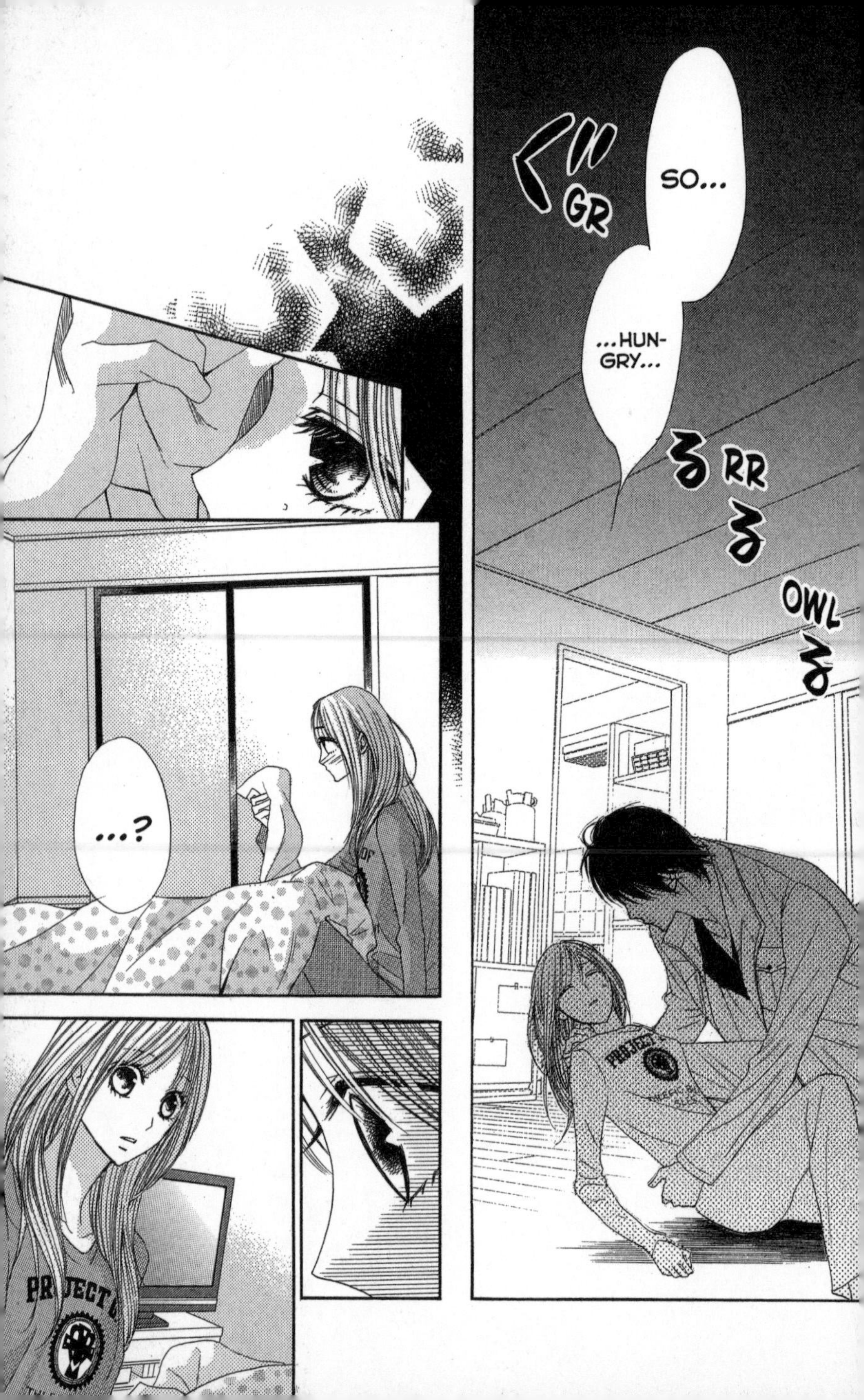

SO...
...HUN-GRY...
ぐ GR
る RR
る
OWL
る
...?

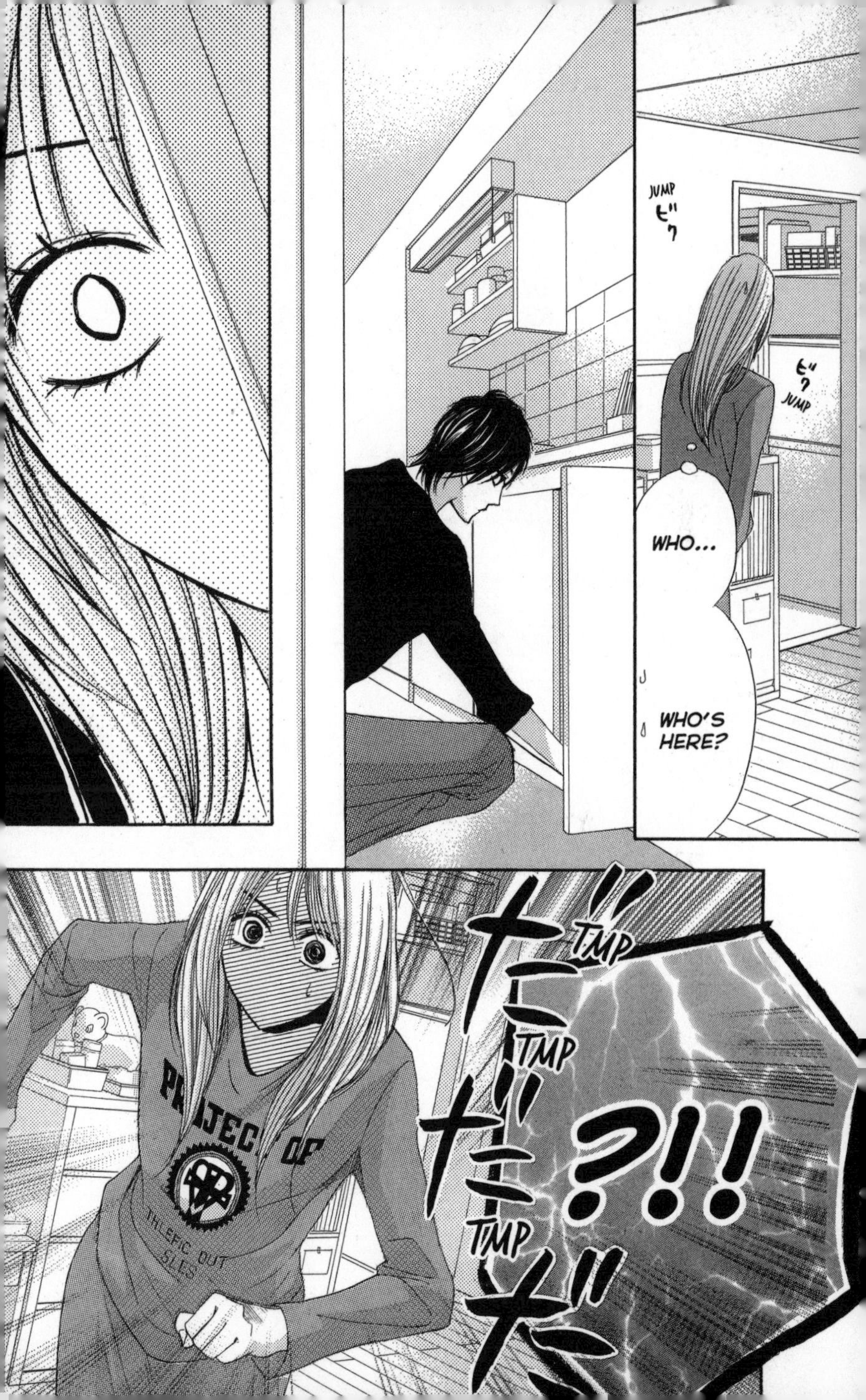
JUMP
ビク
ビク
JUMP
WHO...
WHO'S HERE?
TMP
TMP
TMP
?!!

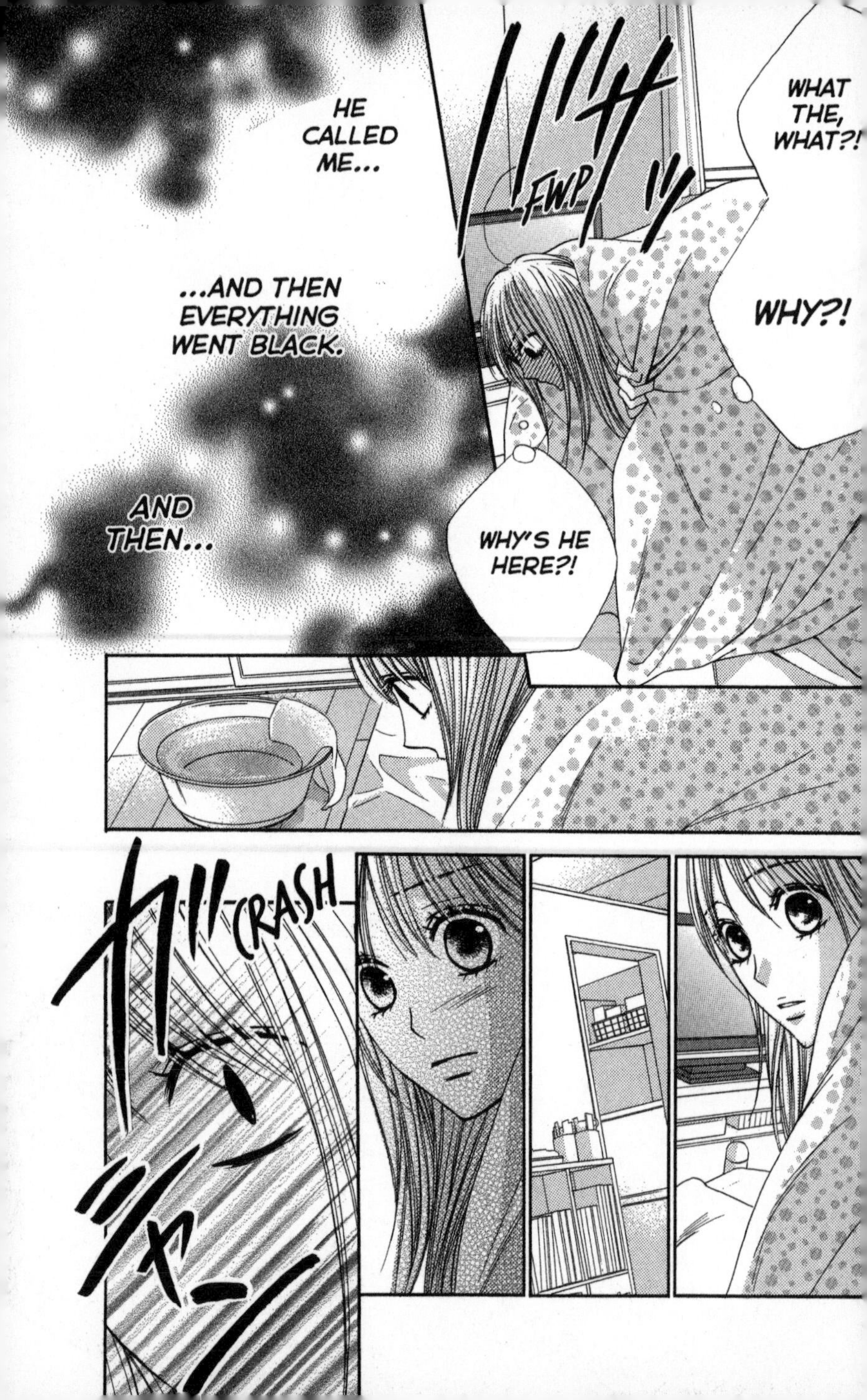
FWP
WHAT THE, WHAT?!
WHY?!
WHY'S HE HERE?!
HE CALLED ME...
...AND THEN EVERYTHING WENT BLACK.
AND THEN...
CRASH

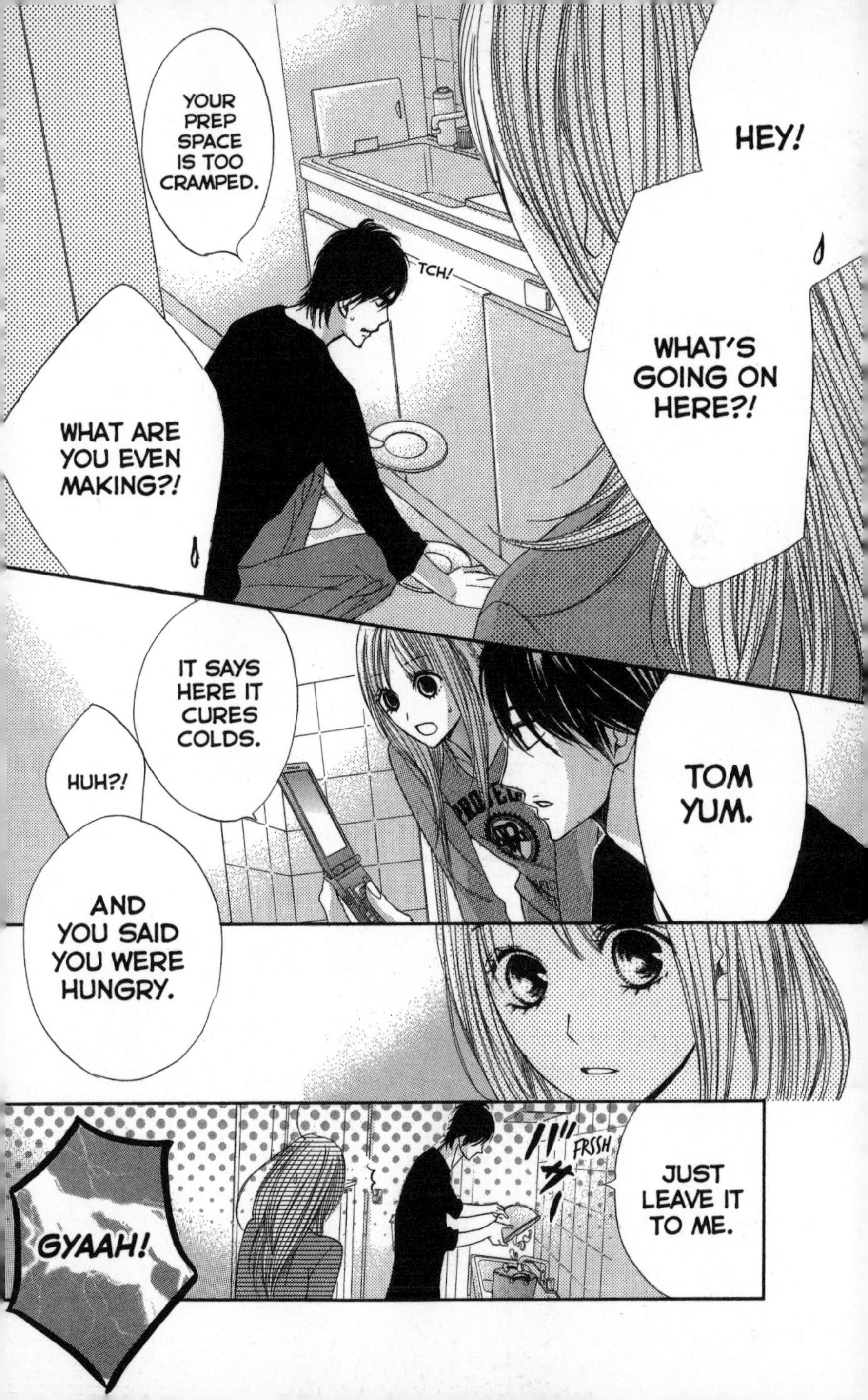
HEY!
WHAT'S GOING ON HERE?!
YOUR PREP SPACE IS TOO CRAMPED.
TCH!
WHAT ARE YOU EVEN MAKING?!
TOM YUM.
IT SAYS HERE IT CURES COLDS.
HUH?!
AND YOU SAID YOU WERE HUNGRY.
JUST LEAVE IT TO ME.
FRSSH
GYAAH!

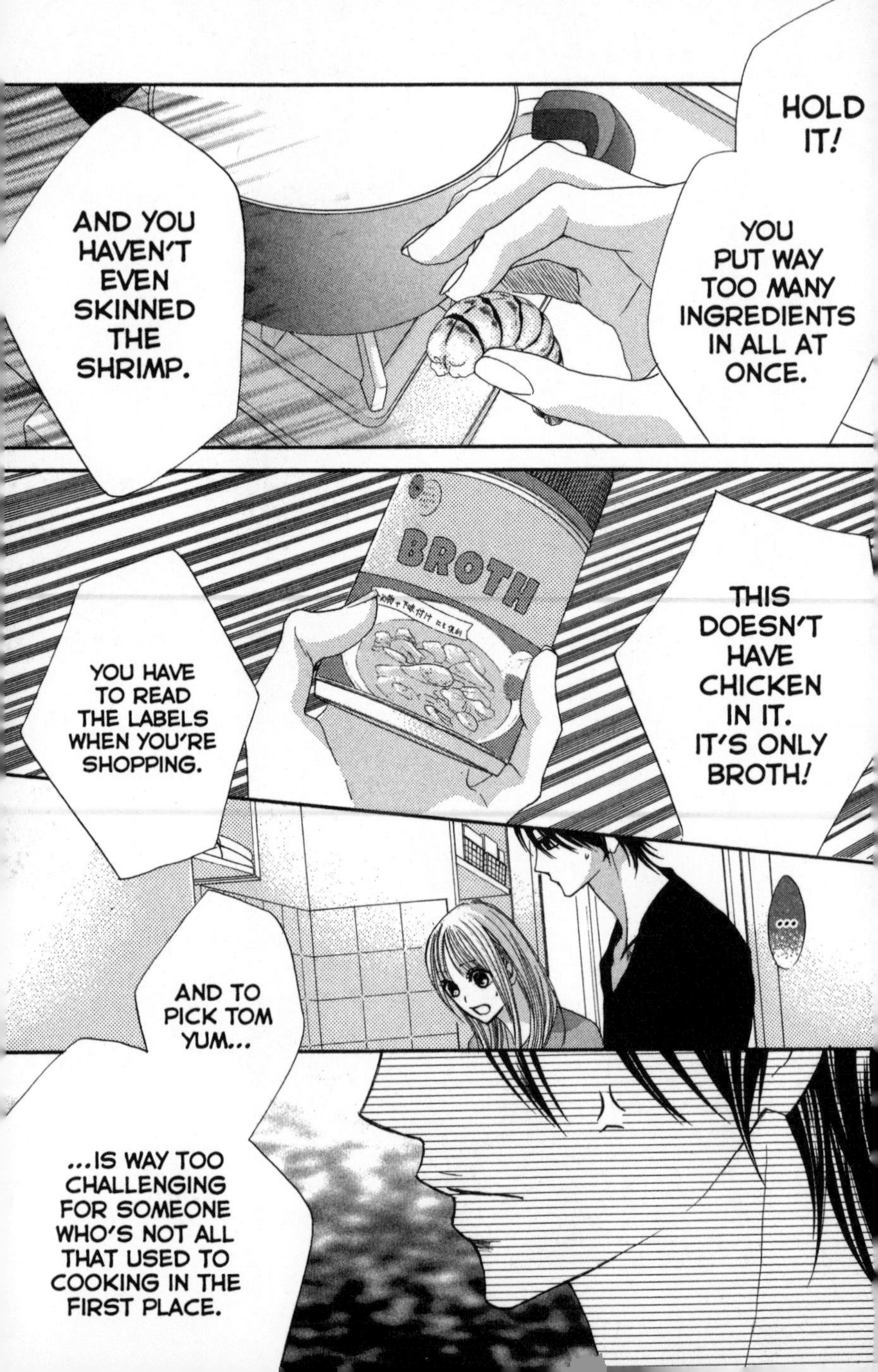
HOLD IT!
YOU PUT WAY TOO MANY INGREDIENTS IN ALL AT ONCE.
AND YOU HAVEN'T EVEN SKINNED THE SHRIMP.
BROTH
THIS DOESN'T HAVE CHICKEN IN IT. IT'S ONLY BROTH!
YOU HAVE TO READ THE LABELS WHEN YOU'RE SHOPPING.
...
AND TO PICK TOM YUM...
...IS WAY TOO CHALLENGING FOR SOMEONE WHO'S NOT ALL THAT USED TO COOKING IN THE FIRST PLACE.

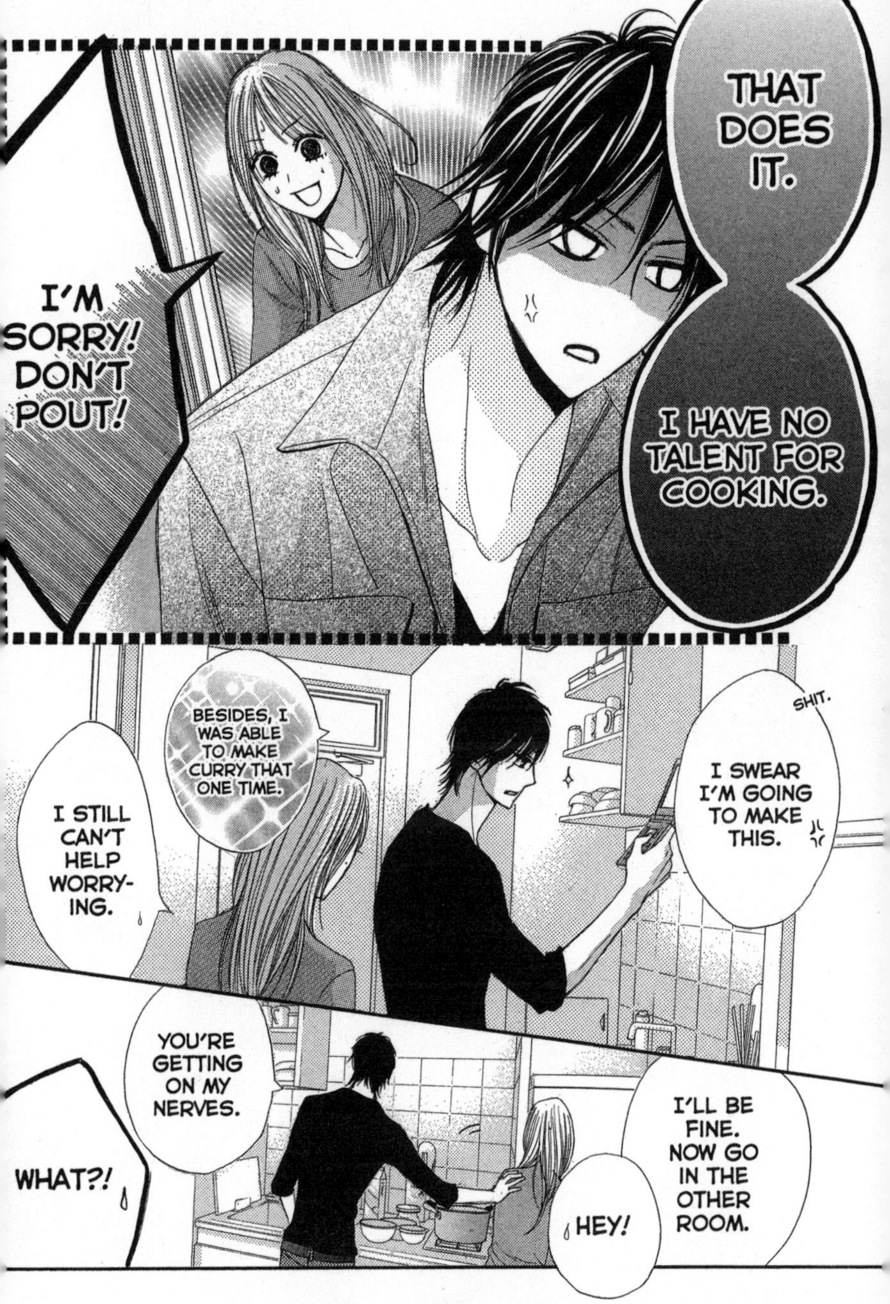
THAT DOES IT.
I HAVE NO TALENT FOR COOKING.
I'M SORRY! DON'T POUT!
SHIT.
I SWEAR I'M GOING TO MAKE THIS.
BESIDES, I WAS ABLE TO MAKE CURRY THAT ONE TIME.
I STILL CAN'T HELP WORRYING.
I'LL BE FINE. NOW GO IN THE OTHER ROOM.
HEY!
YOU'RE GETTING ON MY NERVES.
WHAT?!

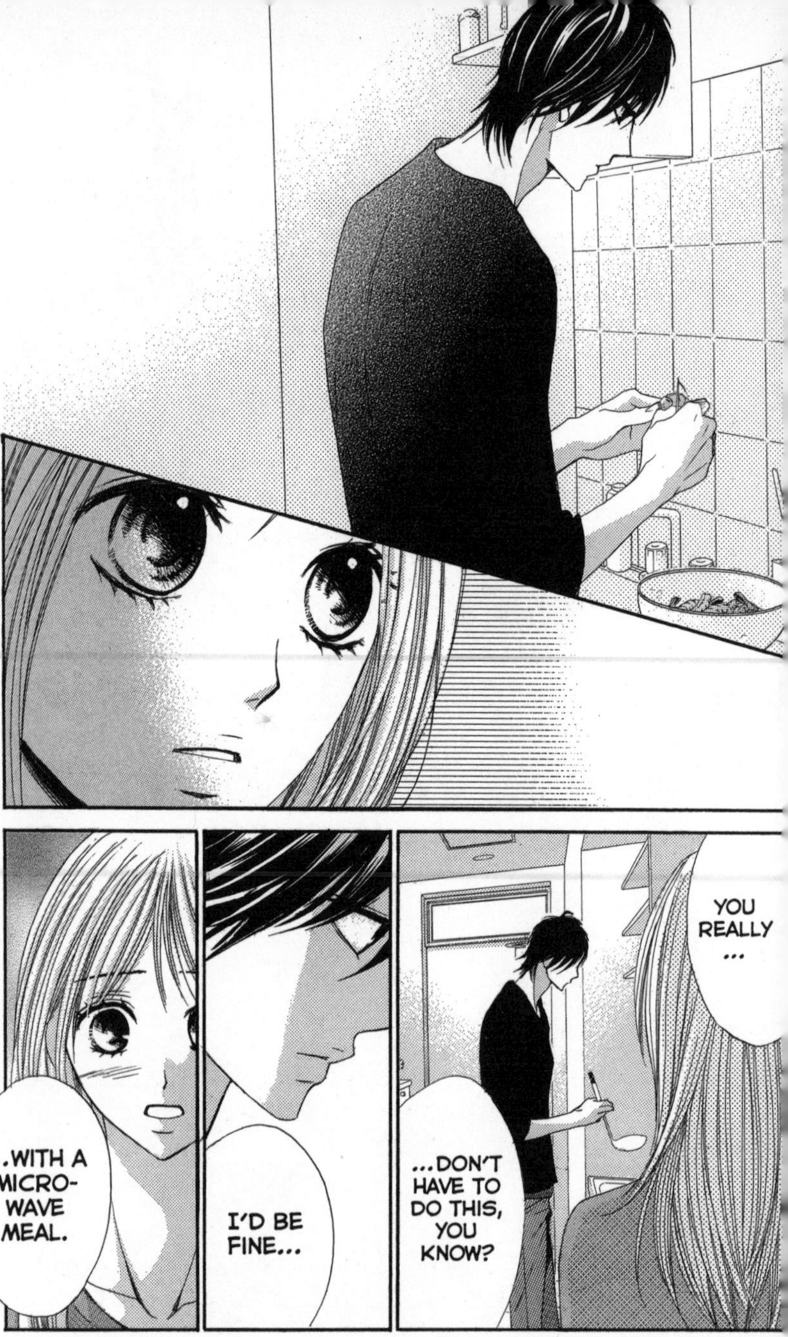
YOU REALLY ...
...DON'T HAVE TO DO THIS, YOU KNOW?
I'D BE FINE...
...WITH A MICRO-WAVE MEAL.

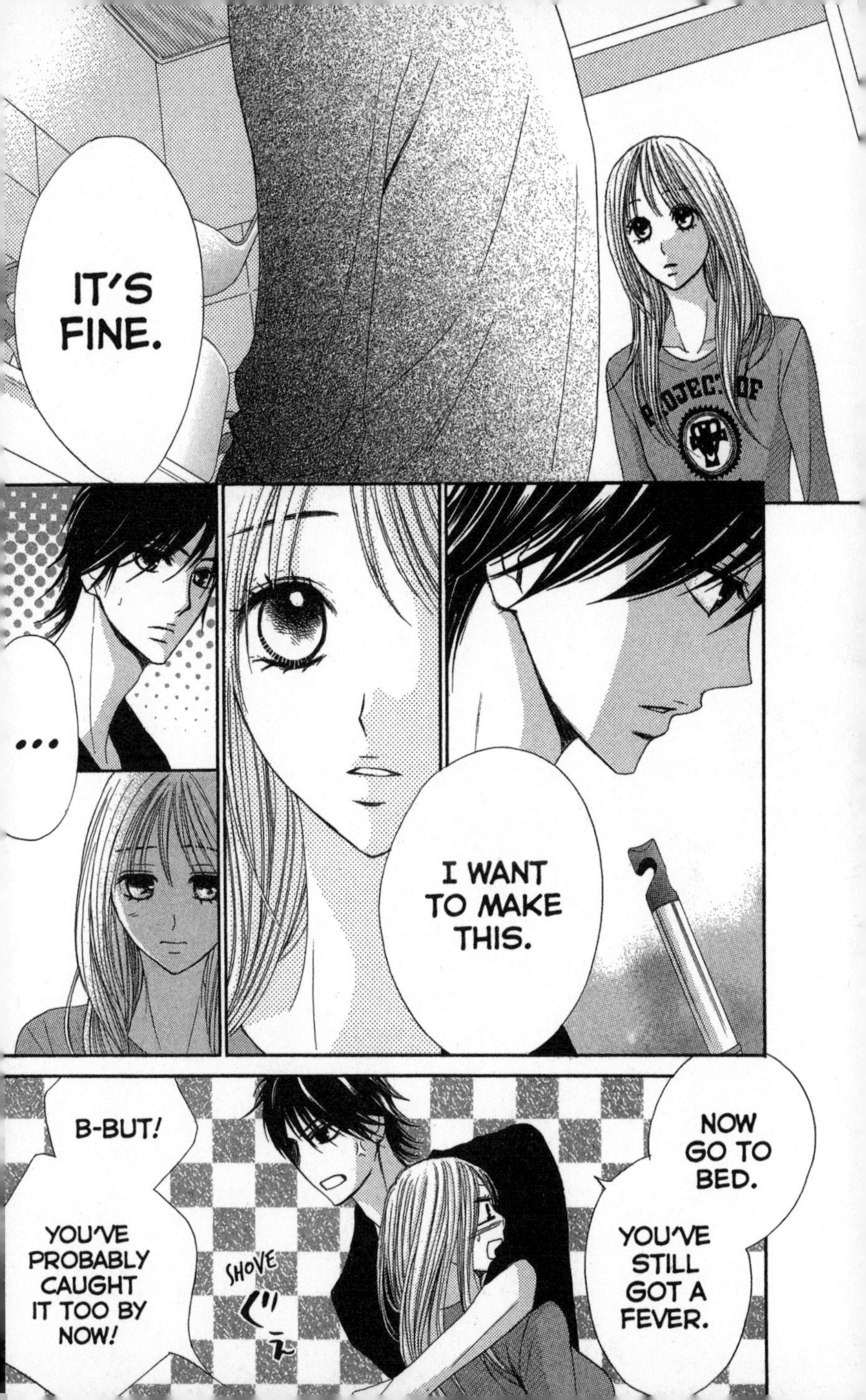
IT'S FINE.
I WANT TO MAKE THIS.
...
NOW GO TO BED.
YOU'VE STILL GOT A FEVER.
B-BUT!
YOU'VE PROBABLY CAUGHT IT TOO BY NOW!
SHOVE

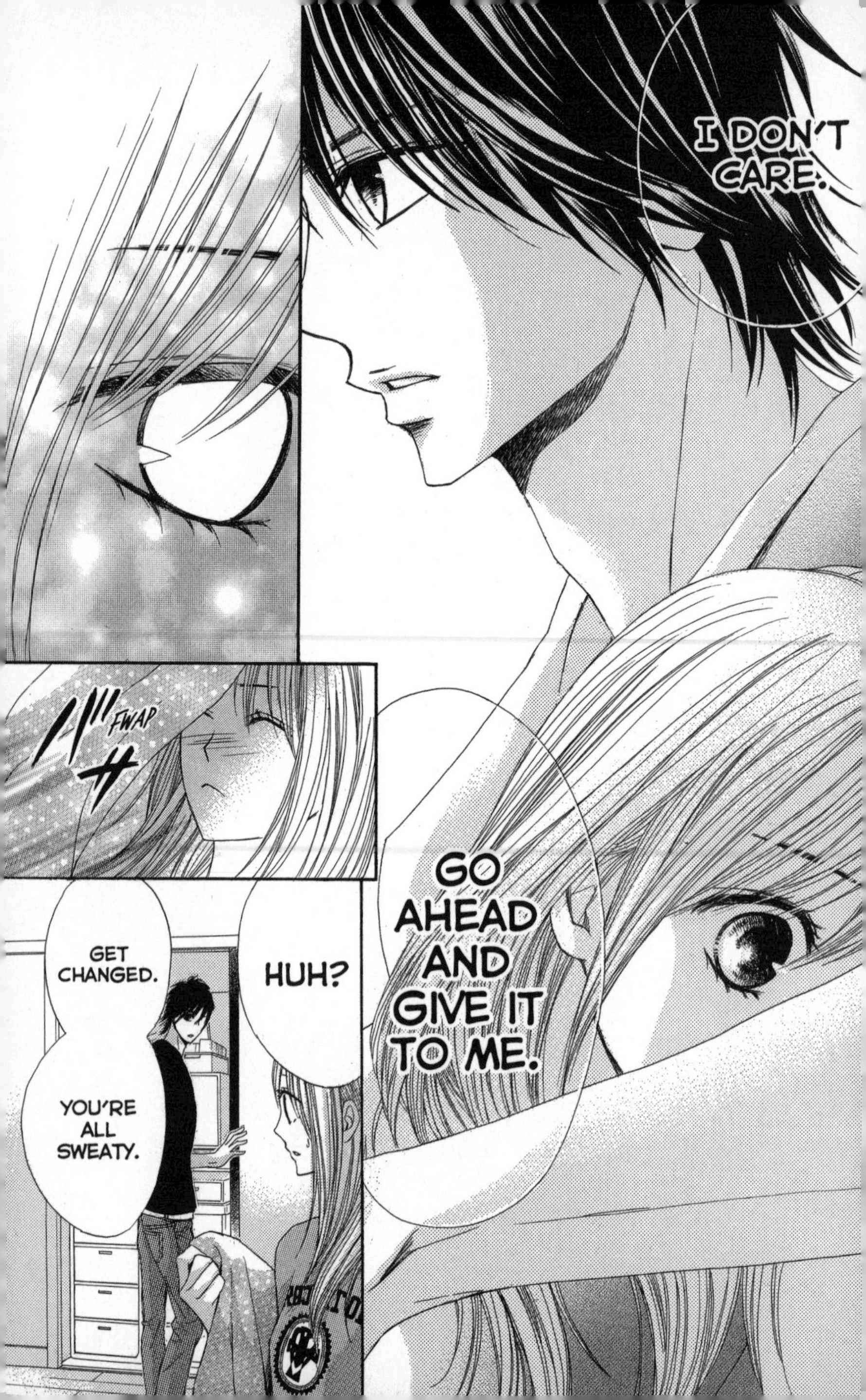
I DON'T CARE.
GO AHEAD AND GIVE IT TO ME.
FWAP
HUH?
GET CHANGED.
YOU'RE ALL SWEATY.

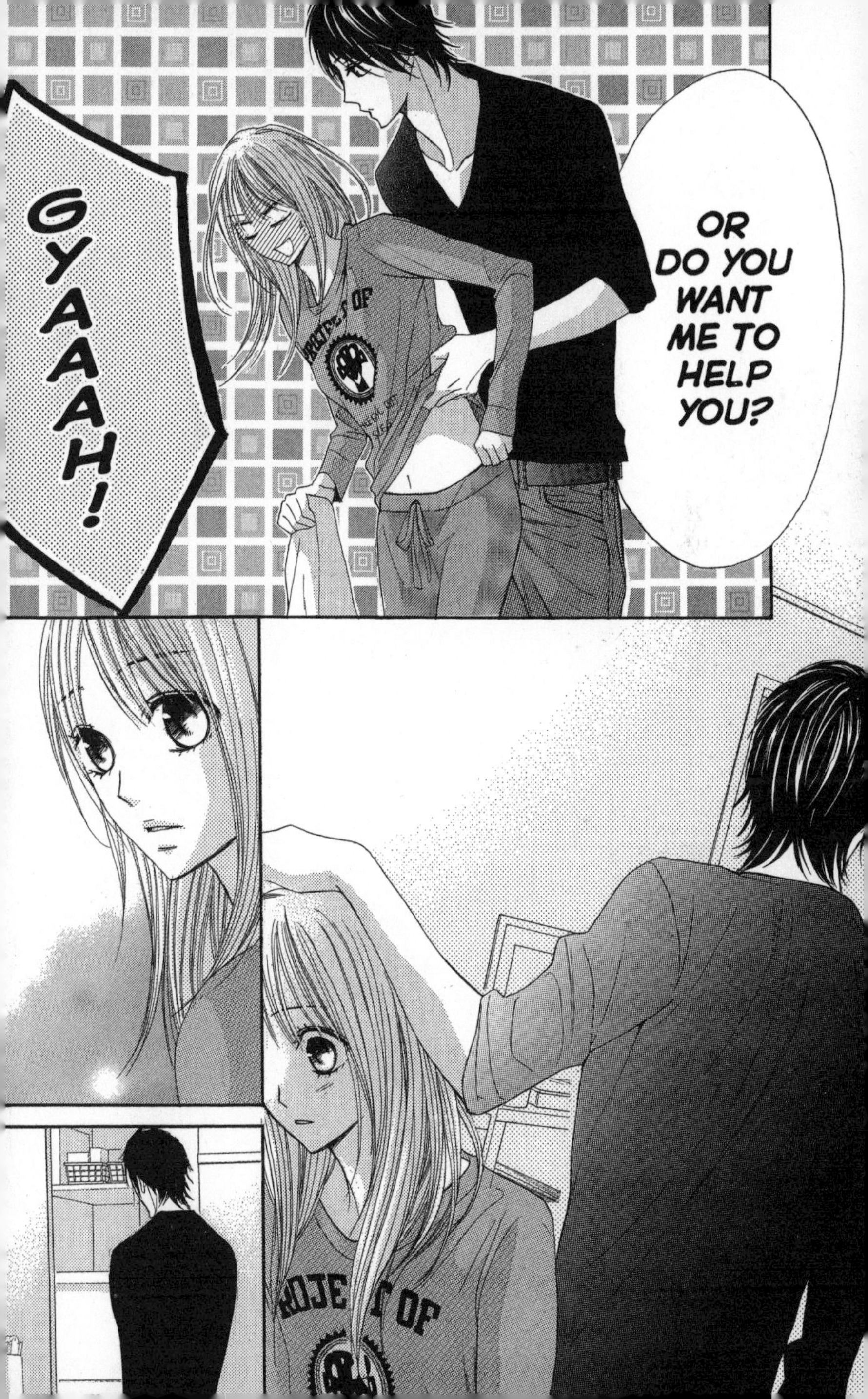
OR DO YOU WANT ME TO HELP YOU?
GYAAAH!

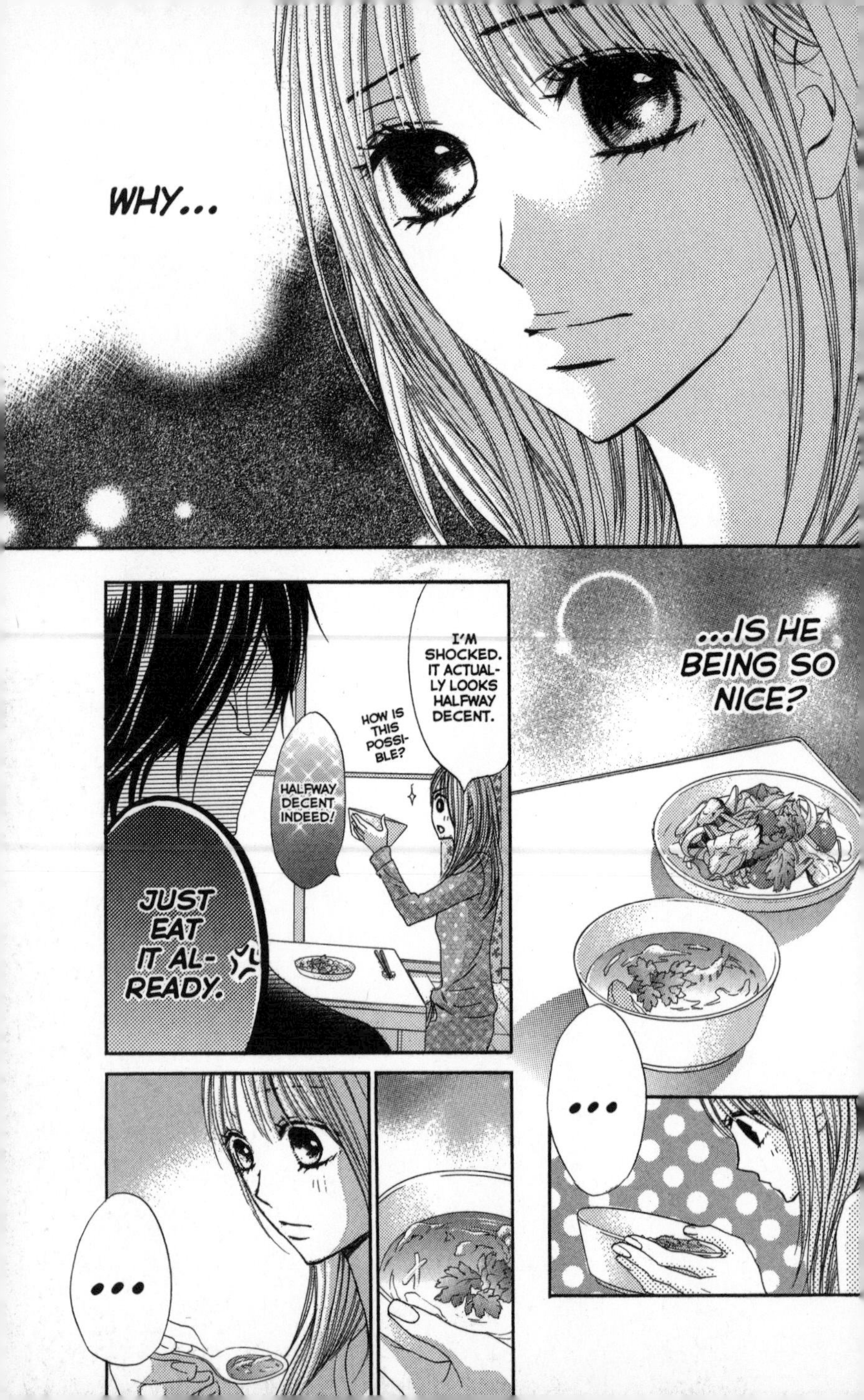
WHY...
...IS HE BEING SO NICE?
I'M SHOCKED. IT ACTUAL-LY LOOKS HALFWAY DECENT.
HOW IS THIS POSSI-BLE?
HALFWAY DECENT INDEED!
JUST EAT IT AL-READY.
...
...

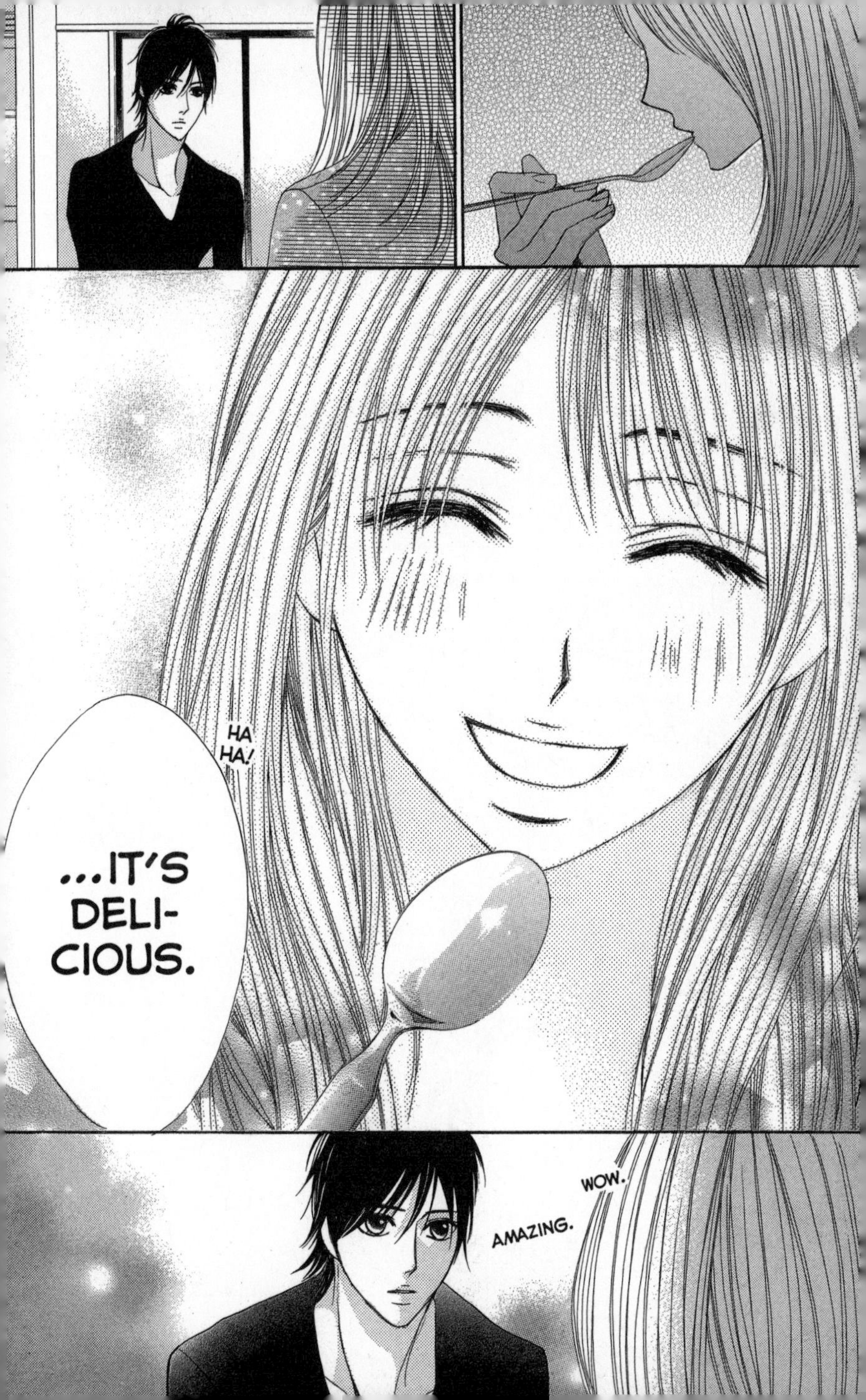
HA HA!
...IT'S DELI- CIOUS.
WOW.
AMAZING.

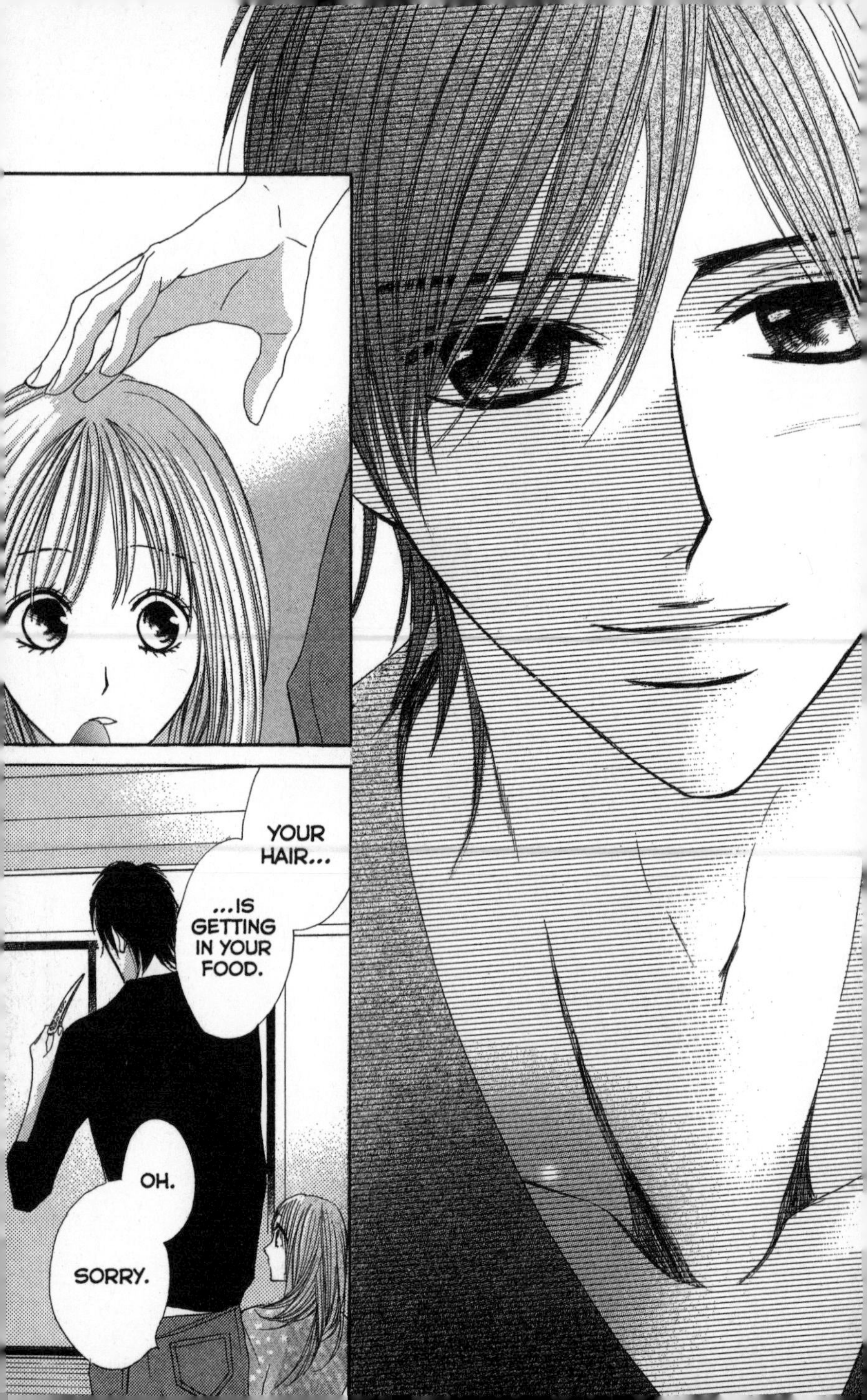
YOUR HAIR...
...IS GETTING IN YOUR FOOD.
OH.
SORRY.

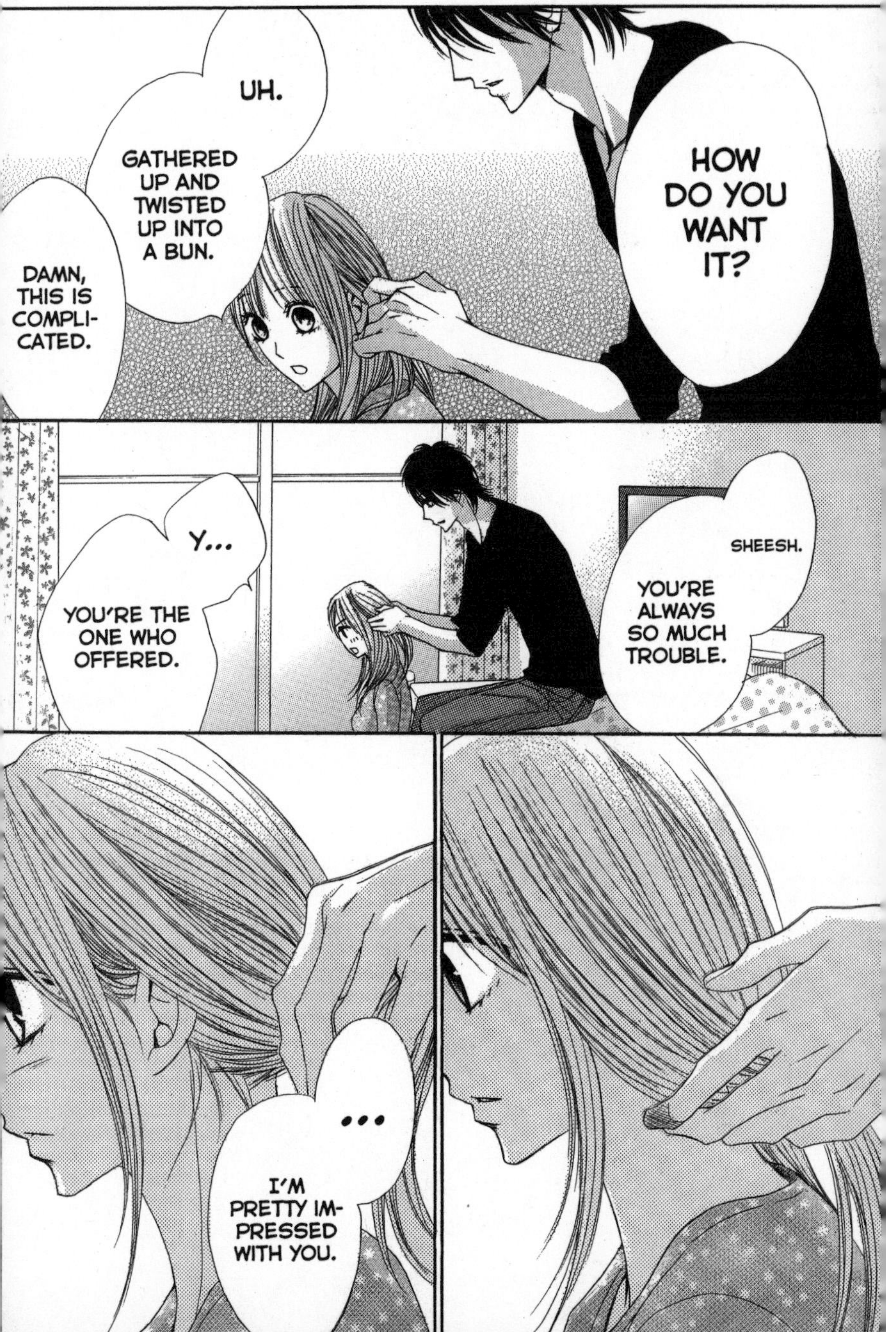
HOW DO YOU WANT IT?
UH.
GATHERED UP AND TWISTED UP INTO A BUN.
DAMN, THIS IS COMPLICATED.
SHEESH.
YOU'RE ALWAYS SO MUCH TROUBLE.
Y...
YOU'RE THE ONE WHO OFFERED.
...
I'M PRETTY IMPRESSED WITH YOU.

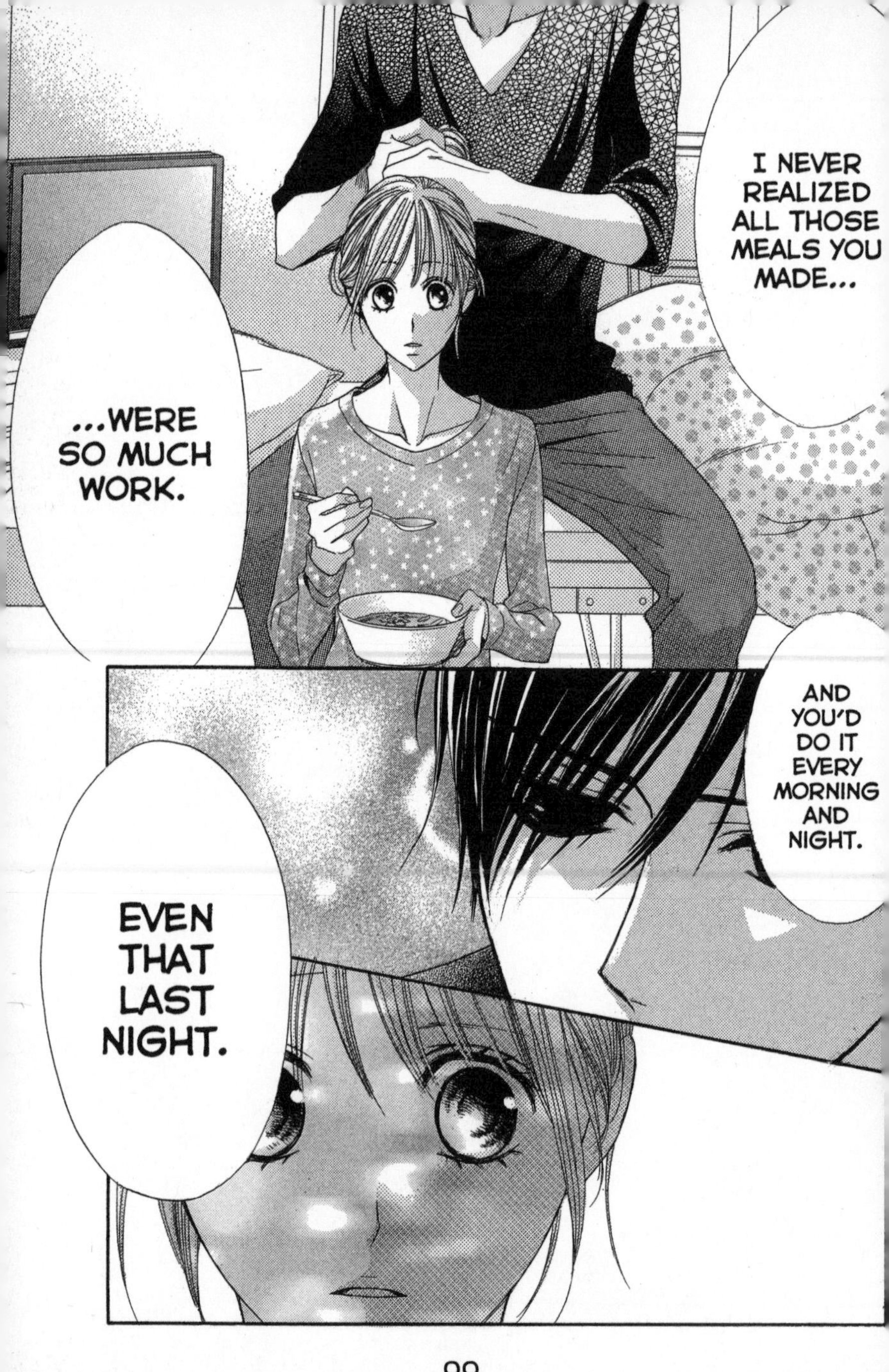

I NEVER REALIZED ALL THOSE MEALS YOU MADE...
...WERE SO MUCH WORK.
AND YOU'D DO IT EVERY MORNING AND NIGHT.
EVEN THAT LAST NIGHT.

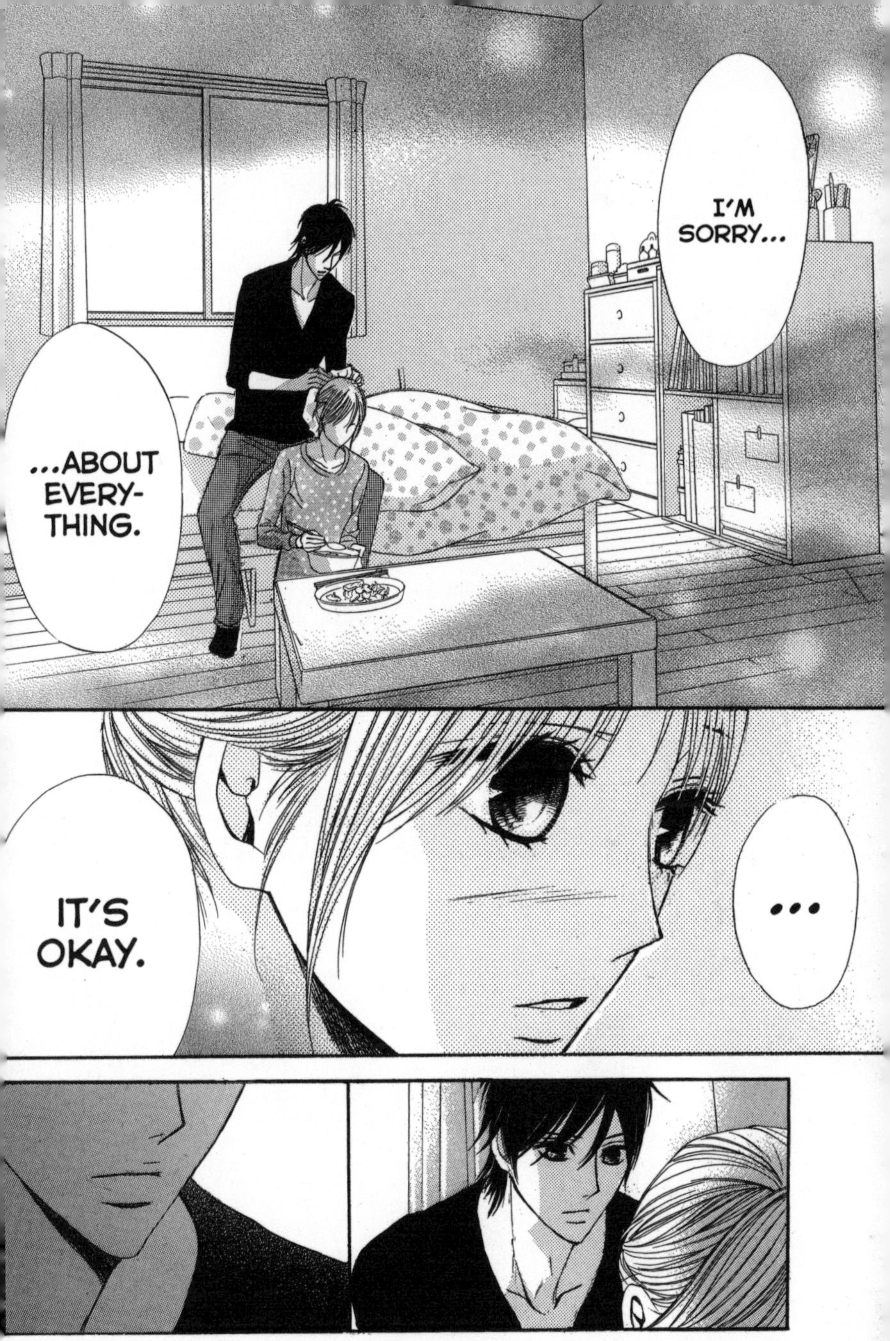
I'M SORRY...
...ABOUT EVERY-THING.
...
IT'S OKAY.

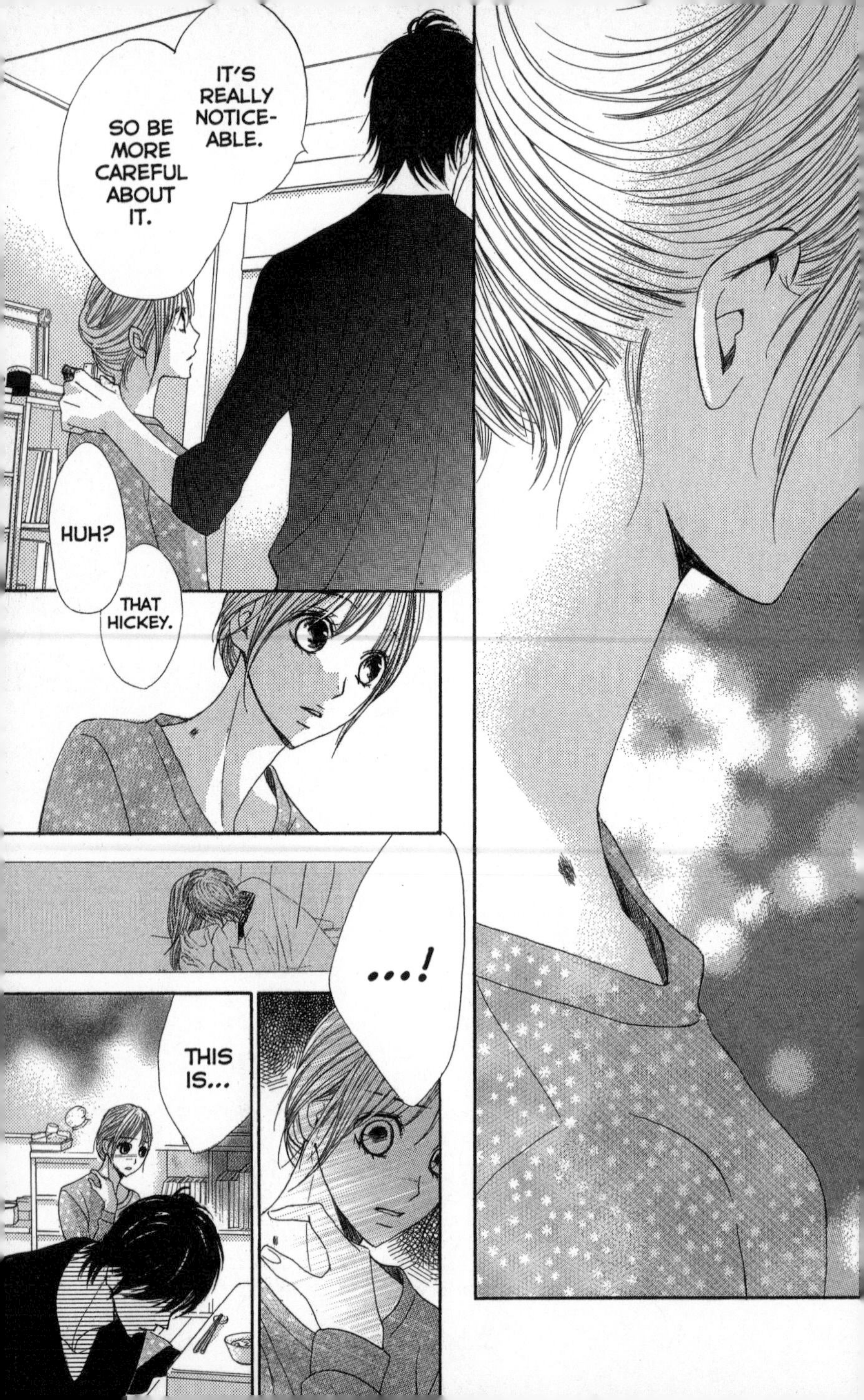
IT'S REALLY NOTICE-ABLE.
SO BE MORE CAREFUL ABOUT IT.
HUH?
THAT HICKEY.
...!
THIS IS...

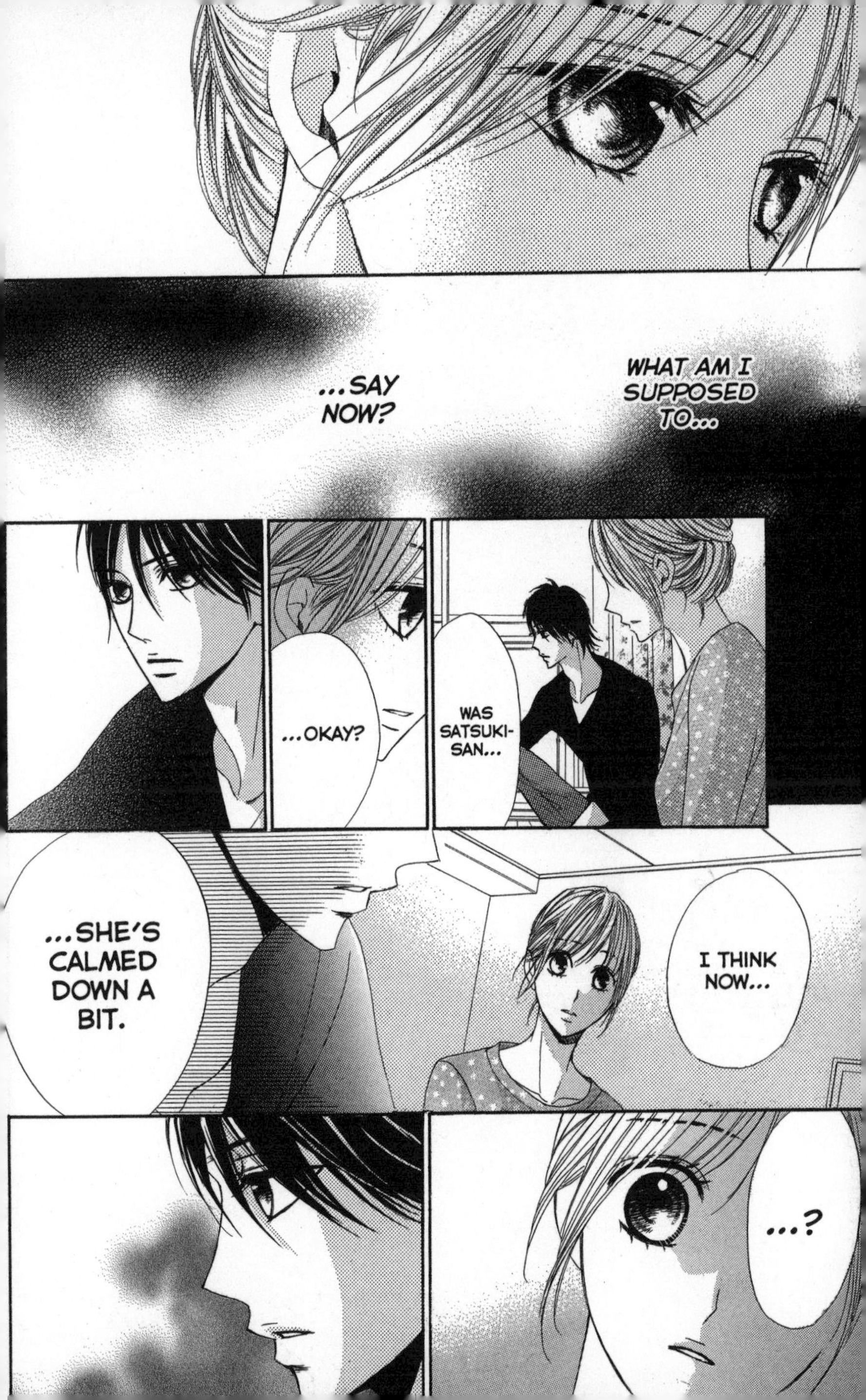
WHAT AM I SUPPOSED TO...
...SAY NOW?
WAS SATSUKI-SAN...
...OKAY?
I THINK NOW...
...SHE'S CALMED DOWN A BIT.
...?

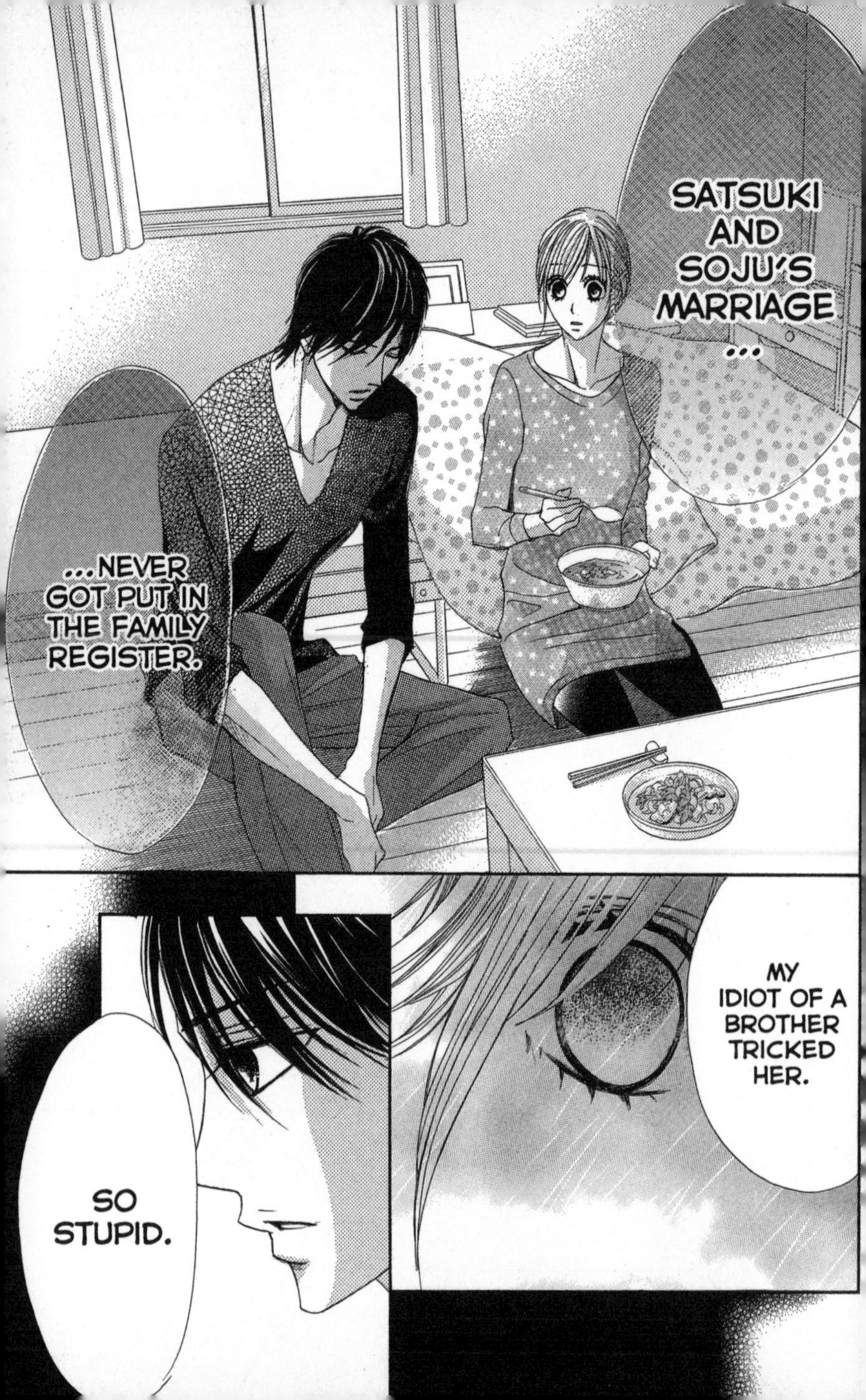
SATSUKI AND SOJU'S MARRIAGE...
...NEVER GOT PUT IN THE FAMILY REGISTER.
MY IDIOT OF A BROTHER TRICKED HER.
SO STUPID.

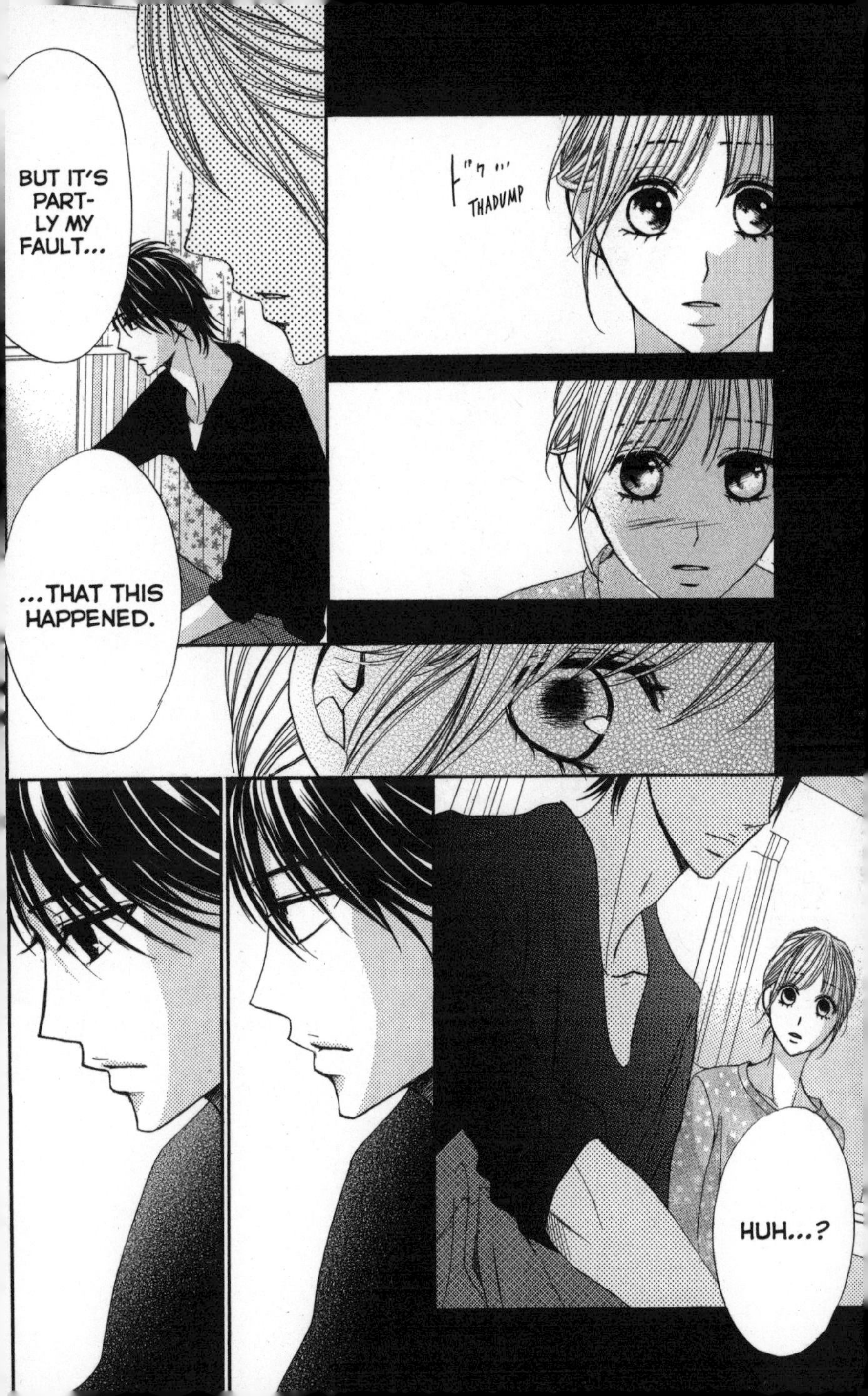
THADUMP
BUT IT'S PART-LY MY FAULT...
...THAT THIS HAPPENED.
HUH...?

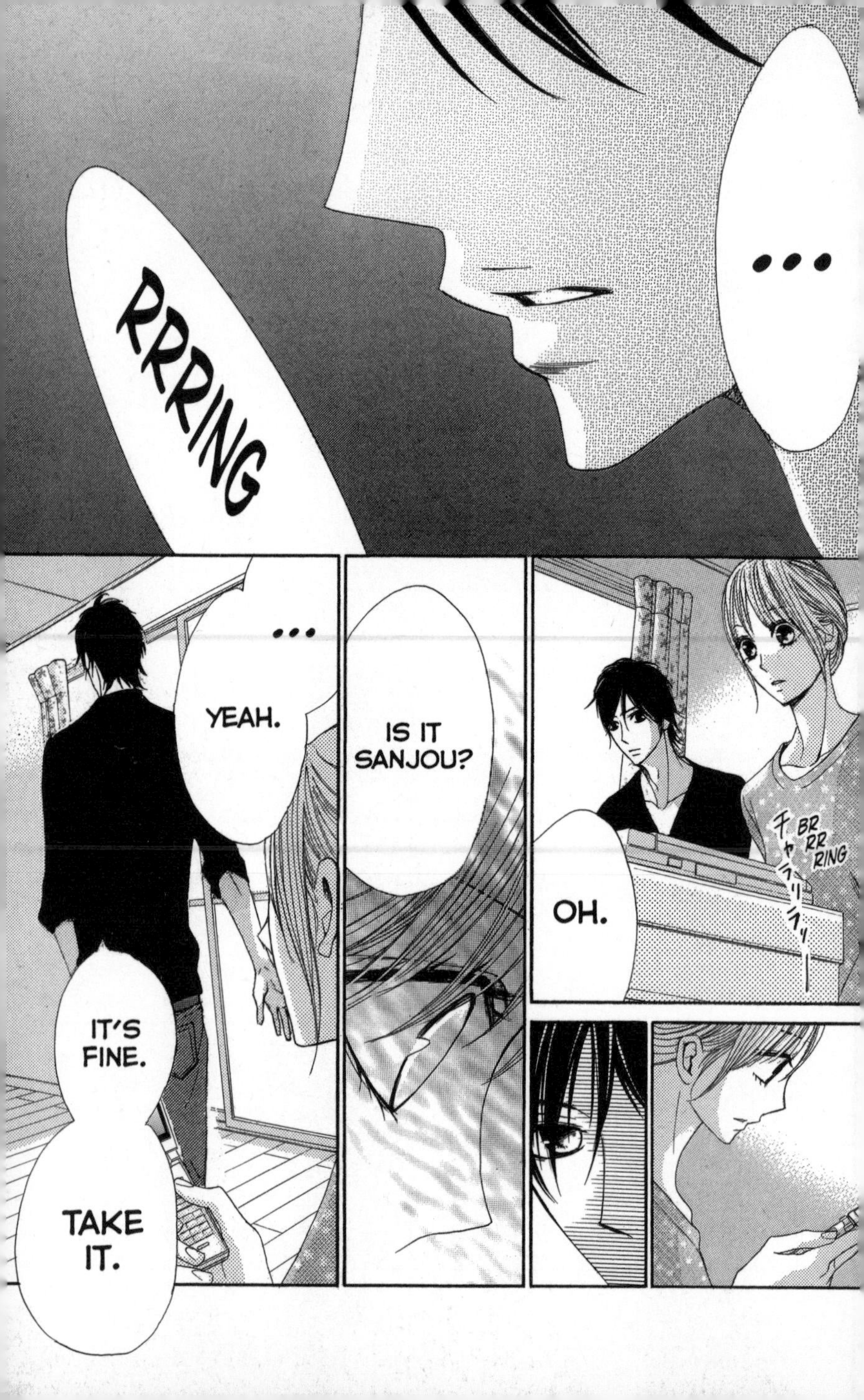
...
RRRING
BR RR RING
OH.
IS IT SANJOU?
...
YEAH.
IT'S FINE.
TAKE IT.

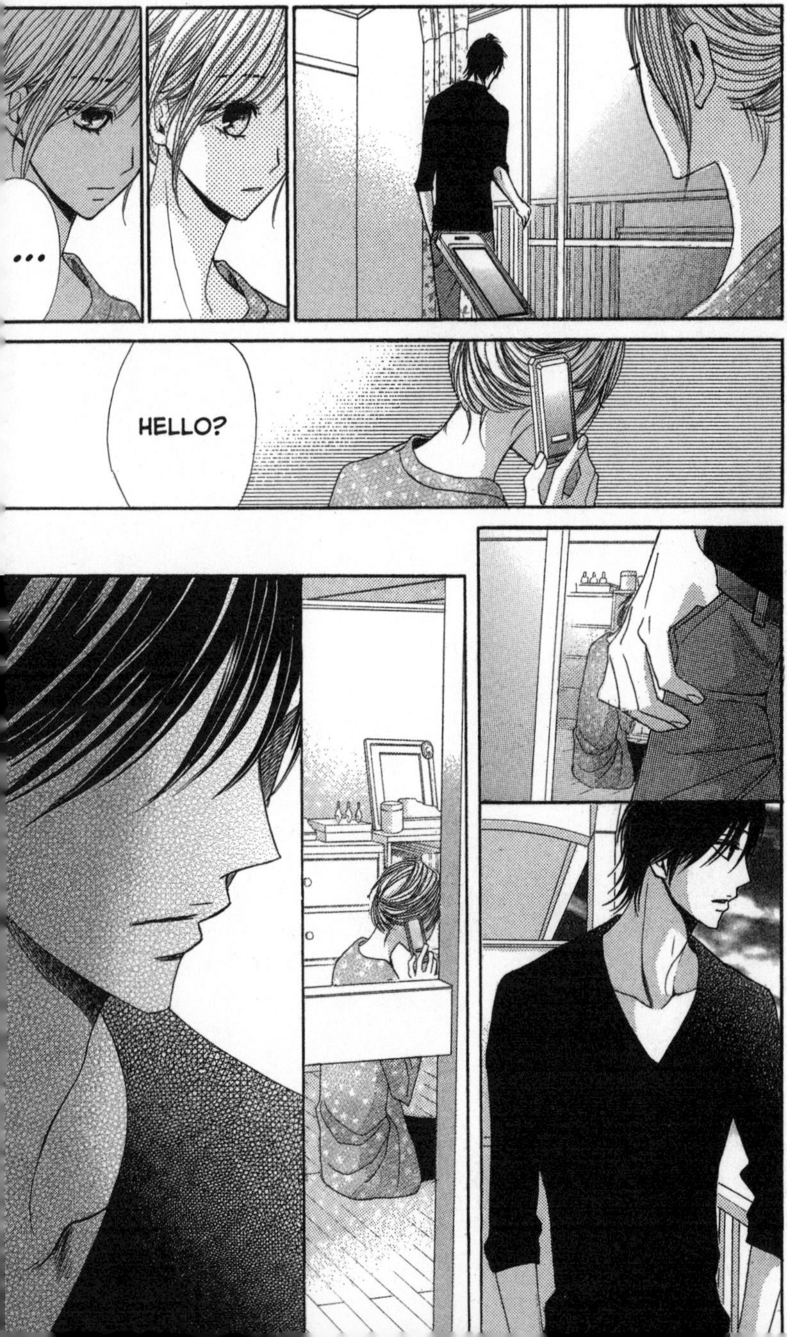
...
HELLO?

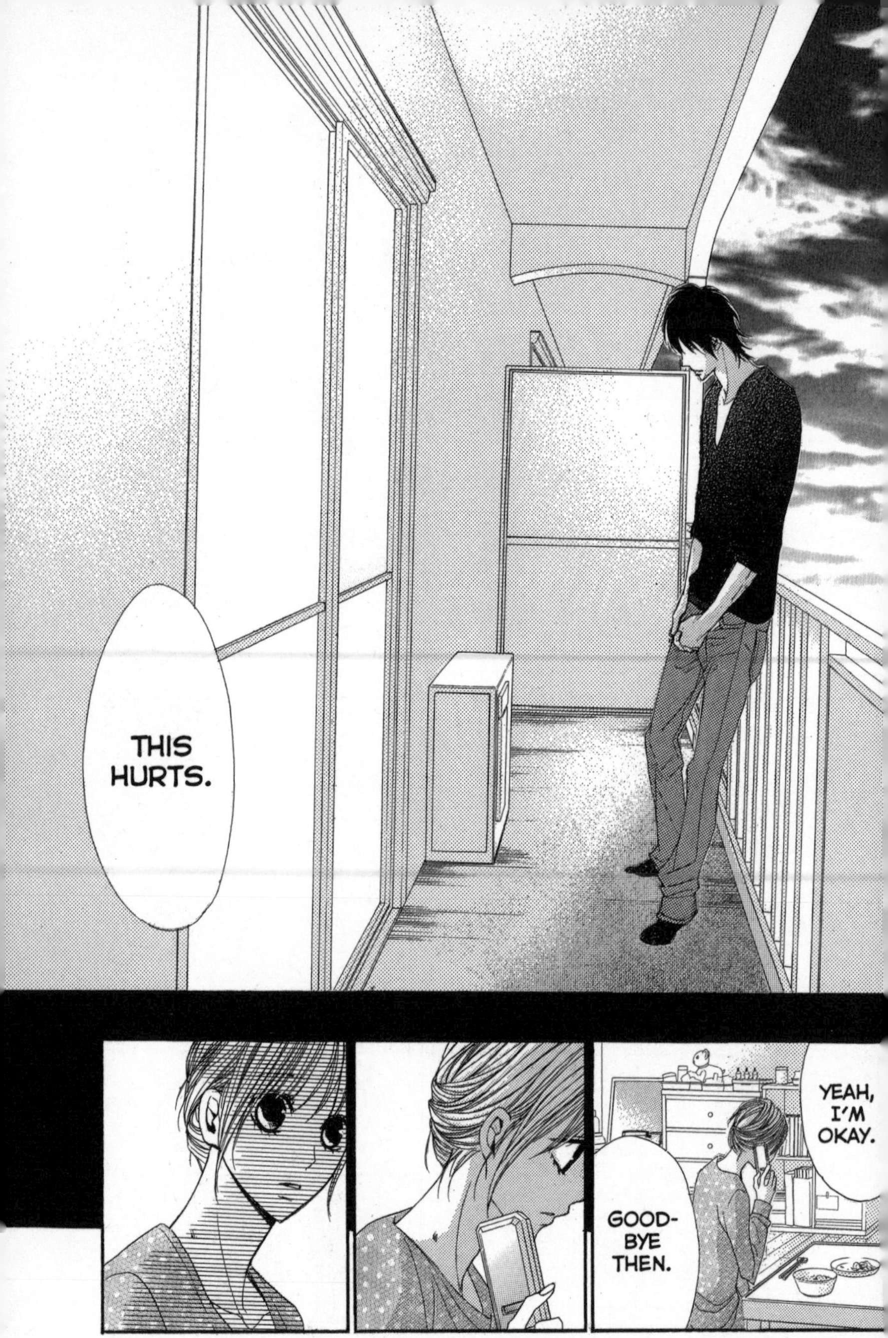
THIS HURTS.
YEAH, I'M OKAY.
GOOD-BYE THEN.

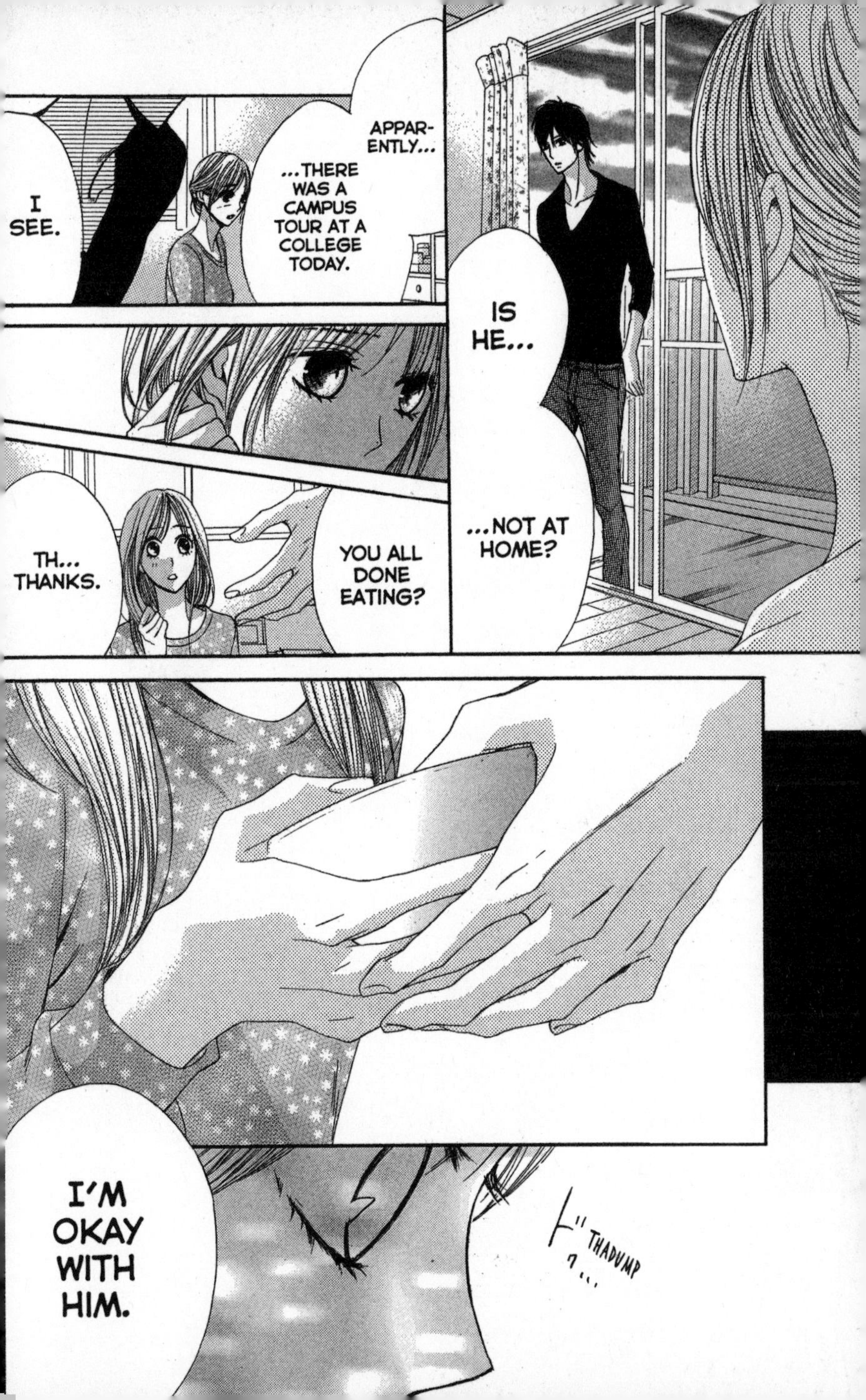
IS HE...
...NOT AT HOME?
APPARENTLY...
...THERE WAS A CAMPUS TOUR AT A COLLEGE TODAY.
I SEE.
YOU ALL DONE EATING?
TH... THANKS.
I'M OKAY WITH HIM.
THADUMP

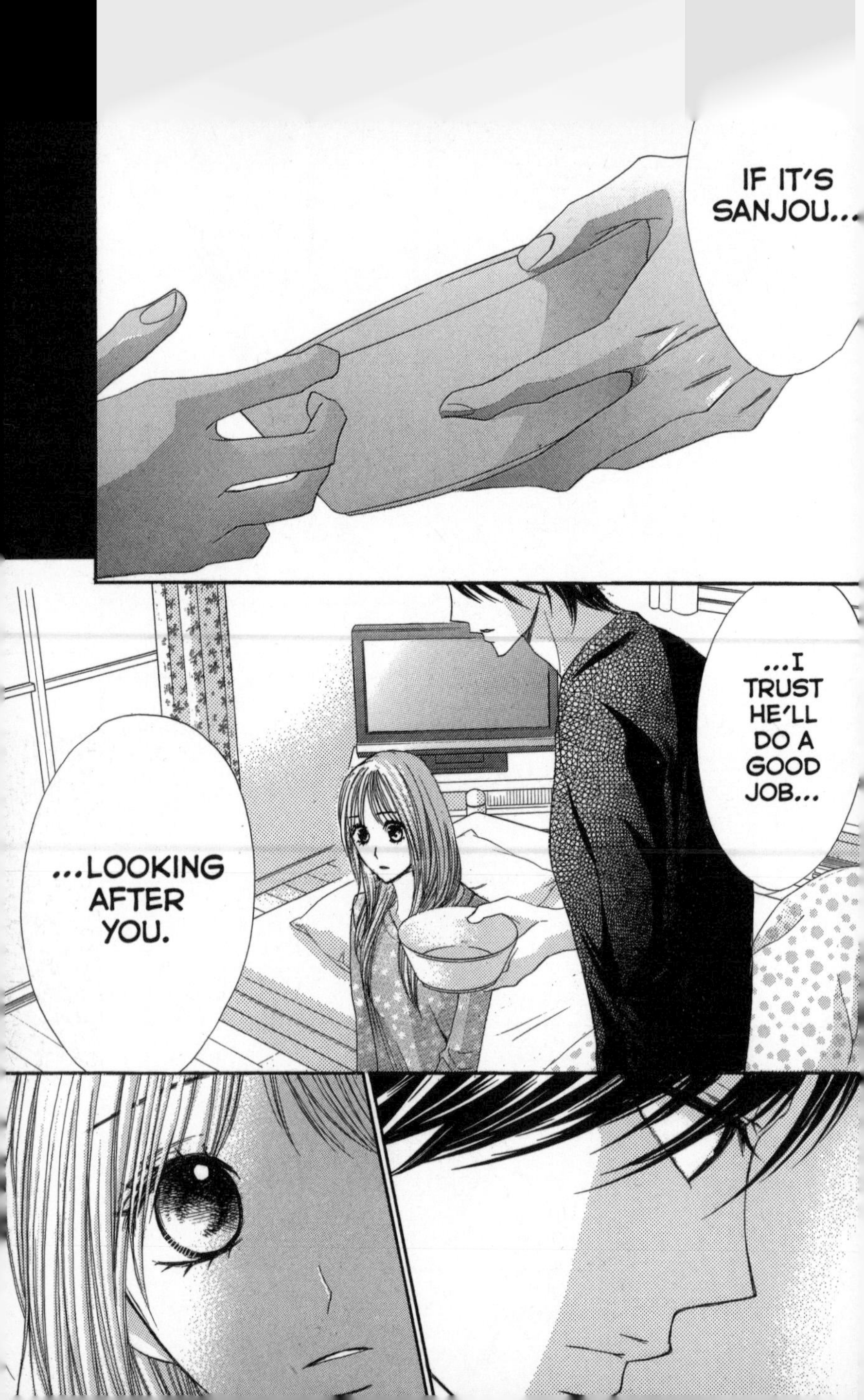
IF IT'S SANJOU...
...I TRUST HE'LL DO A GOOD JOB...
...LOOKING AFTER YOU.

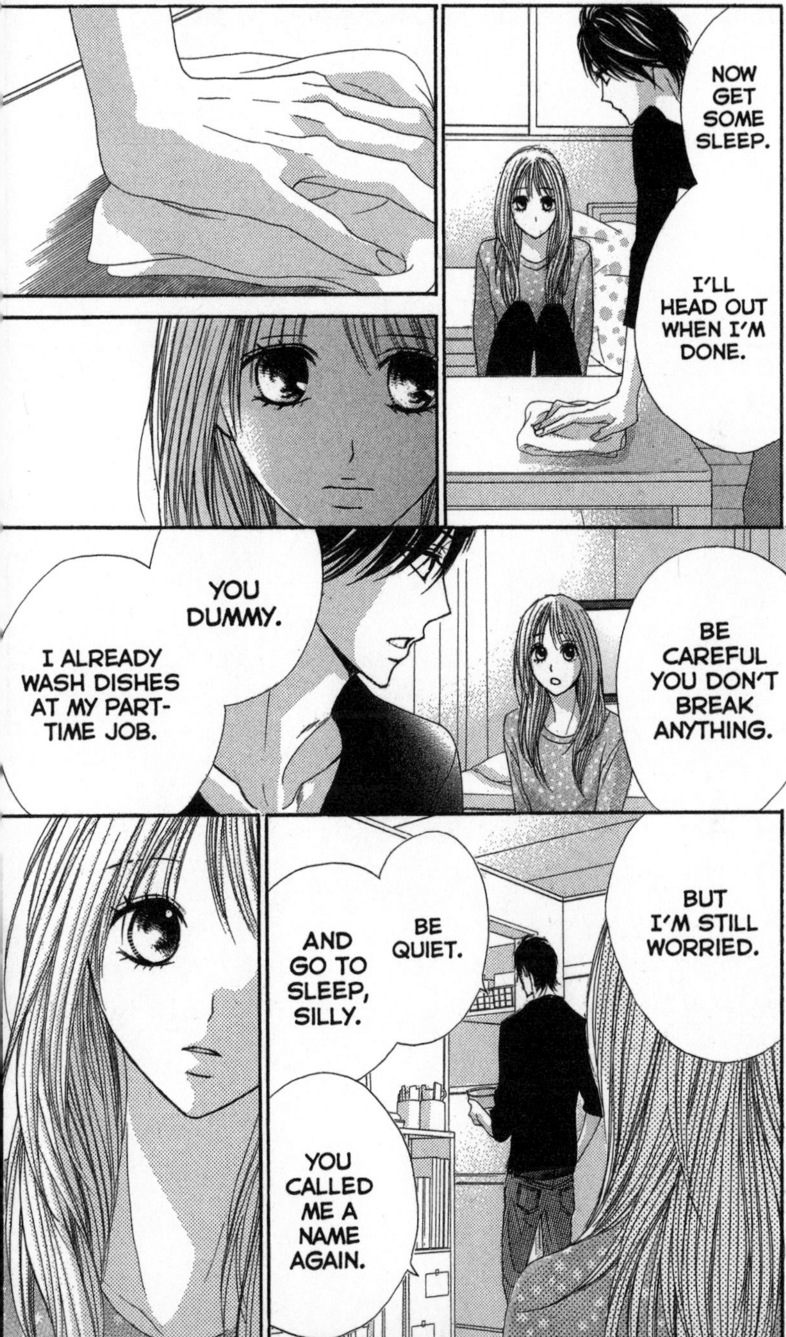
NOW GET SOME SLEEP.
I'LL HEAD OUT WHEN I'M DONE.
BE CAREFUL YOU DON'T BREAK ANYTHING.
YOU DUMMY.
I ALREADY WASH DISHES AT MY PART-TIME JOB.
BUT I'M STILL WORRIED.
BE QUIET.
AND GO TO SLEEP, SILLY.
YOU CALLED ME A NAME AGAIN.

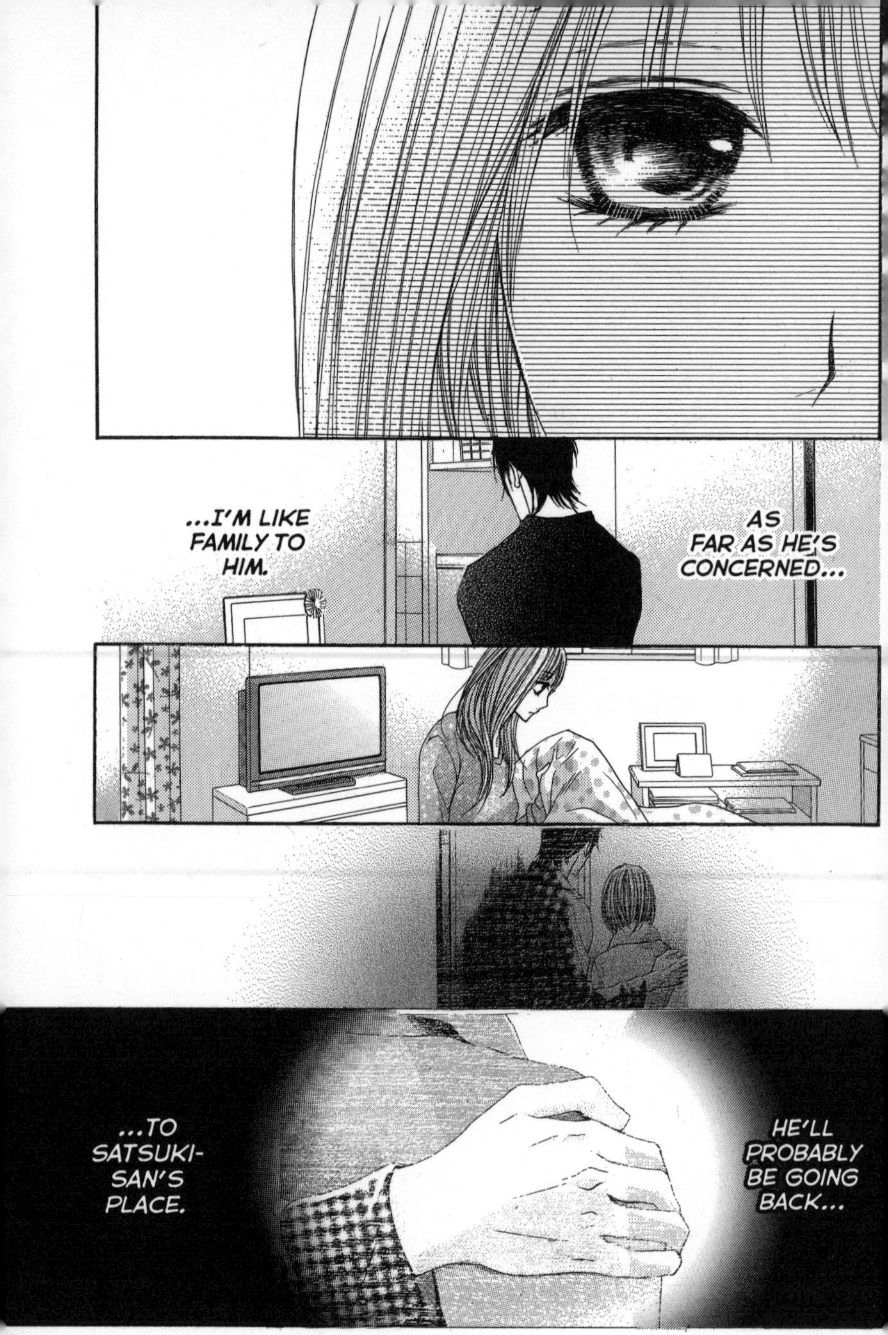
AS FAR AS HE'S CONCERNED...
...I'M LIKE FAMILY TO HIM.
HE'LL PROBABLY BE GOING BACK...
...TO SATSUKI-SAN'S PLACE.

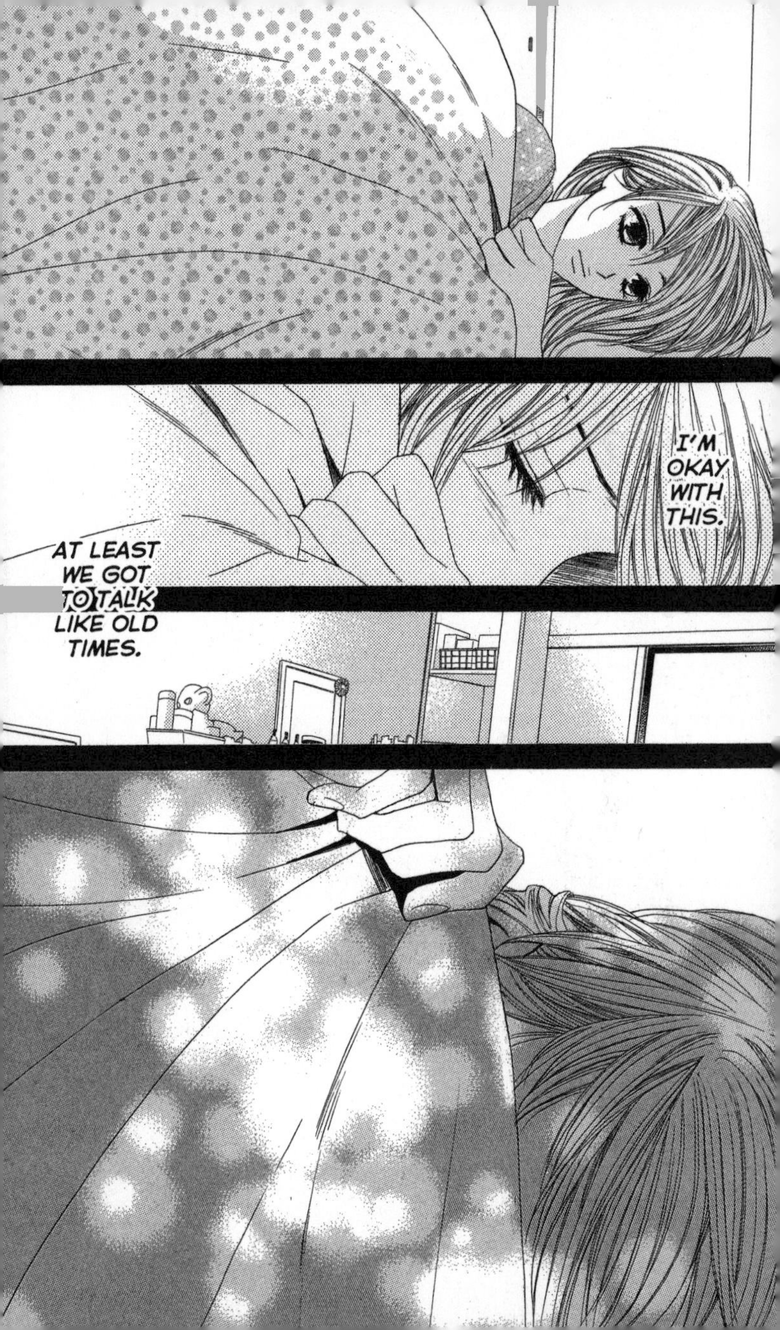
I'M OKAY WITH THIS.
AT LEAST WE GOT TO TALK LIKE OLD TIMES.

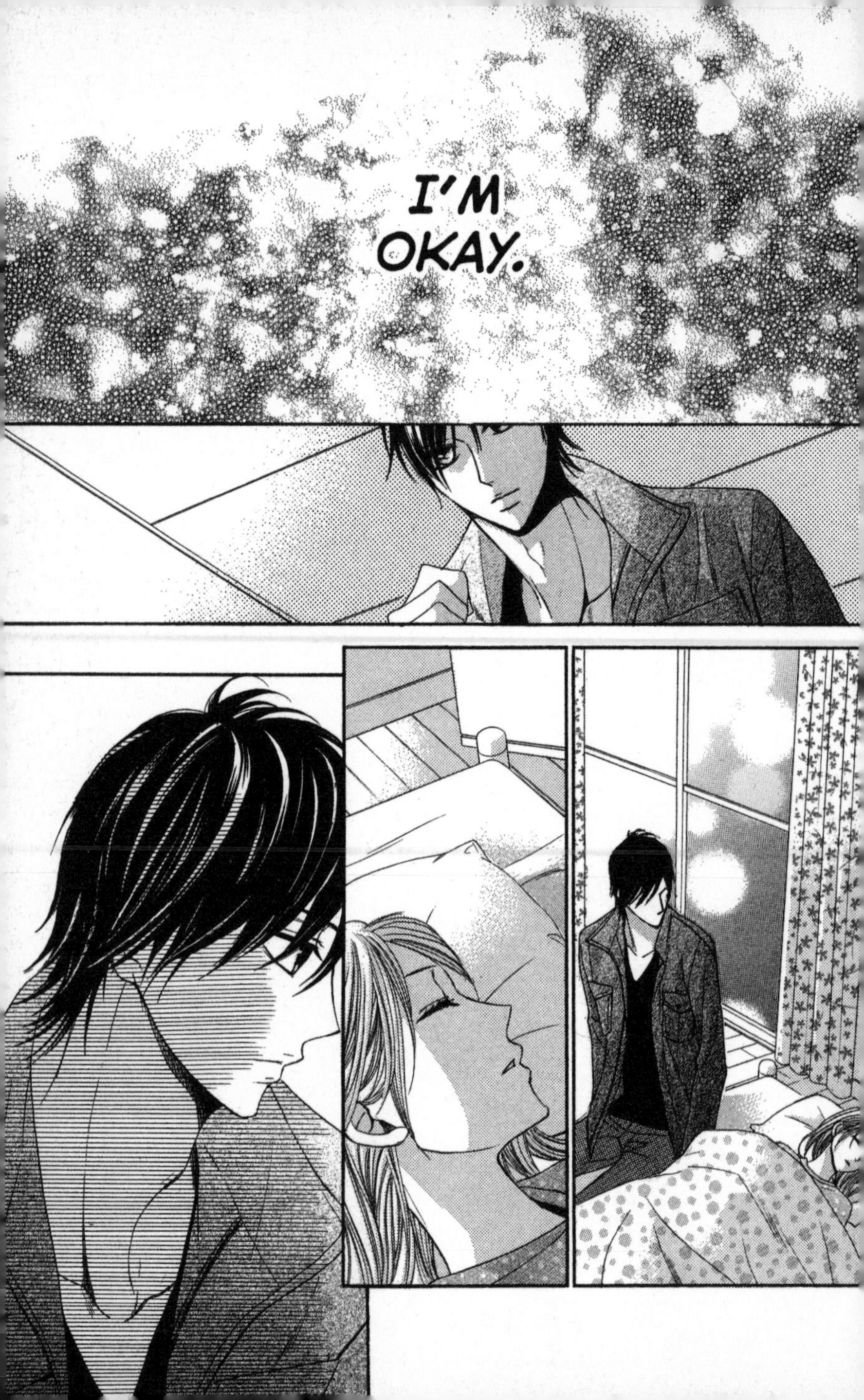
I'M OKAY.

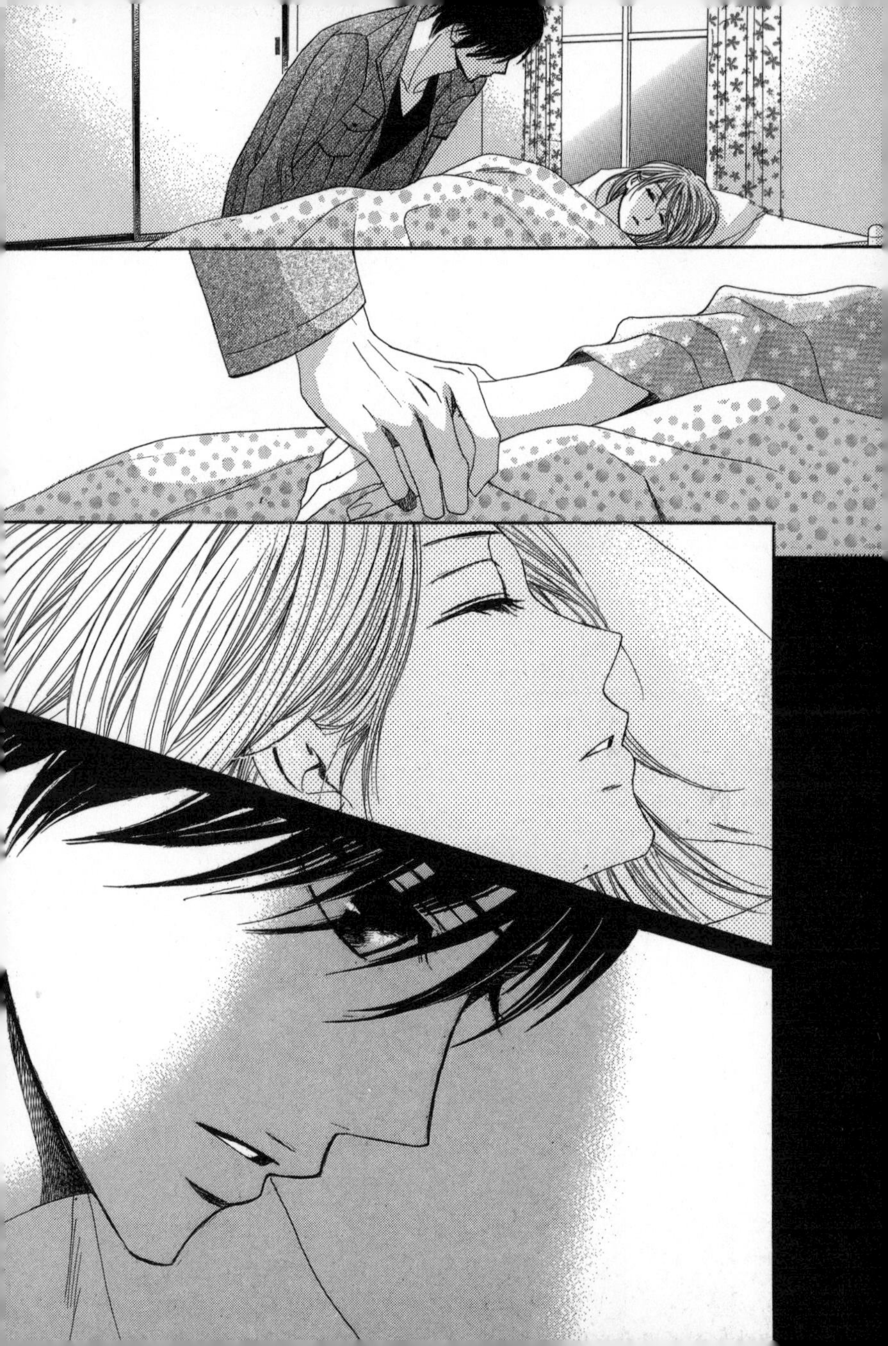

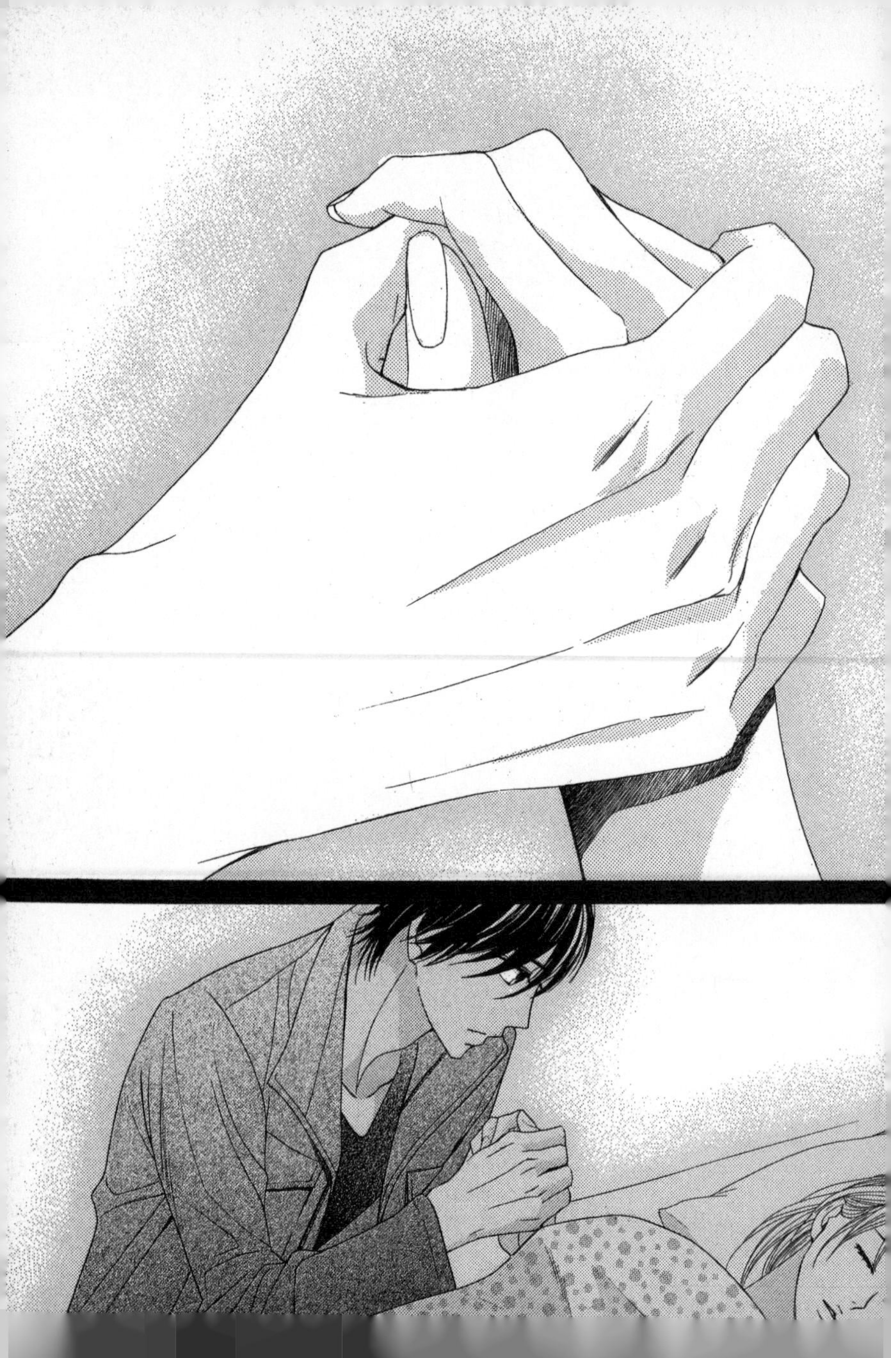

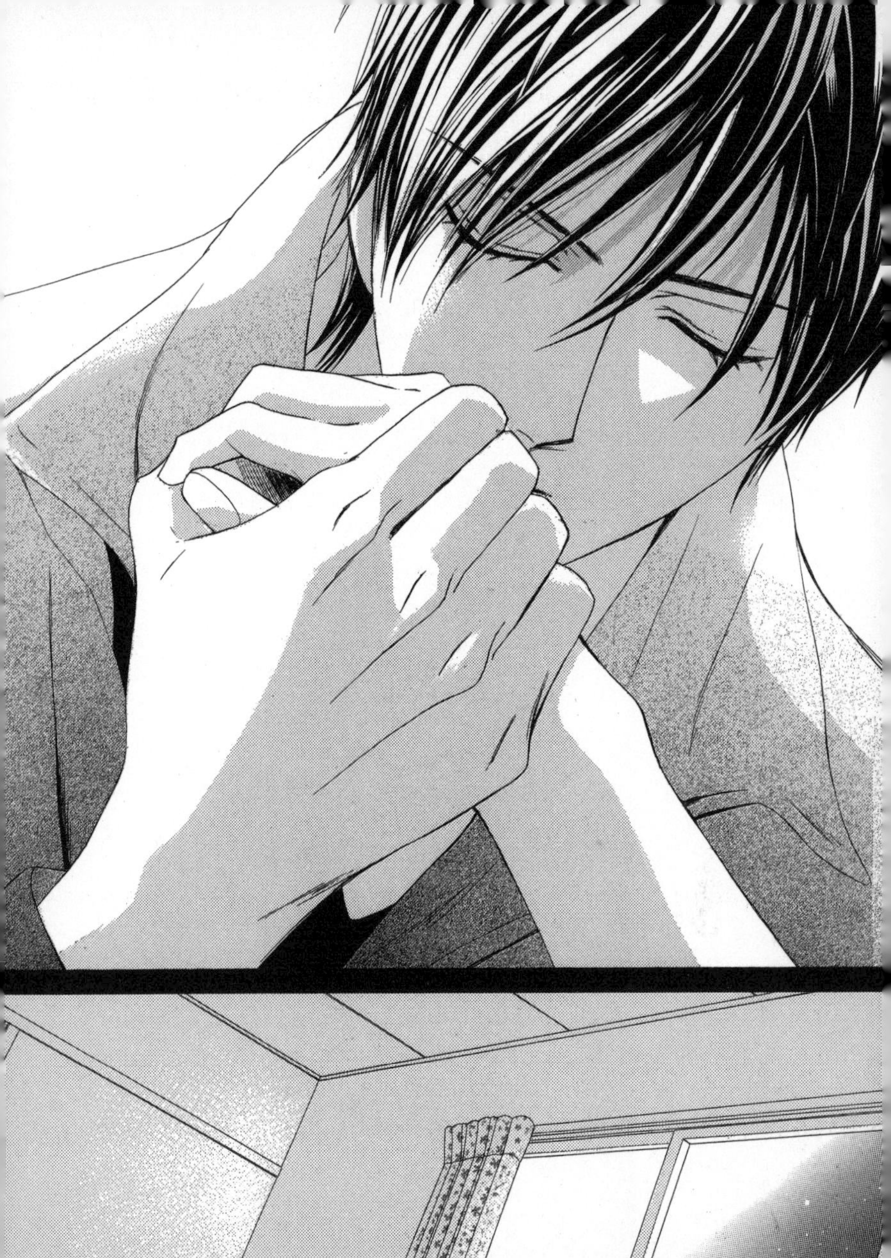

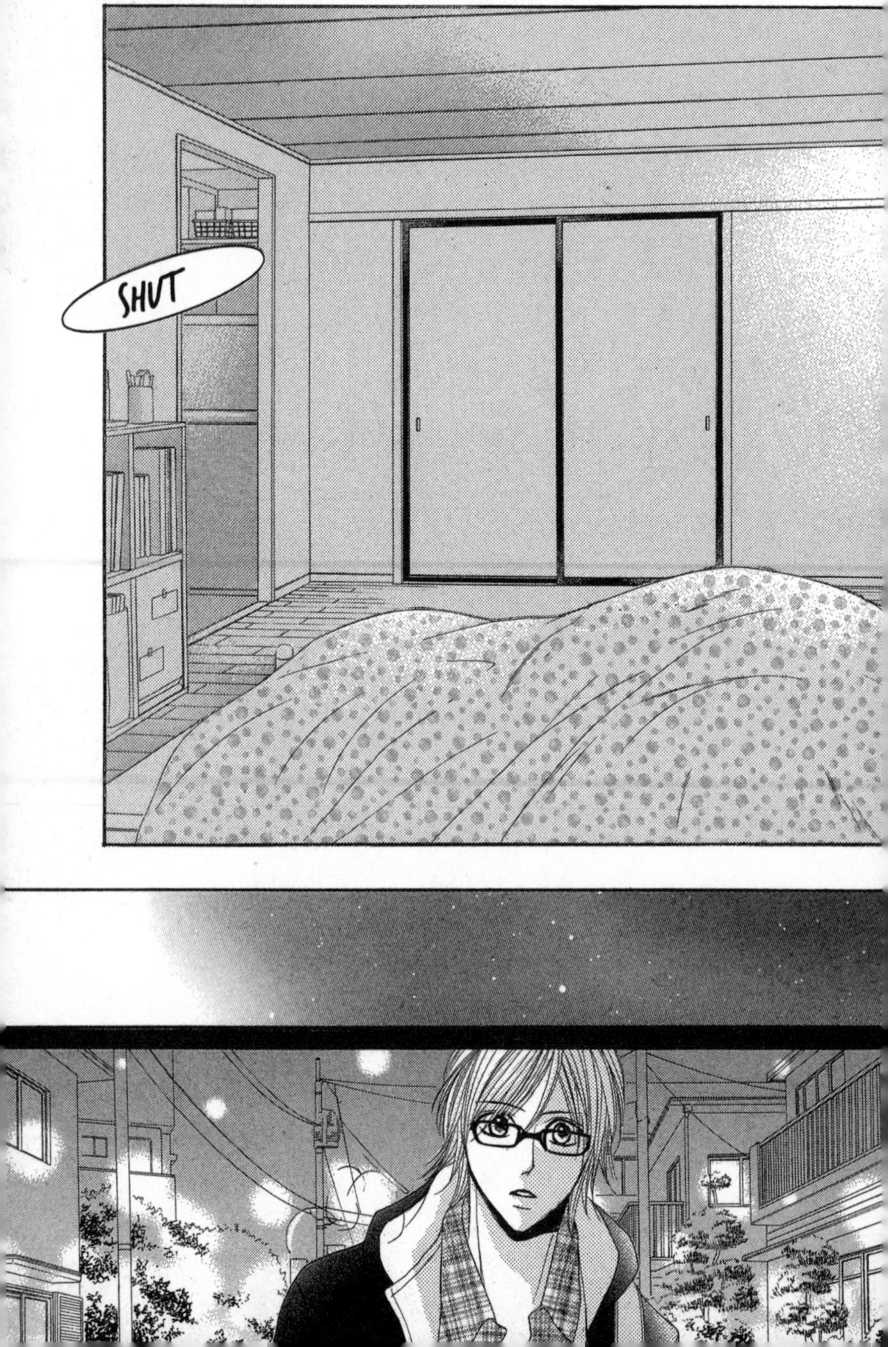
SHUT

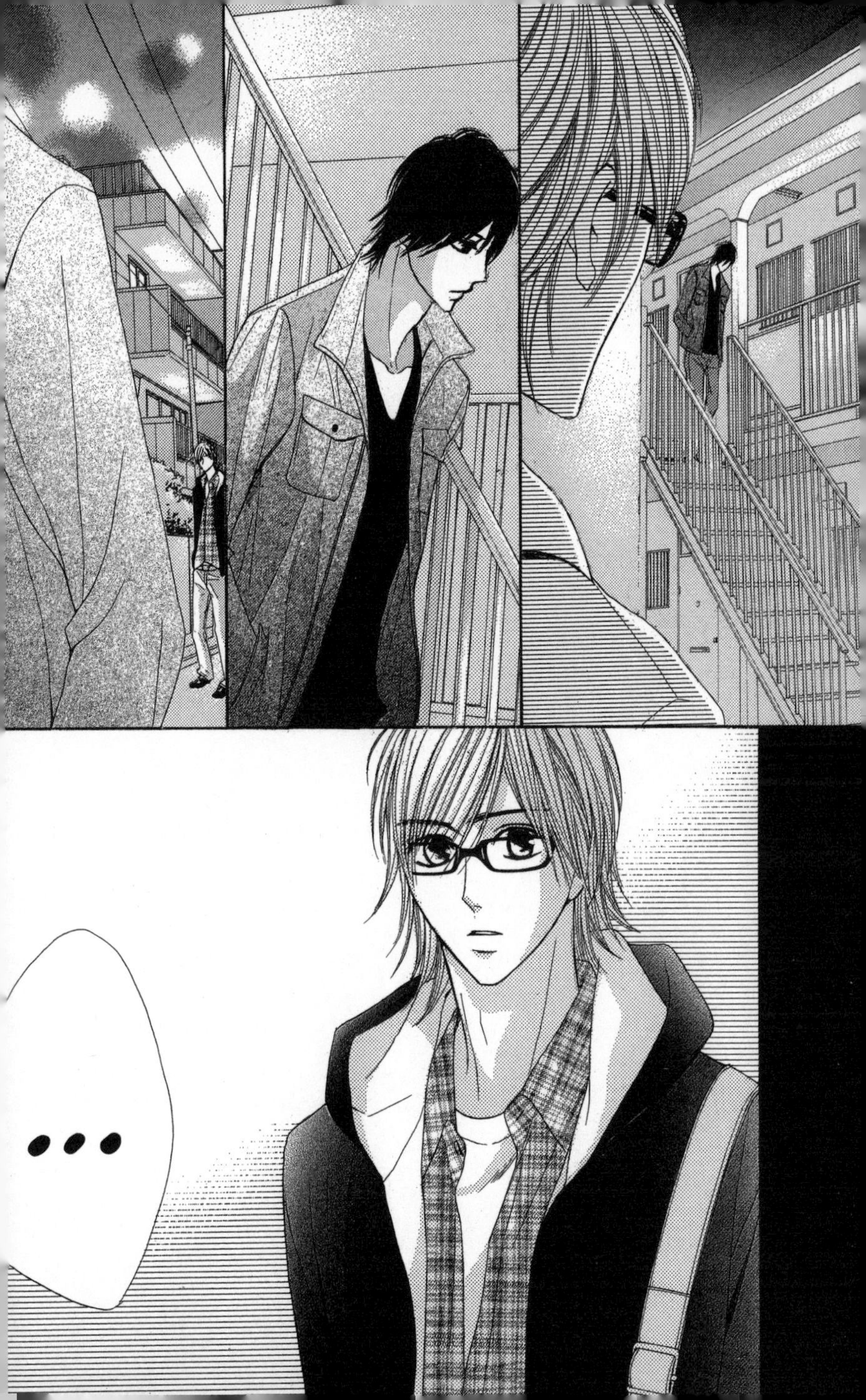
...

L♥DK

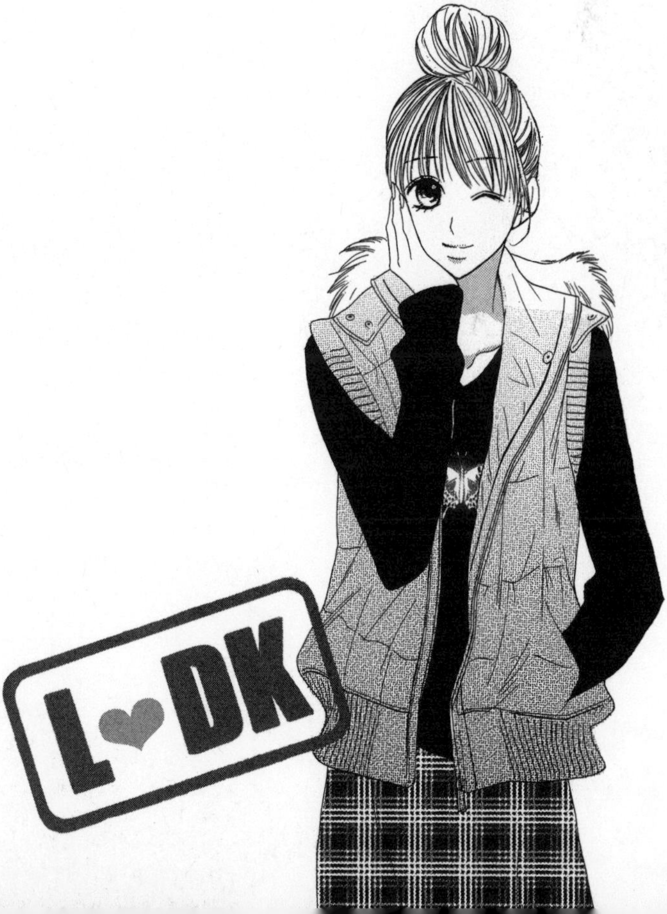
L♥DK

#28 Night of Shooting Stars

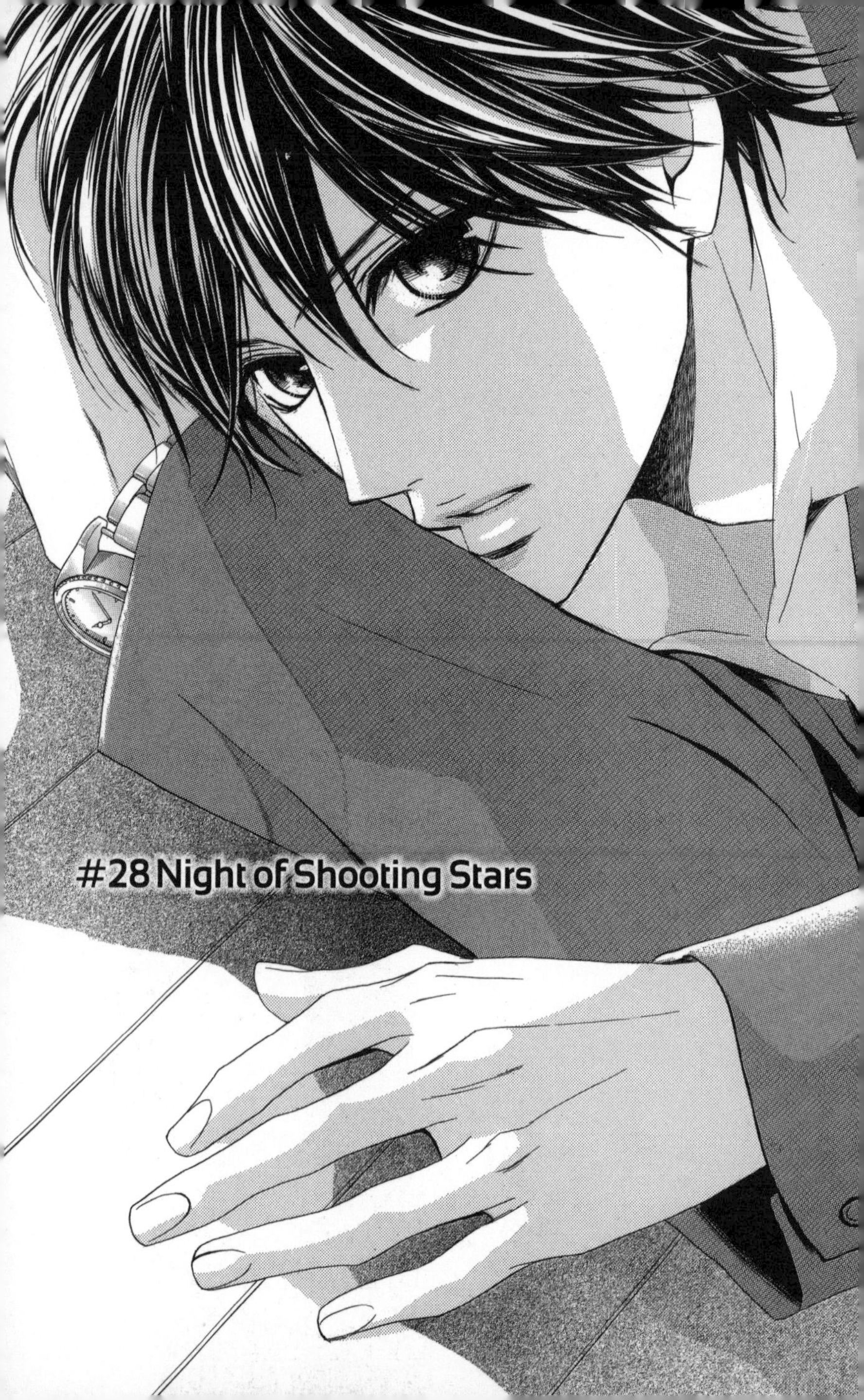

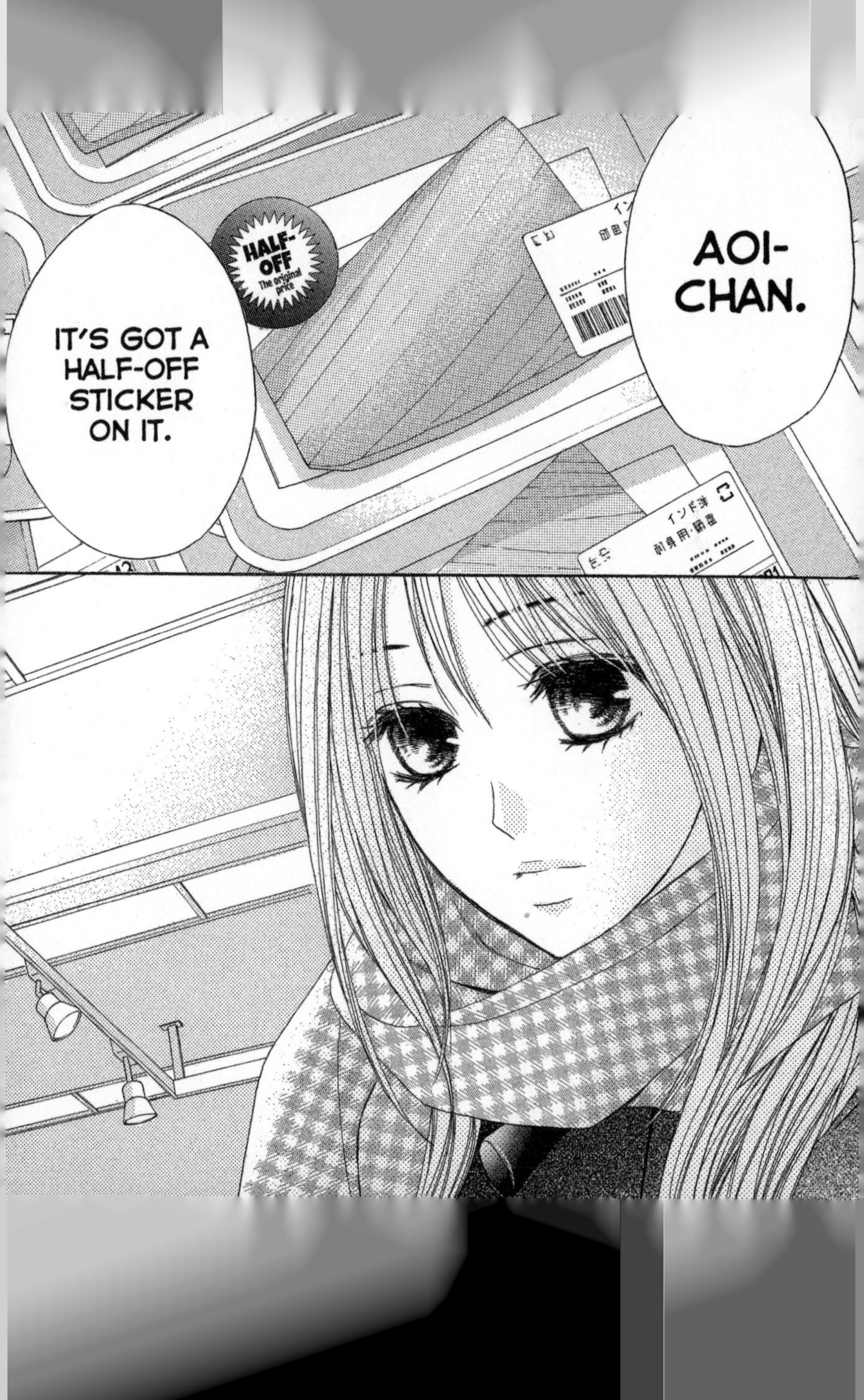
AOI-CHAN.
HALF-OFF The original price
IT'S GOT A HALF-OFF STICKER ON IT.

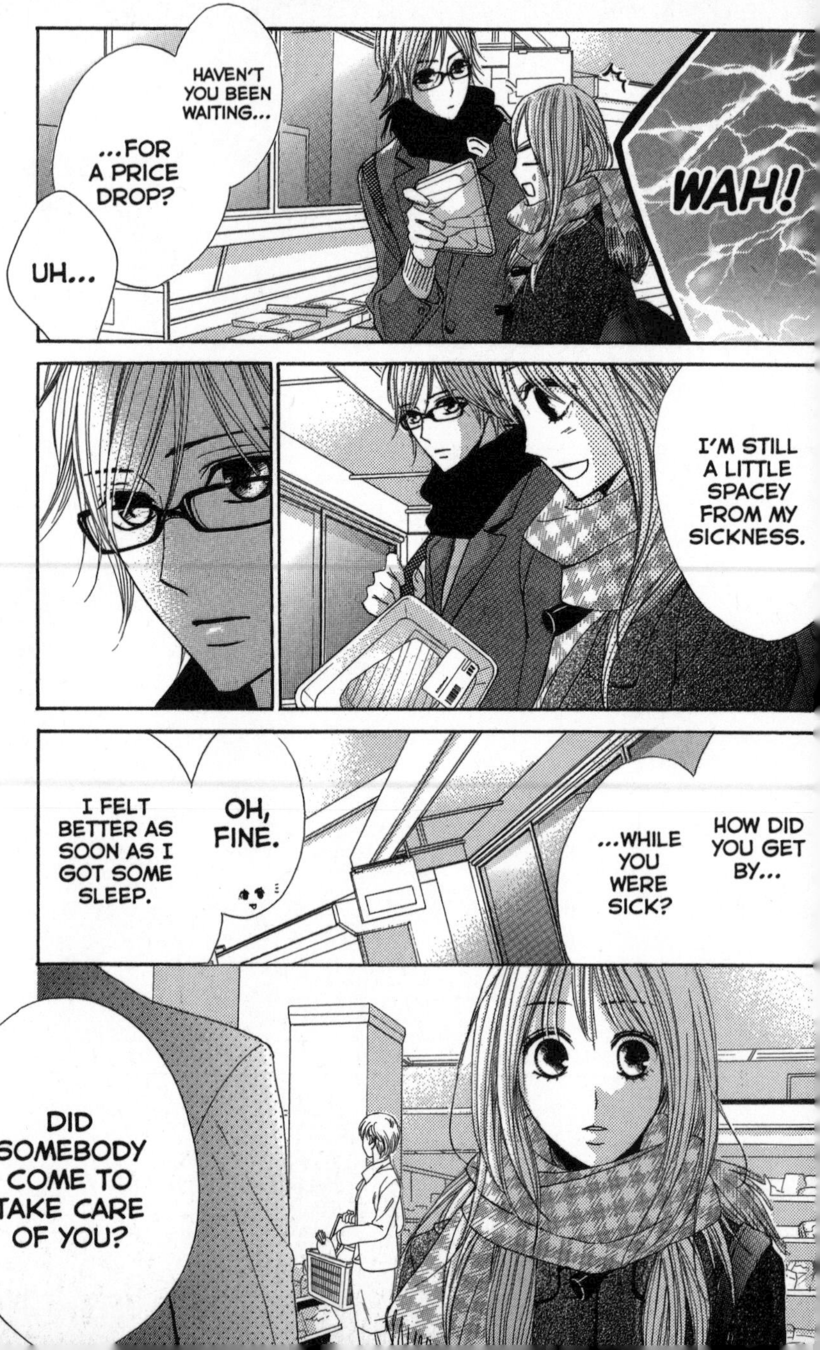
HAVEN'T YOU BEEN WAITING...
...FOR A PRICE DROP?
UH...
WAH!
I'M STILL A LITTLE SPACEY FROM MY SICKNESS.
HOW DID YOU GET BY...
...WHILE YOU WERE SICK?
OH, FINE.
I FELT BETTER AS SOON AS I GOT SOME SLEEP.
DID SOMEBODY COME TO TAKE CARE OF YOU?

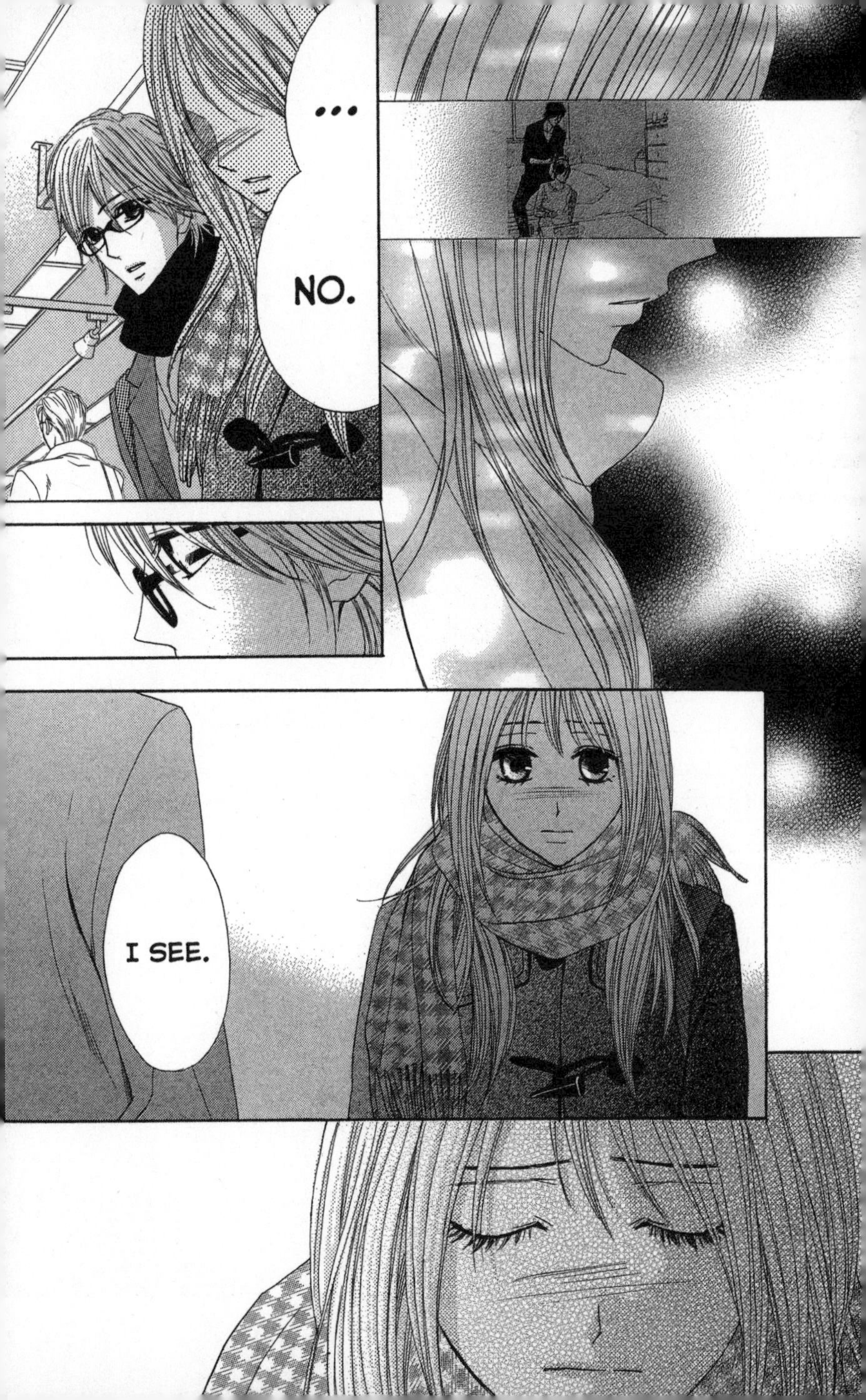
...
NO.
I SEE.

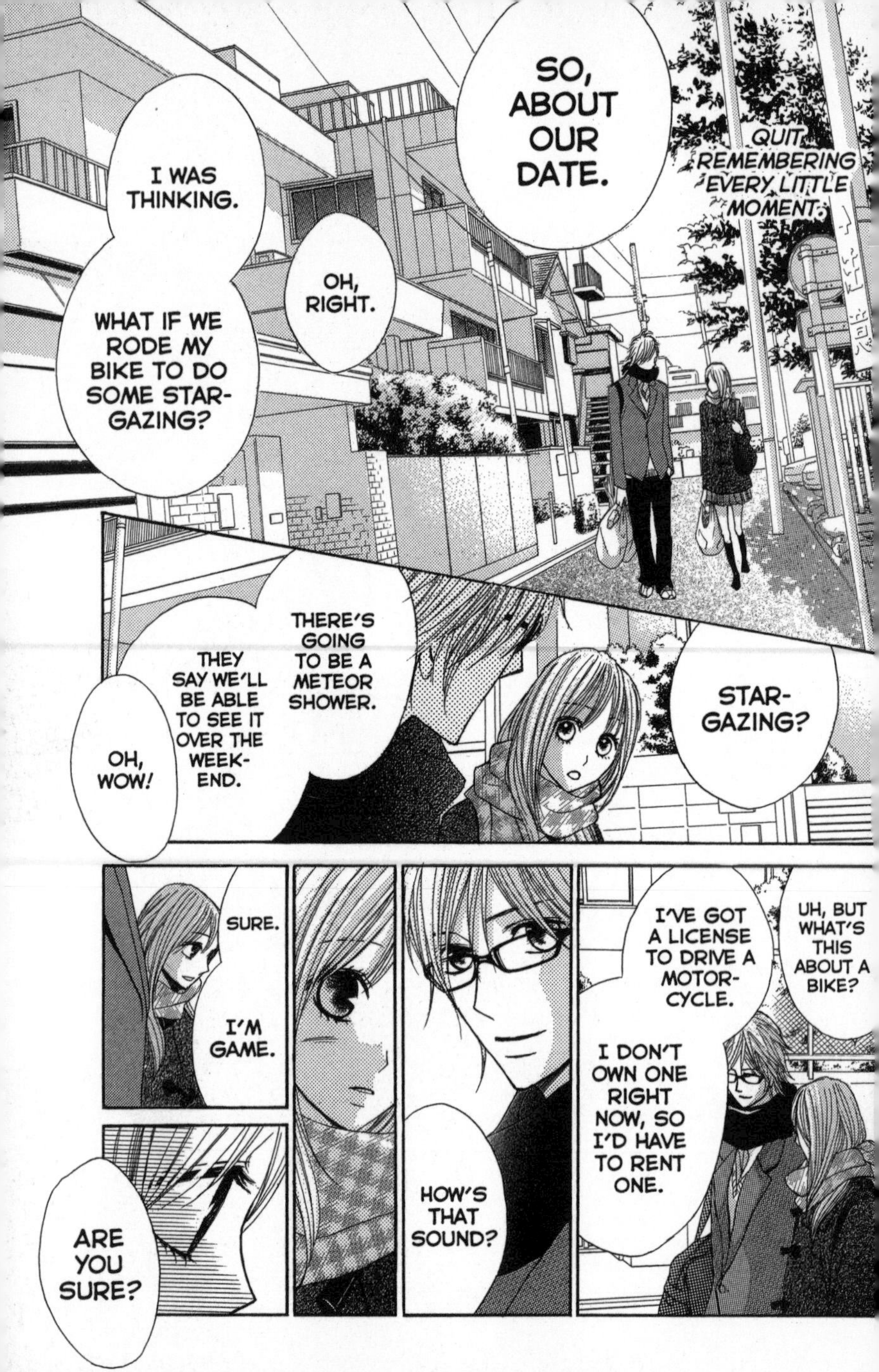
QUIT REMEMBERING EVERY LITTLE MOMENT.
SO, ABOUT OUR DATE.
OH, RIGHT.
I WAS THINKING.
WHAT IF WE RODE MY BIKE TO DO SOME STAR-GAZING?
STAR-GAZING?
THERE'S GOING TO BE A METEOR SHOWER.
THEY SAY WE'LL BE ABLE TO SEE IT OVER THE WEEK-END.
OH, WOW!
UH, BUT WHAT'S THIS ABOUT A BIKE?
I'VE GOT A LICENSE TO DRIVE A MOTOR-CYCLE.
I DON'T OWN ONE RIGHT NOW, SO I'D HAVE TO RENT ONE.
HOW'S THAT SOUND?
SURE.
I'M GAME.
ARE YOU SURE?

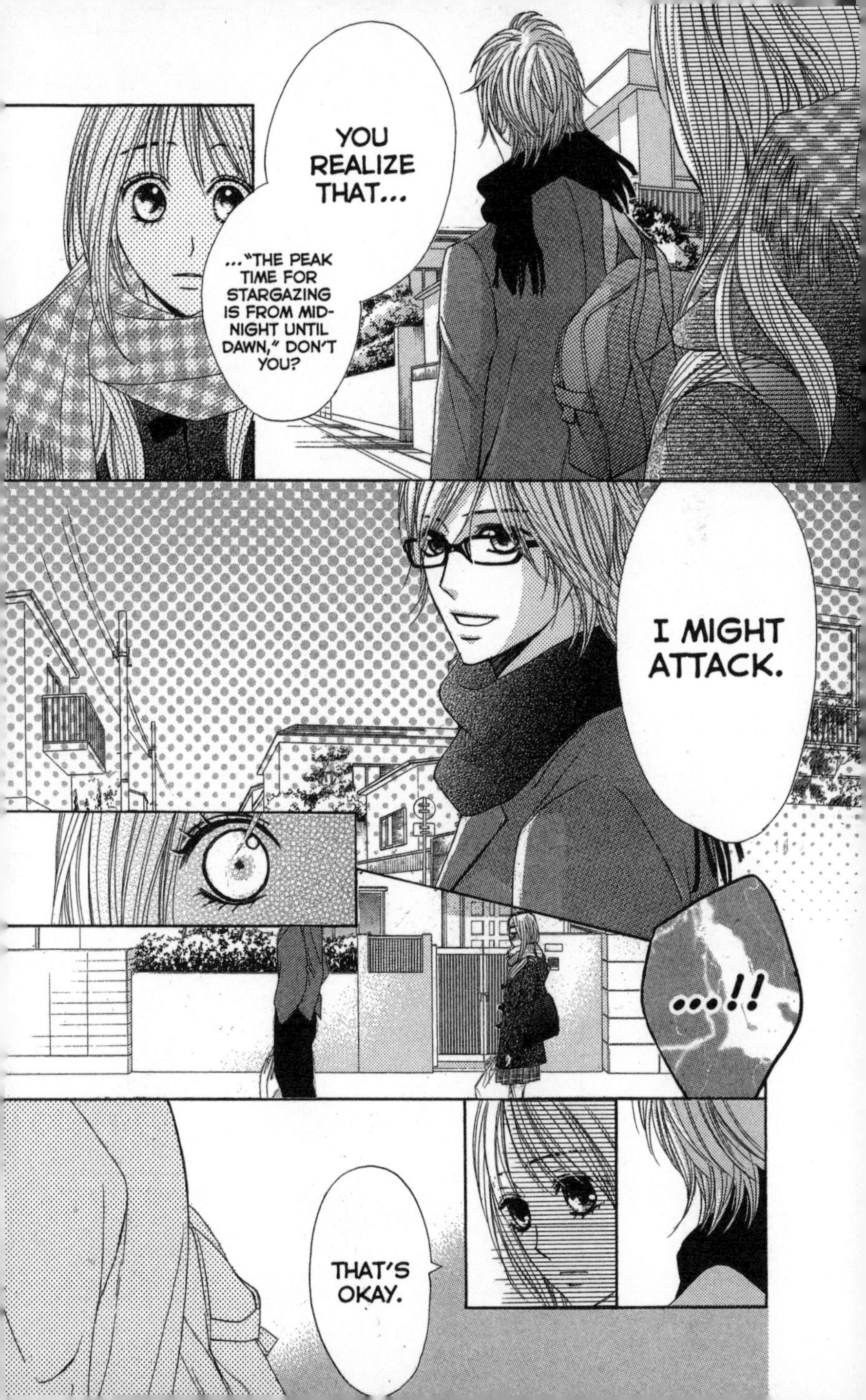

YOU REALIZE THAT...
..."THE PEAK TIME FOR STARGAZING IS FROM MID-NIGHT UNTIL DAWN," DON'T YOU?
I MIGHT ATTACK.
...!!
THAT'S OKAY.

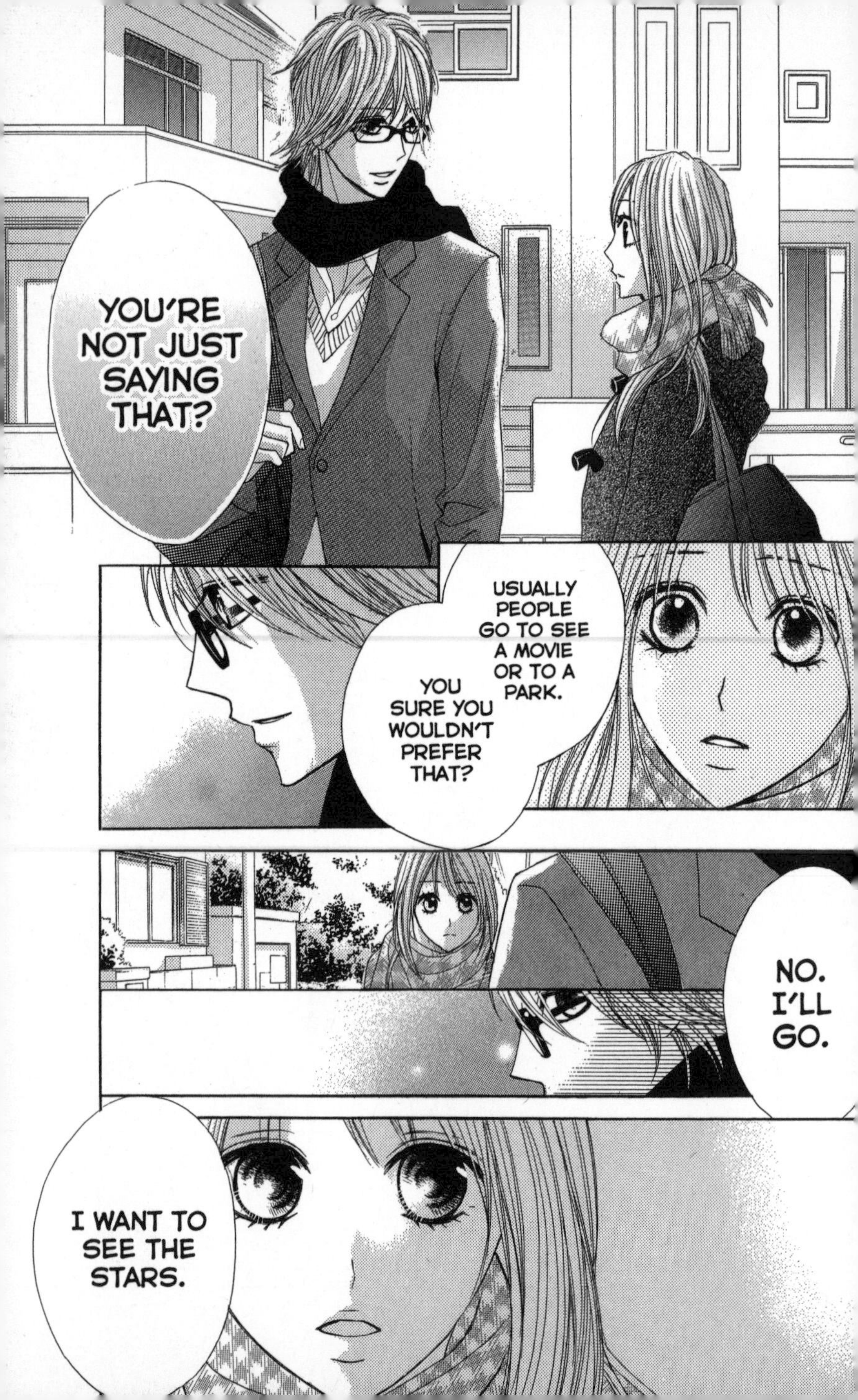
YOU'RE NOT JUST SAYING THAT?
USUALLY PEOPLE GO TO SEE A MOVIE OR TO A PARK.
YOU SURE YOU WOULDN'T PREFER THAT?
NO. I'LL GO.
I WANT TO SEE THE STARS.

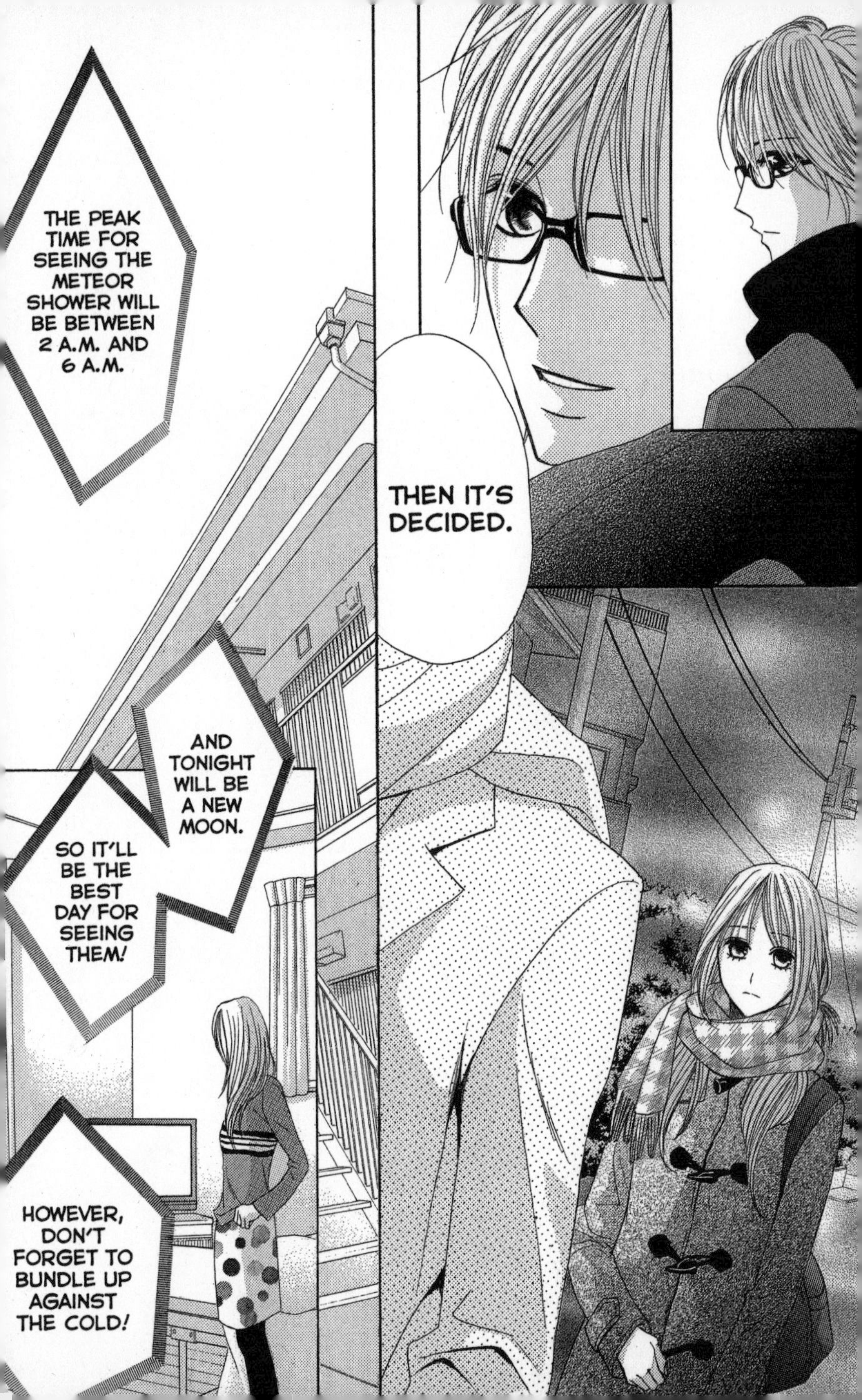
THEN IT'S DECIDED.
THE PEAK TIME FOR SEEING THE METEOR SHOWER WILL BE BETWEEN 2 A.M. AND 6 A.M.
AND TONIGHT WILL BE A NEW MOON.
SO IT'LL BE THE BEST DAY FOR SEEING THEM!
HOWEVER, DON'T FORGET TO BUNDLE UP AGAINST THE COLD!

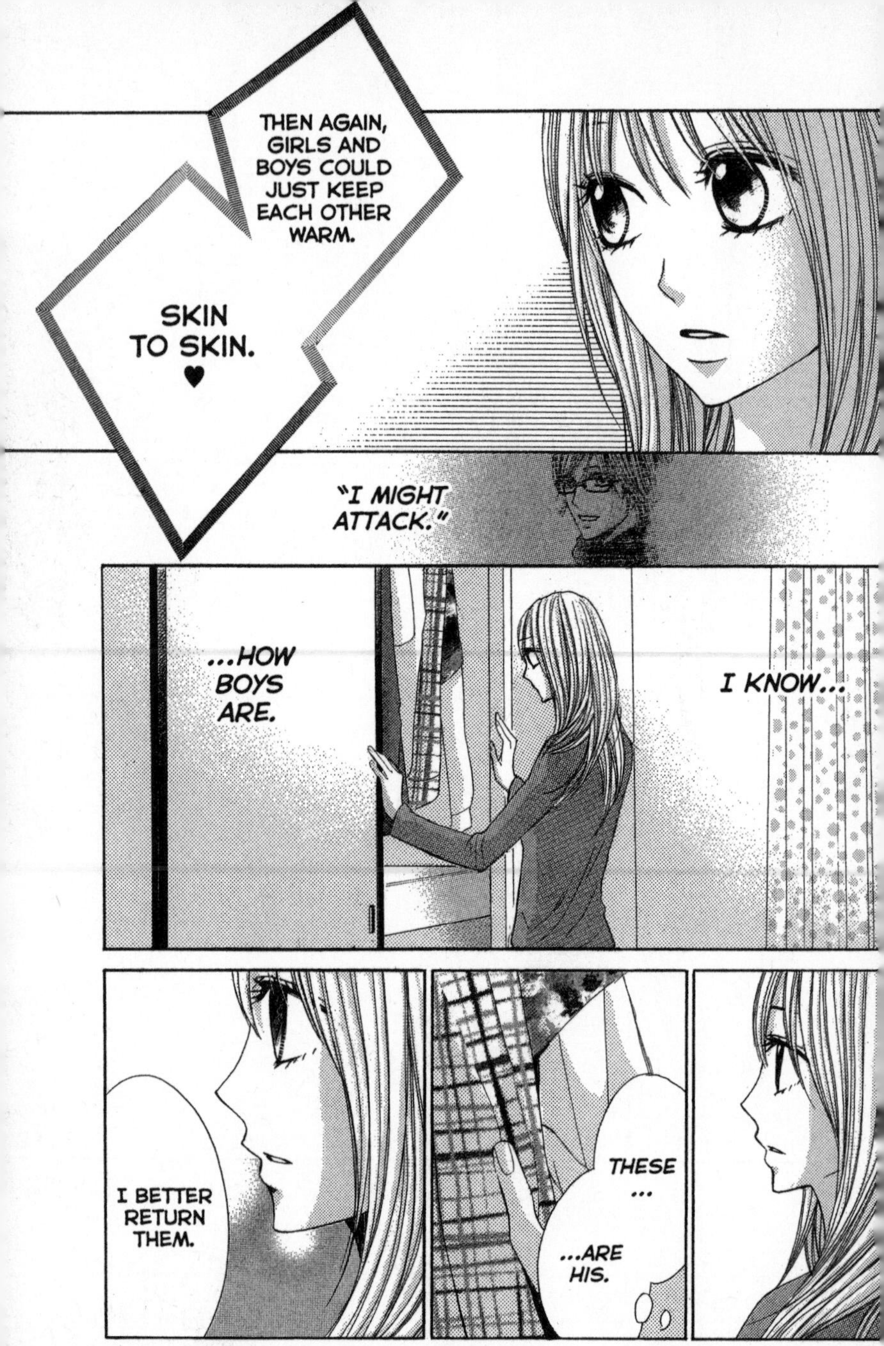
THEN AGAIN, GIRLS AND BOYS COULD JUST KEEP EACH OTHER WARM.
SKIN TO SKIN. ♥
"I MIGHT ATTACK."
I KNOW...
...HOW BOYS ARE.
THESE ...
...ARE HIS.
I BETTER RETURN THEM.

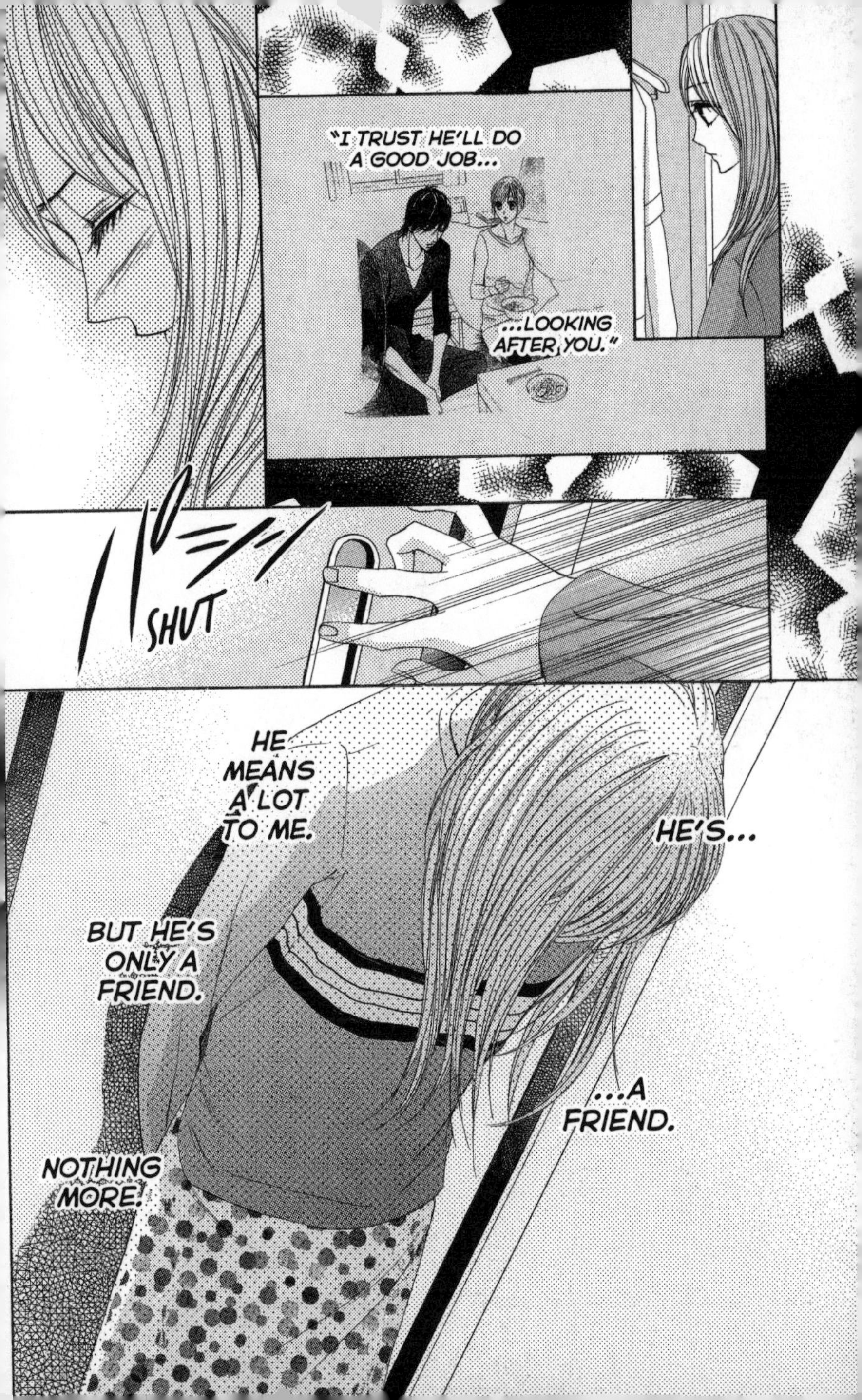
"I TRUST HE'LL DO A GOOD JOB...
...LOOKING AFTER YOU."
SHUT
HE'S...
...A FRIEND.
HE MEANS A LOT TO ME.
BUT HE'S ONLY A FRIEND.
NOTHING MORE.

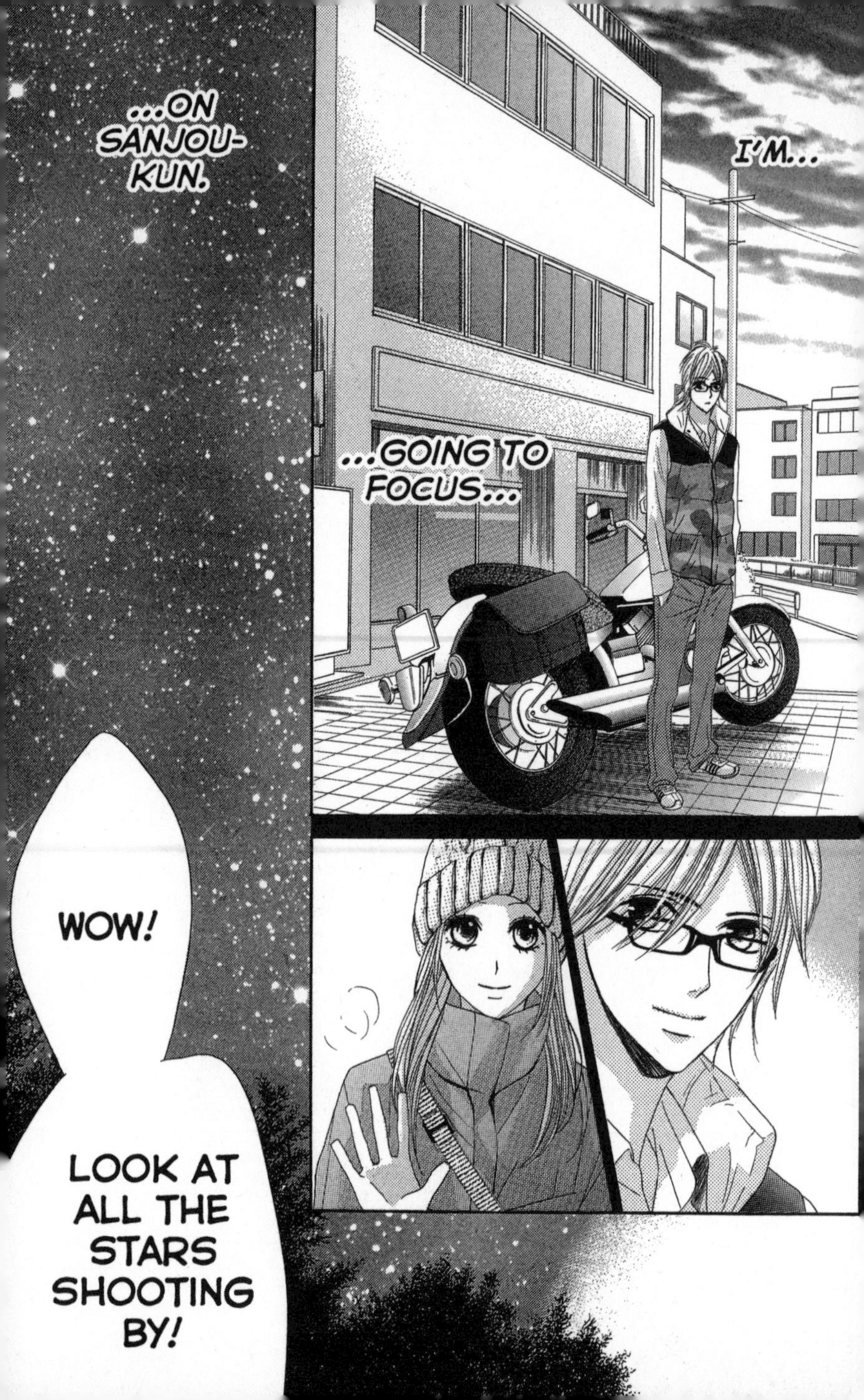
I'M...
...GOING TO FOCUS...
...ON SANJOU-KUN.
WOW!
LOOK AT ALL THE STARS SHOOTING BY!

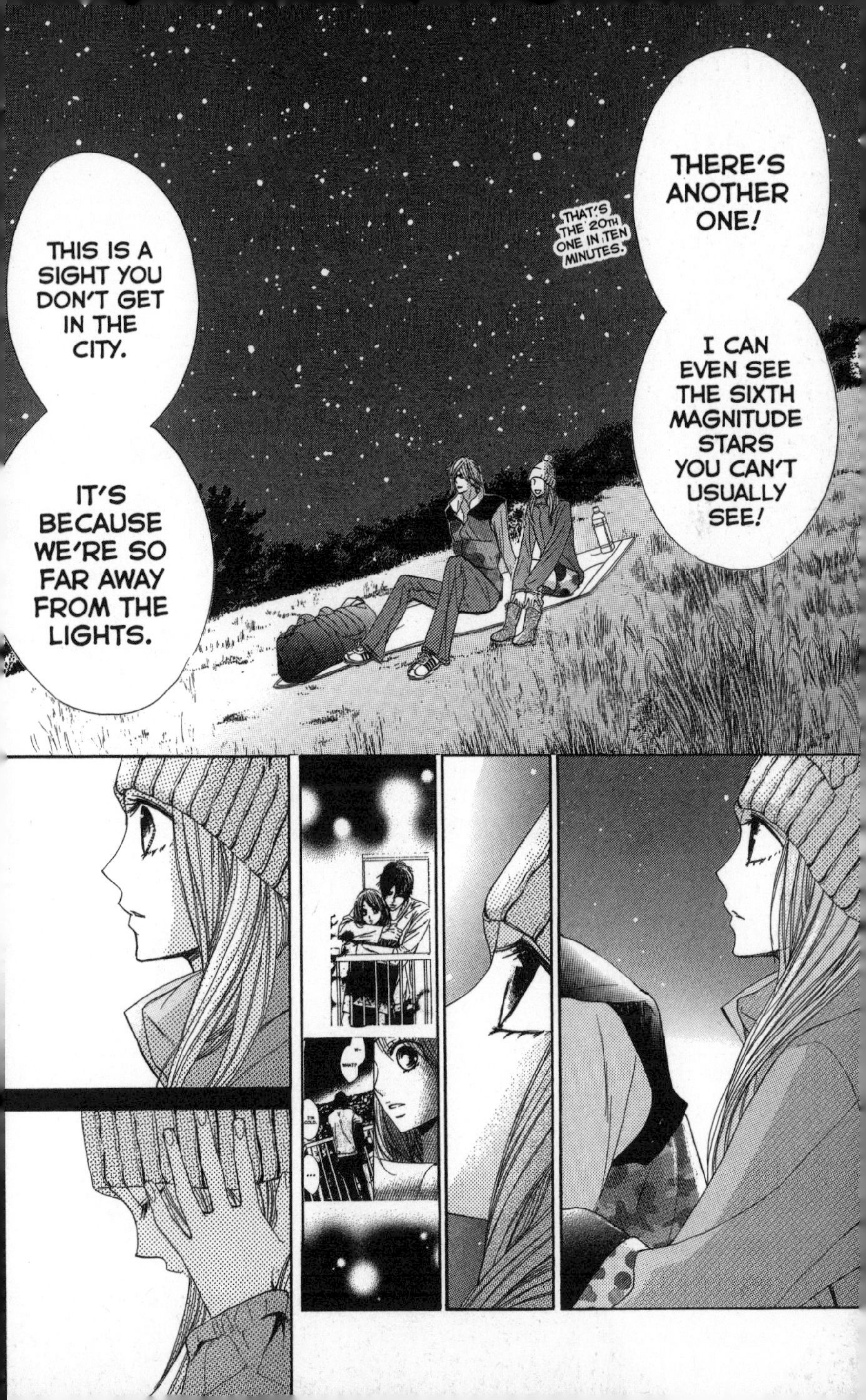
THERE'S ANOTHER ONE!
THAT'S THE 20TH ONE IN TEN MINUTES.
I CAN EVEN SEE THE SIXTH MAGNITUDE STARS YOU CAN'T USUALLY SEE!
THIS IS A SIGHT YOU DON'T GET IN THE CITY.
IT'S BECAUSE WE'RE SO FAR AWAY FROM THE LIGHTS.
W- WHAT?
...

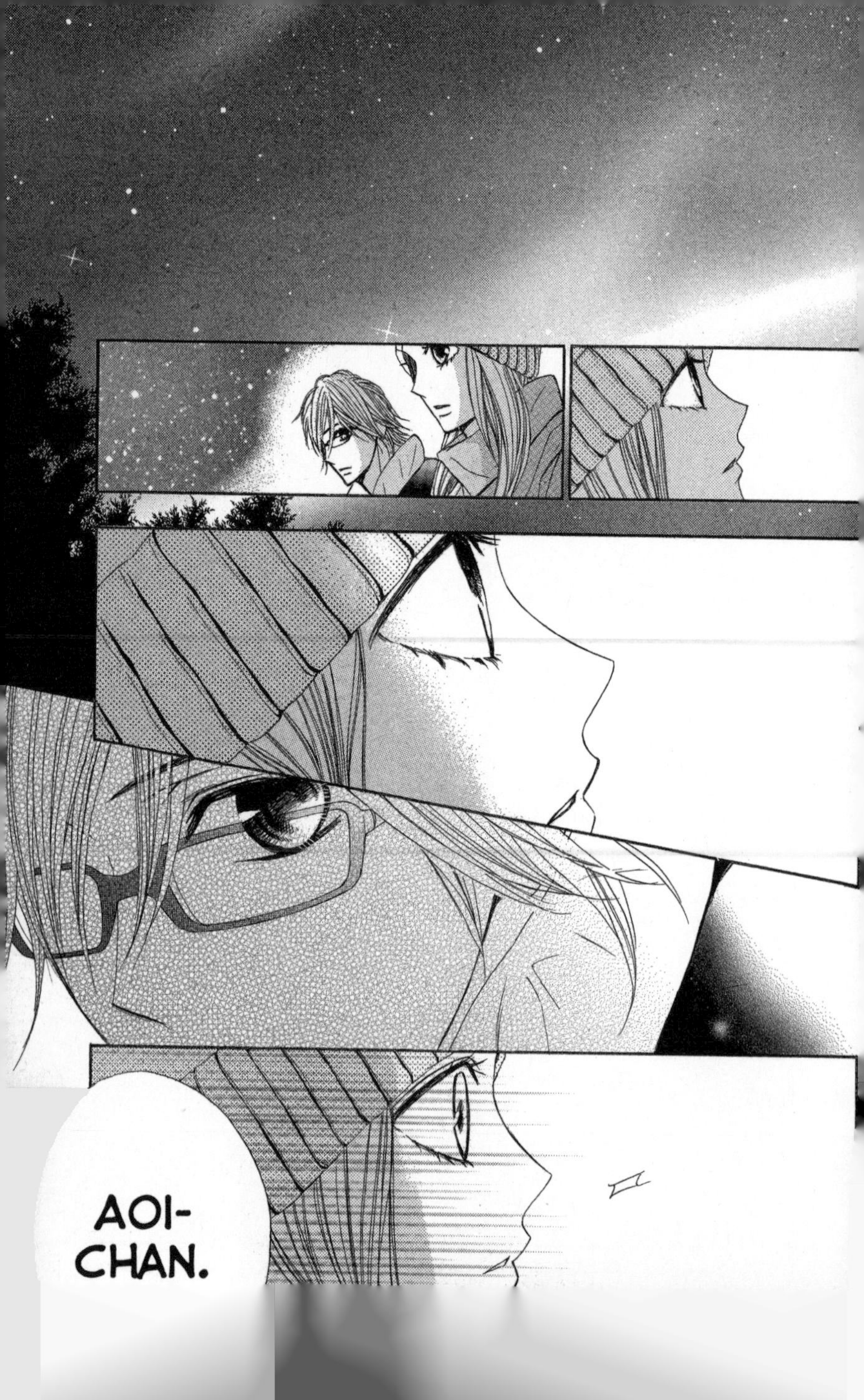
AOI-
CHAN.

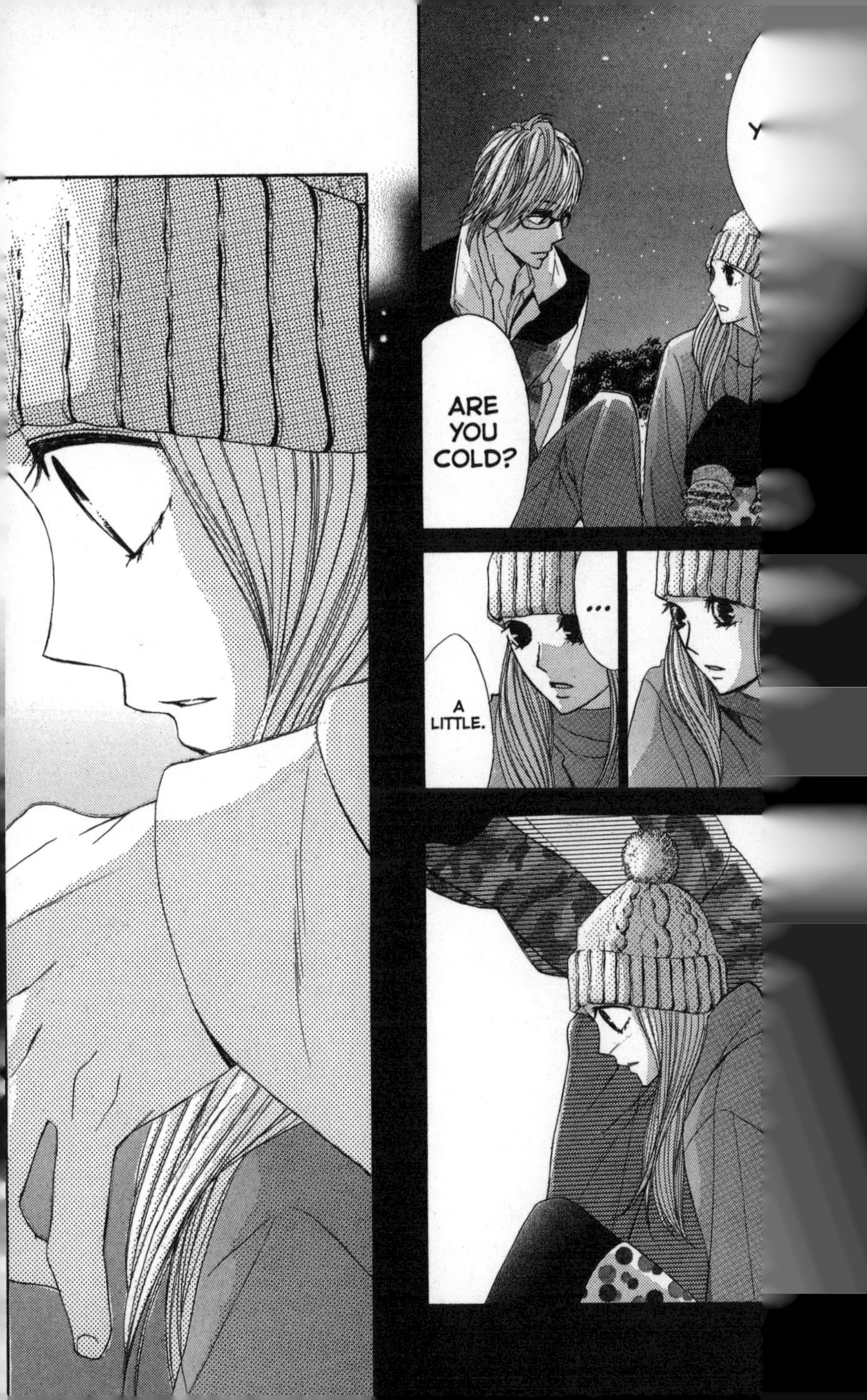
ARE YOU COLD?
...
A LITTLE.

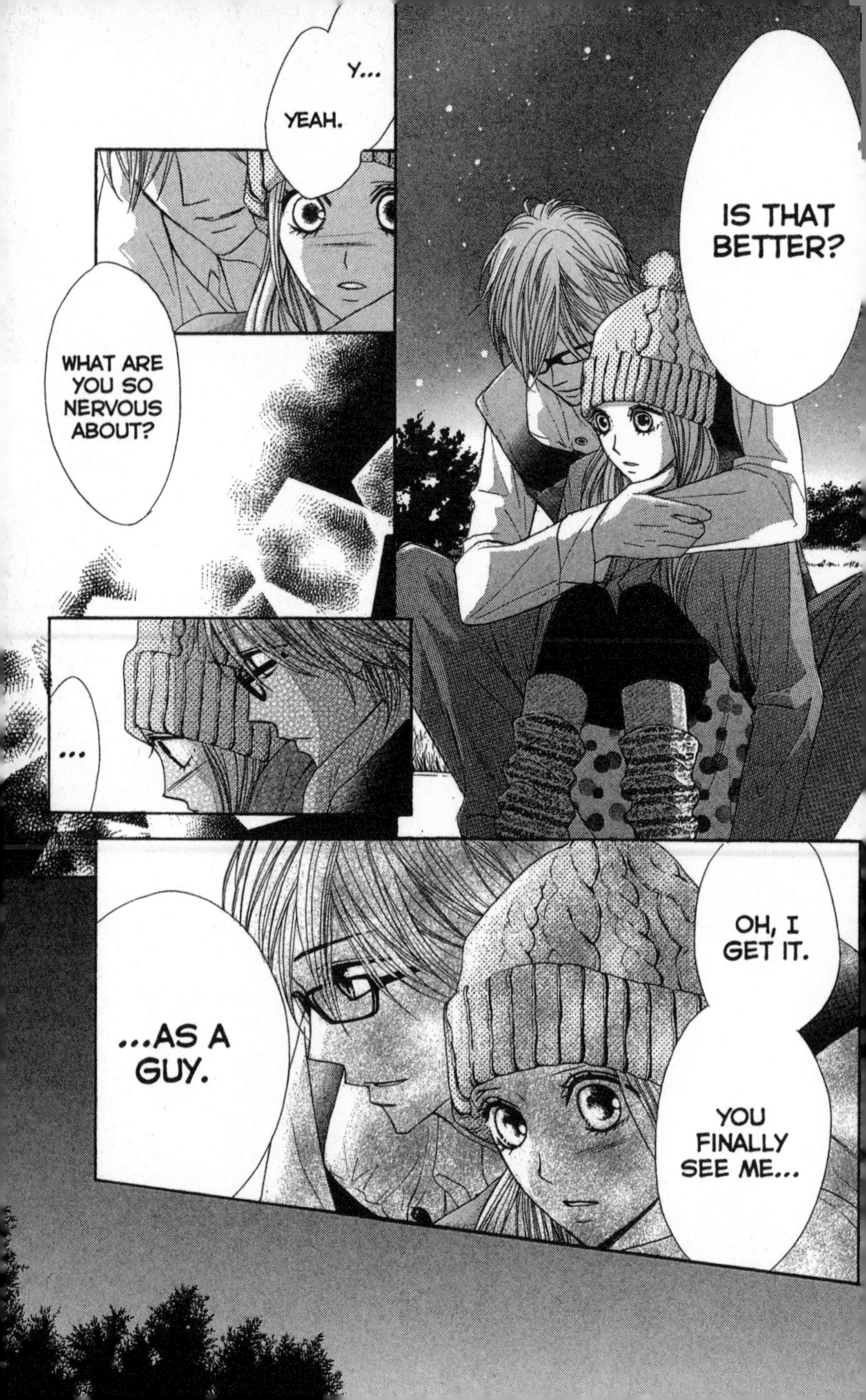
IS THAT BETTER?
Y... YEAH.
WHAT ARE YOU SO NERVOUS ABOUT?
...
OH, I GET IT.
YOU FINALLY SEE ME...
...AS A GUY.

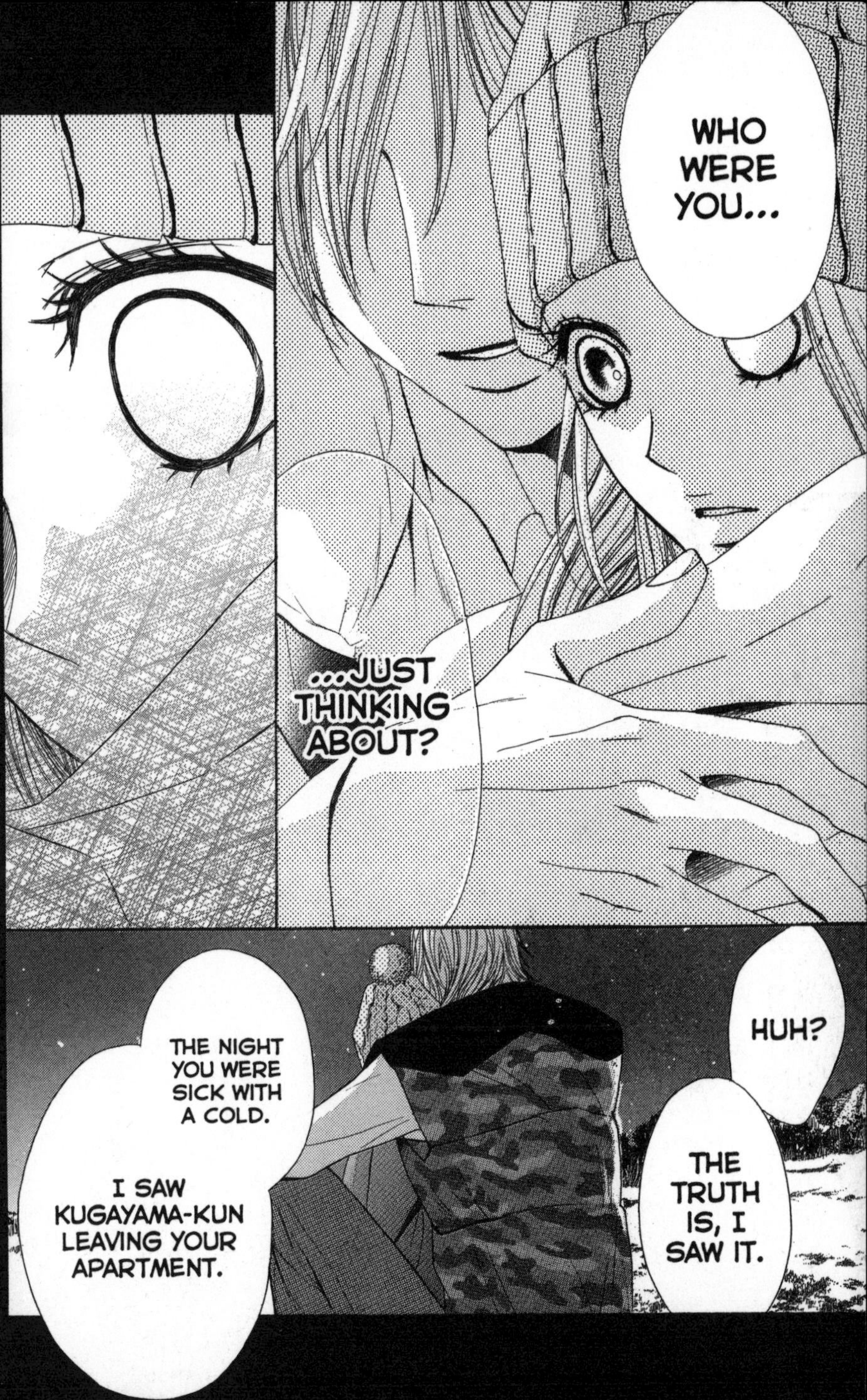
WHO WERE YOU...
...JUST THINKING ABOUT?
HUH?
THE TRUTH IS, I SAW IT.
THE NIGHT YOU WERE SICK WITH A COLD.
I SAW KUGAYAMA-KUN LEAVING YOUR APARTMENT.

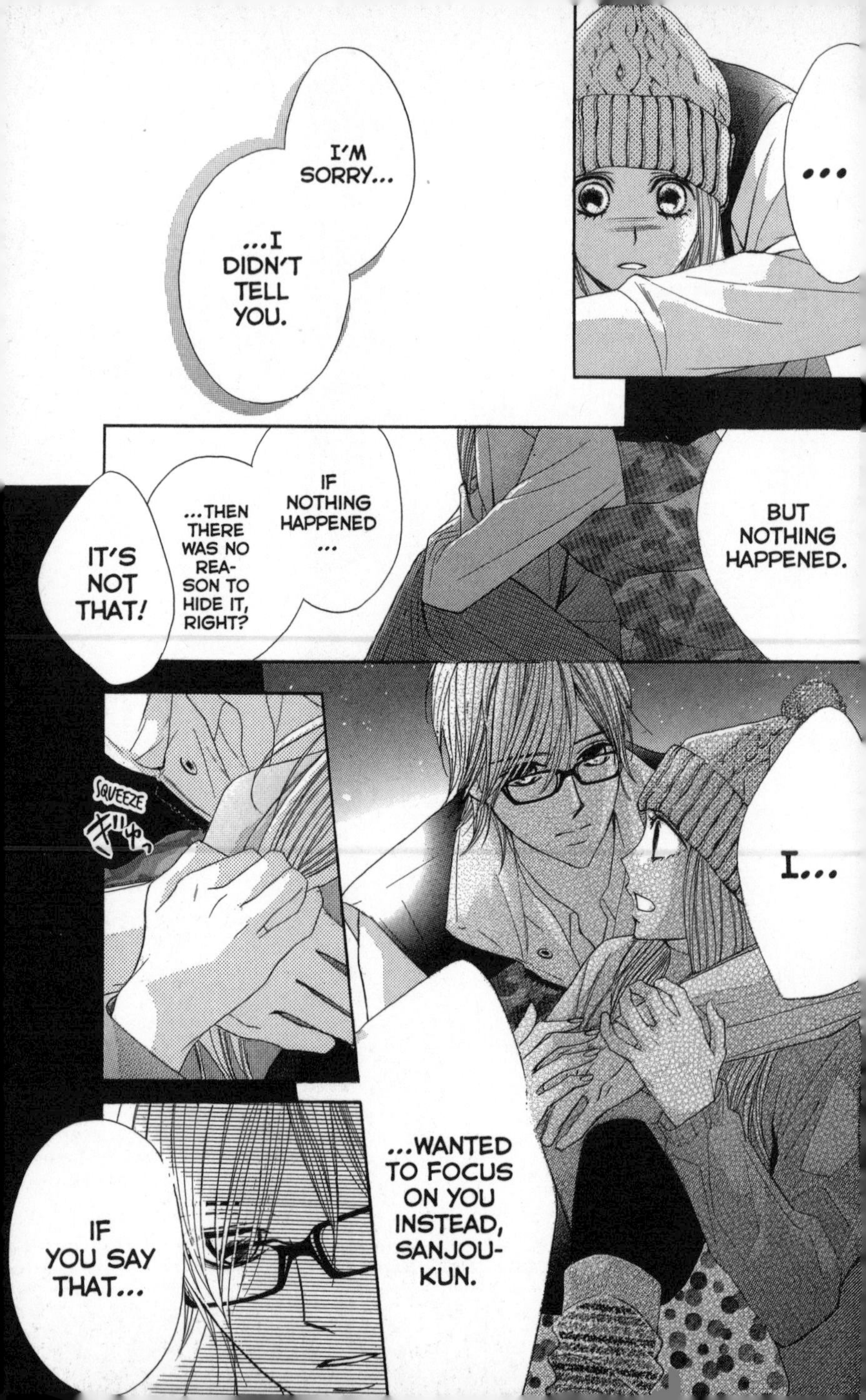
...
I'M SORRY...
...I DIDN'T TELL YOU.
BUT NOTHING HAPPENED.
IF NOTHING HAPPENED ...
...THEN THERE WAS NO REA-SON TO HIDE IT, RIGHT?
IT'S NOT THAT!
I...
...WANTED TO FOCUS ON YOU INSTEAD, SANJOU-KUN.
SQUEEZE
IF YOU SAY THAT...

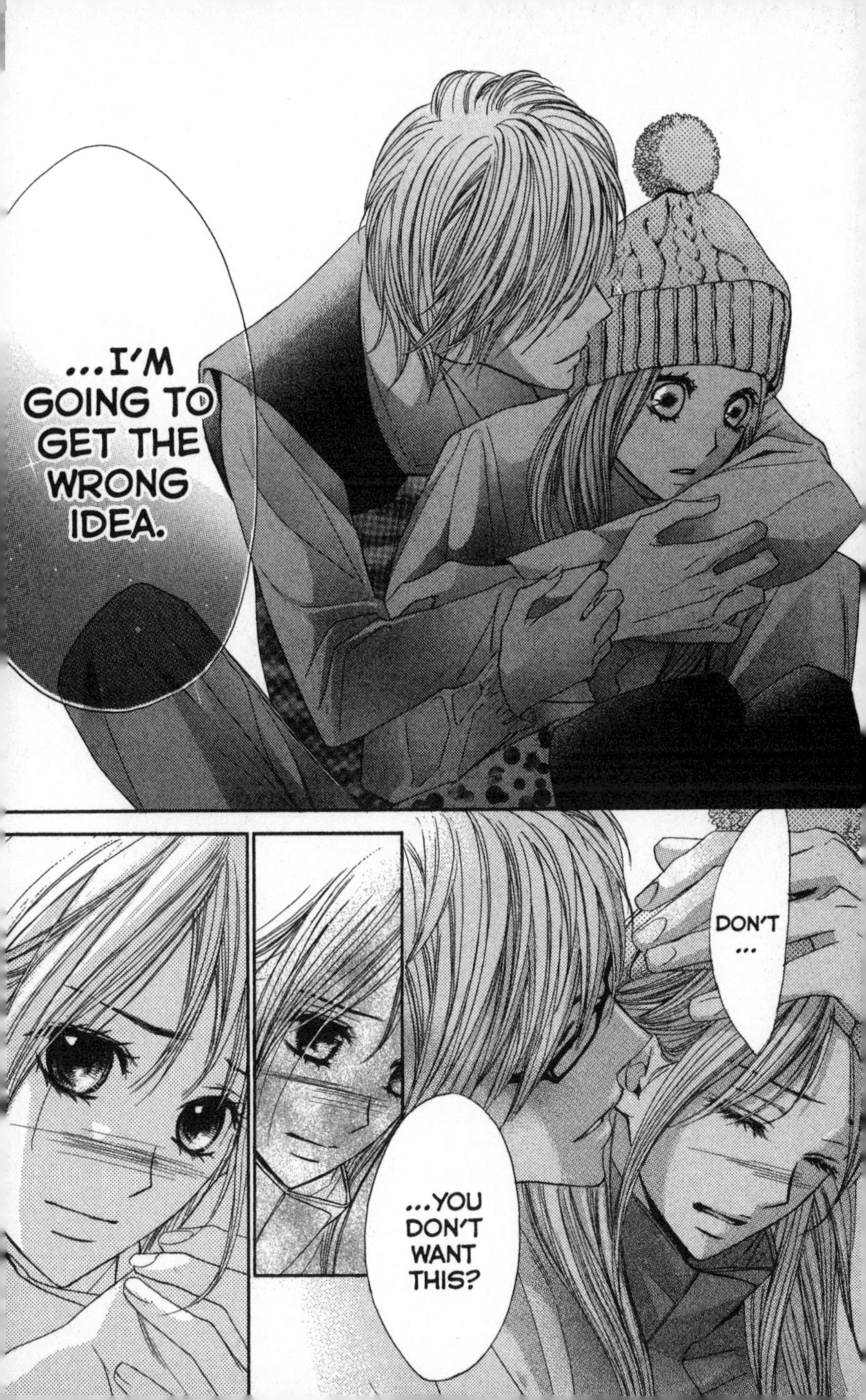
...I'M GOING TO GET THE WRONG IDEA.
DON'T ...
...YOU DON'T WANT THIS?

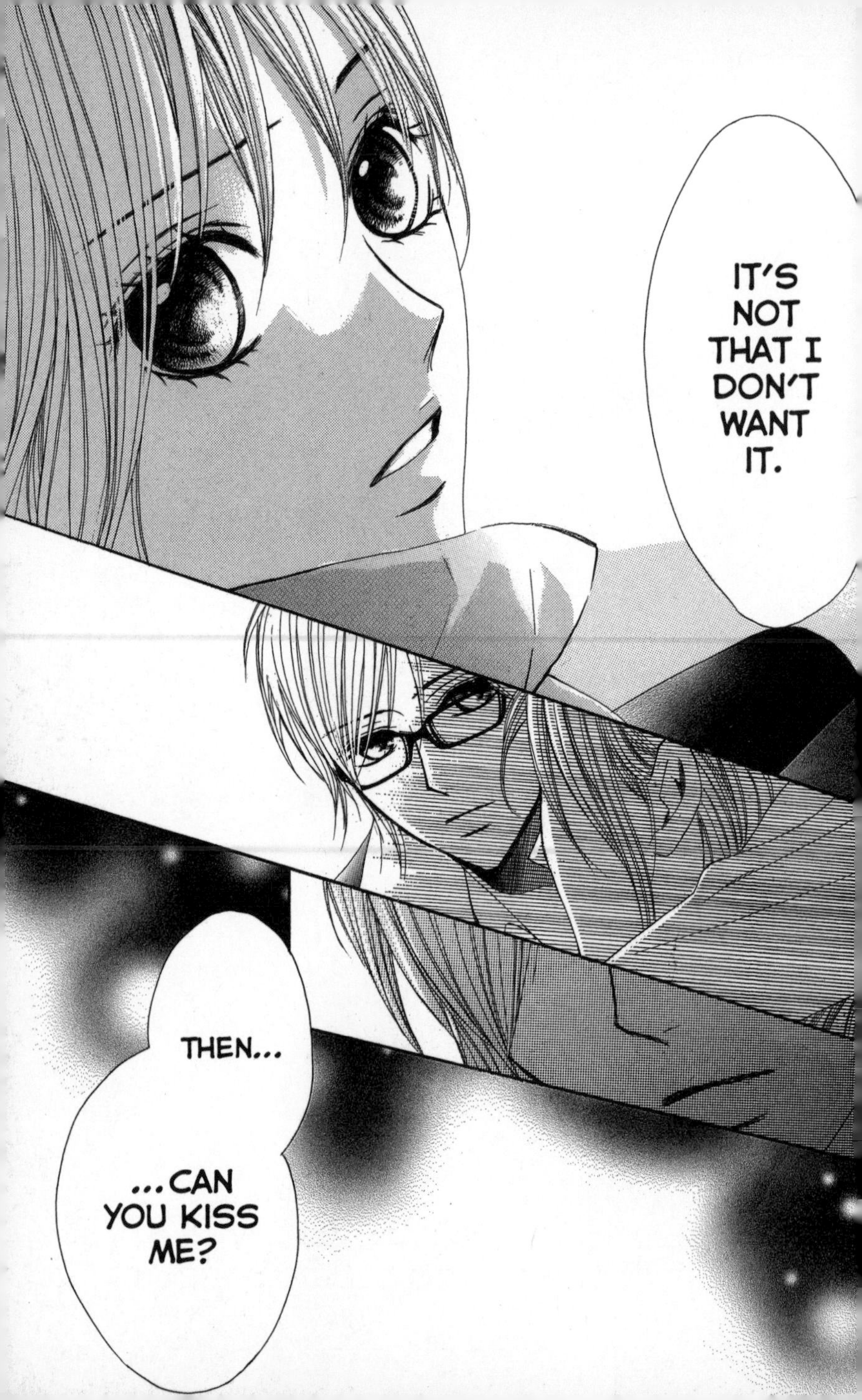
IT'S NOT THAT I DON'T WANT IT.
THEN...
...CAN YOU KISS ME?

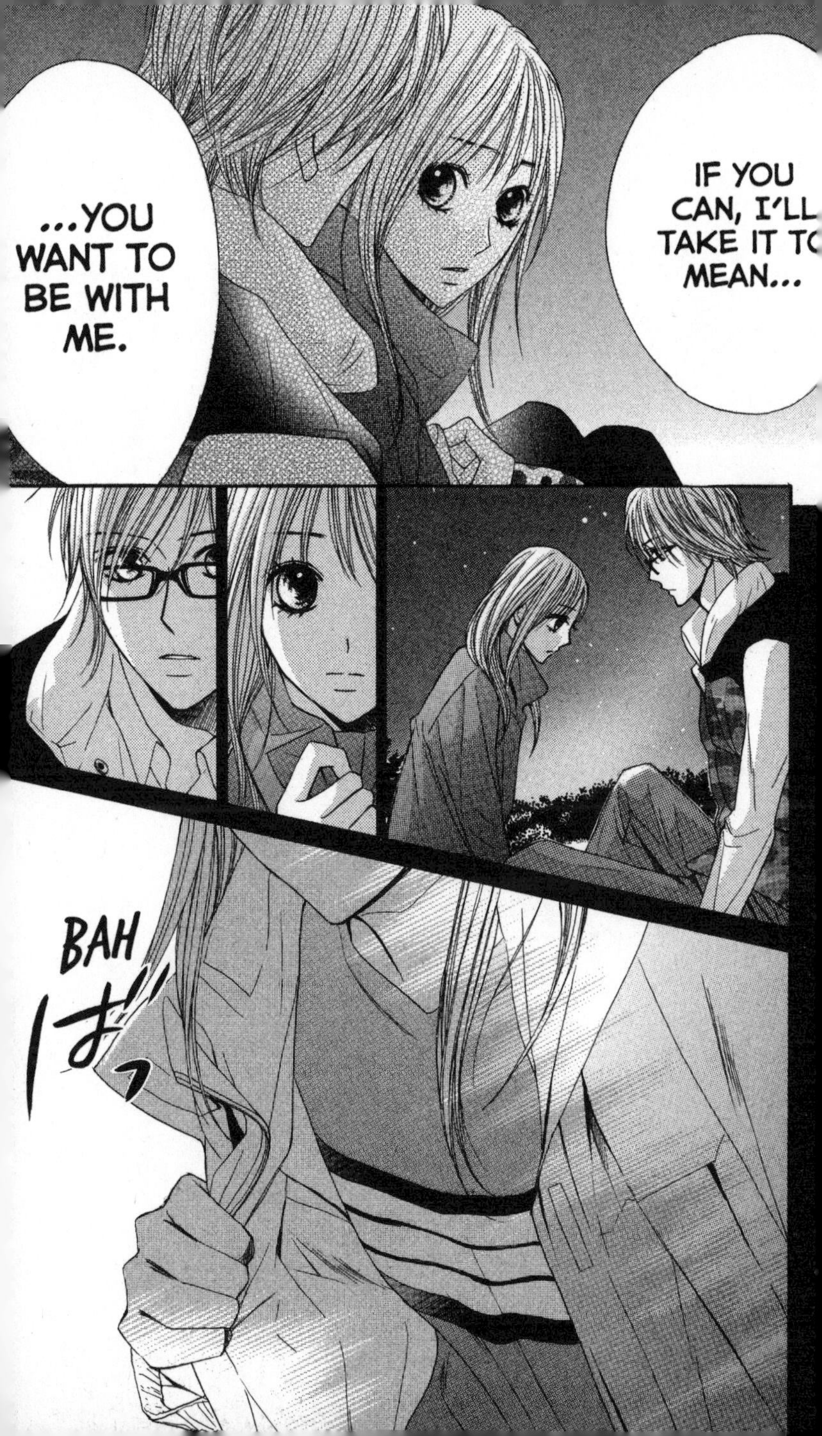
IF YOU CAN, I'LL TAKE IT TO MEAN...
...YOU WANT TO BE WITH ME.
BAH
ばっ

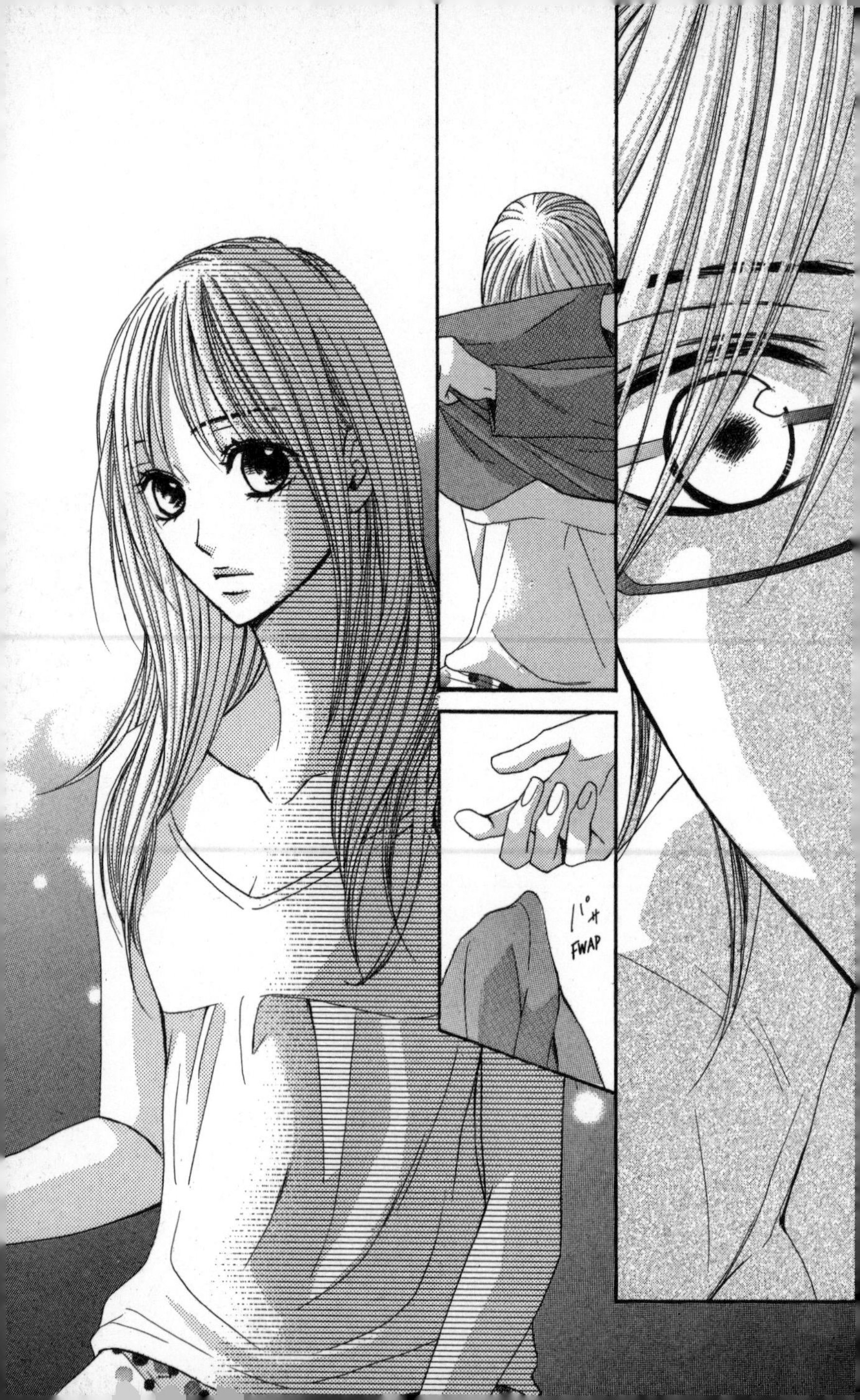
パッ
FWAP

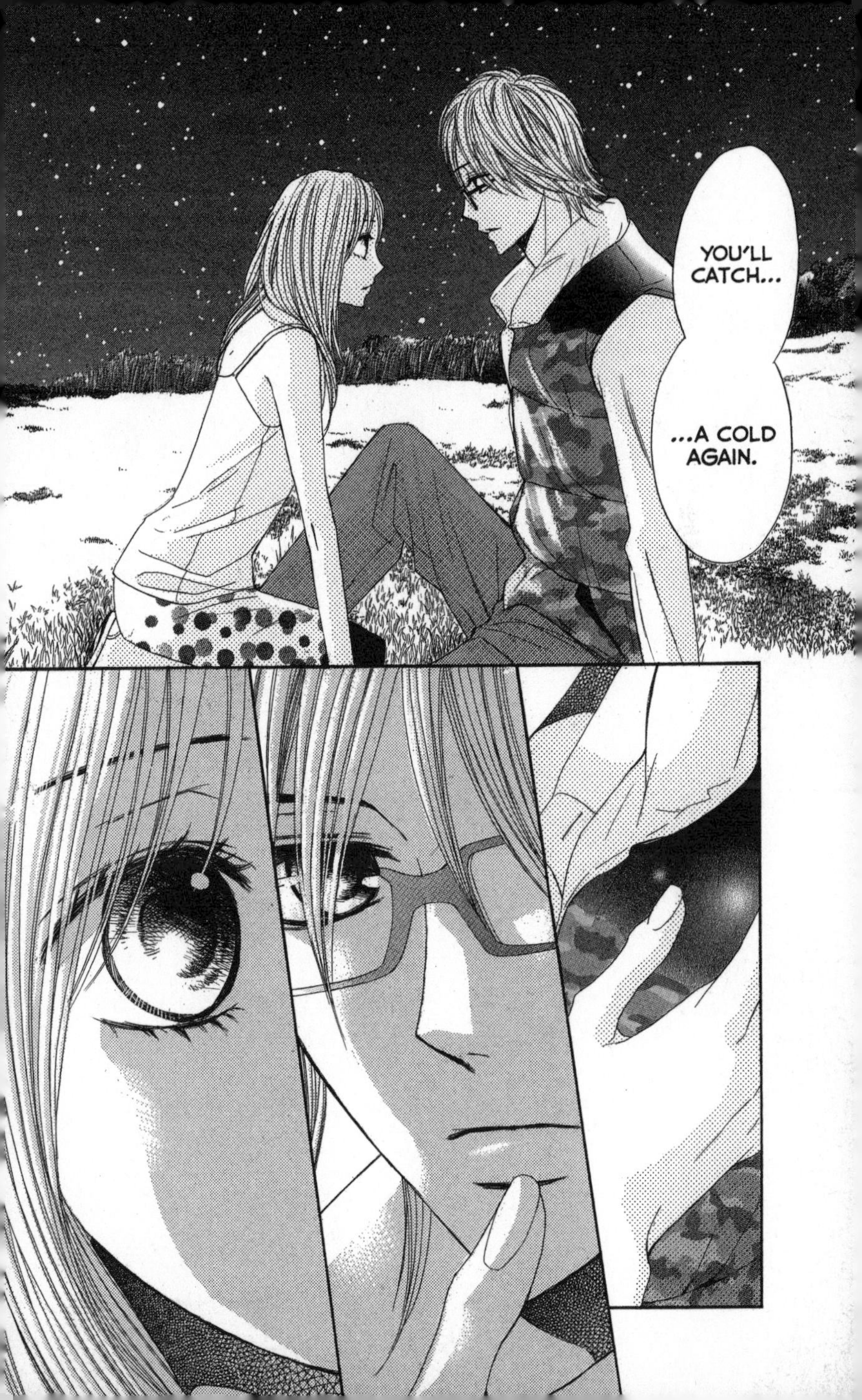
YOU'LL CATCH...
...A COLD AGAIN.

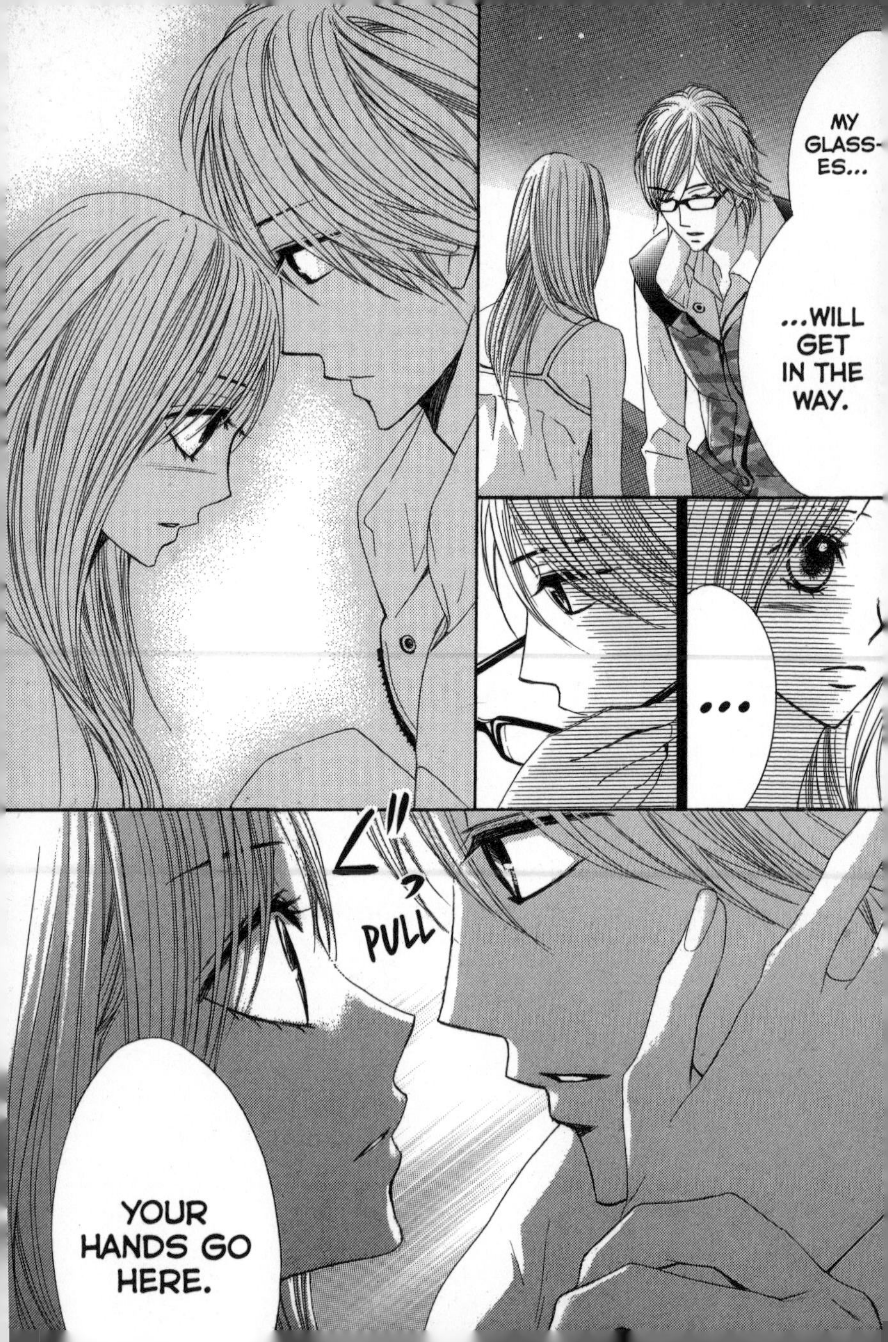
MY GLASSES...
...WILL GET IN THE WAY.
...
ぐっ
PULL
YOUR HANDS GO HERE.

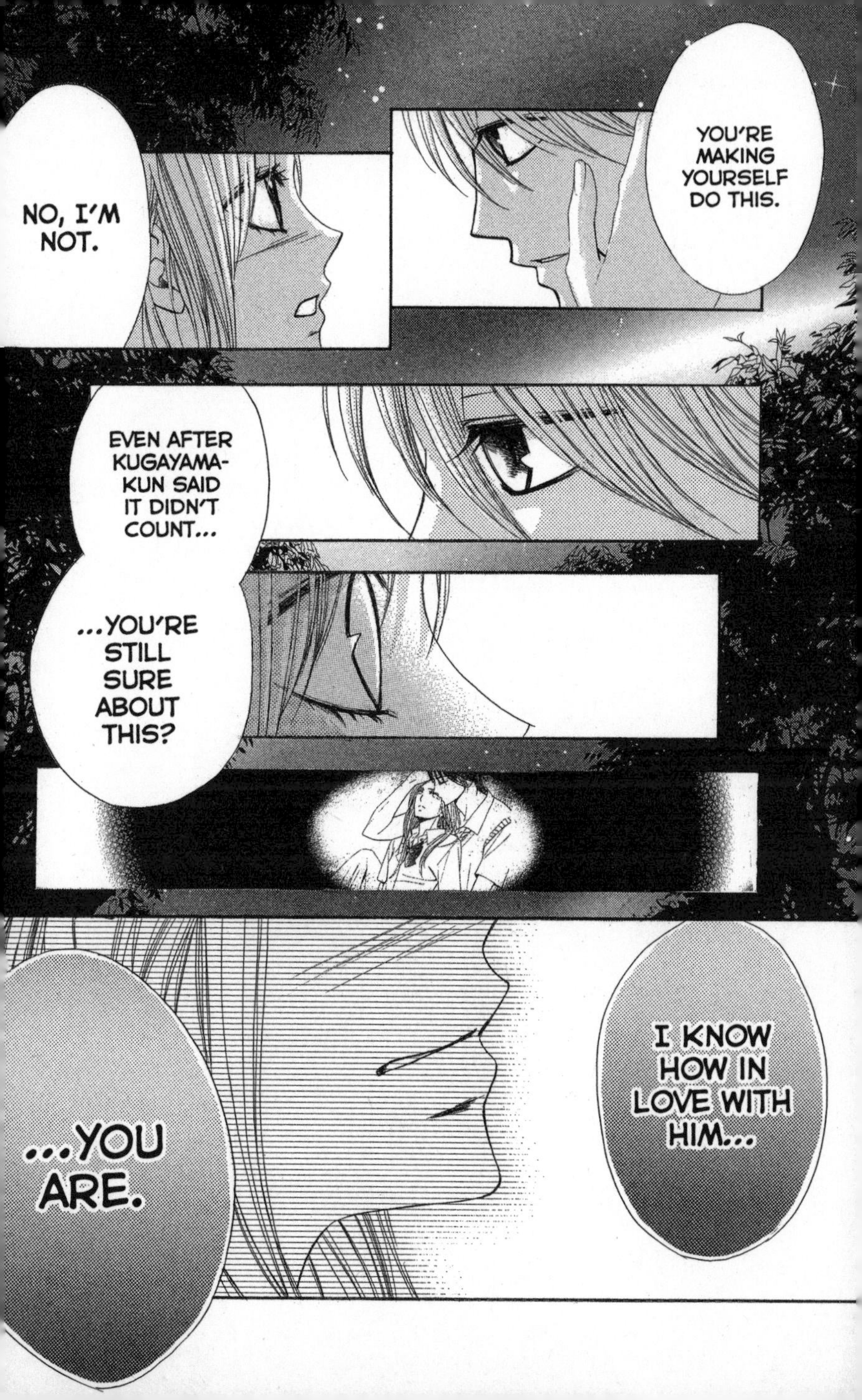
YOU'RE MAKING YOURSELF DO THIS.
NO, I'M NOT.
EVEN AFTER KUGAYAMA-KUN SAID IT DIDN'T COUNT...
...YOU'RE STILL SURE ABOUT THIS?
I KNOW HOW IN LOVE WITH HIM...
...YOU ARE.

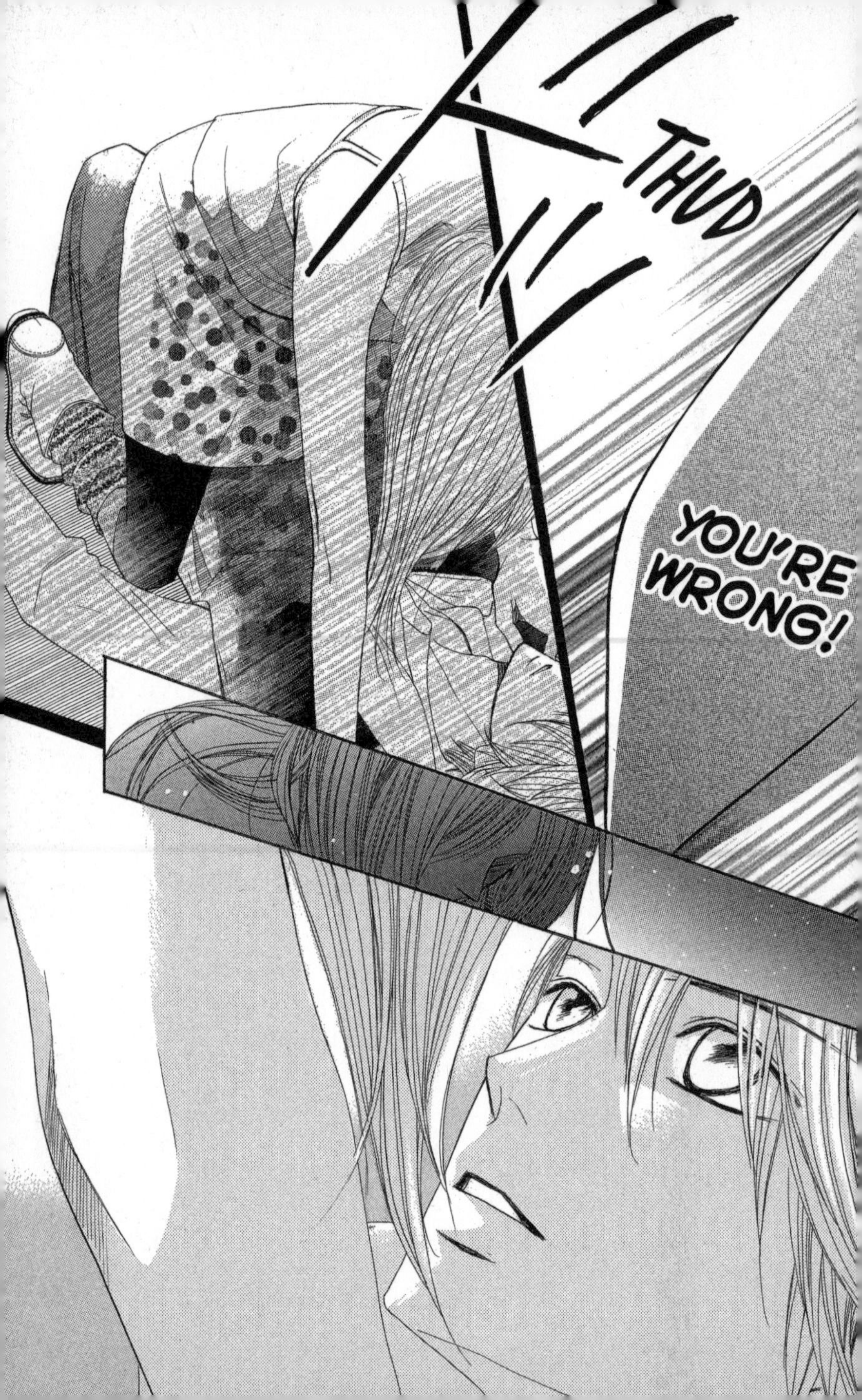
THUD
YOU'RE WRONG!

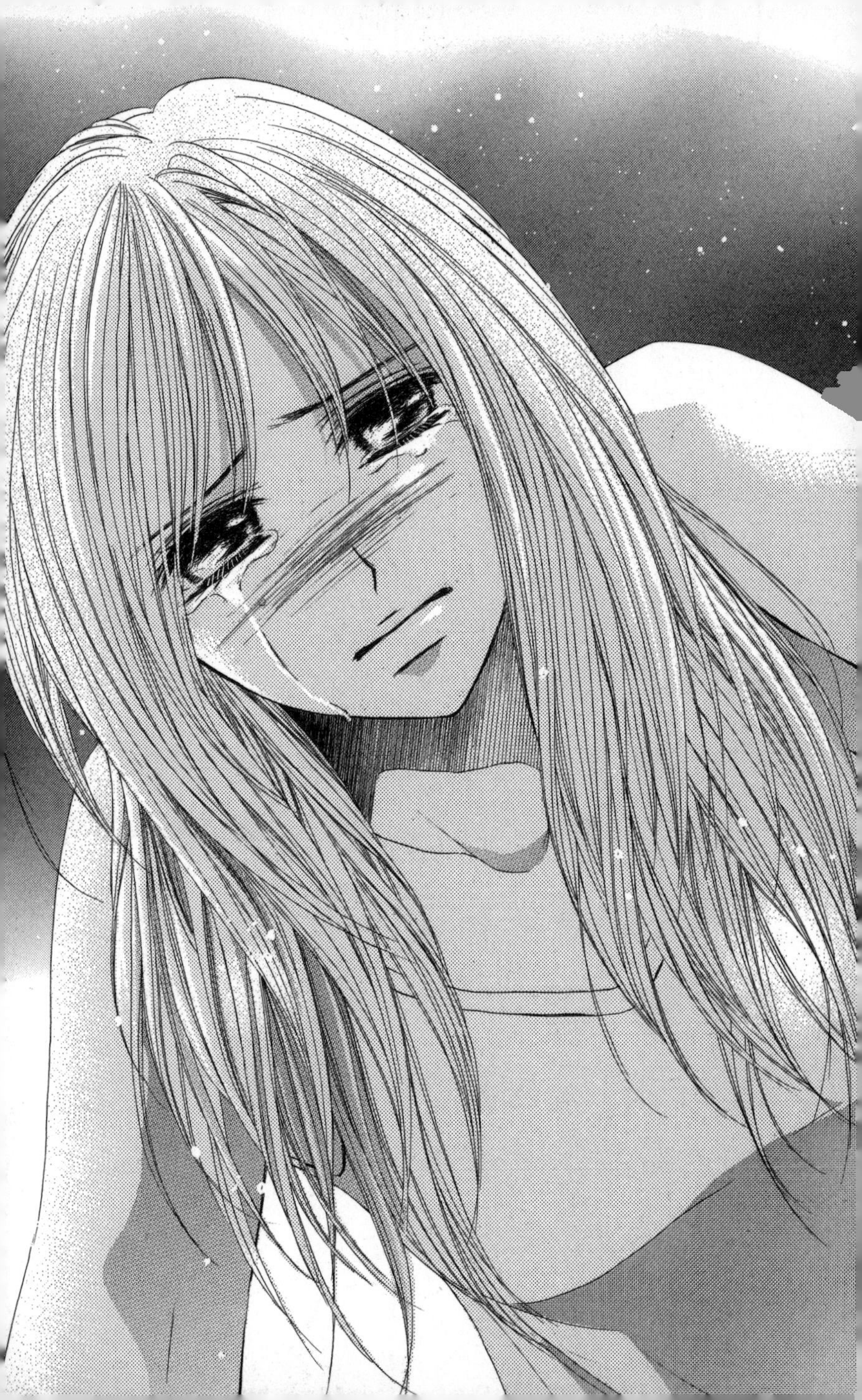

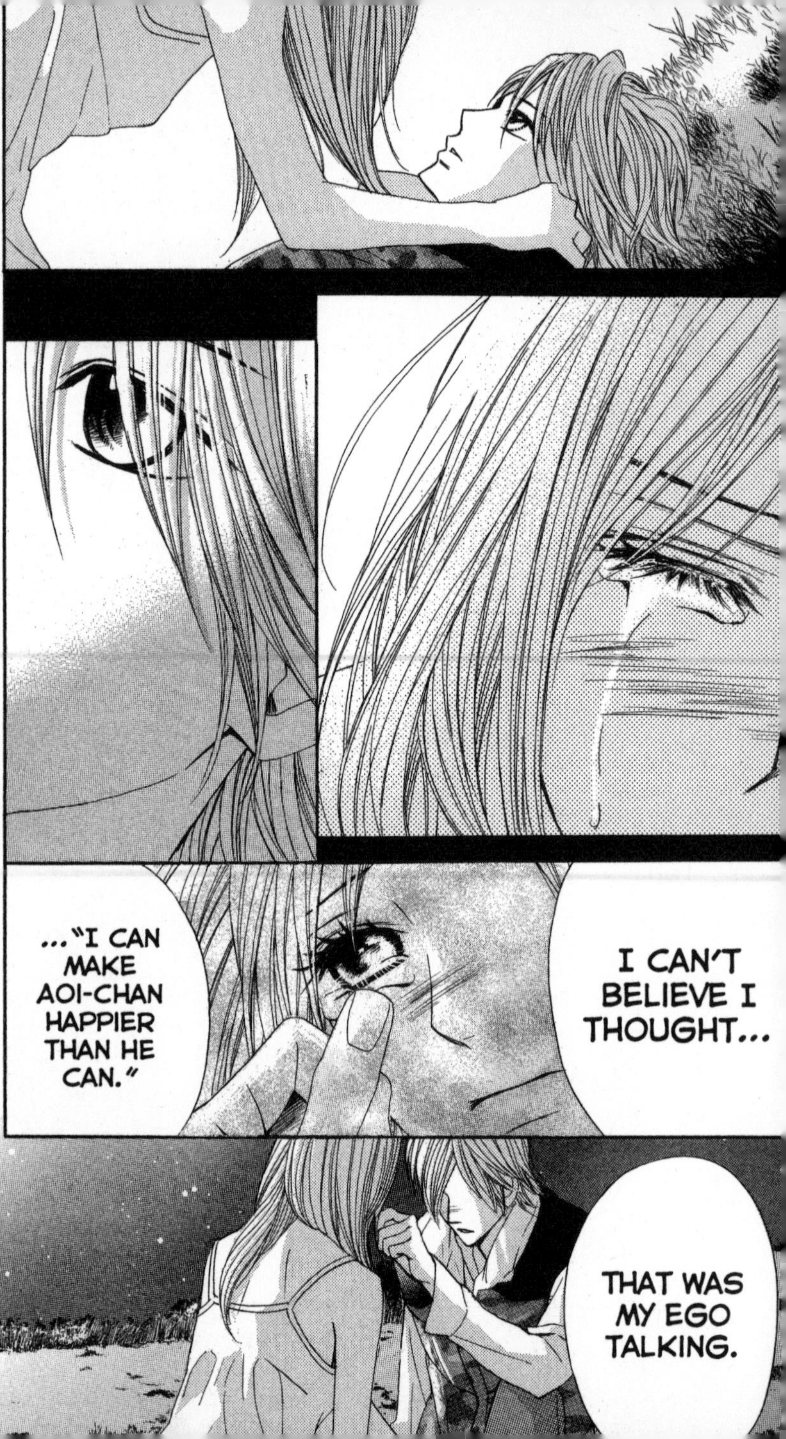
I CAN'T BELIEVE I THOUGHT...
..."I CAN MAKE AOI-CHAN HAPPIER THAN HE CAN."
THAT WAS MY EGO TALKING.

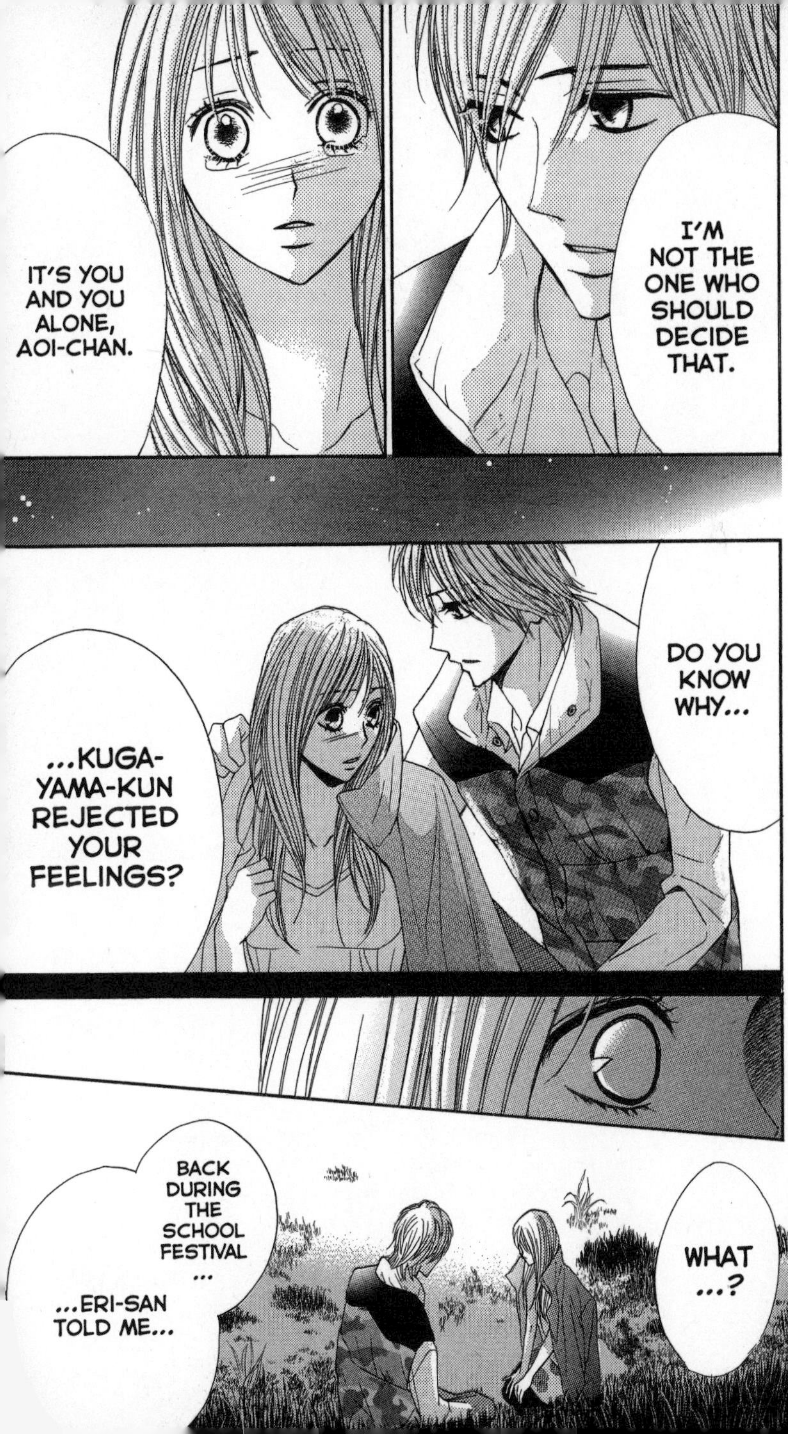
I'M NOT THE ONE WHO SHOULD DECIDE THAT.
IT'S YOU AND YOU ALONE, AOI-CHAN.
DO YOU KNOW WHY...
...KUGA-YAMA-KUN REJECTED YOUR FEELINGS?
WHAT...?
BACK DURING THE SCHOOL FESTIVAL...
...ERI-SAN TOLD ME...

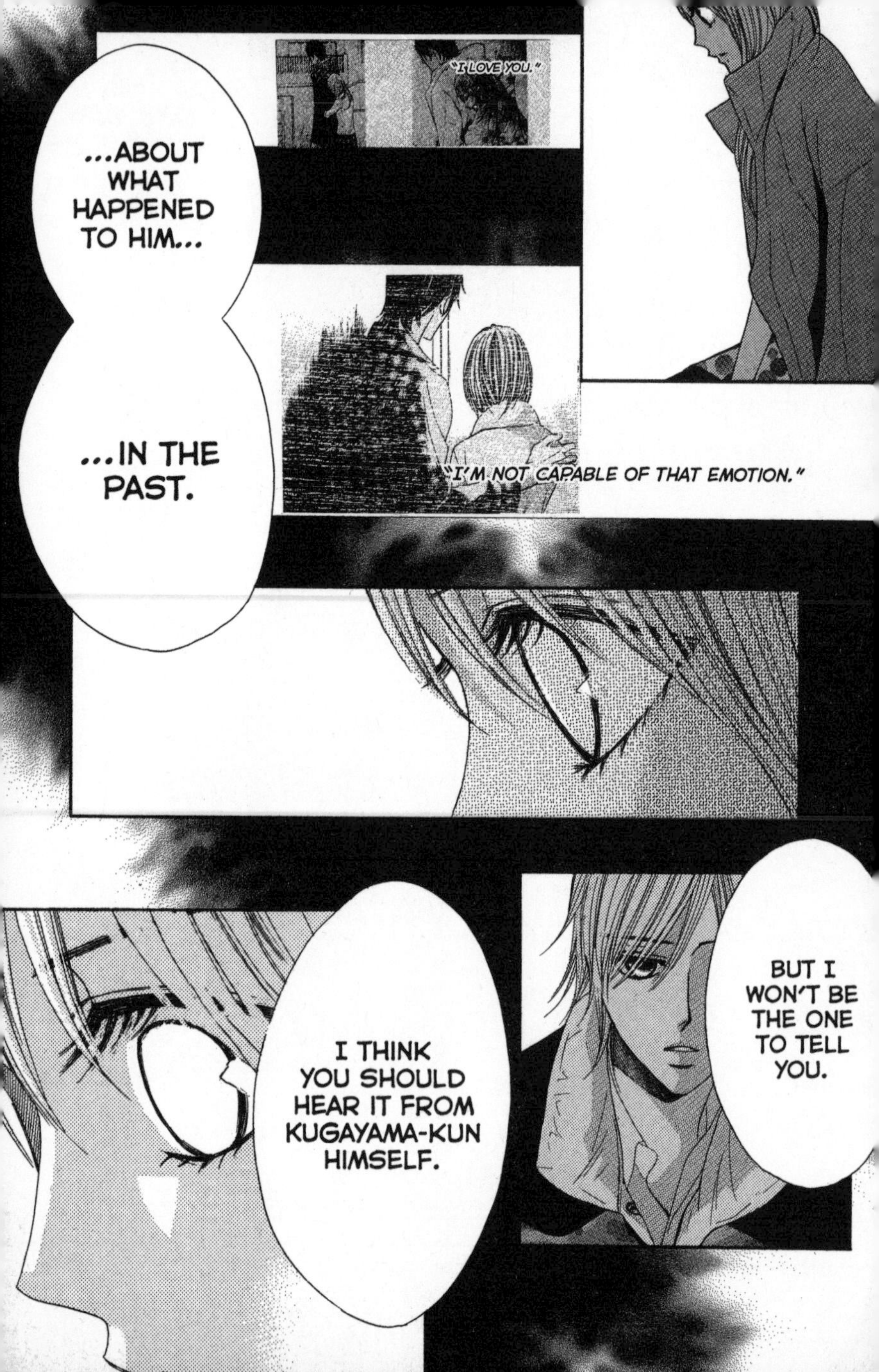

"I LOVE YOU."
...ABOUT WHAT HAPPENED TO HIM...
"I'M NOT CAPABLE OF THAT EMOTION."
...IN THE PAST.
BUT I WON'T BE THE ONE TO TELL YOU.
I THINK YOU SHOULD HEAR IT FROM KUGAYAMA-KUN HIMSELF.

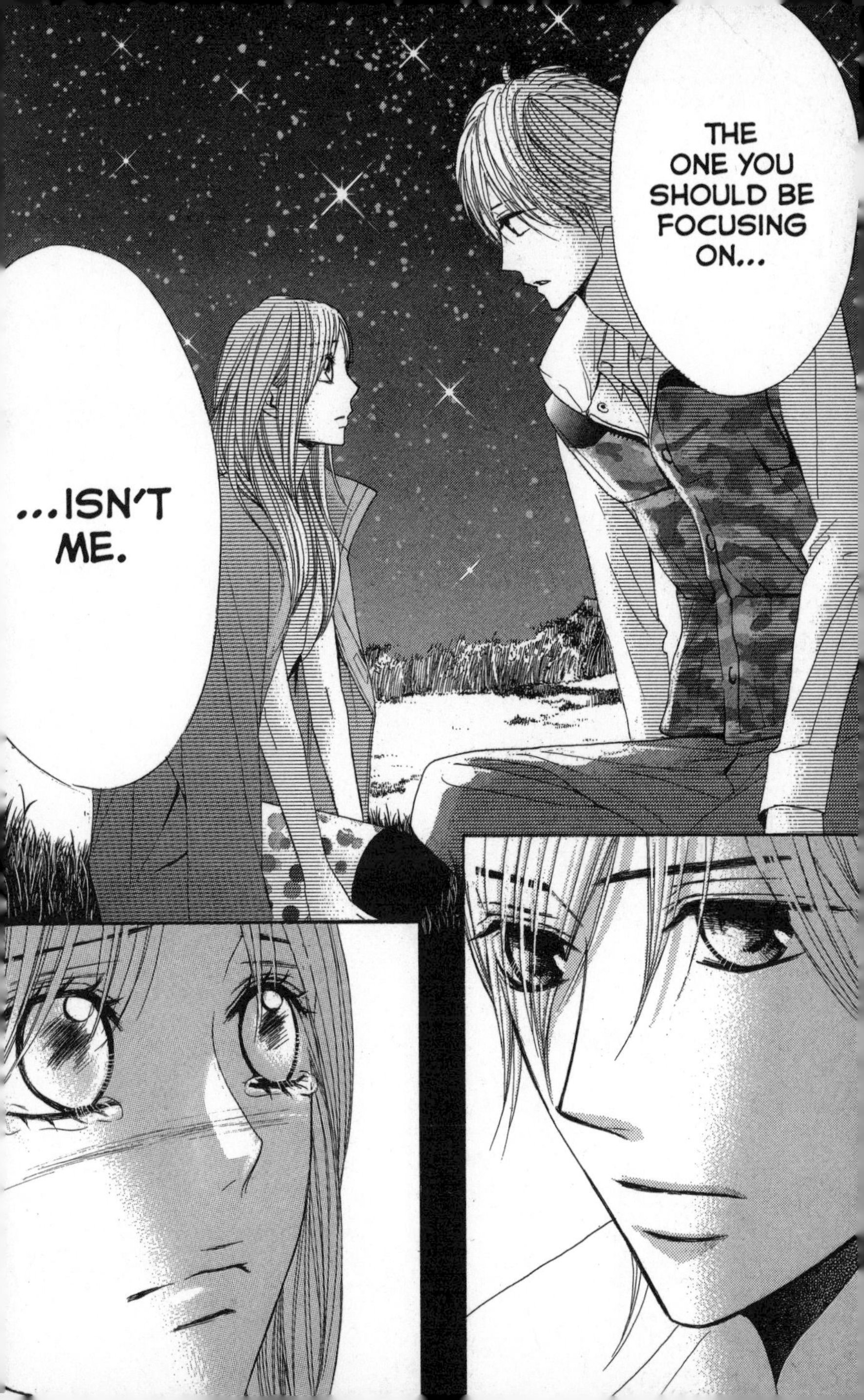
THE ONE YOU SHOULD BE FOCUSING ON...
...ISN'T ME.

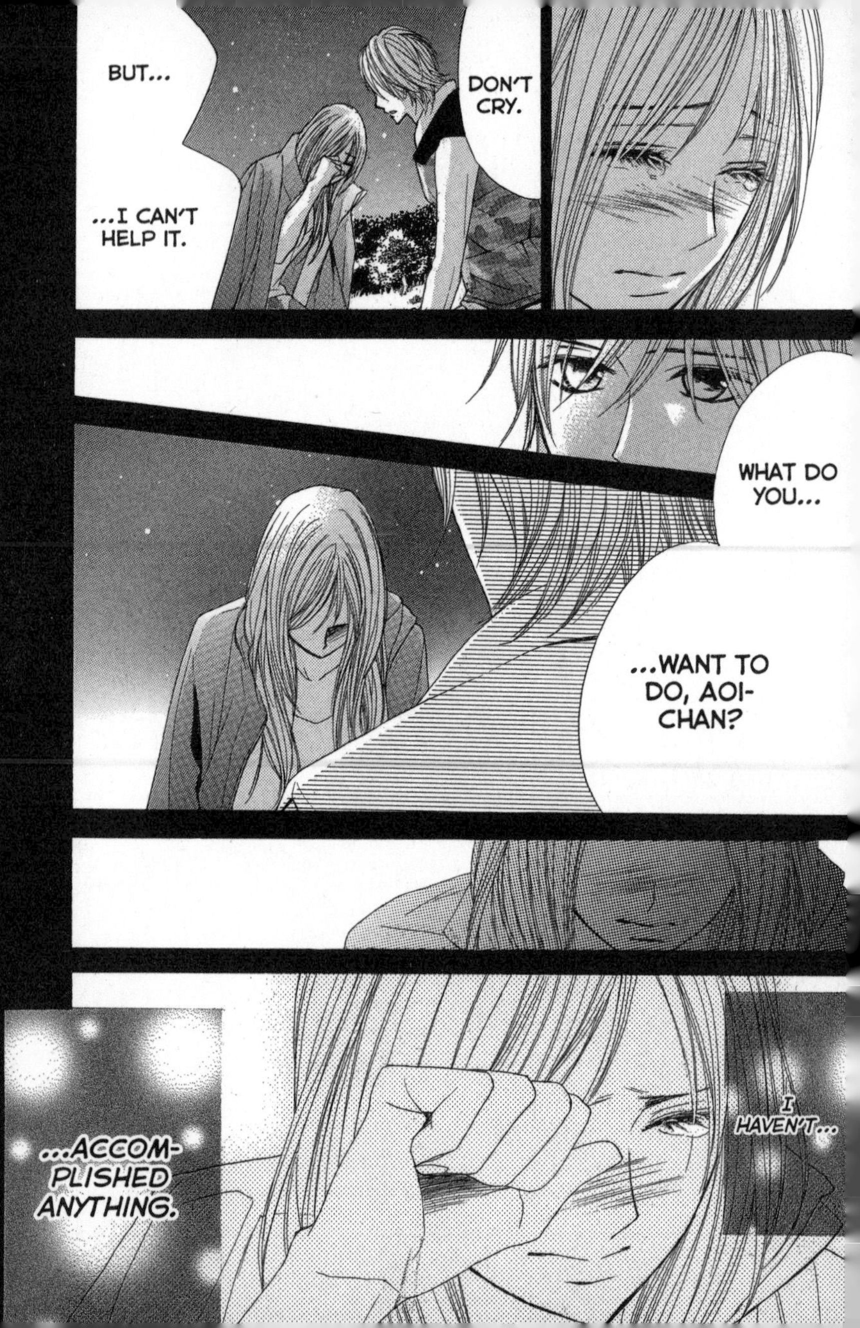
DON'T CRY.
BUT...
...I CAN'T HELP IT.
WHAT DO YOU...
...WANT TO DO, AOI-CHAN?
I HAVEN'T...
...ACCOM-PLISHED ANYTHING.

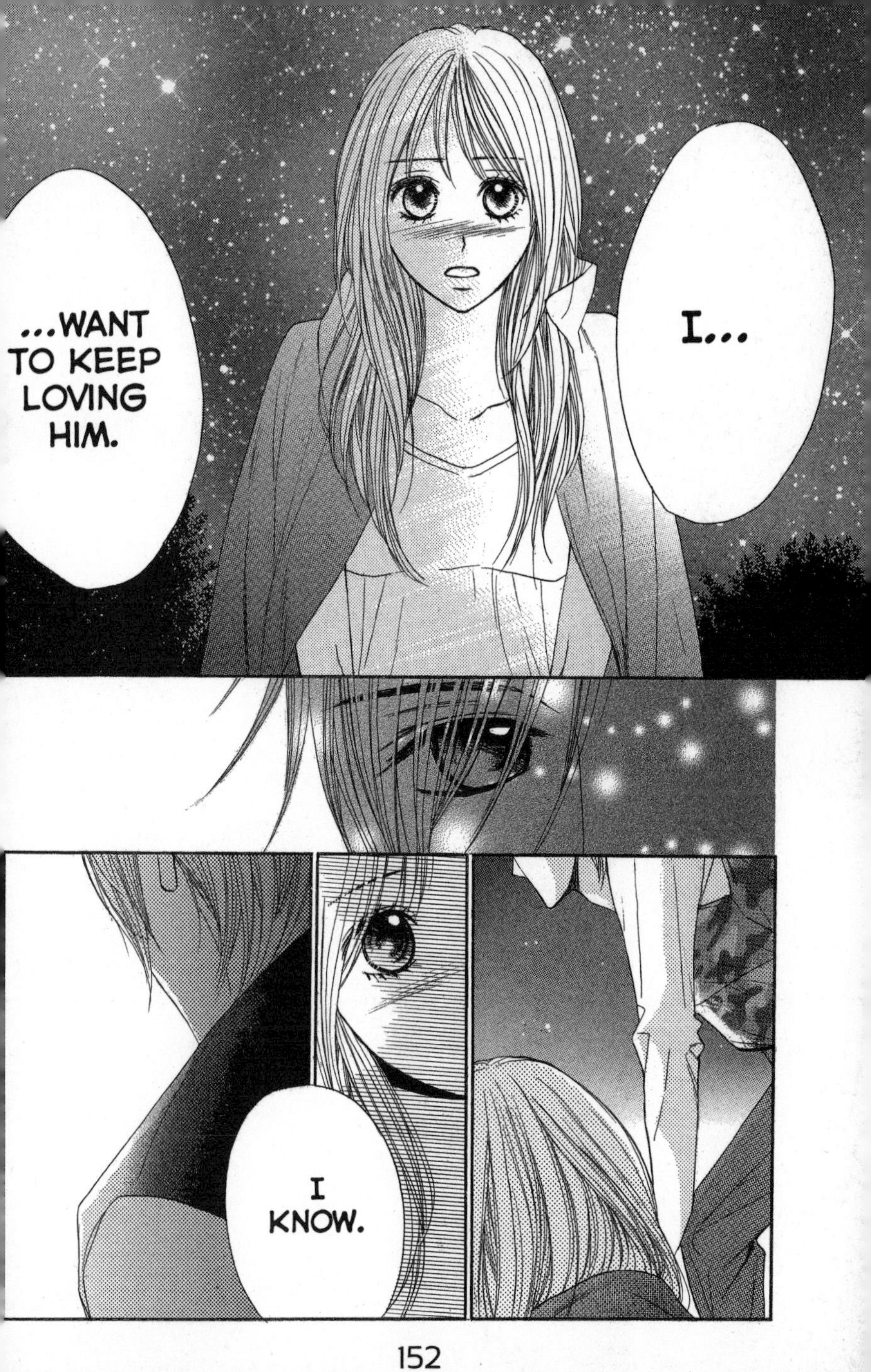
I...
...WANT TO KEEP LOVING HIM.
I KNOW.

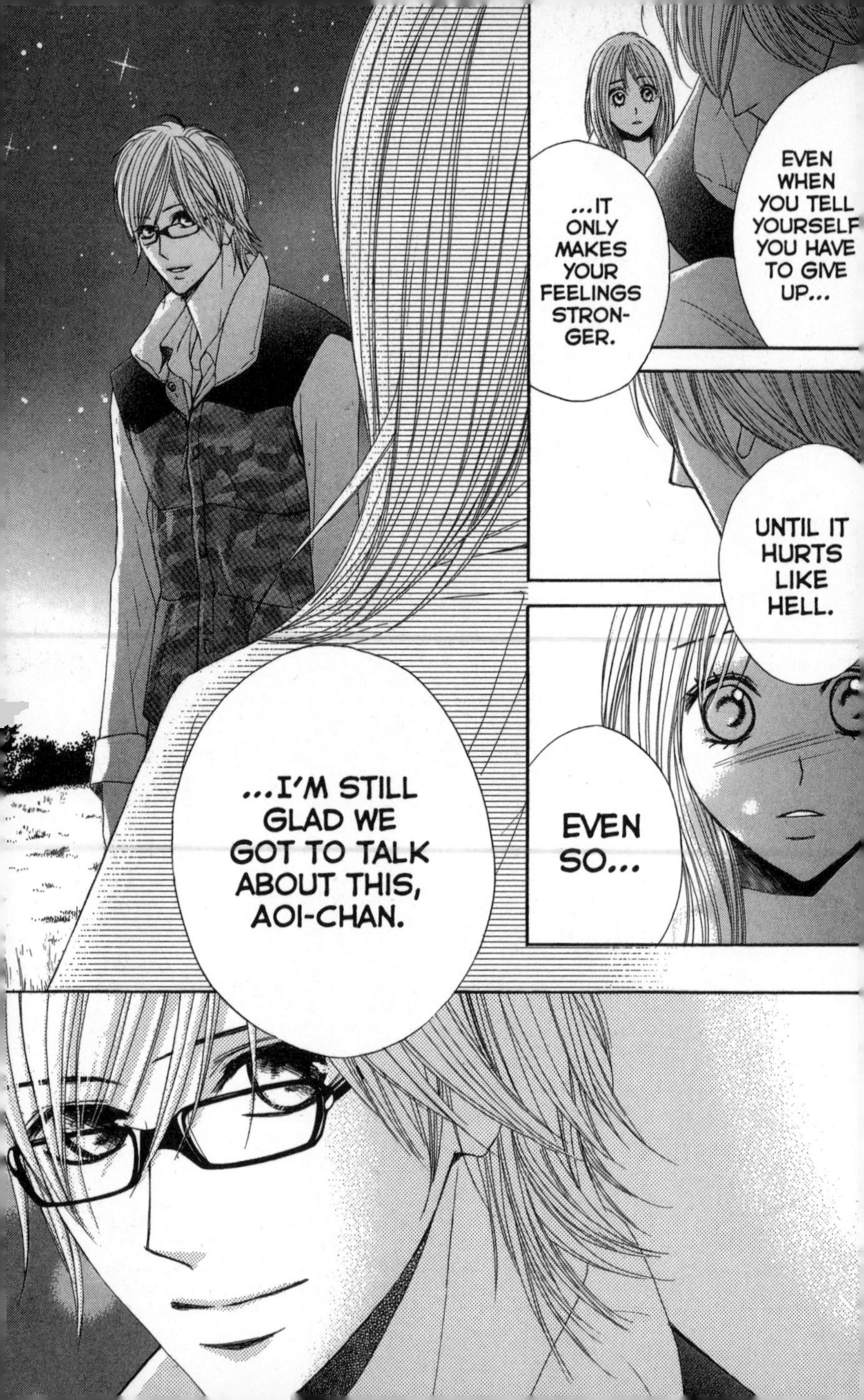
EVEN WHEN YOU TELL YOURSELF YOU HAVE TO GIVE UP...
...IT ONLY MAKES YOUR FEELINGS STRONG-ER.
UNTIL IT HURTS LIKE HELL.
EVEN SO...
...I'M STILL GLAD WE GOT TO TALK ABOUT THIS, AOI-CHAN.

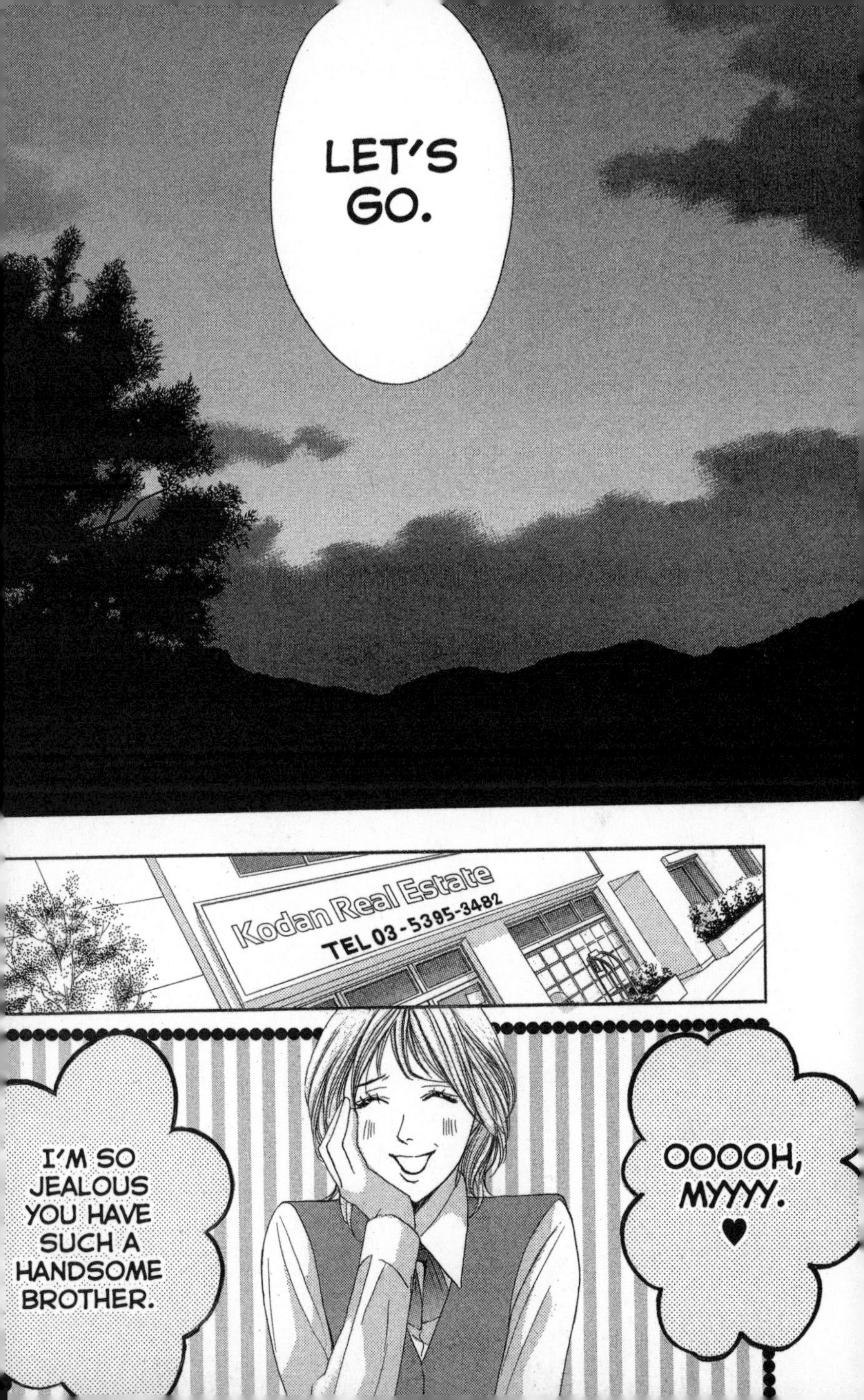
LET'S GO.
Kodan Real Estate
TEL 03-5395-3482
OOOOH, MYYYY. ♥
I'M SO JEALOUS YOU HAVE SUCH A HANDSOME BROTHER.

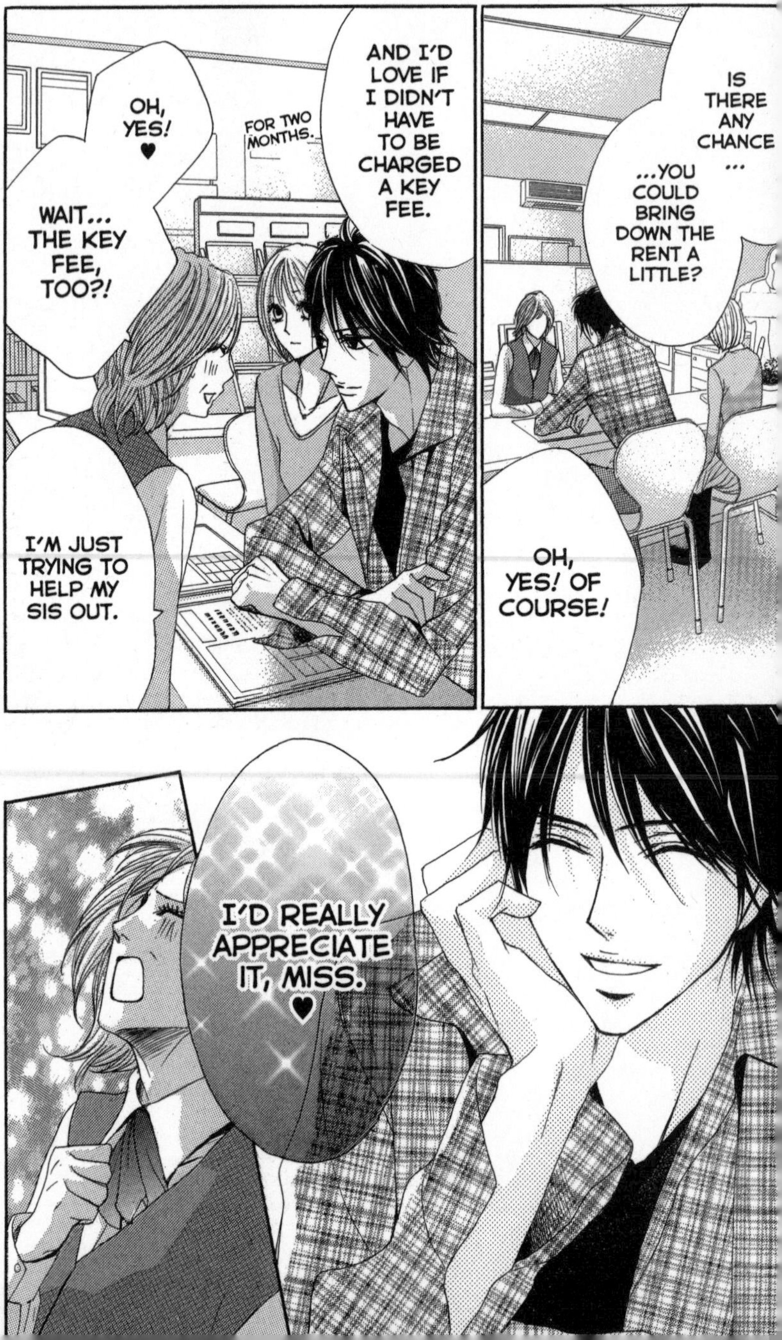
IS THERE ANY CHANCE...
...YOU COULD BRING DOWN THE RENT A LITTLE?
OH, YES! OF COURSE!
AND I'D LOVE IF I DIDN'T HAVE TO BE CHARGED A KEY FEE.
FOR TWO MONTHS.
OH, YES! ♥
WAIT... THE KEY FEE, TOO?!
I'M JUST TRYING TO HELP MY SIS OUT.
I'D REALLY APPRECIATE IT, MISS. ♥

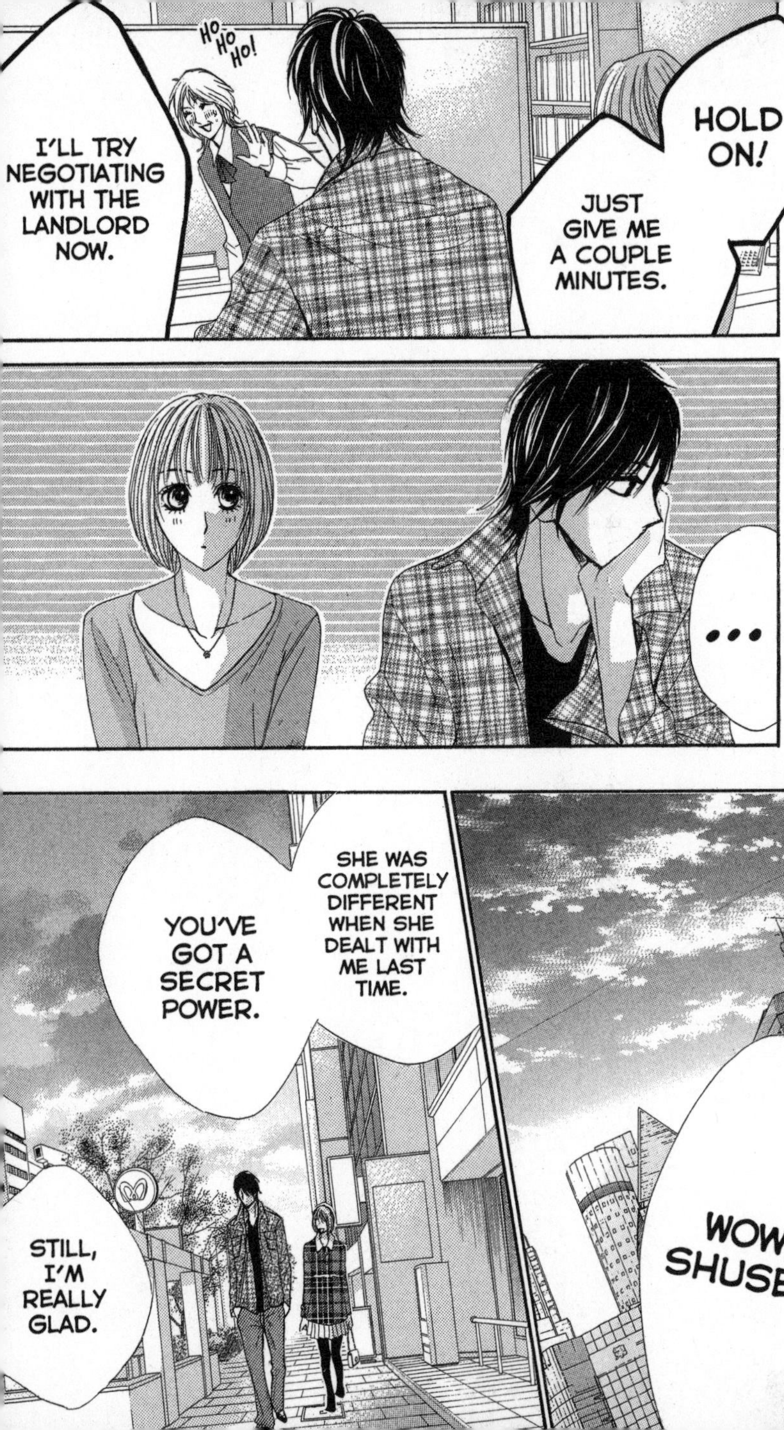
HOLD ON!
JUST GIVE ME A COUPLE MINUTES.
HO HO HO!
I'LL TRY NEGOTIATING WITH THE LANDLORD NOW.
...
WOW, SHUSEI!
SHE WAS COMPLETELY DIFFERENT WHEN SHE DEALT WITH ME LAST TIME.
YOU'VE GOT A SECRET POWER.
STILL, I'M REALLY GLAD.

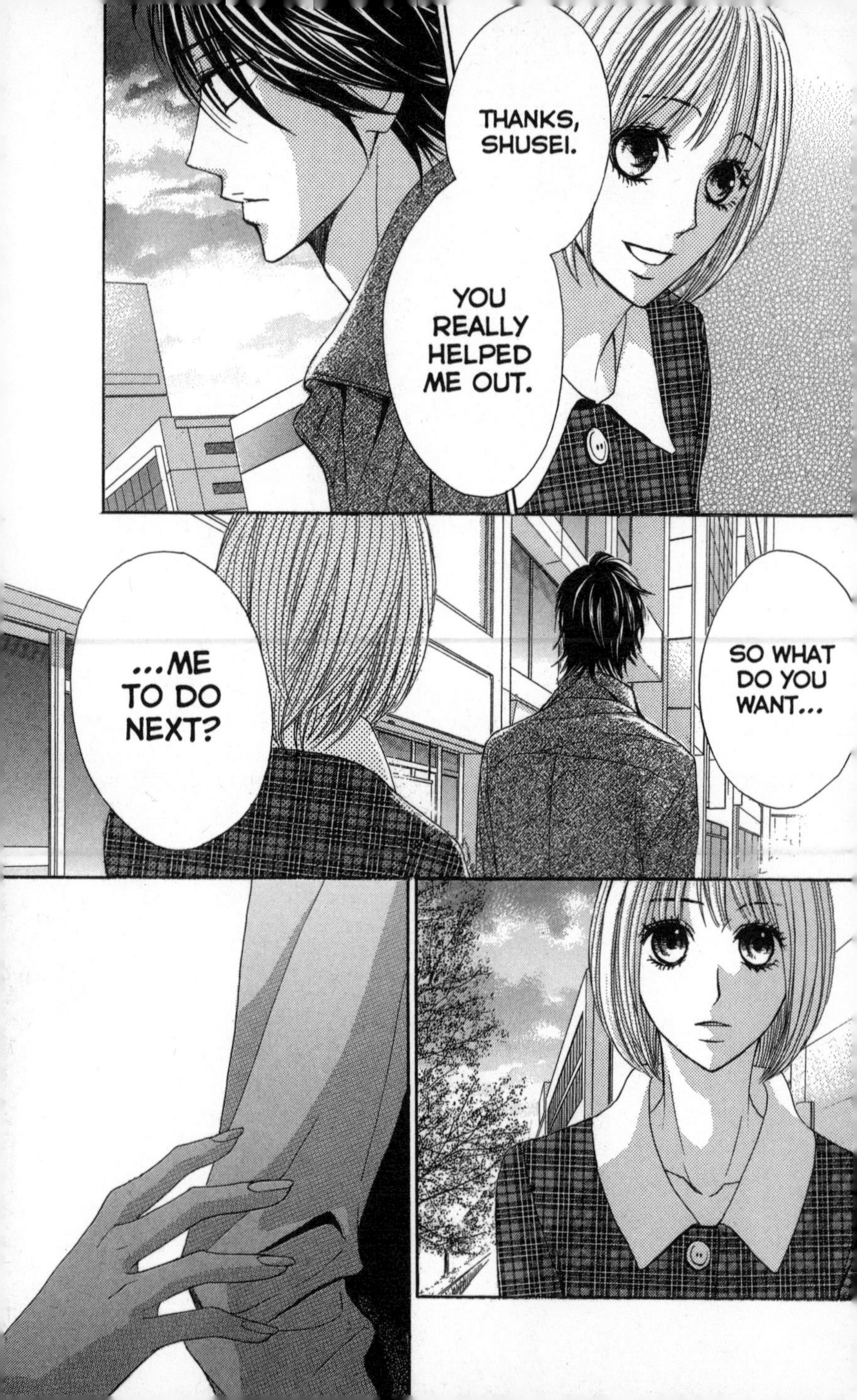
THANKS, SHUSEI.
YOU REALLY HELPED ME OUT.
SO WHAT DO YOU WANT...
...ME TO DO NEXT?

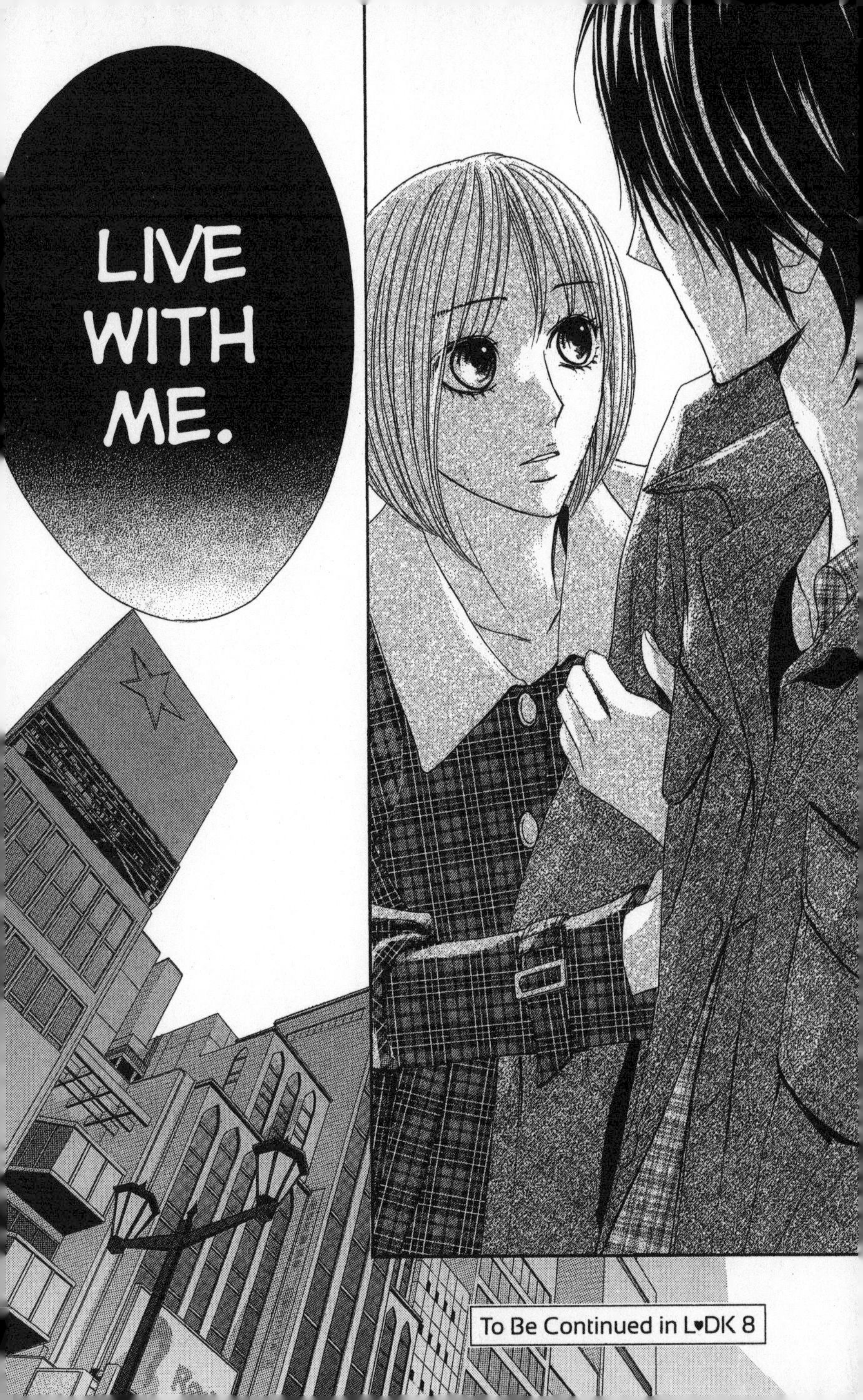

LIVE WITH ME.

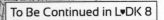

To Be Continued in L♥DK 8

L♥DK

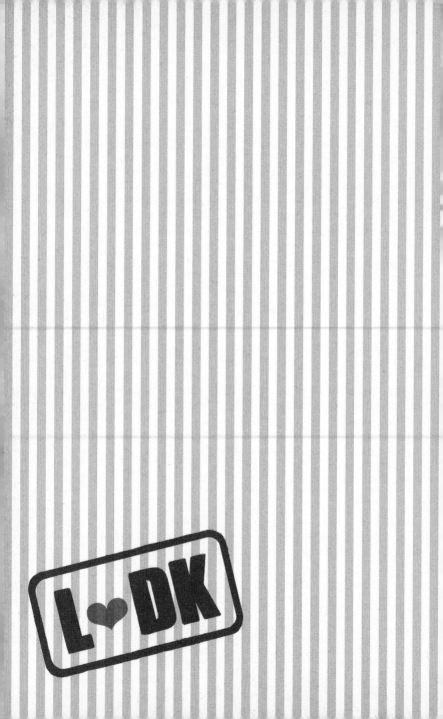

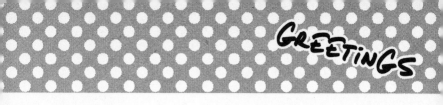

Hello, this is Ayu Watanabe! Thank you for picking up L♥DK Volume 7. We've finally made it to Volume 7! I'm so happy. ♥ In Volume 6, it was a three-company affair between Shueisha, Shogakkan, and Kodansha! So moving!!! It really is thanks to a ton of people that this title is made possible. Before I knew it, it's been two years since the serialization started. And by the time this seventh volume comes out, it'll be August... Time's moving so quickly, I can't even keep up. It's funny because when I was a student, a year didn't feel that long at all... Maybe because it was filled with so many events? When I write in my diary, where day after day I'm working at my desk, it feels like it's nothing but a simple work journal.

Lately, I've been thinking I'd like to get a driver's license for a motorcycle. Even though I can barely drive a car and only have a license in name alone... I want to go on a random trip and let the new landscapes soothe and rejuvenate me. My dream is to ride a Harley, but since I'm so short, it'd probably be hard to handle. The Sportster model I want to ride is close to 260 kilos (approx. 573 lbs) in weight. That's close to how much a sumo wrestler weighs! I'd be absolutely crushed by it. In any case, for now I'll stick to gazing at the catalogs and dreaming.

So, going back to the story, at last the more frightening developments of earlier are drawing to an end. That was long...! It was a route I avoided deep down and couldn't travel, so it took quite a bit of resolution to urge myself to keep drawing. It felt like Aoi always had the most painful looks on her face, which resulted in my shoulders aching while I had to draw it. I really really appreciate all you readers who have been watching over me during this endeavor. Your letters of encouragement always bring a smile to my face. I believe the usual vibe of the story will come back starting in the next volume, so I hope you'll join me for that then.

Well, I'll be praying to see you all again in volume 8...!

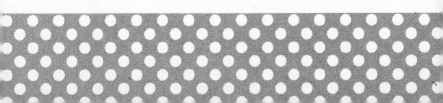

special thanks

K.Hamano
N.Imai
S.Sato
Y.Negishi
I.Kozakura

my family
my friends

M.Morita
A.Ichikawa
A.Yamamoto

AND YOU

Ayu Watanabe
July.2011

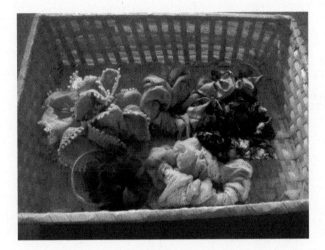

Everyday Essentials, Item 7
Scrunchies

My hair is always pulled back while
I'm working on my storyboards.
The reason I have so many of
these isn't because I'm a collector
or anything. It's because I'm always
misplacing them.

Translation Notes

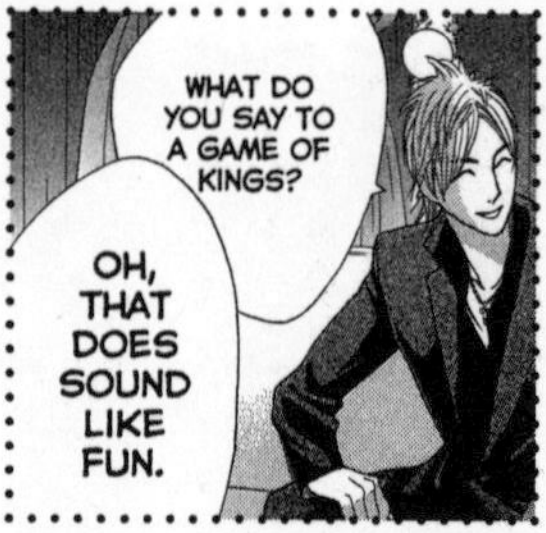
WHAT DO YOU SAY TO A GAME OF KINGS?
OH, THAT DOES SOUND LIKE FUN.

Game of Kings, page 19
The Japanese equivalent of "Truth or Dare" with a little difference. One person is selected to be the "King" (or if it's a female, the "Queen") who can then dictate what the other players in the game have to do.

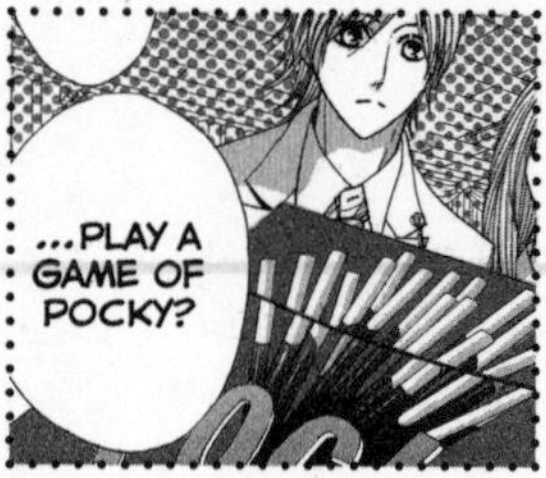
...PLAY A GAME OF POCKY?

Pocky game, page 20
Two people have to eat a Pocky stick from either end, and whoever breaks away first, loses. The game is more or less intended to make (or let) participants kiss, like in the spaghetti scene from *Lady and the Tramp*.

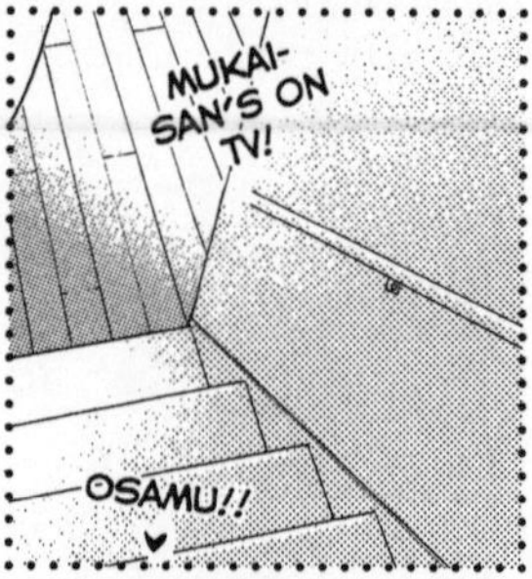
MUKAI-SAN'S ON TV!
OSAMU!!

Osamu Mukai, page 58
A handsome Japanese actor who appeared in TV shows and movies, some of which are based off of famous manga (like *Beck* and *Paradise Kiss*).

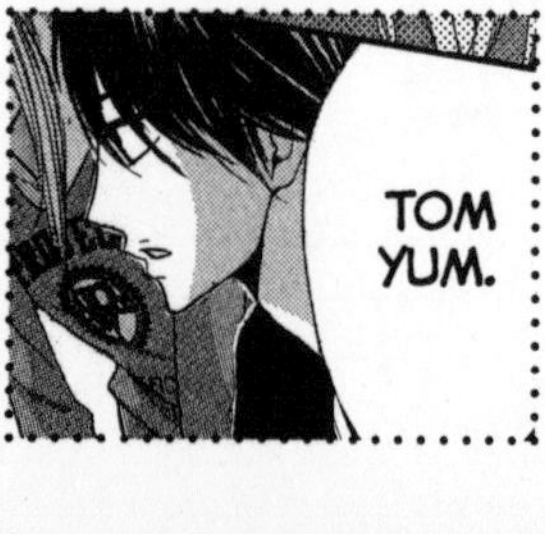
TOM YUM.

Tom yum, page 88
A Thai soup that typically features shrimp.

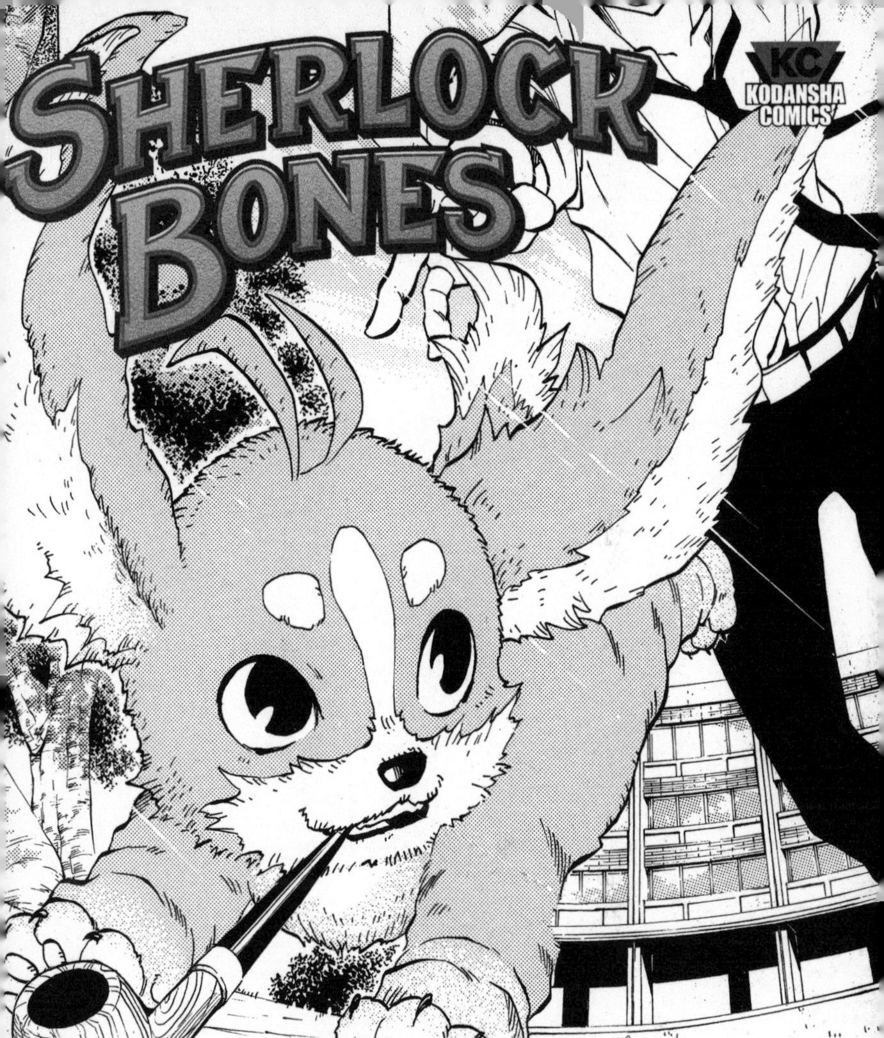

SHERLOCK BONES

KC KODANSHA COMICS

DEDUCTIVE DOG DETECTIVE

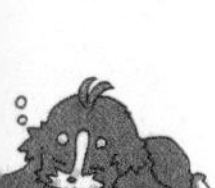

When Takeru adopts a new pet, he's in for a surprise—the dog is none other than the reincarnation of Sherlock Holmes. With no one else able to communicate with Holmes, Takeru is roped into becoming Sherdog's assistant, John Watson. Using his sleuthing skills, Holmes uncovers clues to solve the trickiest crimes. 🐾

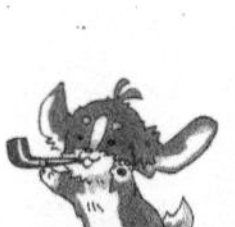

DON'T MISS THE MOST ACCLAIMED ACTION MANGA OF 2013!

"Gripping doesn't begin to describe Vinland Saga. 5 stars."
—ICv2

"Deeply engrossing... If you have any interest at all in Vikings, the Medieval period, or pirates, this is not a series you want to miss."
—Anime News Network

"The art is gorgeous, a combination of beautiful cartooning and realistic backgrounds. Yukimura is also a master of pacing, both in frenetic battle scenes and charged emotional moments."
—Faith Erin Hicks, *Friends With Boys*

"For those who love Berserk, you'll love this too... Worth the long wait."
—A Case Suitable for Treatment

"It will be impossible to stop watching this story unfold."
—Japan Media Arts Awards jury

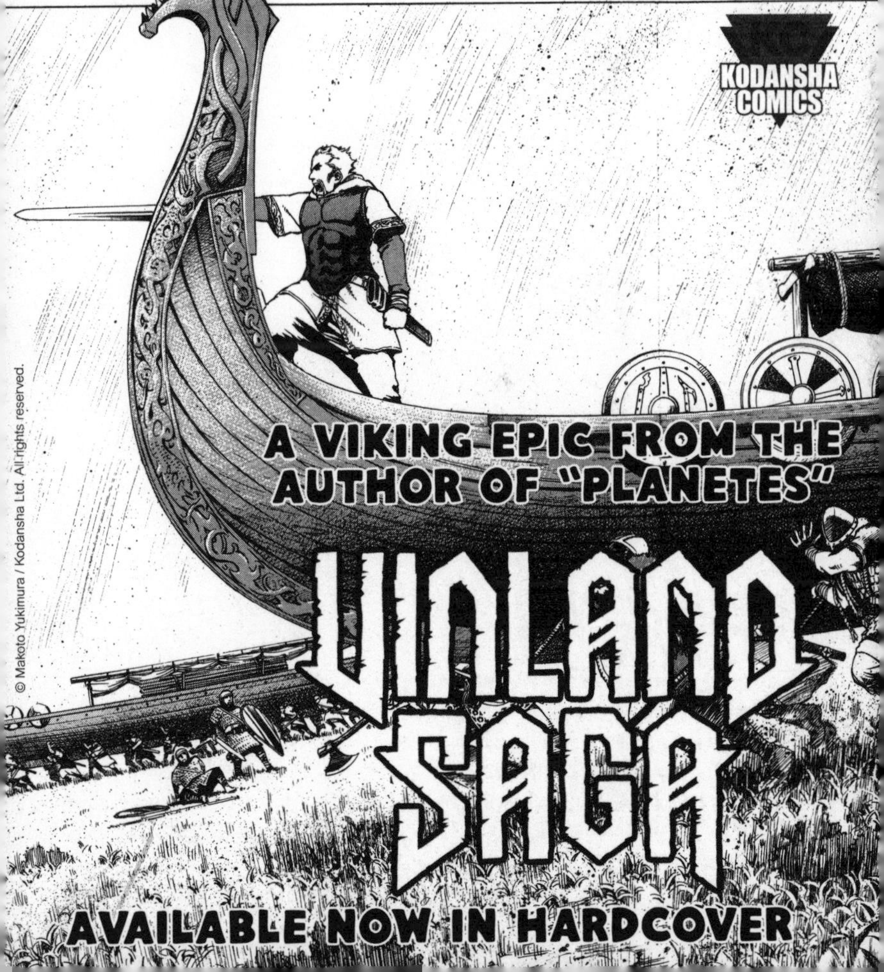
KODANSHA COMICS
A VIKING EPIC FROM THE AUTHOR OF "PLANETES"
VINLAND SAGA
AVAILABLE NOW IN HARDCOVER
© Makoto Yukimura / Kodansha Ltd. All rights reserved.

INUYASHIKI

A superhero like none you've ever seen, from the creator of "Gantz"!

ICHIRO INUYASHIKI IS DOWN ON HIS LUCK. HE LOOKS MUCH OLDER THAN HIS 58 YEARS, HIS CHILDREN DESPISE HIM, AND HIS WIFE THINKS HE'S A USELESS COWARD. SO WHEN HE'S DIAGNOSED WITH STOMACH CANCER AND GIVEN THREE MONTHS TO LIVE, IT SEEMS THE ONLY ONE WHO'LL MISS HIM IS HIS DOG.

THEN A BLINDING LIGHT FILLS THE SKY, AND THE OLD MAN IS KILLED... ONLY TO WAKE UP LATER IN A BODY HE ALMOST RECOGNIZES AS HIS OWN. CAN IT BE THAT ICHIRO INUYASHIKI IS NO LONGER HUMAN?

COMES IN EXTRA-LARGE EDITIONS WITH COLOR PAGES!

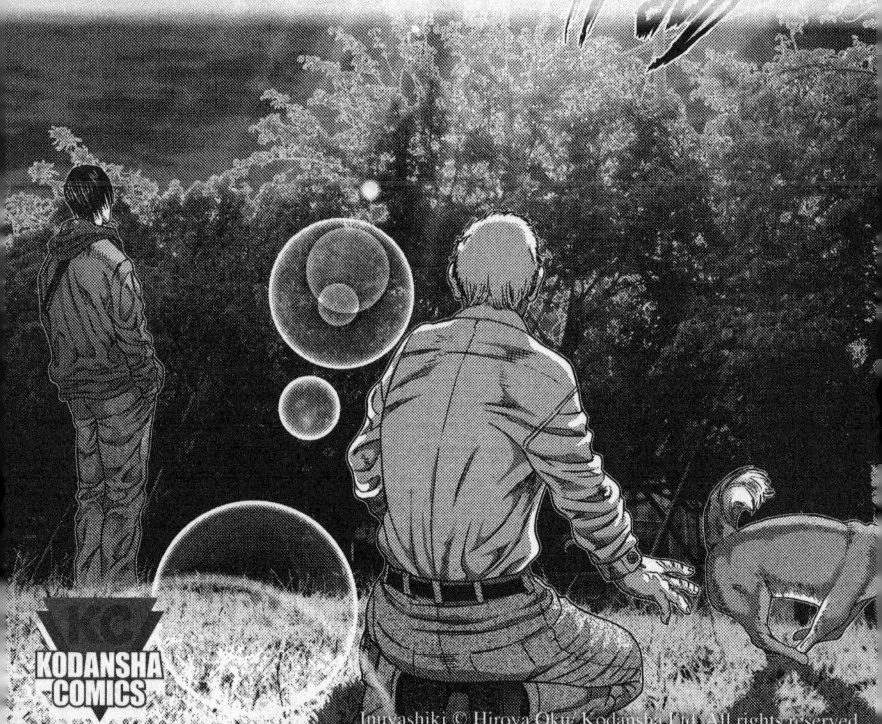
KC
KODANSHA COMICS

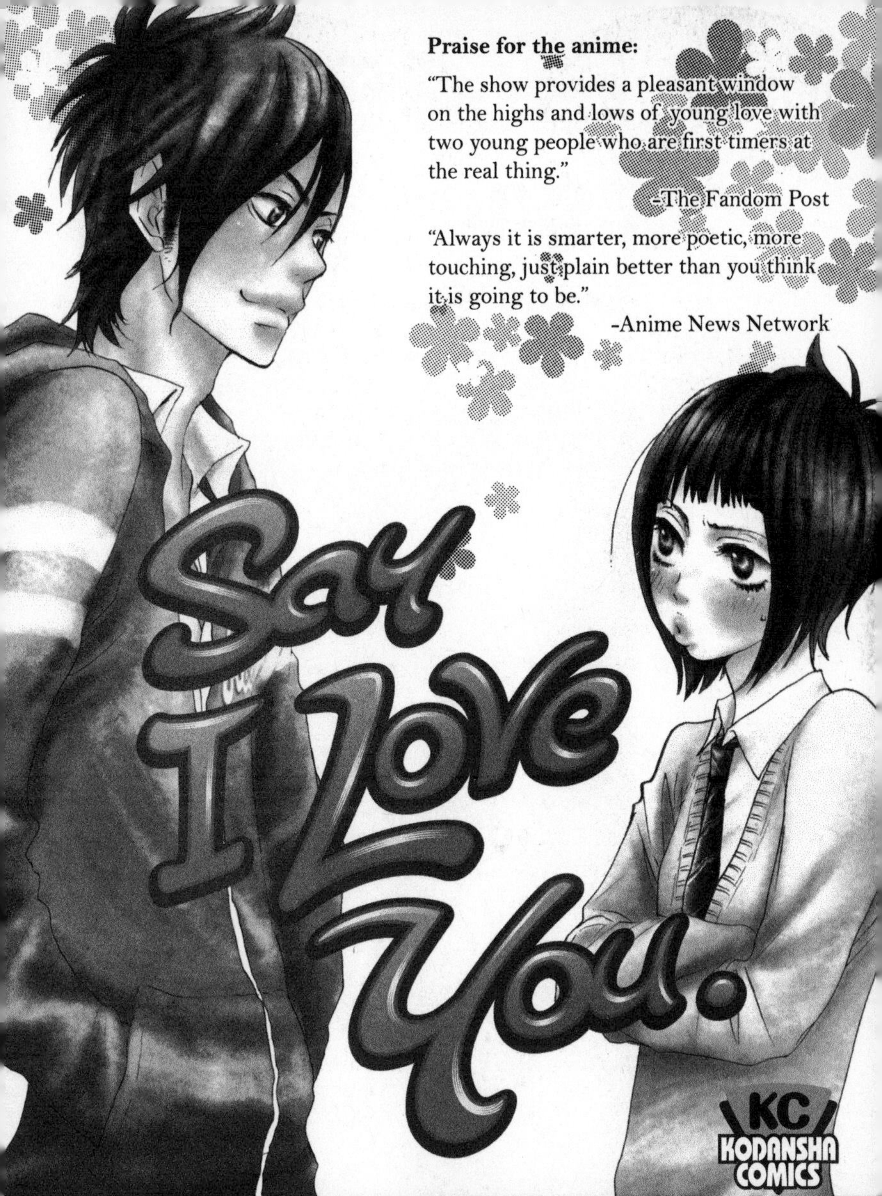

SAY I LOVE YOU.

Mei Tachibana has no friends — and says she doesn't need them!

But everything changes when she accidentally roundhouse kicks the most popular boy in school! However, Yamato Kurosawa isn't angry in the slightest—in fact, he thinks his ordinary life could use an unusual girl like Mei. But winning Mei's trust will be a tough task. How long will she refuse to say, "I love you"?

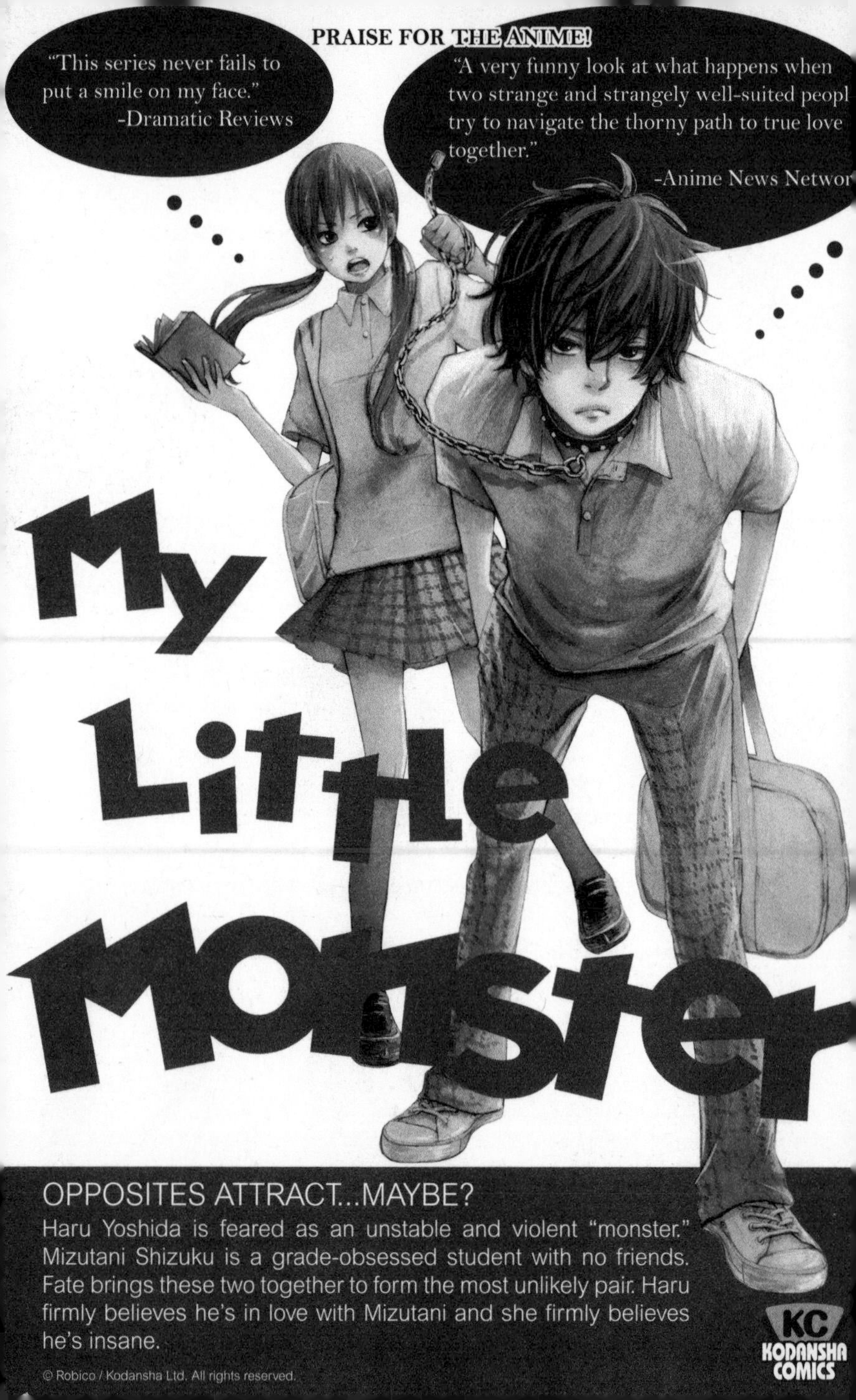
PRAISE FOR THE ANIME!
"This series never fails to put a smile on my face." -Dramatic Reviews
"A very funny look at what happens when two strange and strangely well-suited peopl try to navigate the thorny path to true love together." -Anime News Networ
My Little Monster
OPPOSITES ATTRACT...MAYBE?
Haru Yoshida is feared as an unstable and violent "monster." Mizutani Shizuku is a grade-obsessed student with no friends. Fate brings these two together to form the most unlikely pair. Haru firmly believes he's in love with Mizutani and she firmly believes he's insane.
© Robico / Kodansha Ltd. All rights reserved.
KC KODANSHA COMICS

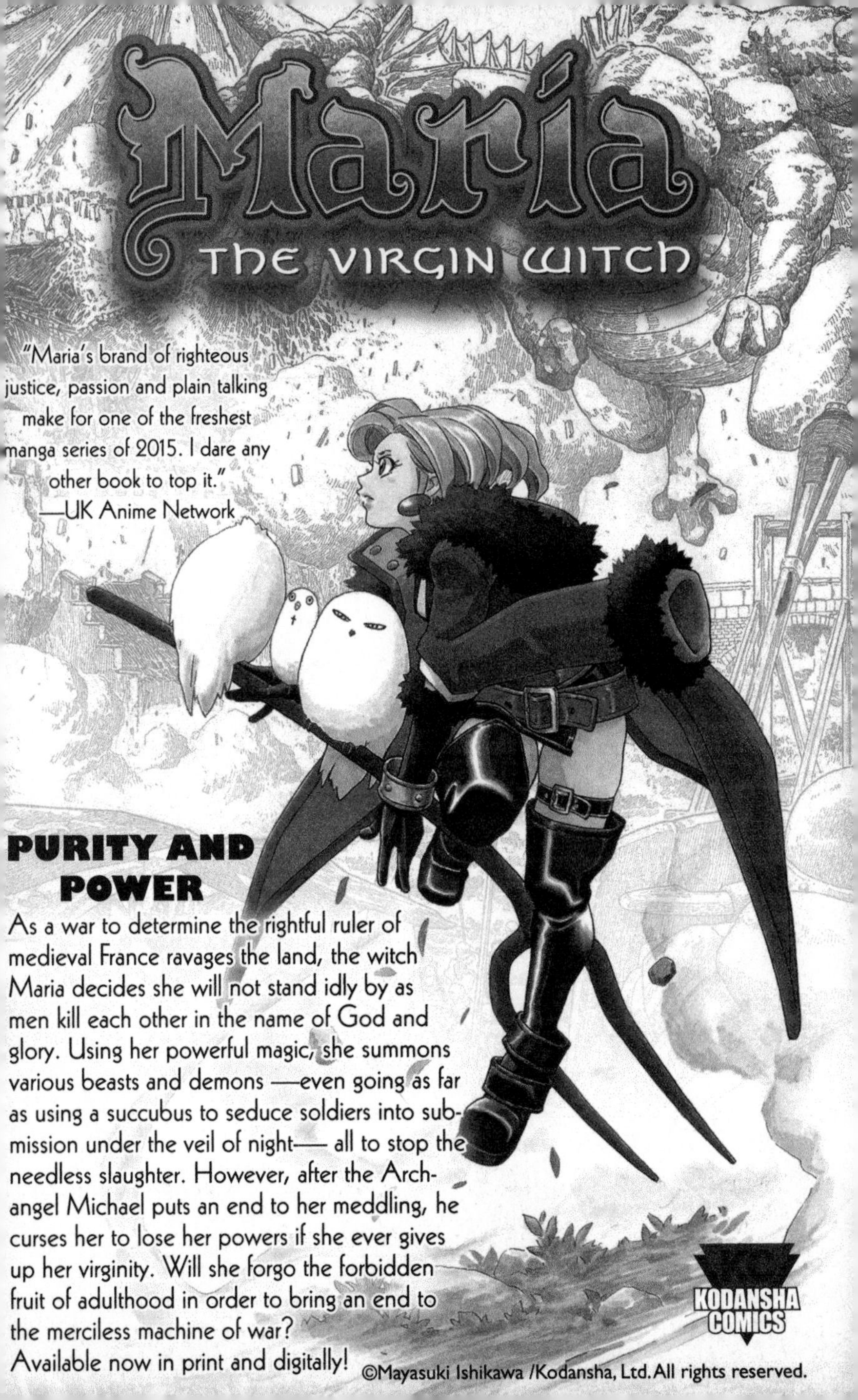
Maria
THE VIRGIN WITCH
"Maria's brand of righteous justice, passion and plain talking make for one of the freshest manga series of 2015. I dare any other book to top it."
—UK Anime Network
PURITY AND POWER
As a war to determine the rightful ruler of medieval France ravages the land, the witch Maria decides she will not stand idly by as men kill each other in the name of God and glory. Using her powerful magic, she summons various beasts and demons —even going as far as using a succubus to seduce soldiers into submission under the veil of night— all to stop the needless slaughter. However, after the Archangel Michael puts an end to her meddling, he curses her to lose her powers if she ever gives up her virginity. Will she forgo the forbidden fruit of adulthood in order to bring an end to the merciless machine of war?
Available now in print and digitally!
KODANSHA COMICS
©Mayasuki Ishikawa /Kodansha, Ltd. All rights reserved.

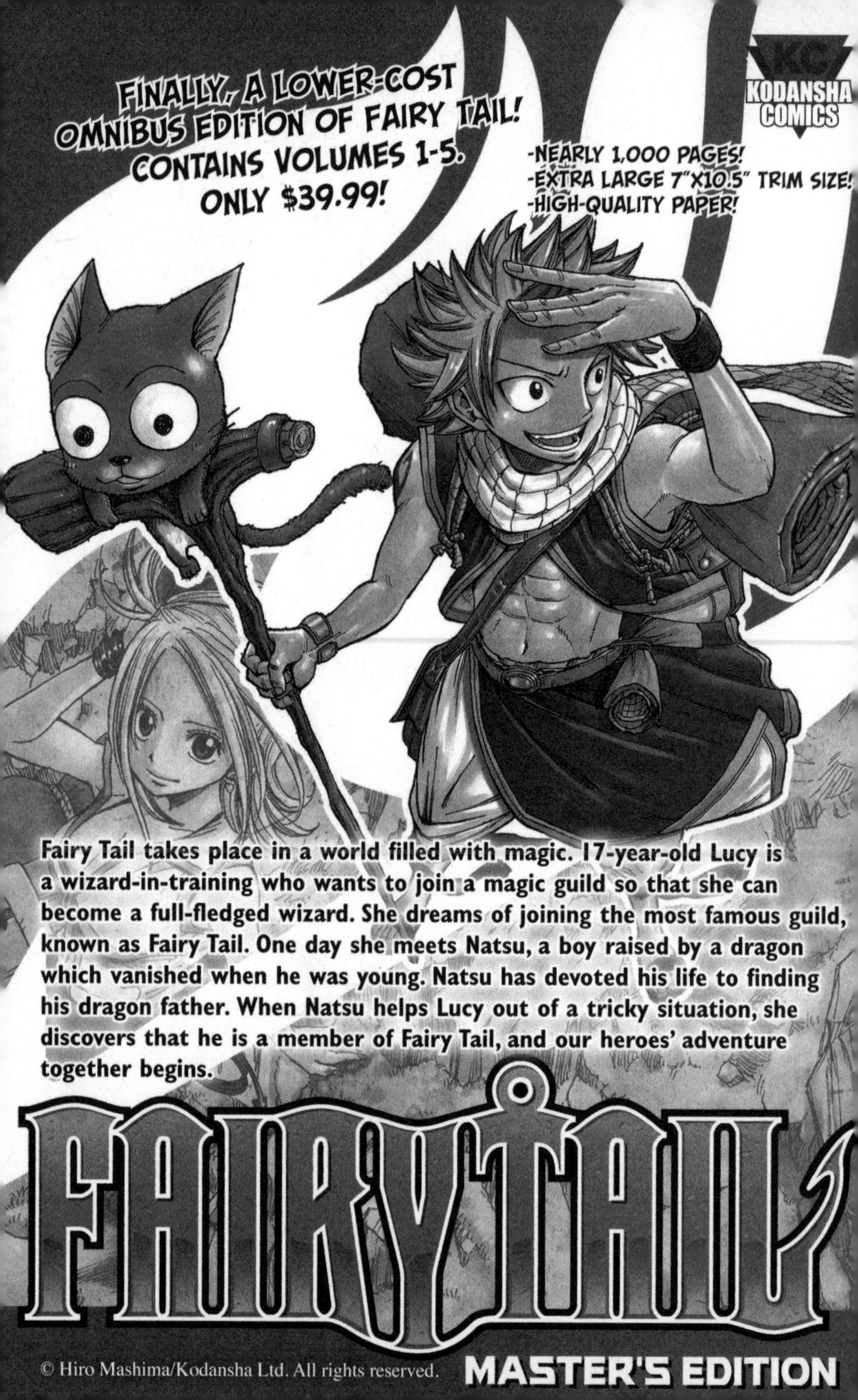
KC
KODANSHA COMICS
FINALLY, A LOWER-COST OMNIBUS EDITION OF FAIRY TAIL!
CONTAINS VOLUMES 1-5.
ONLY $39.99!
-NEARLY 1,000 PAGES!
-EXTRA LARGE 7"X10.5" TRIM SIZE!
-HIGH-QUALITY PAPER!
Fairy Tail takes place in a world filled with magic. 17-year-old Lucy is a wizard-in-training who wants to join a magic guild so that she can become a full-fledged wizard. She dreams of joining the most famous guild, known as Fairy Tail. One day she meets Natsu, a boy raised by a dragon which vanished when he was young. Natsu has devoted his life to finding his dragon father. When Natsu helps Lucy out of a tricky situation, she discovers that he is a member of Fairy Tail, and our heroes' adventure together begins.
FAIRY TAIL
© Hiro Mashima/Kodansha Ltd. All rights reserved.
MASTER'S EDITION

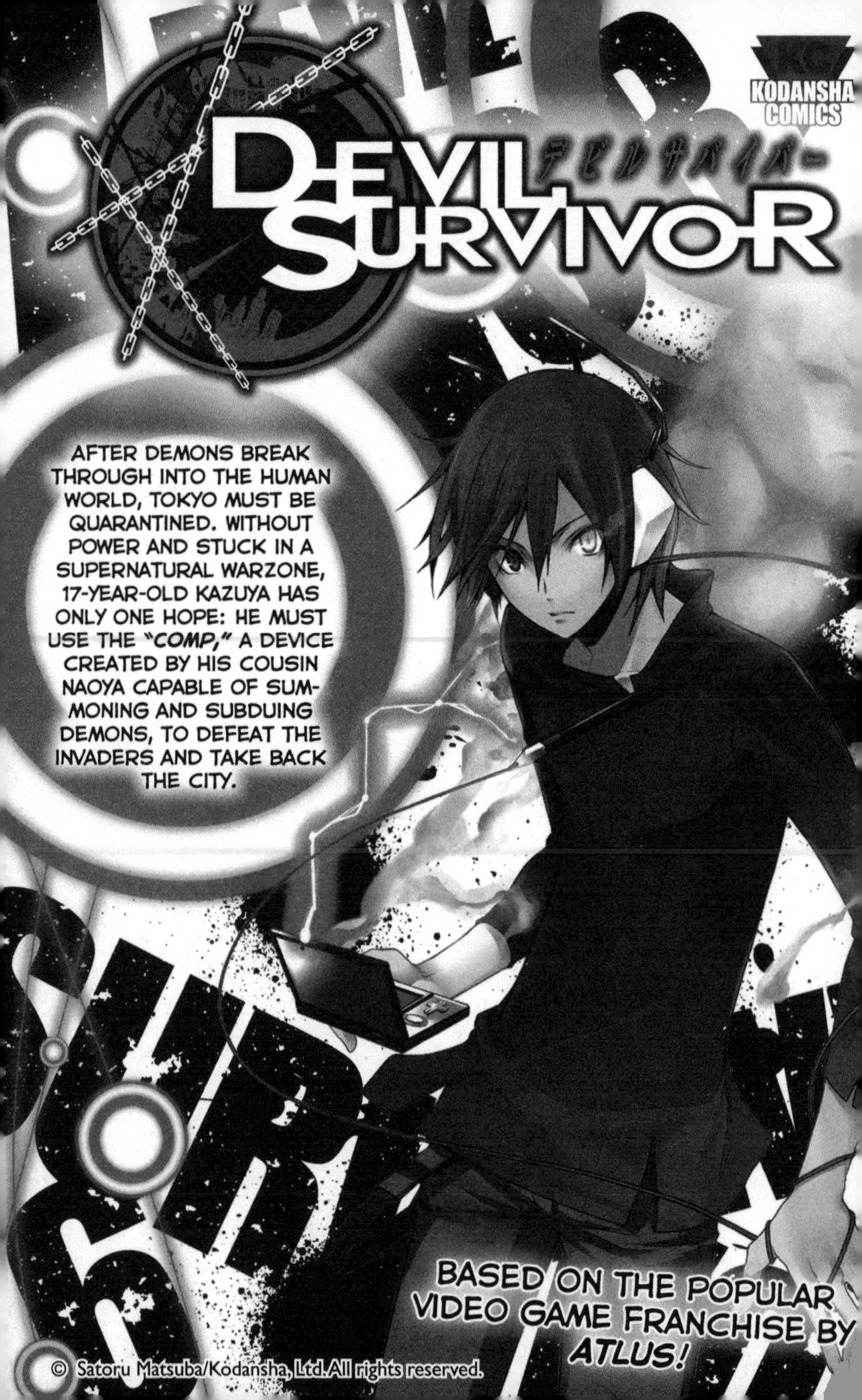
KODANSHA COMICS
DEVIL SURVIVOR
デビルサバイバー
AFTER DEMONS BREAK THROUGH INTO THE HUMAN WORLD, TOKYO MUST BE QUARANTINED. WITHOUT POWER AND STUCK IN A SUPERNATURAL WARZONE, 17-YEAR-OLD KAZUYA HAS ONLY ONE HOPE: HE MUST USE THE "COMP," A DEVICE CREATED BY HIS COUSIN NAOYA CAPABLE OF SUMMONING AND SUBDUING DEMONS, TO DEFEAT THE INVADERS AND TAKE BACK THE CITY.
BASED ON THE POPULAR VIDEO GAME FRANCHISE BY ATLUS!
© Satoru Matsuba/Kodansha, Ltd. All rights reserved.

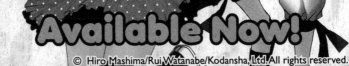

LDK volume 7 is a work of fiction. Names, characters, places, and incidents are the products of the author's imagination or are used fictitiously. Any resemblance to actual events, locales, or persons, living or dead, is entirely coincidental.

A Kodansha Comics Trade Paperback Original.

Published in the United States by Kodansha Comics, an imprint of Kodansha USA Publishing, LLC, New York.

Publication rights for this English edition arranged through Kodansha Ltd., Tokyo.

First published in Japan in 2011 by Kodansha Ltd., Tokyo, as *L♡DK*, volume 7.

ISBN 978-1-63236-160-8

Printed in the United States of America.

www.kodanshacomics.com

9 8 7 6 5 4 3 2 1

Translation: Christine Dashiell
Lettering: Sara Linsley
Editing: Paul Starr
Kodansha Comics Edition Cover Design: Phil Balsman